The Indian Postcolonia

India has often been at the centre of debates on and definitions of the postcolonial condition. Offering challenging new directions for the field, this *Critical Reader* confronts how theory in the Indian context is responding in vital terms to our understanding of that condition today.

The Indian Postcolonial is made up of four sections looking in turn at:

- visual cultures
- translating cultural traditions
- the ethical text
- global/cosmopolitan worlds.

Each section is prefaced with a short introduction by the editors that locate these interdisciplinary articles within the contemporary national and international context. Showcasing the diversity and vitality of current debate, this volume collects the work of both established figures and a new generation of cultural critics.

Challenging and unsettling many basic premises of postcolonial studies, this volume is the ideal Reader for students and scholars of the Indian Postcolonial.

Contributors include: Dipesh Chakrabarty, Partha Chatterjee, Vinayak Chaturvedi, Amit Chaudhuri, Ranajit Guha, Aniket Jaaware, Udaya Kumar, Nivedita Menon, Aamir R. Mufti, Ashis Nandy, M. Madhava Prasad, Gayatri Chakravorty Spivak, Rajeswari Sunder Rajan, and new work by Santanu Das, Tapati Guha-Thakurta, and Robert J. C. Young.

Elleke Boehmer is Professor of World Literature in English at the University of Oxford. Her previous publications include *Colonial and Postcolonial Literature: Migrant Metaphors* (2nd edn 2005), and *Empire, the National, and the Postcolonial, 1890–1920* (2002).

Rosinka Chaudhuri is Fellow in Cultural Studies at the Centre for Studies in Social Sciences, Calcutta. She is author of *Gentlemen Poets in Colonial Bengal: Emergent Nationalism and the Orientalist Project* (2002) and editor of *Derozio, Poet of India: The Definitive Edition* (2008).

The Indian Postcolonial

A Critical Reader

**Edited by Elleke Boehmer
and Rosinka Chaudhuri**

LONDON AND NEW YORK

First edition published 2011
by Routledge
2 Park Square, Milton Park, Abingdon, Oxon OX14 4RN

Simultaneously published in the USA and Canada
by Routledge
270 Madison Ave, New York, NY 10016

Routledge is an imprint of the Taylor & Francis Group,
an informa business

Typeset in Baskerville by
Bookcraft Ltd, Stroud, Gloucestershire
Printed and bound in Great Britain by
TJ International Ltd, Padstow, Cornwall

British Library Cataloguing in Publication Data
A catalogue record for this book is available from the British
Library

Library of Congress Cataloging in Publication Data
The Indian postcolonial : a critical reader / edited by Elleke
Boehmer and Rosinka Chaudhuri. -- 1st edn
    p. cm.
    Includes bibliographical references and index.
    1. Indic literature (English)–20th century–History and
criticism. 2. Postcolonialism in literature. 3. Postcolonialism–
India. 4. Nationalism–India. I. Chaudhuri, Rosinka.
II. Boehmer, Elleke, 1961-

    PR9489.6.I538 2010   820.9'35854–dc22
    2010014140

ISBN 10: 0-415-46747-0 (hbk)
ISBN 10: 0-415-56766-1 (pbk)

ISBN 13: 978-0-415-46747-6 (hbk)
ISBN 13: 978-0-415-56766-4 (pbk)

Contents

List of figures

List of contributors

Elleke Boehmer is Professor of World Literature in English at the University of Oxford. She has published the monographs *Colonial and Postcolonial Literature: Migrant Metaphors* (1995, 2005), *Empire, the National and the Postcolonial, 1890–1920* (2002) and *Stories of Women: Gender and Narrative in the Postcolonial Nation* (2005), and the biography *Nelson Mandela* (2008). She is the author of the novels *Screens against the Sky* (1990), *An Immaculate Figure* (1993), *Bloodlines* (2000), and *Nile Baby* (2008), and of the short story collection *Sharmilla and Other Portraits* (2010). She edited or co-edited Robert Baden-Powell's *Scouting for Boys* (2004), the anthology *Empire Writing* (1998), *J. M. Coetzee in Context and Theory* (2009), and *Terror and the Postcolonial* (2009). A book on *fin de siècle* Indian travel to Britain is forthcoming.

Dipesh Chakrabarty teaches History and South Asian studies at the University of Chicago and holds a visiting position at the Australian National University. He is the author of *Provincializing Europe: Postcolonial Thought and Historical Difference* (2000/2007).

Partha Chatterjee is Honorary Professor, Centre for Studies in Social Sciences, Calcutta, and Professor of Anthropology, Columbia University, New York. He is the author of *Nationalist Thought and the Colonial World* (1986), *The Nation and Its Fragments* (1993), *The Politics of the Governed* (2004), and several other books. He is a founding member of Subaltern Studies.

Vinayak Chaturvedi is an Associate Professor in the Department of History at the University of California, Irvine. He is the editor of *Mapping Subaltern Studies and the Postcolonial* (2000) and the author of *Peasant Pasts: History and Memory in Western India* (2007). A book about V.D. Savarkar, Hindutva, and histories of warfare in twentieth-century India is forthcoming.

Amit Chaudhuri has written five novels, including *The Immortals* (2009). He is the author of two critical works, *Clearing a Space: Reflections on*

India, Literature, and Culture and *D. H. Lawrence and 'Difference'*. Among the prizes he has won are the Commonwealth Writers Prize, the Society of Authors' Betty Trask Award and Encore Award, the *Los Angeles Times Book Prize*, and the Indian Government's Sahitya Akademi award. He is Professor of Contemporary Literature at the University of East Anglia, and a Fellow of the Royal Society of Literature. He is a regular contributor to the *London Review of Books*, the *Times Literary Supplement*, and the *New Left Review*, and was one of the judges of the Man Booker International Prize 2009.

Rosinka Chaudhuri is Fellow in Cultural Studies at the Centre for Studies in Social Sciences, Calcutta. She has been visiting fellow at the Southern Asian Institute, Columbia University, and Charles Wallace Fellow at Cambridge University. She has published *Gentlemen Poets in Colonial Bengal: Emergent Nationalism and the Orientalist Project* (Seagull: 2002) and *Derozio, Poet of India: The Definitive Edition* (Oxford University Press: 2008). Her articles have appeared in, amongst others, *Social Text*, *Interventions*, *Studies in History*, *Modern Asian Studies*, the *Times Literary Supplement* and the *Economic and Political Weekly*. She is currently writing a book on issues of authenticity, aesthetics, politics and history in nineteenth-century Bengali poetry.

Santanu Das is a Senior Lecturer in English at Queen Mary, University of London. He has held research fellowships at St John's College, Cambridge, and at the British Academy, London. He is the author of *Touch and Intimacy in First World War Literature* (Cambridge, 2006, pbk 2008) which received a 2007 Outstanding Academic Title Award from *Choice*, USA, and a Philip Leverhulme Prize in England in 2009. He recently completed editing for Cambridge a collection of essays titled *Race, Empire and First World War Writing*, and gave the 2010 British Academy Chatterton lecture on English poetry. He is working towards a monograph on India, empire and the First World War.

Ranajit Guha has held various research and teaching positions in India, England, Australia and the United States. Apart from the Subaltern Studies Series of which he edited the first six volumes, his publications include *A Rule of Property for Bengal: An Essay on the Idea of Permanent Settlement* (1963), *Elementary Aspects of Peasant Insurgency* (1983), *Dominance Without Hegemony: History and Power in Colonial India* (1997), and *History at the Limit of World-History* (2002). A collection of his essays, *The Small Voice of History* (2009) has been edited by Partha Chatterjee. His most recent work, written in Bengali, deals with literature and philosophy. Ranajit Guha now lives in Austria.

Tapati Guha-Thakurta is a Professor in History at the Centre for Studies in Social Sciences, Calcutta. She has written on the art and cultural history of modern India, and on the institutional and disciplinary workings of the fields of archaeology and art history. Her two main books are *The Making of a New 'Indian' Art: Artists, Aesthetics and Nationalism in Bengal* (Cambridge University Press, 1992) and *Monuments, Objects, Histories: Institutions of Art in Colonial and Postcolonial India* (Columbia University Press and Permanent Black, 2004). She is currently completing a book on the Durga Puja festival in contemporary Calcutta

Aniket Jaaware teaches English at the University of Pune. His publications include an edition of *Hamlet* (Pearson/Longman 2008), *NeonFish in Dark Water*, a volume of short stories (Mapinlit, 2007), and a translation into English of Jotirao Phule's *Shetkaryacha Asude* (*The Farmer's Whip-cord*). He translates from English into Marathi.

Udaya Kumar is Professor of English at the University of Delhi. His publications include *The Joycean Labyrinth: Repetition, Time and Tradition in Ulysses* (1991), and papers on literary and cultural theory and on Indian literature. He is preparing a book on history and modes of self-articulation in modern Malayalam writing. His current research addresses norms and practices of vernacular literary cultures, cultural histories of the body, and conceptions of 'public-ness' in the context of modern Kerala.

Nivedita Menon is Professor in Political Thought at the School of International Studies, Jawaharlal Nehru University, Delhi. She is the author of an edited volume *Gender and Politics in India* (1999) and *Recovering Subversion: Feminist Politics Beyond the Law* (2004). Her publications include the edited volume *Sexualities* (2007) and *Power and Contestation: India after 1989* (2007, co-written with Aditya Nigam). She is an active commentator on contemporary issues in newspapers and on the blog kafila.com. She has translated fiction and non-fiction from Hindi and Malayalam into English, and received the A. K. Ramanujan Award for translation instituted by Katha. She is active with non-funded, non-party citizens' forums in India on a range of issues.

Aamir R. Mufti teaches comparative literature at the University of California, Los Angeles (UCLA). He is the author of *Enlightenment in the Colony: The Jewish Question and the Crisis of Postcolonial Culture* (1997) and has edited or co-edited a number of collections, including *Dangerous Liaisons: Gender, Nation and Postcolonial Perspectives* (Minnesota, 1997) and 'Critical Secularism', a special issue of the journal *Boundary 2*. His work reconsiders the secularization thesis in a comparative perspective, with a special interest in Islam, modernity in India and the cultural politics of Jewish identity in Western Europe.

Ashis Nandy works on the political psychology of violence, cultures of knowledge, utopias and visions, alternatives, futures, and genocide. Among Nandy's books are *Alternative Science*, *At the Edge of Psychology*, *The Intimate Enemy*, *The Tao of Cricket*, *The Illegitimacy of Nationalism*, *The Savage Freud and Other Essays in Possible and Retrievable Selves*, and *Traditions, Tyranny and Utopias*. Nandy has edited two books, *Science, Hegemony and Violence* and *The Secret Politics of our Desires*, and co-edited *The Multiverse of Democracy* and *The Future of Knowledge and Culture: A Twenty-first Century Dictionary*. The Oxford University Press is now bringing out an omnibus edition of his works. For the last forty years, Nandy has been a Fellow of the Centre for the Study of Developing Societies, Delhi. He is also a Distinguished Fellow of the Institute of Postcolonial Studies and a Member of the Global Scientific Committee on Higher Education (UNESCO). Nandy has also contributed to major human rights reports and has monitored democratic elections in India, Bangladesh and Pakistan on behalf of grassroots movements.

M. Madhava Prasad, Professor of Cultural Studies, English and Foreign Languages University, Hyderabad, was educated at Bangalore, Syracuse and Pittsburgh. His publications include *Ideology of the Hindi Film: A Historical Construction* (1998), *Cine-politics* (forthcoming), essays on various topics including film, media, literature, electoral democracy and caste, and a number of literary translations. He is currently working on a critical history of the language question in British India and the Indian Republic.

Gayatri Chakravorty Spivak, University Professor in the Humanities, Columbia University, holds honorary degrees from the Universities of Toronto and London, and Oberlin College. Her books are *In Other Worlds* (1987), *Thinking Academic Freedom in Gendered Post-Coloniality* (1993), *Outside in the Teaching Machine* (1993), *Imperatives to Reimagine the Planet* (1997), *A Critique of Postcolonial Reason* (1999), *Death of a Discipline* (2003), *Other Asias* (2007), and *An Aesthetic Education in the Age of Globalization* (forthcoming). She has translated Jacques Derrida, *Of Grammatology* (1976), Mahasweta Devi, *Imaginary Maps* (1993), *Breast Stories* (1997), *Old Women* (1999), *Chotti Munda* (2002), Ramproshad Sen, *Song for Kali* (2000), Aimé Césaire, *A Season in the Congo* (forthcoming). She has been a full-time activist including in primary health care and ecological agriculture, and involved with feminist social movements from the United Nations through academic theory to the grass roots.

Rajeswari Sunder Rajan is Global Distinguished Professor at New York University, in the Department of English. She has also been Reader in the English Faculty at the University of Oxford and a Senior Fellow at the Nehru Memorial Museum and Library, New Delhi. Her publications include *Real and Imagined Women: Gender, Culture and Postcolonialism* (1993), *The Scandal of the State: Women, Law and Citizenship in Postcolonial India* (2003) and, most recently, the co-edited volume *Crisis of Secularism in India* (2007).

Robert J. C. Young is Julius Silver Professor of English and Comparative Literature at New York University. He was formerly Professor of English and Critical Theory at Oxford University. He has published *White Mythologies: Writing History and the West* (1990; 2004), *Colonial Desire: Hybridity in Culture, Theory and Race* (1995), *Postcolonialism: An Historical Introduction* (2001), *Postcolonialism: A Very Short Introduction* (2003) and *The Idea of English Ethnicity* (2008). His edited books include *Untying the Text* (Routledge, 1981), and, with Derek Attridge and Geoffrey Bennington, *Poststructuralism and the Question of History* (1987). The founding editor of *Interventions: International Journal of Postcolonial Studies*, he was also a founding editor of the *Oxford Literary Review* (1977–94).

Acknowledgements

The publisher and the editors would like to thank the following for permission to reprint material under copyright:

Partha Chatterjee, 'Nationalist Icon to Secular Image' in *Traces of India: Photography, Architecture and the Politics of Representation, 1850–1900*, Maria Antonella Pelizzari (ed.), Canadian Centre for Architecture and Yale Center for British Arts 2003, p. 279–329. Reprinted with the permission of the Canadian Centre for Architecture.

M. Madhava Prasad, 'Fan Bhakti and Subaltern Sovereignty: Enthusiasm as a Political Factor', *Economic and Political Weekly*, July 18, 2009, pp. 68–76. © 2009 M. Madhavi Prasad. Reprinted by kind permission of the author.

Nivedita Menon, 'Thinking through the Postnation', *Economic and Political Weekly*, March 7–13 2009, 70–77. © 2009 Nivedita Menon. Reprinted by kind permission of the author.

Aamir R. Mufti, 'Auerbach in Istanbul: Edward Said, Secular Criticism, and the Question of Minority Culture', *Critical Inquiry* 25:1 (Autumn 1998), 95–125. Reproduced by permission of the University of Chicago Press and the author.

Vinayak Chaturvedi, 'Vinayak & me: Hindutva and the politics of naming', *Social History* 28:2 (Jan 5, 2003), 155–173. Reproduced by permission of Taylor and Francis and the author.

Aniket Jaaware, 'Of Demons and Angels and Historical Humans: Some Events and Questions in Translation and Postcolonial Theory', *The European Legacy* 7:6 (Jan 12, 2002), 735–745. Reproduced by permission of Taylor and Francis and the author.

Gayatri Chakravorty Spivak, 'Ethics and Politics in Tagore, Coetzee, and Certain Scenes of Teaching', *Diacritics* 32:3–4 (2002), 17–31. © 2005 The Johns Hopkins University Press. Reprinted with permission of The Johns Hopkins University Press.

Rajeswari Sunder Rajan, 'Gandhian Ethics', from Gilbert Helen and Chris Tiffin, eds. *Burden or Benefit? Imperial Benevolence and Its Legacies*

(Bloomington, IN: Indiana University Press, 2008), pp. 136–159. Reproduced by kind permission of the author.

Ashish Nandy, 'Humiliation: The Politics and Cultural Pshychology of the Limits of Human Degradation', *Time Treks* (Delhi: Permanent Black, 2007), pp. 129–150. Reproduced by kind permission of Permanent Black, Seagull Books and the author.

Amit Chadhuri, 'Cosmopolitanism's Alien Face', *New Left Review* 55 (January–February 2009), 89–106. Reproduced by kind permission of New Left Review and the author.

Ranajit Guha, 'A colonial city and its time(s)'. Originally published in *Indian Economic and Social History Review*, 45:3, 329–51. Copyright © The Indian Economic and Social History Association, New Delhi. All rights reserved. Reproduced with permission of the copyright holders and the publishers, Sage Publications India Pvt. Ltd, New Delhi.

Udaya Kumar, 'Self, Body and Inner Sense'. Originally published in *Studies in History*, 13:2. Copyright © Jawaharlal Nehru University, New Delhi. All rights reserved. Reproduced with permission of the copyright holders and the publishers, Sage Publications India Pvt. Ltd, New Delhi.

Every effort has been made to trace and contact copyright holders. The publishers would be pleased to hear from any copyright holders not acknowledged here, so that this acknowledgements page may be amended at the earliest opportunity.

Introduction

Elleke Boehmer and Rosinka Chaudhuri

There has always been a straightforward political and historicist sense in which the word 'postcolonial' has been used to mean *after* the end of colonization. Yet, especially when coupled with the word 'studies', the postcolonial has also been configured as an academic discourse that relocates that denotation and its attendant political urgency into an interdisciplinary and cross-border mode of reading often extending backwards in time, and finding practices of resistance and subversion in cultural production both before and after the moment of colonization, and in different regions of the once-colonial world.

Faced with the bewildering multifariousness and ambivalence of the category 'postcolonial', most readers and anthologies devoted to postcolonial subjects have almost of necessity, if not convention, been concerned with introducing, or re-inaugurating, right at the start, the very concept of 'postcolonial studies' – its origins and movements, its fields of primary interest (literary-historical, filmic, cultural), its increasing institutionalization, its global provenance, its engagement with late or neo-capitalism, its multi-form politics of dissent, and so on. At the same time, while recognizing that postcolonial studies stands outside the limits of strictly historicist explanations, many such projects also begin, as if regardless, with historical markers, and discuss how the terms of its discourse were established in academia from the 1980s onward, or trace the evolution of the discipline from the urtext which supposedly generated the seeds of its growth, Edward Said's *Orientalism* (1978).

Such attempts at both academic consolidation and periodization have not, however, displaced another, related postcolonial critical practice – one which again is virtually *de rigueur* in anthology introductions – and that is to speak of postcolonialism's loss of force as a heuristic practice and academic approach. Such valedictory accounts note, for instance, its rigidification into an academic orthodoxy, or its increasing lack of impact and relevance in a globalized world where different concentrations of power exist to the ordinarily or conventionally imperial. With the end of the millennium, and the rise of new colonial or imperial configurations, the interpretative and pedagogic moment of the postcolonial has, it is now sometimes claimed, passed. Moreover, the internal discursive contradictions signified by the term postcolonial – hybrid or nationalist, diasporic or indigenous, singular or specific, materialist or poststructuralist – have allegedly unravelled it from within.[1] As one of its chief practitioners, Gayatri Chakravorty Spivak, noted in diagnostic fashion at the very end of the twentieth century, 'Postcolonial studies, unwittingly commemorating a lost object, can become an alibi unless it is placed within a general frame'.[2] To 'alibi' we might here add 'for a particular political or historicist agenda', and Spivak's 'frame' might be understood as comparative as well as 'general'.

So far, from the vantage point of the end of the first decade of the twenty-first century, if a general frame has in any sense emerged for post-colonial criticism, it has done so in curiously self-reflexive yet at the same time non-specified, less than particular ways, which seem only to reiterate its existing contradictions. This, then, apart from its well-known institutional anxiety, is another impetus for what might be called postcoloniality's repetition compulsion. As every postcolonial studies reader or anthology feels compelled to situate and debate the notion of postcoloniality anew (what it comprises, where it is located and manifested, if at all), it inevitably spreads its argument thinly over many, if not all, the diverse, formerly colonial parts of the (largely Anglophone) globe that could possibly lay a claim to the condition, bringing together essays on Latin America, Africa, New Zealand, Australia, the Caribbean, and even Canada, the USA and multicultural Britain as if all were penetrated more or less equally by post-colonial circumstance. In one instance of extreme self-reflexivity, in *The Cambridge Companion to Postcolonial Literary Studies* edited by Neil Lazarus (2004), we see the postcolonial being repeatedly explored – as the titles of the individual essays indicate – through processes of 'postcolonial nation formation' or 'nationalism and postcolonial studies', as well as through such post-1968 theoretical formations as 'post-structuralism and postcolonial discourse', 'postcolonial studies and globalization theory', or 'feminism in/and postcolonialism'.[3] A concern to be faithful to a range of theoretical frameworks, as well as to the pedagogic requirements of the Companion format, has generated postcolonial constructions that move in every direction. In another example, in Ania Loomba and others' *Postcolonial Studies and Beyond* (2005), an entirely laudable attempt is made to move 'beyond' even these diverse established frames ('frankly, beyond the usual suspects'), into a territory marked by the pressure of resistance to the 'new empires of our own times'. That territory, however, is perceived to extend from globalization studies via history, politics, feminist issues, poetry, environmentalism, race, nationhood, multiculturalism and translation theory all the way through to 'Palestinian Terror and the Post/colonial Question'.[4] A postcolonial focus is thinned to the point where it might justifiably be asked whether it has any interpretative force left in it at all.

If the lifespan of postcolonial studies is construed as stretching from Said's *Orientalism* (1978) to, say, Hardt and Negri's Deleuze-inspired celebration of a new decentred and technologized mode of empire in their eponymous 2000 study, then, ten years after that date of so-called demise, what is there left to say on the 'death' of the subject? [5] Here we should straightaway clarify that this *Critical Reader* is not an attempt to map postcolonial life after death. Many such post-postcolonial ventures have already seen light of day, to limited critical effect. Indeed, postcolonial studies must be pre-eminent among the critical disciplines in the number of times its death has been confidently predicted, only for it to live on into yet another academic conference, seminar series, university course, cultural review, or reader, though now coupled with such words as 'beyond', 're-routing', 'transforming', 'transnational'. It is in this sense something of a shape-shifter, and one that often appears perversely to gain in vitality from one change of form (thematic focus, critical perspective, etc.) to another.

On many university syllabuses in the West, the postcolonial now represents the catch-all heading under which 'the other' – meaning, the non-canonical and marginal – is delivered to students, rather than its being transmitted via area studies models (within courses on African or Caribbean literature, for example), as was the case some ten or even twenty years ago. In the non-West, however, in places such as India or South Africa, courses on postcolonial topics occupy the academic mainstream, and so depend upon publications that, unavoidably, are drawn down from the powerful metropolitan publishing networks. Students have therefore to deal with a centralized canon formation that, from the start, insidiously undermines its stated claims to privileging marginality. Mapping a narrative of the multiple rebirths of postcolonial studies in this context is in many ways a redundant exercise, in view precisely of the inequities of 'the new empires of our own times'. Against this background, the significance of an anthology such as ours must lie in the *continuing* heuristic power of postcolonialism's central critical tropes – of cultural translation, of braided temporality, of marginality itself – which grow in pertinence when they are transposed back into specific postcolonial conditions, as so many of the essays collected here set about doing.

The implied oxymoron in our title, *The Indian Postcolonial*, is indicative of the change of focus that animates and sustains our ongoing postcolonial critical practice – the relocation of our 'general frame' so that it does not degenerate, yet again, into 'an alibi'. Traditionally, the political-historical provenance of the postcolonial has referred to a global condition of oppression (although to use the word 'traditional' in the context of postcolonial studies itself seems oxymoronic). This has had as a consequence the at-times-rigorous exclusion of the framing device of national boundaries from the postcolonial critical project. In the specific context of India, the discredit that has accrued to the national narrative in the wake of the postcolonial perspectives produced by the Subaltern Studies project, has also generated a tendency to avoid framing postcoloniality in national terms. In keeping with those perspectives, this book does not entail in any sense a national reframing or nationalist enterprise. Rather, it attempts to interrogate, unsettle and review the premises of postcolonial studies through the prism of India, locating its contents and assumptions in the midst of Indian manifestations of the field.

Considering the postcolonial as coupled with India, the postcolonial *and* the Indian, our concern in this *Critical Reader* is therefore at one level very specific, as well as intentionally circumscribed. Against the claim that might be made that, till quite recently, interpretative frameworks drawn from Indian colonial history, through the Subaltern School of historians for example, or the Indian English novel, moulded the understanding of postcolonial conditions in the West and beyond in influential ways, this *Reader* intends rather to look at how the postcolonial translates into the specificities of Indian history and culture in critical reflections of the near-contemporary moment. It's a question not (or not only) of how this region of South Asia has shaped postcolonial critical concepts across the past three decades, interesting as this question is, but of how postcolonial readings and critical tropes map on to our view of this wide region; or of how postcolonial paradigms and perceptions have been taken up in the subcontinent, and (re-)inflected and refracted to address local and regional conditions.

An evocative analogy may be made with the multi-storeyed family house in A. K. Ramanujan's memorable poem 'Small-Scale Reflections on a Great House', where the great house, much like India in history, accumulates influences, traditions, individual stories, lessons, and also draws back into itself everything it once produced and let go:

> Sometimes I think that nothing
> that ever comes into this house
> goes out. Things come in every day
> to lose themselves among other things
> lost long ago among
> other things lost long ago[6]

Yet it's also a case of 'Nothing stays out':

> ideas behave like rumours,
> once casually mentioned somewhere
> They come back to the door as prodigies

If India has disseminated certain influential postcolonial precepts and paradigms of global postcolonial studies – such as of the subaltern's silence, or of the intimate enemy – it has also now, across the past decade, we propose, received them back again, to review them in a more embedded, localized frame – for instance, of minority histories or of subaltern pasts. Alongside this, India also, at the same time, accepts and accretes postcolonial debates generated elsewhere, concerning abjection or cosmopolitanism, for example, to construct and adapt its own theories under Indian social and cultural conditions. This *Critical Reader* will attempt, to our knowledge for the first time, to showcase portions of this vast and influential body of work that has been produced since 1999 on Indian postcoloniality, and which has emerged in dialogue with postcolonial discourses being carried on elsewhere in the world. The volume both collects and introduces published materials, but also includes new or recent work from Ranajit Guha, Amit Chaudhuri, Udaya Kumar, Nivedita Menon, and Robert J. C. Young, and previously unpublished essays from Dipesh Chakrabarty, Tapati Guha-Thakurta and Santanu Das.

The influence of Indian postcolonial critical discourses in English, peaking around the mid to late 1990s, can be explained with respect to several important and interlocking historical and pedagogical factors, including the status of India within the broad history of independence movements; the international location and prominence of many Indian critics, writers, and theorists, not least Salman Rushdie, Gayatri Chakravorty Spivak and Homi Bhabha; as well as the institutional receptivity of these writers and critics to poststructuralist literary theory. Interestingly, however, such was the global circulation both of what might be termed Indian postcolonial frameworks, and of the Indian critics and writers themselves, that the specific tracery of locale and region their ideas bore tended to be erased either in whole or in part, and their connection with the form-giving cultural geography of India suspended. Following on from this, a leading aim of this *Critical Reader* is to re-establish that connection, and outline once again that influential tracery. If it is true that the acute and searching postcolonial work that India has produced in the last ten years or so has escaped proper notice in the world arenas where the dominant postcolonial conversations are now held, then this collection wishes to draw attention to this wealth of new material, and to showcase debates and conversations that tend to play out across Indian national *and* diasporic international spaces. Our concern is not that postcolonial critical theory is a metropolitan discourse that requires indigenizing in India (a difficult if not objectionable case to make), as that the interdisciplinary, transnational and cosmopolitan inflections of Indian postcolonial discourse, which have, we submit, always been in evidence, merit renewed comparative and intertextual critical attention, as exemplified in these pages not least through the simple juxtaposition of the divers critical voices and approaches.

In some critical works and readers it would appear to be an editorial duty to be as all-inclusive as page limits will permit, so that no one may feel ignored, left out, under-acknowledged, re-marginalized. Resisting these claims of global reach and representativeness, the collective force of the essays gathered together in this *Critical Reader* seeks to complicate, if not in part dislodge, this postcolonial universalism, while at the same time, advisedly, relocating India at the centre of its interrogative field (though as one centre among others). In short, the book aims to re-describe postcoloniality as inflected by India, especially the India of the new millennium and the twenty-first century. As this implies, our fundamental contention is that, while it certainly is true that late capitalism has drawn all societies into the new global world order (and though we recognize, even as we write, that the world has moved beyond late capitalism into a new post-crash political and economic phase), it remains self-evident that the postcolonial situation is experienced and perceived in different ways in different territories. And this stands alongside another contention that is important to us: that it should likewise be possible for interested scholars now and into the future to (re-)map and re-inflect the postcolonial field through other regional locations or national and pan-nationalistic formations, depending upon the historical shifts that govern an intellectual project at any given moment.

Critical contexts

To embed our critical intentions more fully within the Indian context, and also to resist the closed, if not parochial, nature of the global village of Western postcolonial critique, it is also necessary to explore at once the postcoloniality of India and the Indianness of the postcolonial as these have evolved in criticism since Said, and are expressed in these pages. With the term parochialism we designate that species of 'unapologetic' 'general definition' within postcolonial studies such as is traded, for instance, by a 2000 'Companion' to the field, which asserts that postcolonial studies is 'the academic study *in the West* of the cultures and contexts of decolonization' (our emphasis).[7] Another quotation, 'This book was born in an office in Washington DC', may read on one level as a literal statement made by the editors of the volume or others like it, but it also bears the aspect of an apocryphal tale, or just a bald stating of the obvious, given that for most audiences in the former colonies of the Anglophone world the majority of postcolonial readers and companions that have ever been issued to press have emerged out of an office or a conference in some part or other of the metropolitan West.[8] Moreover, such books are by and large conceptualized by academics located there, and contain work by academics also located there, or at the most, located multiply in the West and the rest of the world. Following through the implications of this formulation, postcolonial studies is a field constructed almost exclusively in terms of academic specialization: born in the academy, it is produced by the academy and for the academy. Against this parochialism, and with Spivak's warning in *A Critique of Postcolonial Reason* and elsewhere as to the dangers of slipping into a 'reverse ethnocentrism' firmly in mind, we would seek to reformulate that sentence quoted earlier in the service of this *Critical Reader*, in order to state, simply, that its aim is 'the academic study *in India* of the cultures and contexts of decolonization'.[9]

The emphatic placement of postcolonial studies within academic practice is not, it is worth noting, the template by which all postcolonial polemic measures itself. In 2008, in an editorial that marked ten years of its foundation, the international postcolonial journal *Interventions* spoke of the questions it had sought to ask at its inception, 'about the asymmetries of power and rights, as well as the histories and other archives ... recovered to both address and redress these inequalities'.[10] In 1998, at the end of the twentieth century, the time to which this retrospective view looked back, postcolonial studies was still establishing itself institutionally, while now, the editors opined, 'some have started to talk about "the end of postcolonial theory"', despite the fact that the 'realities of poverty, underdevelopment, injustice, violence and exclusion in those parts of the world that had experienced colonialism of all kinds has not ceased to be relevant'.[11]

As the editors of *Interventions* would no doubt agree, the reconfiguration of postcolonial studies in the present and immediate future requires a rather more practicable agenda than that of envisioning an end to the eternal inequities of humankind – inspiring and important as this aim remains. What can be agreed upon, nevertheless, is the importance at once of keeping such a radical vision alive, as well as the unflagging intention to maintain and enlarge the wide scope of the field – to open it up to new horizons and to 'support the emergence of a broader postcolonial intellectual practice'.[12] The expectation that the practice of postcolonial studies will result in new political directions and goals may of course be a utopian hope at best, yet it remains crucial to concede that, with all its limitations, the arena of postcolonial studies has created pathways and interstices of contestation within the academy which in turn have brought new interdisciplinary formations and cross-border alliances holding important repercussions for the manner in which Western domination may be countered, however partially, in a neo-liberal, globalized world.

In 1993, a small but prestigious niche Indian publishing house based in Calcutta, Seagull Books, brought out a volume that has since become a benchmark in Indian postcolonial studies without overtly allying itself to the terminology of international postcolonial studies: *Interrogating Modernity: Culture and Colonialism in India*.[13] Edited by Indian academics with decidedly theoretical interests, the volume ranged over literary texts, film studies, gender studies, translation theory and colonial discourse analysis in essays written by a spectrum of commentators, none of whom would describe themselves first and foremost as postcolonialists. Its attempt to look at present-day cultural practices in the light of an Indian modernity placed at the intersection of various social, political and other registers was, as postcolonial studies often is, rooted in the cultural studies enterprise, in Raymond Williams's definition of culture as comprising socially constructed meaning, and in the Indian ramifications of such definitions. The yoking together in the Seagull volume of high theory, in the form of 'Benjamin, Williams, Hall, Bourdieu, Foucault', and of the politics of culture as defined through particular formulations of national, communal, caste or gender identities in India, was made possible, it can be said with hindsight, by the powerful conjuncture of postcolonial studies and cultural studies as these were being developed within academic disciplines the world over. Similar theoretical alliances were replicated a few years later in a Western publication with similar concerns, *Dangerous Liaisons: Gender, Nation and Postcolonial Perspectives* (1997), where the word 'postcolonial' made its way into the title, but only after the colon.[14]

That the Seagull book was quickly well known in India but little known in the West was interestingly symptomatic of what Dipesh Chakrabarty (a contributor to this volume), in another context, has called 'asymmetric ignorance' – where third world scholars feel compelled to read a wide variety of Western texts, but Western scholars of Postcolonial Studies feel no such compunction to 'know' third world texts.[15] This *Critical Reader* would seek to interrogate and adjust to some degree such asymmetries. Emerging from our cross-national collaboration as editors and our India-involved materials, on the one hand, and the Western location of our publisher, on the other, we seek, ideally, an interstitial, different, and in-between space in which to situate this enterprise.

It was Vinayak Chaturvedi, one of the contributors to this volume, who in *Mapping Subaltern Studies and the Postcolonial* (2000) first traced the merging of subalternists' concerns with those of the postcolonial critical arena through the lens of such concepts as the subaltern and body politics, taken from Antonio Gramsci and Michel Foucault.[16] As he noted there, it was in the 1990s, almost a decade after it was founded in the early 1980s, that the Subaltern Studies project first arrived in the Anglo-American academy. Edward Said's introduction to a volume of selected subaltern writings, *Selected Subaltern Studies*, had contributed, in part, to a significant shift in academic institutions towards postcolonialist preoccupations, and an attendant turn towards culture and away from purely Marxist concerns with power, poverty and resistance.[17] The cultural turn in subaltern studies, therefore, was taking place at a time when postcolonial studies, too, was establishing itself in the academy.

The mention of *Selected Subaltern Studies* usefully recalls us at this point to postcolonialism's institutional and pedagogic histories. It was two decades ago, two years after the publication of the selected volume, that Robert J. C. Young's *White Mythologies* appeared in Britain, influentially installing the 'holy trinity' of postcolonial studies, Said, Spivak and Bhabha, at the fountainhead of postcolonial critical activity. *White Mythologies* followed close on the heels of the equally influential and more literary *The Empire Writes Back* (1989) in which Bill Ashcroft, Gareth Griffiths and Helen Tiffin tested the application of denationalized, poststructuralist perspectives to what had till then been called Commonwealth books.[18] Preceding this, Young's lucid and incisive introduction to the still-opaque regions of French high theory in *Untying the Text: A Post-structuralist Reader* (1981), had brought many of the critical and poststructuralist antecedents of the postcolonial field into focus, as, too, in cultural materialist terms, had Terry Eagleton's *Literary Theory: An Introduction* (1983).[19] Neither book, predictably, made any mention at all of the word *postcolonial* (with or without the hyphen) – something which now contrasts strongly with the outpouring of definitions, redefinitions and redeployments of the term variously linked to 'thought', 'reason', 'critique', 'analysis' in the many companions to and surveys of the postcolonial field that appeared from 1989/90. Published in 2001, Chakrabarty's *Provincializing Europe: Postcolonial Thought and Historical Difference* marked a moment of confluence between postcolonial and new historicist perspectives representative of an entire range of texts that had appeared across the intervening period.

In the two decades spanning *Untying the Text* and Chakrabarty's keynote study, a host of critics and commentators of Indian background and/ or sharing Indian points of focus – Gayatri Chakravorty Spivak, Homi Bhabha, Lata Mani, Sara Suleri, Gauri Viswanathan, Chandra Talpade Mohanty, Mrinalini Sinha – published cultural analysis that rapidly became constitutive of the postcolonial field, though largely from within the Western academy. An expanded list of names drawn from places beyond India designates further keynote work, including Said's discussion of Kipling's *Kim* in his introduction to the novel's Penguin edition, later included in *Culture and Imperialism* (1993), and Robert J. C. Young's incisive chapter on Gandhi in *Postcolonialism: An Historical Introduction* (2001).[20] In the following decade, the 2000s, Rajeswari Sunder Rajan, Leela Gandhi, Antoinette Burton, Elleke Boehmer, and Aamir R. Mufti, amongst others, produced powerful reflections on the subcontinent's tangled communities and histories, in diverse literary, feminist, activist and archival fields.[21] To this already considerable body of scholarship we must also add the hugely influential Subaltern historians of the period, broadly defined – Partha Chatterjee, Dipesh Chakrabarty, Shahid Amin, Gyan Pandey – and the fierce criticism of the school on the Left, whose most combative representative, Aijaz Ahmad, was from India as well.

Yet, what we wish to underline in the list of critics and theorists mentioned – a list which always remains, of necessity, both incomplete and curtailed in a representational sense – is that very little of this work was conceived of as being first and foremost 'on' or 'about' postcoloniality or the postcolonial condition. The efforts to define or redefine the postcolonial were, in the majority of cases, a spin-off of research focused on local, regional or transnational issues and concerns. Many of the later names also signify the entry into the global postcolonial domain of writers whose work had been produced primarily in the Indian academy, although allied with university departments in the West. These scholars' investigations were often first articulated in papers published in the Indian academic press and were firmly grounded in Indian networks of research, reference and publishing. Ashis Nandy, again collected between these covers, whose work stood, *sui generis*, outside the circle of Subaltern theorists, was another major India-located interpreter of Indian postcolonial maladies in the period, bringing psychoanalytic perspectives to cultural material in a series of definitive readings, such as of the 'loss and recovery of self under colonialism'.[22]

To an area of study beset by situational ironies we might therefore add another paradox, derived from our India-refracted perspective on the field, namely, that some of postcolonialism's most influential work has been accomplished by those not overtly seeking to sign up to a postcolonial position. Conversely put, writing from outside the postcolonial fold can on occasion generate a more nuanced understanding of the postcolonial than from within the field. While this may be as contentious and extreme a statement to make as Salman Rushdie's infamous (and untrue) assertion, in *The Vintage Book of Indian Writing in English*, that the best of Indian postcolonial writing was that which had been written in English, it nonetheless remains the case that some of the contributors to this volume wanted to have nothing to do with the term 'postcolonial'. More than one contributor articulated the thought that one respondent put into an email:

> I fear that by contributing an essay ... I would be allowing my work to serve as an example of postcolonial scholarship, which it is of course, technically speaking, but not in the sense that the word carries in the academy internationally. If as you say, you want to present new work and pull away from the older names, perhaps the name that one needs to pull away from more urgently than any other, is precisely 'postcolonial'?

In reply, our response elucidated that while it is true that much work in postcolonial studies has been excessively homogenizing in its effects and Western in its assumptions, we are not of the opinion that the solution is to junk the term, as suggested, but rather to shift and focus more closely on the discursive frameworks that organize the field, as well as on the connections of field and framework. Certainly this *Critical Reader* proposes to try to carry this through, which is why work is collected that looks through an Indian lens on visual cultures, on regional and vernacular literatures, on film and translation theory, on the ethics of texts, and on cosmopolitan as well as minority stances and identities. (Inevitably, and regrettably, there are omissions – pioneering work on gender studies, urban culture, politics and performance theory, to name only a few fields, has remained unrepresented.) We also bring together critics who are well known in India but relatively emergent in the West, who have been trying out new or revised applications of postcolonial perspectives, such as Udaya Kumar, Nivedita Menon, Madhava Prasad and Aniket Jaaware, none of whose positions would map easily onto a standard postcolonial description. A further expanded list of younger critics who have produced work that is deliberately and productively focused on India in the context of literary and print cultures and that exists in a tangential but dynamic relation to the postcolonial frame, would include Priya Joshi, Milind Wakankar, Francesca Orsini, Rosinka Chaudhuri and Rochelle Pinto, to mention only a few names that have not been anthologized under a postcolonial heading so far.[23]

The established, not to say household, names who have contributed to the volume, from both outside the academic postcolonial fold, as in the case of Amit Chaudhuri, and from within the postcolonial arena – Partha Chatterjee, Dipesh Chakrabarty, Gayatri Chakravorty Spivak, Robert J. C. Young – have done so in a new avatar that marks a departure from the established procedures of their existent genres. While Chaudhuri's academic work, in books such as *D.H. Lawrence and 'Difference': Postcoloniality and the Poetry of the Present* (2003) and *Clearing A Space: Reflections on India, Literature, and Culture* (2008), has wrestled with the paradigmatic frames of postcolonial discourse, his essay collected here develops a nuanced account of twentieth-century cosmopolitanism that suggests a new departure from postcolonial vocabularies. Spivak's meticulous and closely read essay on 'Ethics and politics in Tagore, Coetzee and certain scenes of teaching', reads how 'disgrace' is interpreted not only translocally, but also as it moves between different social and cultural discourses and conversations. Similarly, Partha Chatterjee, quoted extensively in the postcolonial arena, presents an essay on the sacred circulation of photographic images in the service of national historiography that breaks unfamiliar ground outside of his own oeuvre.

In so far as these well-known postcolonial commentators apply themselves to an expansion of postcolonial preoccupations and methodologies in India, Dipesh Chakrabarty and Aamir R. Mufti, too, in their different ways, produce a deliberate 'fuzzy' making of postcolonial terminologies, especially in processes of cultural translation of different kinds – for instance, in creative repetition across widely different contexts; in the cultural and political displacement of texts that translation occasions; and in the politically demonic affinities that are revealed by translation. While Robert J. C. Young's reading of ways of seeing in Satyajit Ray decisively takes him away from the for-him-familiar textual sphere and towards the visual, Ashis Nandy's study of 'the politics and cultural psychology of the limits of human degradation' also explores fresh ground by considering situations of humiliation both in South Asia and in a globalized world. Evidently, the best-known postcolonialists in this collection have been made to serve a different purpose from their usual role – in almost every instance, the work chosen from them is not representative of the mode in which they are most recognizable.

Our selections are admittedly culturalist, as postcolonial work often is, but that is a self-conscious choice, coming out of our own personal trajectories. In defence, one could quote again Said's well-known quotation from Gramsci in his *Prison Notebooks*: 'The starting-point of critical elaboration is the consciousness of what one really is, and is "knowing thyself" as a product of the historical process to date, which has deposited in you an infinity of traces, without leaving an inventory'. As Said points out in the Introduction to *Orientalism*, the only available English translation at the time left Gramsci's comment at that, whereas the Italian text concluded by adding, 'therefore it is imperative at the outset to compile such an inventory'.[24] Inventories have many incarnations: ours may be found sedimented in our own individual body of works and reflect, as in this *Critical Reader*, our related Indian, contextual, and postcolonial interests.

Notes

1   For a Deleuzian development of this point, see Peter Hallward, *Absolutely Postcolonial: Writing Between the Singular and the Specific* (Manchester: Manchester University Press, 2001).

2   Gayatri Chakravorty Spivak, *A Critique of Postcolonial Reason: Toward a History of the Vanishing Present* (Cambridge, MA, London: Harvard University Press, 1999), p. 1.

3   Neil Lazarus (ed.), *The Cambridge Companion to Postcolonial Literary Studies* (Cambridge: Cambridge University Press, 2004).

4   Ania Loomba, Suvir Kaul, Matti Bunzl, Antoinette Burton, Jed Esty, *et al.* (eds), *Postcolonial Studies and Beyond* (Duke University Press, 2005).

5   Michael Hardt and Antonio Negri, *Empire* (Cambridge, MA, and London: Harvard University Press, 2000).

6   A. K. Ramanujan, 'Small-Scale Reflections on a Great House', *The Arnold Anthology of Post-Colonial Literatures in English*, John Thieme (ed.) (London: Hodder Headline, 1996), pp. 712–15.

7   Henry Schwartz and Sangeeta Ray (ed.), *A Companion to Postcolonial Studies* (Oxford: Blackwell, 2000) p. 6. The following sentence concedes the point:

'Inevitably, these have been seen to date through the prevailing intellectual paradigms of Western universities'.

8 Ibid., p. xxiii.
9 Gayatri Chakravorty Spivak, *A Critique of Postcolonial Reason: Towards a History of the Vanishing Present* (Cambridge, MA: Harvard University Press, 1999).
10 *Interventions* 10.1 (2008): pp. v–vi.
11 *Interventions* 10.1 (2008): pp. v–vi.
12 *Interventions* 10.1 (2008): pp. v–vi.
13 Tejaswini Niranjana, P. Sudhir, Vivek Dhareshwar (eds), *Interrogating Modernity: Culture and Colonialism in India* (Calcutta: Seagull, 1993).
14 Anne McClintock, Aamir R. Mufti, Ella Shohat (eds), *Dangerous Liaisons: Gender, Nation, and Postcolonial Perspectives* (Minneapolis: University of Minnesota Press, 1997).
15 See Dipesh Chakrabarty, *Provincializing Europe: Postcolonial Thought and Historical Difference* (Delhi: Oxford University Press, 2001).
16 Vinayak Chaturvedi (ed.), *Mapping Subaltern Studies and the Postcolonial* (Oxford: Verso, 2000).
17 Ranajit Guha and Gayatri Chakravorty Spivak (eds), *Selected Subaltern Studies* (New York and Oxford: Oxford University Press, 1988).
18 Bill Ashcroft, Gareth Griffiths and Helen Tiffin, *The Empire Writes Back* (London: Routledge, 1989).
19 Robert J. C. Young, *White Mythologies: Writing History and the West* (London: Routledge, 1990); Robert J. C. Young (ed.), *Untying the Text: A Post-Structuralist Reader* (London: RKP, 1981); Terry Eagleton, *Literary Theory: An Introduction* (Oxford: Basil Blackwell, 1983).
20 Edward Said, *Culture and Imperialism* (London: Cape, 1993); Robert J. C. Young, *Postcolonialism: An Historical Introduction* (Oxford: Blackwell, 2001), pp. 317–34.
21 Rajeswari Sunder Rajan, *The Scandal of the State: Women, Law and Citizenship in Postcolonial India* (Durham and London: Duke University Press, 2003); Leela Gandhi, *Affective Communities: Anti-Colonial Thought, Fin-de-Siècle Radicalism and the Politics of Friendship* (Durham and London: Duke University Press, 2006); Antoinette Burton, *At the Heart of Empire: Indians and the Colonial Encounter in Late Victorian Britain* (Berkeley: University of California Press, 199); Elleke Boehmer, *Empire, the National and the Postcolonial: Resistance in Interaction* (Oxford: Oxford University Press, 2002); Aamir R. Mufti, *Enlightenment in the Colony: The Jewish Question and the Crisis of Postcolonial Culture* (Princeton and Oxford: Princeton University Press, 2007).
22 Ashis Nandy, *The Intimate Enemy: Loss and Recovery of Self under Colonialism* (Oxford: Oxford University Press, 1988).
23 Priya Joshi, *In Another Country: Colonialism, Culture, and the English Novel in India* (New York: Columbia University Press, 2002; New Delhi: Oxford University Press, 2003); Milind Wakankar, *Subalternity and Religion: The Prehistory of Dalit Empowerment in South Asia* (London: Routledge, 2010); Francesca Orsini, *The Hindi Public Sphere 1920–1940. Language and Literature in the Age of Nationalism* (Delhi: Oxford University Press. 2002); *Print and Pleasure: Popular literature and entertaining fictions in colonial north India* (New Delhi: Permanent Black, 2009); Rosinka Chaudhuri, *Gentlemen Poets in Colonial Bengal: Emergent Nationalism and the Orientalist Project* (Calcutta: Seagull, 2002); Derozio, *Poet of India: The Definitive Edition* (Delhi: Oxford University Press, 2008); Rochelle Pinto, *Between Empires: Print and Politics in Goa* (Delhi: Oxford University Press, 2007).
24 Edward Said, *Orientalism: Western Conceptions of the Orient* (London: Penguin, 1978), p. 26.

Part I

Visual cultures

Introduction

Elleke Boehmer and Rosinka Chaudhuri

The study of the visual cultures of Indian modernity belongs to a relatively recent though fully developed genre of scholarship that has come to
signify the most prominent, contemporary face of South Asian postcolonial and cultural studies. The field has been devoted, so far, to analyses of
the popular public cultures that have shaped the nuanced histories of the
multiple modernities of colonial, nationalist and present-day India, investigating the variety of manifestations and practices of which it is constituted. The celebrated 'visual turn' in modern Indian cultural studies rests
upon an abundance of works that have shown how visual iconographies
have played a fundamental role in nationalist and postcolonial representations across a variety of pictorial, architectural and performative arenas,
demonstrating how this image-field, comprised of posters, calendar art,
photography, popular prints, drama, cinema and television, has become a
fundamental key to the understanding of the nature of the Indian modern.

In a number of publications from within this area, the claim is made that
the ground should be shifted from the primacy of written sources to that
of visual practices – that popular visual culture constitutes a definitive, not
a supplementary site of knowledge in the construction of the histories of
India's many modernities. This discrete field of study allies the analysis of
popular visual culture to the disciplines of art history, film, and television
studies, while borrowing from the resources of cultural theory and the
interdisciplinary fields of postcolonial scholarship an array of concerns
that complicate received notions of elite and popular culture, high and
low art. The bringing together in this section, therefore, of two essays on
iconography and two on film is a fortuitous conjunction that depends
for its efficacy on certain shared notions of the idea of 'public culture' as
put forward by Arjun Appadurai and Carol Breckenridge in the 1990s
in their influential journal of the same name. Emphatically, the driving
force in this project was the desire to chart the trans-national flows that
energized local sites of the performance and production of the modern
and to study new forms of electronic media and popular entertainment
and their spaces of consumption and reception.

The range of scholars co-opted into this enterprise of 'interrogating' or 'consuming' modernity was extensive, as was the diverse eclecticism of the practices brought within its fold.[1] Nevertheless, certain seminal works and theorists came to dominate certain sub-fields within this overall schema. In the area of popular printed texts and images, their production and consumption, and their place within the nation, Christopher Pinney established himself as an important theorist in his carefully nuanced study of the aesthetic conceptions that govern popular photography and visual culture in India. *Camera Indica: The Social Life of Indian Photographs* (1997) was followed by another significant study on the social history of Indian chromolithography, *Photos of the Gods: The Printed Image and Political Struggle in India* (2004), where he theorized his notion of how corporeal engagement and the sensory aesthetics of devotion signify the world of popular pictures of the gods in India. Invaluable contributors to the richness and depth of this academic field investigating the visual practices of Indian modernity also include Jyotindra Jain, Sumathi Ramaswamy, Kajri Jain, Tapati Guha-Thakurta and Raminder Kaur, to name only a few.[2]

The study of popular visual culture in India has long had an investment in the framing debates of Indian cinema. Writing about the relation between cinema and the viewing culture of the Indian public sphere boasts a historiography that goes back at least to the early 1960s, when directors such as Satyajit Ray and film critics such as Chidananda Das Gupta wrote about popular cinema and popular culture in relation to their own practices that were located in a rationalist-realist framework in contradistinction to the popular films of mass entertainment. Ashis Nandy then offered the contentious thesis that the non-modernity of certain tropes in popular Indian cinema signalled, in fact, the last remaining traces of traditional viewing practices that were holding out against the onslaught of globalization. The position that has developed in the last decade or so amongst a group of highly productive film studies, academics in India, however, has developed into a distinct lineage of its own, where the transformation of both popular cinema and its audiences has been studied in relation to the modernization of available narrative forms within a modern technological mode. Their contribution to the burgeoning area of Indian film studies marshals a wide range of Marxist, political, and film theories about ideology, the Indian state, melodrama, realism, and narrative form to trace the contemporary construction of Indian cinema outside the box of the usual historicist approaches derived from a nationalist, 'postcolonial' consciousness. Ravi Vasudevan's *Making Meaning in Indian Cinema* (2000), Arvind Rajagopal's *Politics after Television: Religious Nationalism and the Reshaping of the Indian Public* (2001), Ashish Rajadhyaksha's *Encyclopaedia of Indian Cinema* (1994) and the recent *Indian Cinema in the Time of Celluloid* (2009), and Madhava Prasad's *Ideology of the Hindi Film* (1998) are incompletely representative of a field where the most important contributions are often made in individual articles (such as

Rajadhakshya on D. G. Phalke, the founding father of Indian cinema) or path-breaking anthologies (such as those edited by Moinak Biswas, Rachel Dwyer and Christopher Pinney or Preben Kaarsholm).[3]

The research in both fields of popular print culture as well as film studies, therefore, is involved in a common consideration of how the visual, performative and mediated sites of culture have constituted multi-perspectival programmes in historical and contemporary India. Tapati Guha-Thakurta's chapter in this volume comes out of the established parameters of studies on the visual realm and the public sphere in contemporary India. It analyses the resurrection of religion as a key player in political affairs, and the manner in which such an emergence complicates the practices of civil society and the secular premises of artistic productions. Looking at two very disparate instances, that of the case of M. F. Husain, India's most celebrated artist, and of the festival of the Durga Puja in the city of Calcutta, she investigates the manner in which a broader set of debates and paradoxes have arisen from the recurring blurring of distinctions between the 'artistic' and the 'religious' object across different institutional and public sites in contemporary India. What happens to the qualities of 'iconicity' and 'sacredness', she asks, in the modern spaces of contemporary India, where these can be seen to belong as much to the 'artwork' as to the 'religious object'? The porous fences demarcating one from the other disallow 'art' its autonomous zone of creative licence in the one case, while allowing the aura of the religious icon, in another, to be dissipated into the commercial complexes of festival celebration. The chapter by Partha Chatterjee comes to its subject of the sacredness of images constituted as national icons from outside of the field of visual culture studies, adding, thereby, an intriguing dimension to an arena that, by its very provenance, welcomes interventions from cultural critics across a broad spectrum. His is a famous name in postcolonial studies generally, cited repeatedly in the context of his best known work on nationalism and the politics of the governed. Here, however, he looks at images of the great monuments of India in history textbooks from the colonial to the post-Independence era, showing how photographs of this architecture reveal the inescapable ways in which the practice of image-making is aligned with the purposes of power, as the representations accrue an iconic status in a nationalist context where the original presumptions that imbued the encounter with the strangeness of the random and the everyday have no place.

In the two chapters that deal with film, too, we have a similar dichotomy in that the one comes from within the discipline, the other from without. Madhava Prasad teaches film and cultural studies and has published extensively on cinema, literary theory, postcolonial questions and critical theory. His book on post-Independence Hindi cinema used dense theoretical analysis and detailed empirical evidence to discuss, for instance, the ban on kissing in these films as a symptom of national unity, or to show how the narrative structure of popular film is perpetuated by the Bombay industry's mode of manufacture. In the essay included here, he deals with the problem of popular sovereignty, which he says needs to be investigated beyond the confines of republican institutions in fields where supplementary, virtual formations of sovereignty create community effects that compensate for their lack in the proper political structure per se. Using the occasion of the Tamil superstar Rajnikanth's film release in 2007, he shows how the emergence of sovereignty formations around film stars such as these may be analysed in the context of the challenge posed to such formations by a newly triumphant commodity logic, which, far from solving the problem, however, may be expected instead to create new political crises.

In a completely divergent frame, Robert J. C. Young, one of postcolonial theory's leading critics, writes here for the first time on the legendary film director, Satyajit Ray, using a short story by him to elaborate upon the theme of ventriloquism and illusion, image-making and its production of effect. Investigating what is different about the photography in Ray's early films, Young maintains that thinking about the relation of the ventriloquist to his dummy, the director to his camera, helps us to understand that distinctiveness of the illusion that is produced. Focusing on the mediating role of the animating machine, he shows how the distinctiveness of Ray's image-making came both from his belief that 'seeing' was more important than technique and from the giant Mitchell camera used in *Pather Panchali*, which achieved a different kind of monumentality in the images of that film. It was the machine, which remained almost immovable, that then directed the stillness of the images of this early film, thus acquiring – like the ventriloquist's come-alive dummy – an agency that is absent from the later films that used a standard Arriflex camera, which brought with it a more standardized all-seeing eye.

Notes

1   Tejaswini Niranjana, P. Sudhir and V. Dhareshwar (eds), *Interrogating Modernity: Culture and Colonialism in India* (Calcutta: Seagull Books, 1993); Arjun Appadurai and Carol Breckenridge (ed.), *Consuming Modernity: Public Culture in Contemporary India* (1996).
2   To name only one book per writer, Jyotindra Jain, *Indian Popular Culture, 'The Conquest of the World as Picture'* (2004), Sumathi Ramaswamy, *Beyond Appearances?: Visual Practices and Ideologies in Modern India* (2003), Kajri Jain, *Gods in the Bazaar: The Economies of Indian Calendar Art* (2007), Tapati Guha-Thakurta, *The Making of a New 'Indian' Art: Artists, Aesthetics and Nationalism in Bengal, c. 1850–1920*, (1992), Raminder Kaur, *Performative Politics and the Cultures of Hinduism: Public Uses of Religion in Western India* (2003).
3   Ashish Rajadhyaksha, 'The Phalke Era: Conflict of Traditional Form and Modern Technology' in *Interrogating Modernity* (Calcutta: Seagull Books,1993); Moinak Biswas (ed.), *Apu and After: Re-visiting Ray's Cinema* (Calcutta: Seagull Books, 2006); Rachel Dwyer and Christopher Pinney (eds), *Pleasure and the Nation: The History, Politics and Consumption of Public Culture in India* (Delhi: Oxford University Press, 2001); Preben Kaarsholm (ed.), *City Flicks: Indian Cinema and the Urban Experience* (Calcutta: Seagull, 2007).

1 The sacred circulation of national images

Partha Chatterjee

In 1962, India went to war with China over a piece of disputed territory up in the Himalayas. I was in high school at the time and impressionable enough to be swept away by the patriotic fervour. Our cause was right, we believed, because the territory in question was clearly ours: wasn't there a McMahon Line, drawn on a map solemnly signed in 1914 by representatives of the governments of British India and Republican China? What greater proof did one need to support our claim? Of course, the military campaign went disastrously for India and, along with millions of my compatriots, I smarted under the national humiliation. Later, when the scales of adolescence fell from my eyes, I realized we had been fighting not over territory – after all, the land in question was up in the mountains and completely uninhabited – but over its representation. We had been fighting over maps. The image wielded has far greater power over our imaginations and passions than the real thing.

It is the same story everywhere with national images. What is interesting is the special way in which a particular national culture turns an image into an icon, to be reproduced, distributed, displayed and sacralized. What is it about an image that allows it to be multiplied and disseminated as a national icon while fully retaining its quality of sacredness? Let me pursue this question by looking at the way national monuments have been displayed in school textbooks in Bengal. I cannot claim deep familiarity with textbooks used in other parts of India, yet I would be surprised to find they were radically different.

My choice of sources is deliberate. I will be looking at official nationalism, materials produced as an ideological ensemble within the institutional ambit of a nation-state regime. Most of the elements in this ensemble can be traced back genealogically to earlier formations in colonial and sometimes even precolonial histories. But they were reconstituted in a new order of discourse by the official nationalism of the postcolonial nation-state. This ideological function, while it is supervised and directed by the state, is not necessarily confined only to formal state institutions. When successful, the official ideology proliferates in the practices of non-state institutions such as schools, clubs, professional associations, cultural organizations, media, etc. Most secondary schools in Bengal, for instance, have been run as private trusts, sometimes with government grants but often without. Textbooks were provided by private publishers in accordance with syllabi laid down by a public school board.

Official nationalism has a performative as well as a pedagogical function.[1] In the performative mode, it must display the unity and singularity of the nation and the equal place within it of all citizens. In the pedagogical mode, however, official nationalism must reckon with the fact that not all citizens can be treated equally, because all are not yet 'proper' citizens; they must be educated into full membership of the 'true' body of national citizens. Under official nationalism, schools become a crucial site for both functions. In the performative mode, schoolchildren frequently participate in events that play out the simultaneous and equal participation in the national space of diverse groups of Indians: the 'unity in diversity' theme is the most common trope for performing the national. Here the school largely replicates practices that are more effectively played out on other sites, such as the parades held on Republic Day, or in cinema and television. In the other mode, however, the school, with its curriculum, its texts and its expository and disciplinary regime, is the place where the pedagogical function of official nationalism can be observed in its purest form. It is thus not surprising that the content of school textbooks has been so often a bone of political contention in contemporary India.

Before nationalism

Bibidhartha samgraha (literally, Collection of Diverse Knowledge) founded in 1851 and edited by the polymath Rajendralal Mitra, was the first illustrated Bengali journal that regularly published articles on places of archaeological and historical interest. Besides being a leading figure in the Asiatic Society of Bengal, the most prominent editor in his day of Sanskrit manuscripts, and a leading historian of art and architecture, Mitra was also a pioneer in the publication of Bengali maps and the founder of the Photographic Society of India. Both the engraved illustrations and the historical articles in *Bibidhartha samgraha* were based on current English writings. The illustrations of monuments have the same picturesque quality that was the hallmark of both colonial illustrative art and early colonial photography (figures 1.1 and 1.2; for comparison see figure 1.3).[2] The age of nationalism was yet to appear in Bengal.

When the gods Brahma, Indra, Narayana, and Shiva visited Delhi in 1879, after catching the train from Saharanpur, they were taken on a tour through the city by the rain god Varuna who, judging by the account of the visit, had probably memorized Baedeker's or Thomas

Cook's guide to India (Baedeker's guide was published in the 1850s, Thomas Cook's in the 1860s).[3] He knew, for instance, that the great mosque of the city was 201 feet long and 120 feet wide and that the Red Fort was spread across two and a half miles. Objective knowledge was colonial knowledge; the objective gaze was the colonial gaze. Few among the new English-educated Indians were questioning these truisms of the times.

In Bengal, nineteenth-century school textbooks in history rarely carried illustrations. Metal engraving, lithography and halftone printing were still expensive and textbooks had to be cheap. Halftone printing was patented in France in 1857 and was commercially used in Europe and the United States by the 1880s. The first halftone press was set up in Calcutta in the 1900s, but some publishers were printing halftone blocks made for them in Europe. Wood engravings were, of course, both cheap and widely used, but they were rarely employed in textbooks, possibly because of their association with the pulp literature of the bazaar. We have to move forward to the 1920s to find illustrated history books for schoolchildren. By then, nationalism in Bengal was well advanced. On the one hand, revolutionary groups were carrying out daring attacks on British officials and when these rebels were tried and hanged they became national martyrs. On the other hand, the Indian National Congress, under the leadership of C. R. Das, launched a very successful mass campaign of non-cooperation with the colonial government. In literature, theatre, art and music, the nationalist agenda was being pushed forward vigorously.

The school curriculum was, of course, still under official control and no hint of disloyalty was tolerated on the pages of textbooks. Flipping the pages of a widely read textbook on Indian history from 1924, we find engraved illustrations of rulers and monuments – in fact, exactly the same sort of engravings we would have found in older colonial histories and travel accounts.[4] The monuments have the same picturesque quality and some of the engraved blocks look well-worn from repeated use (figure 1.4; for comparison see figure 1.5). If national icons were being produced at this time, they had still not entered into mass circulation in school textbooks. This particular book, however, established a pattern for historical illustrations that would henceforth be repeated: ancient India (called the 'Hindu period') would be represented by Hindu and Buddhist religious architecture and medieval India (called the 'Muslim period') by forts, victory towers and royal tombs. (The exception for ancient India was the headless statue, lodged in the museum at Mathura, of the Kushana ruler Kanishka, a source of endless mirth for generations of schoolchildren; see figure 1.10.) Interestingly, the modern or 'British' period was illustrated not by monuments but by portraits of viceroys.

Nationalist transformations

There is a moment soon after Indian independence in 1947 that appears to be something like a nodal point in the telling of this story. One is as yet unsure which way the plot will move. Official nationalism was still being constituted. Ultimately, the plot does, of course, advance in one particular direction.

In the handling of illustrations, the textbooks of the early 1950s mark one important change. Line engravings are replaced by photographs printed from halftone zinc blocks. A textbook of 1950 written by the well-known historian Kalidas Nag, a specialist on the art and archaeology of Southeast Asia, is copiously illustrated by photographs.[5] But they have one curious feature. The picturesque quality has disappeared; there are no trees or reflections on water or stray human figures in the foreground (figure 1.6). Historical monuments are acquiring an iconic quality. What else can one say about the photographed image of the Taj, obviously printed from a metal block that has long outlived its aesthetic appeal?

The contrast is brought out sharply by comparing this textbook with another publication of the same time that was also meant for children but was not a prescribed school textbook. *Biswa parichay* (Introduction to the World), brought out by one of the largest publishers of children's books, was meant as an upmarket publication, printed on glossy paper with photographs on every page, to be bought as a gift or given as a prize.[6] The photographs here have a self-consciously artistic quality about them; they are not intended to serve any iconic function. Notice, for example, the photograph of the Qutb Minar shot through a ruined gateway (figure 1.7), or that of the Taj Mahal from the bank of the river Yamuna. These images would not get into officially prescribed textbooks intended for the first generation of Indian children born after independence.

What happens next is inexplicable in terms of any theory of modernization or development. Technologically, it is a reversal, a throwback. But it is not caused by any technological gap or absence. From the late 1950s or early 1960s, photographs disappear from history textbooks, to be replaced by images that look like etchings or engravings but are actually pen-and-ink drawings made to look like engravings and transferred photographically onto metal blocks. They are not, however, artists' sketches: there is not the slightest trace of an individualized aesthetic gaze. These are representations of historical monuments as icons.

Let me present some random selections, because almost any textbook published in the last 40 years will do. Take the picture of the temple at Thanjavur (figure 1.8) or of the Qutb Minar or the Taj Mahal (figure 1.9).[7] They are clearly drawn from photographic images – the angle of vision, the perspective and the framing all suggest this. But they are not photographs; they are drawings. Even Kanishka, the 'headless monarch', is represented in the form of his museum statue (figure 1.10). What can be the reason for this strange denial of the advantages of photographic reproduction?

I suggest that the answer lies in the way in which the effect of sacredness is produced in the national icon. There is an economy of this iconicity that requires that the image be cleansed of all traces of a self-conscious artistic aesthetic. There must be no hint of the picturesque or the painterly, no tricks of the camera angle, no staging of the unexpected or the exotic. The image must also be shorn of all redundancy: any element that does not have a specific place within the narrative economy of this national iconography must be removed from the image. Hence, no superfluous foliage or shimmering reflections on water, no lazy dog sleeping in the shade or stray passers-by going about their daily business. The 'artistic' has no place within the visual domain of the sacred.

The sacredness of national icons plays a curious role within the pedagogical apparatus of history. It is well known, for instance, that a common trope in the narration of history is the romantic one of imaginatively inhabiting a past era. The effort here is to close the distance in time by travelling back into another period and, in a sense, participating in the experience of another time and another people. The historical romance – in the form of novels, ballads, dramas – is the most obvious literary genre in which this imaginative anachronism is practised. But it is also a common pedagogical tool employed by history teachers and is not infrequently, or so at least I suspect, a powerful affective impulse that drives the work of many professional historians. This romantic attitude towards the historical object encourages proximity; it invites the reader or viewer to enter the world to which the object belonged. The attitude is the same as that which impels modern-day travel as distinct from traditional pilgrimage. Not surprisingly, it promotes a visual language that emphasizes not just vividness or a life-like quality but also the exotic and the picturesque.

The attitude of sacredness I am considering here in connection with national icons is diametrically opposed to that of the romantic. It is founded on a reverential distance of the viewer from the object. But that distance cannot be one of time, for then the object would be consigned irretrievably to some lost period peopled by others. To enter the sacred domain of 'our' national treasures, the object must be recovered for 'our' worshipful gaze. I suggest that this recovery is effectively accomplished by the iconic image of the monument. An iconic image is not merely an easily recognized depiction or a conventional logo. It is the representation of a sacred object in which the image itself partakes of the sacred quality of the original. To imagine, as it were, a treasure-house of national monuments, the schoolchild must be presented with a gallery of iconic images that are situated in no particular place or time but in fact belong to the whole of the national space and to all time. After all, as the nationalist is the first to remind us, has not the nation existed from time immemorial? In contrast with the imaginative anachronism of the romantic trope, the iconic image produces a visual anachronism in which the real object is taken out of its context in a specific place and time and located in an abstract and timeless space. The image now becomes the pure and sacred original, compared to which the real object can only be observed (by the tourist, for example) in its corrupt and utterly profane real-life context.

Judith Mara Gutman has argued that photographs made by Indian photographers reflect a completely different and distinctly Indian conception of reality unlike the Western realist aesthetic.[8] The painted photograph is the example most commonly cited to show how, in this case, paint is used not to supplement but in fact to hide the technologically produced likeness of the real object. It has, of course, been correctly pointed out that Gutman's claim of a radically different Indian aesthetic is hugely simplistic and overstated.[9] But her argument that in Indian photographs everything within the picture field happens at once, as though in an idealized and timeless space, appears to hold for the iconic images of national monuments I have been talking about. To achieve that effect, photography itself is avoided, for its very life-like quality threatens to introduce into the image elements that suggest a specific time and context within which the monument actually exists. The iconic drawing allows for much greater control, so that all that is redundant to the sacred economy of the image can be carefully eliminated.

Consider, for instance, a picture of the Red Fort in Delhi in a textbook published in 1987 (figure 1.12).[10] The Mughal fort, once the seat of imperial sovereignty, first entered the sacred geography of Indian nationalism when officers of Subhas Chandra Bose's Indian National Army were tried there for treason and cruelty to prisoners by the colonial government in the last days of British rule. Those convicted as traitors by the British were regarded as national heroes by Indians. Since India became independent in 1947, it has become an annual ritual for the Prime Minister to address the nation from the fort's ramparts on Independence Day (figure 1.11). On that day, the national flag flies from the flagstaff on top of the fort. The illustration of the Red Fort freezes this moment, elevating it into an abstract ideality by eliminating everything from the picture field except for the bare architectural facade and the national flag flying from an impossibly high flagstaff. Such is the process by which the sacred iconicity of the monument is produced. No photograph could have achieved the effect with such controlled economy.

I should add that there are two other categories of images in history textbooks that are also reproduced, virtually without exception, as line drawings: the maps (always redrawn by artists from unacknowledged originals) and the portraits of national leaders that fill the pages of the 'modern period' (even though they commonly serve as the basis for the artist's line drawings, photographs are almost never used).

It might be supposed that there are economic or technological reasons for the preference for line drawings over photographs. Are they cheaper to print? Not really; both are printed from zinc blocks made by the same photographic process. There is some substance to the claim that line blocks produce better prints on inferior paper than halftone blocks. But if there were a clear pedagogical or aesthetic case to be made for the representational superiority of the photographic image, there is no reason to believe that it would not have been used in textbooks, even if it meant a slightly higher price. In fact, the use of line drawing is so ubiquitous that block-makers manufacture and sell readymade printing blocks of historical monuments for textbook use (figure 1.13). It seems to me that the pedagogical purpose of nationalist education is believed to be served far more effectively by such idealized drawings than by the suspiciously profane realism of photographs.

I should emphasize that we are talking about a professional practice within a pedagogical regime that has acquired the consensual form of a convention. When we try to decode the underlying order of meanings, we do not imply that the artists, publishers or teachers participating in the practice are conscious of that underlying structure, or even curious about it. Such is the commonsensical obviousness of every conventional practice.

My argument would be clinched if I could show that even after the latest technological revolution in the Bengali textbook industry, namely, the rapid introduction of phototypesetting and offset printing in the last decade or so, historical illustrations continue to follow the same pattern I have described. The evidence on this point, however, is still somewhat ambiguous. Most history textbooks I have seen published in the last five years do, in fact, contain the same line drawings, even when their texts are phototypeset and the books are printed by the photo-offset process.[11] One significant novelty is the introduction of glossy colour photographs of monuments on the covers. One textbook has a section of colour photographs printed on glossy paper inserted in the middle of the book: the photos of the Sanchi stupa or the Taj Mahal are the same as one finds on picture postcards.

I have, however, found one book that appears to have broken from the convention by abandoning line drawings and reintroducing photographs – a half century after the early days of the Indian republic.[12] This book has a sheaf of colour photos (once again of picture-postcard quality) and coloured maps. It also has black-and-white photographs of monuments strewn across its pages, many with a deliberately vivid and picturesque quality that suggests proximity and everyday familiarity rather than abstract remoteness and sacred iconicity (figure 1.14). Does this mark a new trend? It is too early to tell. It is possible that there is a recognition that with the proliferation of colour magazines, cinema and television, even schoolchildren in small towns and villages are now exposed to a visual language that makes the iconic drawing seem archaic and jaded. Perhaps new pedagogical techniques, enabled by the most recent technologies of mechanical reproduction, will be fashioned to create the effect of sacredness by which alone an imagined national space, dotted by timeless images, can exist in its spectral purity, purer even than the real-life originals.

Or could it be that that iconic space is being desacralized? Perhaps the romantic trope has finally won the day, making room for those familiar techniques of historical reconstruction by which an object can be imaginatively grasped in the here-and-now while, at the same time, it is located in a specific time and place in the past? Yet, I see no reason to believe that that is the case. Were the artistic photograph to find a place in history textbooks, my guess would be that sacred images would be produced and circulated by other means. What those means might be, I cannot tell. At the moment, I see that the old line-drawn images have still not yielded their place on the pages of Bengal's school textbooks. I also notice that Indians, as before, and like many other people, are still prepared to fight over maps.

Figure 1.1 The fort of Shah Jahan (Red Fort), Delhi, showing the residence of Empress Nur Jahan. Unknown artist. Engraving. Page 218 in *Bibidhartha samgraha* (Collection of Diverse Knowledges; Shaka era 1776 [1854]). The flag flying above the turret on the left cannot be identified. Before the suppression of the revolt of 1857, the Red Fort was the seat of the Mughal emperor, even though effective sovereignty in most of India had passed to the British.

Figure 1.2 The Riverfront at Varanasi. Unknown artist. Engraving. Page 67 in *Bibidhartha samgraha* (1852).

Figure 1.3 The Manikarnika Burning Ghat, Varanasi, c. 1858–60. Felice Beato, photographer. Albumen silver print from an albumen-on-glass negative; 23.7 × 28.5 cm. From a disbound album of views of Northern India, Egypt, and the Middle East with portraits of British soldiers. Canadian Centre for Architecture, Montréal.

Figure 1.4 The Taj Mahal, Agra. Unknown artist. Engraving. Page 111 in Bijaychandra Majumdar, *Bharatbarsher itihas* (History of India; Calcutta: Sen Brothers, 1924).

Figure 1.5 The Taj Mahal with fountains, Agra, c. 1858–60. Felice Beato, photographer. Albumen silver print from an albumen-on-glass negative; 28.6 × 25.2 cm. From a disbound album of views of Northern India, Egypt, and the Middle East with portraits of British soldiers. Canadian Centre for Architecture, Montréal.

Figure 1.6 The Shiva Temple at Thanjavur. Photoengraving. Page 107 in Kalidas Nag, *Swadesh o sabhyata* (Our Land and Civilization; Calcutta: Modern Book Agency, 1950).

Figure 1.7 The Qutb Minar, Delhi. Photoengraving. Page 72 in *Biswa parichay* (Introduction to the World; Calcutta: Deb Sahitya Kutir, 1953).

Figure 1.8 The Shiva Temple at Thanjavur. Unknown artist. Engraving. Page 103 in Dilip Kumar Ghosh, *Bharat o bharatbasi* (India and Indians; Calcutta: New Book Stall, 1974). Though it is a line drawing, is there a hint of the painterly here? Notice the somewhat unusual angle of view and the trees, especially in comparison with figure 1.6. A photograph from this angle would have firmly situated the temple in real time and space, as the line drawing does not.

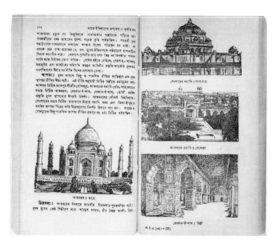

Figure 1.9 The Taj Mahal, Agra. Unknown artist. Engraving. Page 112 in Dineschandra Sarkar and Kalipada Hore, *Bharat-itihaser ruprekha* (Outline of Indian History; Calcutta: Vidyoday, 1973). The right column shows, from top to bottom, the tomb of Sher Shah Sur, Sasaram; the tomb of Akbar, Sikandra; and the *Diwan-i-Khas* in the Red Fort, Delhi.

Figure 1.10 The headless statue of Kanishka. Unknown artist. Engraving. Page 30 in Ghosh, *Bharat o bharatbasi* (1974).

Figure 1.11 Address to the nation by Prime Minister Nehru on Independence Day from the ramparts of the Red Fort, Delhi, 1970s. Unknown artist. Calendar: 35.5 × 28 cm. Private collection. The three figures in the sky are, at left and right, the Maratha ruler Shivaji and the Rajput ruler Rana Pratap, both of whom resisted Mughal domination. Between them is Subhas Chandra Bose, the nationalist leader who fought the British in the Second World War at the head of the Indian National Army. The military display that fills the skies provides an umbrella of protection over the new state leaders.

Figure 1.12 The fort of Shah Jahan (Red Fort), Delhi. Unknown artist. Engraving. Page 182 in Sobhakar Chattopadhyay, *Bharater itihas* (History of India; Calcutta: Narmada Publication, 1987).

7176 Rs. 3·00

Figure 1.13 Image sample of the fort of Shah Jahan (Red Fort), Delhi, in a sales catalogue of metal printing forms. Unknown artist. Calcutta: Dass Brothers, 1960.

Figure 1.14 The fort of Shah Jahan (Red Fort), Delhi. Unknown photographer. Engraving. Page 152 in Atulchandra Ray, *Bharater itihas* (History of India; Calcutta: Prantik, 2001). Notice the parked bicycle and people sitting under the tree in the foreground.

Notes

This chapter previously appeared in *Traces of India: Photography, Architecture and the Politics of Representation, 1850–1900*, edited by Maria Antonella Pelizzari (Yale University Press, 2003).

1 The distinction has been made by Homi Bhabha, 'DissemiNation', in Bhabha (ed.), *Nation and Narration* (New York: Routledge, 1990).
2 The connection between the picturesque and the scientific in early colonial representations of Indian monuments is discussed by Tapati Guha-Thakurta in chapter one of *Monuments, Objects, Histories: Institutions of Art in Colonial and Pre-Colonial India* (New York: Columbia University Press, 2004).
3 Durgacharan Ray, *Debganer martye agaman* (The Gods' Visit to Earth, 1880; reprint edn, Calcutta: Dey's Publishing, 1984), pp. 45–57. This is one of the first travel guides in Bengali, written as an account of a visit by the gods keen to find out how their creation was faring under British rule.
4 Bijaychandra Majumdar, *Bharatbarsher itihas* (History of India; Calcutta: Sen Brothers, 1924).
5 Kalidas Nag, *Swadesh o sabhyata* (Our Land and Civilization; Calcutta: Modern Book Agency, 1950).
6 *Biswa parichay* (Introduction to the World; Calcutta: Deb Sahitya Kutir, 1953).
7 The Thanjavur image is from Dilip Kumar Ghosh, *Bharat o bharatbasi* (India and Indians; Calcutta: New Book Stall, 1974), p. 103. The Qutb and the Taj pictures are from Dineschandra Sarkar and Kalipada Hore, *Bharat-itihaser ruprekha* (Outline of Indian History; Calcutta: Vidyoday, 1973), pp. 70, 112.
8 Judith Mara Gutman, *Through Indian Eyes: Nineteenth- and Early Twentieth-Century Photography from India* (New York: Oxford University Press, 1982).
9 For instance, by Christopher Pinney, *Camera Indica: The Social Life of Indian Photographs* (London: Reaktion, 1997), pp. 95–6.
10 Sobhakar Chattopadhyay, *Bharater itihas* (History of India; Calcutta: Narmada Publication, 1987), p. 182.
11 Among popular textbooks today that continue to use line drawings instead of photographs are Nitish Ranjan Ray, *Bharat parichay* (Introduction to India; Calcutta: Allied Book Agency, 2001); Jiban Mukhopadhyay, *Swadesh parichay* (Introduction to Our Land; Calcutta: Nababharati, 2002); and Prabhattangshu Maiti, *Bharater itihas* (History of India; Calcutta: Sridhar Prakashani, 2001).
12 Atulchandra Ray, *Bharater itihas* (History of India; Calcutta: Prantik, 2001).

2 The blurring of distinctions

The artwork and the religious icon in contemporary India[1]

Tapati Guha-Thakurta

Posing the problem

This chapter explores a set of contentions and paradoxes that have arisen from the repeated blurring of distinctions between the 'artistic' and the 'religious' object across different institutional and public sites in contemporary India. This is the central, recurrent problem that I track across two divergent sites of art production and reception. In the first case, I revisit the unabated Hindu right-wing campaign against India's veteran modern artist, Maqbool Fida Husain, that began to snowball from 1996 around Husain's 'offence' of painting Hindu divinities in the nude (figure 2.1). Notwithstanding two definitive rulings of the Delhi High Court and Supreme Court of India (in May and September 2008) that have acquitted the artist of the many 'criminal' charges that were levelled against him,[2] the campaign has refused to let go of its target, forcing the artist into a life of self-imposed exile in Dubai.[3] If the 'Husain affair' has come over time to exemplify the siege of culture by the Hindu Right and the beleaguered state of the 'secular' in contemporary India, it also throws into the open a deep instability in the status of the nation's 'artistic' and 'religious' imagery, in the representational licences they enjoy and in the public fields of their circulation.

While the first part of the chapter maps this shrinking space of artistic autonomy and authority, the second part turns to a set of other tropes of conflations between the 'sacred' and 'secular' designation of objects, as they move in and out of a vortex of overlapping identities in new public fields of display and spectatorship. From the worlds of art, it enters a separate domain of a public festival in the city of Calcutta: one organized each autumn around the worship of goddess Durga. I take up here a recent trend of the striking reconfiguration of Durga icons as 'works of art' in the streets of Calcutta during this annual event (figure 2.2) that comes out of a longer history of the growing secularization of this domain of festivity and visual productions. What is involved here is less a situation of contention and conflict, more one of porous boundaries that allow the 'artistic' and the 'religious' the liberty to trespass into and inhabit each other's domains.

While the qualities of 'iconicity' and 'sacredness' can be seen to belong as much to the 'artwork' as to the 'religious object', modern history (not just in the West but equally in India) produced a series of crucial distinctions that set apart these different orders of iconicity, the practices that support them and the discursive spheres they inhabit. These distinctions, introduced and fine-tuned by modernity, are both ontological and institutional, and the relative weight of these differentiating criteria has been a subject of continuing debate in aesthetic and sociological theories of art.[4] In India, as elsewhere, the very identity of 'art' in the modern era has been grounded on this separation of domains between the 'secular' and the 'religious', on the elaborate distilling of the new 'secular' worlds in which both the art of the ancient and medieval past as well as the modern art of the nation came to be positioned. Together, the evolving discipline of art history and modern art practices served to render art into one of the most powerful secular-ritual objects of national life. The modern epistemology of 'art', we find, could accommodate as effectively the religious productions and iconographies of the nation's past as the new repertoire of divine and mythological imagery in the art of the present. If the Indian art tradition came to be invested with a uniquely 'spiritual' and 'transcendental' character, the 'spiritual' served here as a markedly secular designation, one that would give a body of the religious objects of the past a new sacral stature of 'art'.[5]

We need to remind ourselves of this well-established history to guard against a lingering trend of Orientalist and nationalist projections that emphasize the quintessentially 'religious' nature of India's artistic traditions as against the secularization of art in the West. Of longstanding prestige is a distinctly separate domain that we denominate as 'art' in India, and treat apart from the fields of both organized religion and popular faith. And it is only through recognizing this categorical distinction that we can grapple with the spectre of violation and threat, or with the conflation of identities that the current collapsing of this boundary presents to visual objects and subjects across this divide. As we shall see, the allegations against the paintings of Maqbool Fida Husain have forced us to rethink how we draw the line, not just between 'art' and 'obscenity', but also between the 'artistic' and 'religious' image – a line that may never have existed in earlier tradition, but fell powerfully in place in modern Indian history, and now needs to be redrawn and policed with great urgency. Using the case of new kinds of ritual art productions for the Durga Puja festival in contemporary Calcutta, I will also show how this line between the 'artistic' and the 'religious' keeps strategically shifting and disappearing in other public contexts, to enable a new order of modern practices to permeate the existing field of the 'religious'.

It is important that we do not confuse the current collapsing of 'religious' and 'artistic' identities of images as a clash between 'traditional' and 'modern' dispensations. For, as we know, what is countering the secular entity of contemporary art is not its religious other, but a political and communal entity of 'Hindus', who share many of the same markers of contemporaneity as the artists they detest. The modernity of the new regimes of religious identities and productions will repeatedly reappear, in the escalating attacks on M. F. Husain and in the spectacles produced around Durga Puja in different urban locations in Calcutta. In the case of the anti-Husain campaign, notions of the 'religious' can be seen to surface within a wholly modern political register of rights and claims, with its vocabulary of offence and outrage, and its claims to objects and iconographies. In the case of the Durga creations in the city of Calcutta, the 'religious' will be shown to take on a new set of modern vanities of 'art', its hankering for a spiritual aesthetic, and often its distinctly modernist nostalgia for the retrieval of disappearing rural and folk art practices. The claims of artistic production and the markings of the 'secular' labour are to leave their imprints in a festival field that remains constitutively grounded in the performance of the ritual event. The result is a continuous re-inscription of devotional affect – surrounding the homecoming of the goddess – within the body of the urban spectacle. An ongoing concern of the article will be with the vexed interface of the 'artistic' and the 'religious' across these domains, with the public fields of locations of these varied bodies of art practice, and the kinds of iconographic transgressions that these enable or foreclose.

The nudes that offend: more notes on the 'Husain affair'[6]

The offence and the allegations

In September 1996, a line drawing of the goddess Saraswati by M. F. Husain, one of the artist's large repertoire of stylized female nudes done in the 1970s (figure 2.1) became the object of sudden moral outrage among local activists of the Vishva Hindu Parishad (VHP), a right-wing political group allied to the Bharatiya Janata Party (BJP). It produced a spiralling curve of violence against the artist's works and property that moved over time from Indore and Bhopal to Ahmedabad, Mumbai, New Delhi and, more recently, to London. What came to be dragged into the centre of the country's fanatical *Hindutva* politics as a result was the hallowed world of modern Indian art, and its most cherished object of representation: the female nude. Why was M. F. Husain targeted, and what were the particular political circumstances that propelled this 'pogrom' against him and his art? What made Husain's nude goddesses any the less defensible from those that we encounter in traditional Indian painting and sculpture, or in the works of several other modern Indian artists? Continuously raised and debated, these questions have remained dangerously unresolved.

M. F. Husain (born in 1915) has been the most flamboyant and effervescent artistic personality of post-Independence India: one of the last surviving figures of the modernist era of progressive art movements in Calcutta, Bombay and Madras that coincided with India's independence.[7] His biographers highlight the way in which this Muslim artist, born in the small western Indian town of Pandharpur, emerged from his early working-class background and worlds of practising faith to reinvent himself as a secular and modernist artistic persona. It is in this capacity that he then proceeded to draw freely on Hindu religious and mythic iconographies as a source of inspiration for his art. That he could visualize the Hindu pantheon with such empathy and candour became the surest mark of his secular identity. Over the years, this lanky, bearded, barefoot artist, once a painter of cinema hoardings, acquired an iconic stature, no less than his signatorial array of horses, his images of Mother Teresa and Indira Gandhi, or his pageant of playful divine heroines (figure 2.3). It was precisely his celebrity stature, public visibility and showmanship, compounded by the accident of his religion, that made Husain most vulnerable to the cultural bigotry of the country's Hindu right-wing during the mid and late 1990s. Through the attack on Husain, it was the whole privileged world of modern art and the privileged stature of the artist as 'super-citizen' that were being called into question within a new politicized public domain that staked its own control over artistic representation.[8]

These attacks on Husain, as has been widely commented upon, were triggered by external factors that had nothing to do with either art or religion. In 1996, there was a series of a specific animosities brewing between Husain and the BJP government of Madhya Pradesh, led by Sunderlal Patwa, over the running of a major art institution in the state (Bhopal's Bharat Bhavan) and the allocation of land for Husain's art gallery at Indore, that directly motivated the first protestors and the first wave of attacks.[9] These hostilities were then quickly transmitted on to the local units of the Shiv Sena in Mumbai and the Bajrang Dal in Ahmedabad who turned their ire on Husain's flat in Mumbai and on his art gallery at Ahmedabad (the Husain-Doshi Gufa). It became all too clear that what was at work against Husain was a Hindu right-wing political vendetta, of the most violent kind, riding on trumped-up concerns about licence and morality in art and the norms of Hindu iconography. Yet, the sheer virulence with which these 'extra-artistic' factors have come to repeatedly disrupt the secure practices of modern art forces one to take stock of the flow of charges against these artistic representations and the construction of the 'crimes' of the artist. What the allegations did expose was the wide rift that existed between the nude as a symbol of high art and the nude as a target of popular, public disapproval, straining the thin boundary that marks out the 'artistic' from the 'obscene', testifying to the perennially contentious status of the unclothed body (especially the naked female body) in the public domain.[10]

Nudity has been held out as Husain's cardinal and most pernicious offence. His audacity, it was alleged, lay not only in the public depiction of nude female bodies but also in labelling these figures with names of Hindu goddesses like Saraswati, Lakshmi or Parvati. This act of disrobing the goddesses was seen not just as a gross misrepresentation of Hindu mythology (so he would paint a near-naked Draupadi even where legend protected her from being fully disrobed) but also as sign of outright disrespect (figure 2.4). Worse still (we are told) is Husain's predilection for depicting goddesses in sexual union with the animals that carry them. Cast into the stereotypical image of the Muslim sexual predator, nudity in his hands came to be construed as acts of sexual violation: acts tantamount to the 'rape of Hindu goddesses'. And the root cause for such mischief was shown to reside in 'the nature of the religion and culture which Husain embraces'.[11] The entire campaign revolved around the naming of Husain as a Muslim artist, producing a terrifying equation between the painter's religion, his immoral passion for nude female figures and his urge to disrespect Hindu sentiments.

In the years that have followed, the target of attack moved from Husain's paintings of Draupadis and Sitas to his figuration of 'Bharat-Mata' ('Mother India'), where a hot-red nude female body is morphed on to the map of India, flanked by the topography of the Himalayas and the oceans, and inscribed with the names of cities and the official national symbol of the Buddhist wheel (figure 2.5). The offence to Hindu religion is seen to expand here into an even graver insult and abuse of the nation. To prove that he uses nudity as an instrument of deliberate humiliation, there are websites that lay out pairs of Husain's paintings, where he is shown to paint his mother, his daughter, the Prophet's daughter Fatima and all Muslim ladies (i.e. all women he respects) fully clothed while stripping all his Hindu goddesses and his figure of Bharat-Mata.[12] From the local and national, the campaign against Husain moved on to a global arena. In 2006, an exhibition of his paintings of Hindu divinities at the Asia House was stalled by a Hindu human rights group. An even more crucial marker of the 'global' is cyber-space, which now serves as the main site for the proliferation and circulation of anti-Husain propaganda – an endlessly expansive space from where a new global political community of Hindus is being mobilized in moral defence of the nation and its iconographies.

Right from the start of the campaign, the protestors have been vocal in their assertion of Husain's 'crime'. While there is no clear legal definition of what constitutes 'obscenity' in art, the legal proscriptions work around the purported offence and disorder that a work deemed to be obscene can cause in the public domain. The contestation of what constitutes the public spaces of viewing and circulation of art has remained at the heart of the debates. A number of clauses from the Indian Penal Code – relating to the 'Indecent Representation of Women', 'Offences Relating to Religion' and 'Offences against Public Tranquillity' – were invoked to frame the charges. The last of these was the most insidious, where the concrete evidence for offended religious sentiments was seen to lie in the public disorder that this injury incited. The burning of the artist's effigy, the destruction of his painting, the ransacking of his gallery and apartment – all became 'proof' of the public outrage that Husain's paintings were causing, providing a ready reason for their removal from the public scene. The legal defenders of the artist have been arguing, all along, that if this was at all an 'art-crime', it was less a crime *by* art, far more a crime *against* art.[13] It has been argued, for instance, that the prime offender in the Husain case should have been the person who, in the first instance, searched out and dragged into the public domain and published in the local periodical of Bhopal, *Vichar Mimansa*, the so-called 'offensive' painting of the nude Saraswati. The charges of criminal offence need to be turned on those who have instigated and perpetrated the attacks on Husain's paintings and property, prevented the exhibition and sale of his paintings, banned the screening of his film, *Gaja-Gamini*, in theatres in Mumbai and Ahmedabad, and threatened the artist with murderous assault.

The defence and the apology

Coming in the wake of the *fatwa* against Salman Rushdie and India's banning of *The Satanic Verses*, these attacks on Husain raised the spectre of a global siege of artistic freedom. Armed with a battery of counter-arguments, the artistic and intellectual community in India mobilized itself in a huge show of solidarity around Husain.[14] What is instructive, though, is the way that this defence has had to constantly shift its grounds from what was most directly at stake – the 'freedom of artistic expression' – to justify instead the Indian authenticity and legitimacy of Husain's nudes. The nature of the charges made it imperative that scholars corrected the falsified notions of tradition that were being used against Husain, to explain that there was nothing about his imagery that transgressed the bounds of either 'art' or Indian religious iconography. The crux of this art historical defence lay in looking back to India's long artistic tradition of the female nude, highlighting the ritual validity of nudity in Indian sculptural iconography, pointing to the innumerable instances of unclothed female figures (divine and semi-divine) in Indian sculpture and temple architecture. In his interviews of 1996–7, the artist himself participated actively in this mode of self-legitimization, projecting his art as an integral 'part of India's five-thousand-year-old culture', going to lengths to show how heavily his vocabulary was informed by the past traditions of Indian sculpture, and how as 'a quintessential Indian' he had internalized the spirit of Hindu myths and icons.[15]

These counter-stances, however, did little to change public perceptions or stem the tide of the assaults. The celebration of the sexual feminine imagery of ancient Indian art, especially the erotic temple sculptures of a site like Khajuraho, could go hand in hand with the continued polemics against Husain's nudes in another public sphere, allowing the elaborate construction of the artistic legitimacy of the one versus the perceived illegitimacy of the other (figure 2.6a, b).[16] The female nude, it has been argued, stands 'not only at the centre of the definition of art, but also on the dangerous edge of the category, brushing against obscenity. The female nude is the border, the *parergon* as Derrida calls it, between art and obscenity'.[17] What the shifting art historical fortunes of the temple maidens of Khajuraho and the nude goddesses of Husain point to are the tenuousness of such borders – and the highly contingent and motivated nature of the charge of the 'obscene' in the way it accretes around a certain body of imagery in a particular time and place, and absolves others. Such contingencies are what enabled Khajuraho's gradual passage from the 'shame and stigma' to the pride of its erotic sculptures in the art history of post-Independence India. They have also allowed for a range of far bolder and eroticized representations of the mythic female form to thrive in the work of several other modern Indian artists, while suddenly placing under censure Husain's fairly innocuous, taut and bony line drawing of Saraswati.

The moot issue lay in determining which body of imagery could seek the immunities and licences of modern art, and remain in this insulated sphere, and which others were to be inappositely thrust into an unprotected public domain. The autonomy of the sphere of modern art practices is what came most severely under threat in the campaign against Husain. Its freedoms and authority faced the greatest checks. From a secure, fortified shield, the 'modern' would become a slippery and unstable ground for Husain. This is why neither he nor his defenders could take effective refuge in the legacy of the nation's modern and contemporary art history. To hold on to the arrogance and prerogatives of modern art would not have been a commendable stance in a political environment where the *Hindutva* prejudice against Husain's nudes reflected a larger hostility to the very object of modern Indian art and the licences it enjoyed. To cite the cases of innumerable other more lascivious modernist nudes in the works of Husain's contemporaries, or to argue that 'Hindu' modern artists have as unabashedly unclothed their goddesses as this 'Muslim', would have exposed them all to the same dangers and violations. So, paradoxically, the best defence for this distinctly modernist artist and his peers was to justify his imagery in terms of ancient sculptural precedents and religious iconography. The motivated force and direction of the attacks on him left him few options, and made the claims to 'artistic freedom' a particularly treacherous ground to stand on. With his back to the wall, he could publicly indulge in none of the modernist daring about the inversions of tradition, about laying bare bodies and sexualities, or about playfully mocking one's gods and goddesses. Whatever may have been the artistic intention of these images, the proud options of transgression and irreverence (the founding premises of modernist aesthetics, and of all 'avant-garde' art) were not open to Husain in the face of these attacks.[18] Instead of holding to his modern artistic licence to disrespect or break with tradition, he could only offer up for his detractors his deep 'respect' for the goddesses he had portrayed, and the 'innocence' and 'spirituality' of his erotic representations. He has had to declare, for instance, that the title 'Bharat-Mata' was not one that he had given the painting under attack, but one given without his knowledge by the organizers of the art auction. Worst of all were the string of apologies that Husain had to offer to the Shiv Sena for the offence his paintings had inadvertently caused.

In rounding off this discussion of the 'Husain affair', let me pose the problem of transgression on a different register, by pushing it away from the content of Husain's images on to the ontological status of his works within a public domain. What was being violated, all through this controversy, was not only the authority of the 'work of art', but also the all-important boundaries between 'art' and 'non-art'. Husain's paintings were being dragged out of the sphere of modern art practices to answer charges in a public political domain to which they never belonged. It is important to labour the point that Husain's goddesses were 'works of art' that were never intended to serve as religious icons, even as we struggle to demarcate a legitimate public domain that his artworks can occupy, without encountering public wrath or offending the religious sentiments of worshippers. There are generic distinctions to be made between the visualization of goddesses in Husain's art and those in popular print-productions and calendar art, equally between the fields of reception and circulation of these divergent genres of images. While he has worked with a series of popular referents, culled especially from film posters and hoardings, Husain's images have also unsettled these idioms in a way that resist their easy reception by consumers of popular culture.[19] The point to reiterate is that a work of modern art has seldom been able to comfortably inhabit this unbounded domain of the 'popular'. The situation is particular paradoxical in the case of Husain, who, more than any other contemporary artist, has consciously courted the popular – obsessively drawing on the fantasies and indulgences of Bollywood cinema (as in his famous Madhuri series of paintings and film) and spraying his imprint across prints, posters, tin cans and designer drapes to produce a 'cottage industry' of his own images in the market (figure 2.7).[20] Yet, in all these citations and interventions, Husain would never have wished to have dissolved the divide that kept his artistic oeuvre securely apart from these many other genres of mass-productions, nor to have given up the vantage position of the 'secular modern' from which he operated. The popular public sphere has claimed him in a way that he could never have bargained for. It has eroded his high ground of autonomy and immunity, leaving him and his art dangerously vulnerable before a hateful and inapposite public.

Goddesses that have become 'art': Notes from the Durga Pujas of contemporary Calcutta[21]

If the campaign against M. F. Husain has allowed the new claims of the 'religious' to intrude into the secularized domain of modern art, the field of Durga Puja celebrations in today's Calcutta is marked by a pointedly opposite trend – the conspicuous secularization of a religious festival and its metamorphosis into a public 'art event'. The transforming nature of this public field can be seen to both preserve and erase the markings of the ritual occasion within the body of the urban festival, continuously deflecting the ambience of worship into one of display and spectacle. In the context of this article, it is instructive to see how this field of festivity has assumed a special artistic character in recent times, and has generated its own discourse on 'art' production and reception, even as it has remained categorically distanced from the sequestered worlds of contemporary art practices in the city.[22]

During the days and nights of the festival, the entire topography of the city undergoes a magical transfiguration, with the streets taken over by myriad shapes and forms of *pandals* (temporary pavilions that are erected to house the images of the goddess). These *pandals* (as all of us who live in this city know) serve primarily as exhibition sites, taking on spectacular forms of architectural replicas, remakes of temples, forts and palaces, theme parks and craft villages (figure 2.8). For several years now, a defining feature of such spectacles has been an unfettered local licence to copy, reassemble and reinvent whatever monument or site catches the fancy of organizing clubs, producers and publics. From the pre-historic cave sites of Bhimbhetka in central India to distant African villages, from the temples of Orissa or Khajuraho to the Opera House of Paris, all of India and the world are laid open for free 'tours' to the people of the city during the week of the festival (figures 2.9, 2.10). In keeping with these tableaux, the images of the goddess and her entourage take on newer and newer forms (figure 2.11) each icon competing with its rivals as an object for viewing and photography. The ambience is increasingly that of public art installations – so like art exhibitions, Pujas these days are routinely 'opened' by invited celebrities, designed by art school trained artists or set design professionals, often organized by professional event managers, and drawn into competitions for a growing number of awards for excellence of production offered by media groups and commercial houses in the city.

At the same time, there is a public, popular and, most importantly, an ephemeral dimension to the field of production that firmly sets it apart from the established enclaves of modern art: its circuit of art galleries, exhibitions, catalogues, critics and collectors. For all its endeavours to innovate, experiment and inculcate new artistic tastes in the spectator, all Durga Puja tableaux must take their place within an unenclosed and unbounded public domain, and must struggle to find popular approbation alongside connoisseurial attention. The locations being the open street and roadside parks, all *pandal* structures, however elaborate, must also come down at the end of the festival week, just as every Durga clay idol, however beautiful, must be ritually immersed at the end of the Puja. The new publicity and prestige that surround this domain of 'festival' art, just like the new artistic identities that are staked around it, tend to be as fleeting and seasonal as the event itself. The lack of durability and permanence gives this body of creations a status that does not brook any easy or sustained equation with the more entrenched worlds of 'art' and 'artists'. So, even as the Durga Puja festivities have taken on the form of a major public art event in the city, there is still a crucial line of distinction to be maintained between the objects of modern art and these Durga Puja productions: a line that keeps blurring but is also continuously renegotiated by artists and publics on either side of the divide.

Of central importance to this discussion is the long-established nomenclature of the Durga Puja as a 'festival': as a time of public congregation, conviviality, and the intricate enmeshing of worship with mass celebration. The process of secularization of the festival in and around the city of Calcutta has a long history that goes back to the early twentieth century, when the Puja moved from elite households to the open streets, from *zamindari* patronage to community sponsorship, and when, in select areas, the community or the *sarbojanin* Puja also became an important platform for anti-colonial nationalist gatherings and mobilization.[23] Over the latter half of the twentieth century, it is this category of the community or the *sarbojanin* Puja, organized by neighbourhood clubs which grew to unprecedented scales, drawing on a growing corpus of funds from subscriptions and sponsorships, jostling with each other to provide the season's most spectacular tableaux of *pandals*, decoration and lighting. The declining weight of the religious within the changing body of the urban festival is now part of a long, familiar lament. The argument can always be pushed both ways. At one level, it can be pointed out that the ritual calendar continues to set the dates for the annual event – that the prescribed icon of Durga, surrounded by her four children, continues to feature as the centrepiece of the ever-new forms of *pandal* designs; and however innovative be the image of the goddess and the structures that house her, what continues is the performance of all the rituals of worship through the five days of the Puja. On the other hand, it can also be shown that the Puja is often no more than an excuse for a huge spurt of consumption, for a flood of new productions and releases, and a mega show of lights, sights and sounds that have increasingly obscured the religious event and the sanctity of its performance. Taking for granted, then, the now long-standing identity of Calcutta's Durga Puja as a secularized festival and the city's most extravagant mass public event, the main contemporary shift that I wish to foreground is the entry into the field of a distinct set of claims and discourses about 'art' production. This artistic identity is one that has had to struggle to assert itself both within the structure of the religious event and within the space of mass display and spectacle.

The recent career of a particular genre of production, which is locally termed the 'art' or the 'theme' Puja, provides the main lead for tracking the new artistic profile of the festival. There are multiple markers of 'art' that energize these productions and give them a cognitively distinctive status in local perceptions. One clear marker lies in the kinds of forms given to the iconography of the goddess and the nature of the *pandal* tableaux constructed around the icon. There are broadly two standardized forms – one, the realistic, movie-heroine type appearance of the goddess, with muscle-flexing *Asuras* and growling life-like lions; the other, the large-eyed traditional stylized faces of the goddess ensemble under one frame (*ekchaala*) (figures 2.12, 2.13) – against which the newness of conceptions are staged each season. One needs to look more closely, though, into what constitutes the 'new wave' within this genre of productions, and what kinds of licences and novelties find acceptance within this field. Unlike the parallel field of modern Indian art, here, the modernity or contemporaneity of the new productions constantly have to seek out a base in traditional authenticities, whether classical or folk. Examples of distinctly modernist Puja installations or images of the goddess turn out on the whole to be far less effective than the different archaeological and craft ensembles and a flourishing variety of 'folk-art' Durgas that have swept the field (figure 2.14 a, b).

There is also, often, a distinct contemporary category of the 'secular' (a recognizably political ideology of 'secularism') that is profiled in these Durga Puja tableaux – as we see in the 'Communal Harmony' installation set up in 2002 in a south Calcutta venue, where the designer blended the architectural styles and décor of a temple and a mosque to highlight the 'cross-fertilization of Islamic and Hindu cultures' (figure 2.15) where the Durga image took on the look of a Mughal miniature painting, and her sari the patterning of Persian carpets, and where the idol at the far end was set off at the entrance by the most famous media photograph of the Gujarat carnage of 2002 (the face of Mohammad Ansari pleading for police protection). It is in the same contemporary spirit of the 'secular' that that another neighbouring Durga Puja tableau, the same year, laid claims on the early nineteenth-century Muslim millenarian peasant rebel of Bengal, Titumeer (of the Faraizi movement), and reconstructed with great aplomb in a small local park Titumeer's legendary bamboo fortress, one that is said to have been felled in a single night by Bentinck's army (figure 2.16). For the designer of this Puja, the choice of Titumeer and his imaginary fort was made in a clear-cut present-day stance of anti-coloni-alism and anti-communalism – by these terms, by this reading, Titumeer (a militant *Jihadi*, an iconoclast and Islamic puritan) can be non-contro-versially appropriated as an archetypal subaltern nationalist rebel and his story easily accommodated within the space of a Durga Puja *pandal*.

Such overt anti-communal stances apart, the 'secular' dimensions of today's festivities, I would argue, find their most powerful manifestation in the name of 'art'. Even in the traditional milieu of the production and worship, the Durga Puja always involved the work of several Muslim rural artisans, who would supply different elements of the goddess's arms, ornaments or *pandal* decorations. This has long been a part of the inclu-sive syncretic flavour of the festival. In recent times, this image is given an altogether new 'secular' and 'artistic' orientation by a novel type of crea-tive personnel who have captured the field of Durga Puja designing, side by side with the communities of hereditary idol-makers or the suburban firms of *pandal*-decorators who had long dominated the trade. The field now attracts in growing numbers a diverse group of artists and designers, ranging from the successful art-college trained professionals and film and television set-producers, to local amateurs, to a type who stand ambiva-lently strung between identities of 'artist' and 'artisan'. Cut off from the cosmopolitan, national and international circuits of modern art activity, deprived equally of access to the worlds of high design or advertising, this provincial group has found in the local sphere of Durga Puja productions a main avenue of earning and acclaim. It is in their conscious capacity as 'modern artists' that they have intervened in this field of public art, and brought with them a new concept of production. Under this new dispen-sation, the Puja in its entirety – the image, the *pandal*, the surrounding tableaux, the colours, the decoration and even the music – is conceived of and laid out as an integrated 'theme' (hence the nomenclature of 'theme' Pujas) either by an individual artist with the help of artisan labour, or by an art designer and his team, or sometimes by event-impresarios who mobilize supervising artists and rural craft persons from near and far to work on these projects. There is a close complementarity, here, between these different types of creative personnel, their work processes and their styles of productions, within the rapidly spreading domain of 'art' Pujas in the city.

There is today a rich graph to be plotted of artistic careers, authorial styles and design typologies within the phenomenon of the 'art' Pujas, just as there are new maps to be tracked of its spread and proliferation across the extended space of the festival city. We could cite the instance of two of the most prominent of this new creed of young Durga Puja 'artists' of contemporary Calcutta – Sanatan Dinda and Bhabatosh Sutar – both of whom have worked their way up from humble backgrounds to secure an art college training, and have used their rising credentials in the field of Durga Puja productions to carve out aspiring careers in the alternative circuits of gallery art. Sanatan Dinda came to specialize in a particular style of Tantrik iconography of the goddess, imaginatively drawing on the traditions of Pala period stone sculpture and the bronze statuary of the Himalayan Buddhist pantheon (figures 2.17 a, b) placing his Durga creations within simulated tree shrines and mixed pagoda and temple ensembles, all of which would be fabricated each year in a narrow alley in north Calcutta.

Bhabatosh Sutar, on the other hand, has made his name in the field, by working closely with various local craft and folk forms (like Bankura terra-cotta sculpture, West Dinajpur bamboo and wood carvings or Shantipur handlooms) to spearhead a form of Puja installation that innovatively cites and subsumes these craft idioms within his own signatorial style (figures 2.18 a, b). What holds together their respective styles is a tight authorial control over the entire production, a common premium on the centrality of Durga image with which they begin and around which they plan the larger ensemble, and a deep investment in both the artistry and the religiosity of the Durga imagery they sculpt each year. While Dinda has refused to work in any other medium except the ritually prescribed alluvial clay and has declined an offer for the collection and preservation of one of his images in a museum, Sutar has been open to sculpting his Durgas with durable material like wood or baked and lacquered clay, with the conscious intention of the post-Puja preservation of his works, arranging for the rituals to be performed before a small substitute set of clay idols which are to be immersed. Much to the pride of the first Puja club with which he made his name, Sutar stands out as one of the few Puja designers whose images have found their way into collections for three consecutive years (2003–5) – one was acquired by a five-star hotel, another by a private art collector, and a third for a state craft museum.[24]

We are standing, then, in a public field where the Durga images can be seen to simultaneously inhabit their double identities as worshipped icons and works of art. The claims of ritual and artistic productions can comfortably coalesce, here, without any overt sense of violation and transgression. In the new worlds of Calcutta's Durga Puja, the works of 'artists' like Dinda and Sutar can be seen to stand within a spreading wave of such art styles and fashions – of several varieties of Tantrik-art Durgas with *pandals* replete with Yantra symbolisms and motifs, and an even wider array of primitivist, folk-art Durgas – where artistic liberties with form never seem to push against the basic iconographic tenets of the image of the goddess. We need to ask what allows for such overlaps and fluidities between 'artistic' and 'religious' designations in this genre of imagery and disallows them in others. The clues, one can show, lie in the very conditions that differentiate this field of production and display from the exclusive domain of modern art practices.

If the contemporary festival presents an upsurge of artistic claims and assertions, it also exposes the ambivalence and fragilities of the identities of 'art' in this ephemeral sphere. The category of the Durga Puja 'artist' is one that struggles to find a firm foothold in a world, where (as I have already stated) recognition and success frequently turn out to be as temporary as the event itself, and where few routes open out for admission into the more exclusive national or international modern art circuits. None of the prestige and glamour, little of the social and cultural capital, and certainly nothing comparable to the kinds of prices that the modern Indian artist commands on the art market are available to this circle of designers and their works. One of the oldest and best-known corporate Durga Puja awards, on offer since 1985 by Asian Paints, still searches out winners under the label, 'Best Artisan of the Year' – a label that merges these artists with the community of traditional idol-makers from whom they wish to stand apart, and denies them the very status of 'artist' that they covet. The same anomalies also hover around the Durga image on view in the *pandals*, or on display in a hotel lawn or a craft museum. Whether or not these images can be accorded, the epithet of 'art' is a much-debated subject in Calcutta's artistic circles. In post-Puja settings, in particular, these figures seem to lose their animation and lie in a curious state of liminality: as 'icons' whose lives have passed and as 'artworks' whose lives are still to be defined.[25]

Conclusion: A problem of publics

I highlight these ambivalences that surround Durga Puja 'art' and 'artists' to mark out, once again, its separateness from the contiguous sphere of contemporary art, where the critical lines of distinction between the 'religious' and the 'art' object still fall powerfully in place. In contrast to the field of the Pujas, the distinctions here need constantly to be reaffirmed and resurrected – to stake claims to a special order of artistic privileges vis-à-vis sacred icons, and to mark out a select public as the target of address. The question of publics, their artistic literacy and initiation in certain languages of representation, is centrally at issue. If, in the unbounded space of mass-viewing, the 'art' of the Pujas can never escape the demands of popular appeal and approbation, and must coexist with a host of more mundane or standardized productions, the modern artwork, on the contrary, thrives within its own circles of exclusion and sets its own clear bounds on the publics it cultivates and the connoisseur community to which it belongs. Despite its investment in the transformation of public tastes, there can be no sealing-off of a niche audience for these new Durga Puja productions in the same ways that are possible for modern avant-garde productions. This has direct bearings on the kinds of iconographies that emerge and thrive in these overlapping but distinctly divergent spheres.

In bringing together these two apparently incommensurate worlds of productions and practices, the main intention of this chapter has been to open up a set of oppositional tropes in the kinds of authorities and immunities that 'art' confers on its subjects and objects. One of its broader concerns has been to test the terms and conditions on which 'art' can encode the space of the 'secular' in contemporary India, and the extent to which it can assert its creative prerogatives over images that come out of a supposedly segregated domain of the 'religious'. In its claims on images of divinities, how effectively can modern art deflect the 'religious' into the 'cultural' and produce an alternative category of iconicity? Conversely, how smoothly can images that lie embedded within a different history of worship and popular devotion live out their new lives as objects of 'art'? In engaging with these questions, much is at stake, I have argued, in determining the fields of public location and engagement of these realms of images.

The paradoxes that beset Husain's iconographies of Hindu goddesses and the nation, as they are stripped off their designation as 'art' by a hostile and indignant public, are offset by the paradoxes that hover around the new age iconographies of Durga, as they can only partially be transfigured as 'art' in a shifting zone of public tastes and demands. In each case, there are different battles to be waged in securing for these images their desired publics and in defining the limits to the licences they seek. As contemporary Indian art finds itself periodically pushed into a domain of public accountability and thrown open to a new intensity of public adjudication on its freedoms and responsibilities, there is an urgent need to constitute a different sense of proprietorship over cultures, mythologies and iconographies – one that would legitimize the representational licences of the veteran Husain, as much as those of his younger counterparts who form the contemporary avant-garde, or those of upcoming Durga Puja designers of Calcutta, while also underlining their widely divergent locations in the contemporary art milieu. We would have to keep asking: what kinds of immunity, protection and authority can they varyingly claim or take for granted? And what are the public domains that these many worlds of art can rightfully and comfortably inhabit?

This chapter has been all about contrasts and anomalies. Let me end by juxtaposing, again, two contrary scenarios of limits and possibilities. In one, we have the self-exiled Husain, his celebrity stature undiminished by the unceasing campaign against him, reaching out to the world with élan while contending with an increasingly shrinking national space of inhabitation of his art. If his Hindu right-wing detractors have made capital out of a deliberate misrecognition and non-comprehension of his iconographies, lambasting them as 'immoral' and 'anti-national', a section of his own community of artists, curators and gallery owners in India has also distanced itself from his art, for the needless political controversy it drags into its secure enclaves. Given the regularity with which Husain's works have been vandalized in galleries and exhibitions, there is a strong fear within this community of further endangering these locations of art and their precious rights and privileges. So, during 2008 and 2009, the biggest modern art fair in the capital – the mega Indian art summit at Pragati Maidan – chose to play it safe by not showing any works of Husain, pointedly excluding the very person who had first brought big money into contemporary Indian art. In the other scenario, we have a host of small-time Durga Puja artists, with none of the fame or cultural capital of a Husain, seeking out new artistic designations and public spaces of viewing for their work and basking under a rising spurt of corporate attention, within the very localized milieu of the city's festival. The safety and prestige of the artistic locations that Husain has had to forfeit are being actively claimed by this other group. It is tempting to think of them as playing out, albeit within a very different vernacular forum, Husain's dream of embodying popular tastes and of letting free the modern art object within a more open circuit of reception and consumption. It is specially pertinent to see how the contentious nude, that is rendered into such a vehement target of outrage in Husain's images of goddesses, can comfortably rest within a new register of Tantrik iconography and devotional affect within the ambit of viewing and worship of Calcutta's Durga Puja. So, while Husain's playfully irreverent and erotic Durgas continue to fight the charges of defamation and transgression and live within a precarious politics of risk,[26] a resplendent nude red Durga can unproblematically hold her own as both an aesthetic and worshipped object in a festival that has been able to freely negotiate the boundaries between 'art' and 'religion' (figure 2.19).

Figure 2.1 M. F. Husain, 'Saraswati' (pen and ink on paper, c. 1970). Reproduced courtesy of the artist.

Figure 2.2 Durga pantheon in a North Bengal folk art style – Behala Tapoban Club Puja, 2004. Reproduced courtesy of the visual archive of the Centre for Studies in Social Sciences, Calcutta (CSSSC).

Figure 2.3 M. F. Husain, Goddess Durga astride a tiger (acrylic on canvas, c. 1980). Reproduced courtesy of the artist.

Figure 2.4 M. F. Husain, 'Draupadi in the Game of Dice' (lithograph, 1983), *Mahabharata* series. Reproduced courtesy of the Peabody Art Museum, Salem.

Figure 2.5 M. F. Husain, 'Bharat-Mata' (acrylic on canvas, 2005). Reproduced courtesy of the artist and Apparao Galleries, Chennai.

Figure 2.6a Dancing Surasundari (celestial maiden) putting on an anklet, Parsvanatha temple, Khajuraho (sandstone, tenth century). Photograph, courtesy, American Institute of Indian Studies, New Delhi.

Figure 2.6b M. F. Husain, Untitled (lithograph, 1974). Reproduced courtesy of the artist.

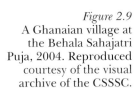

Figure 2.10 The facade of the Paris Opera House at a Salt Lake Durga Puja, 2009. Reproduced courtesy of the visual archive of the CSSSC.

Figure 2.11 The Durga image-group in the style of Pahari miniature painting, in keeping with the Rajasthani architectural tableaux, being photographed by television news reporters – Suruchi Sangha Puja, New Alipore, 2004. Reproduced courtesy of the visual archive of the CSSSC.

Figure 2.12 Example of the realistic style of the goddess and a muscle-flexing Asura – Durga Puja, Barisha, Behala, 2008. Reproduced courtesy of the visual archive of the CSSSC.

Figure 2.13 Example of a more traditional stylized single unit Durga pantheon – Durga Puja, Salt Lake, 2008. Reproduced courtesy of the visual archive of the CSSSC.

Figure 2.14a (left) and *2.14b* (below) A typical 'folk art' Durga in a recreated Bhil and Gond art village – Behala Club Puja, 2006. Reproduced courtesy of the visual archive of the CSSSC.

Figure 2.15 The 'Communal Harmony' temple-mosque fusion tableau at Hindusthan Park Puja, 2002. Reproduced courtesy of the visual archive of the CSSSC.

Figure 2.16 Recreation of Titumeer's bamboo fortress at Babubagan Club Puja, Dhakuria, 2002. Reproduced courtesy of the visual archive of the CSSSC.

Figure 2.17a and b Two Durga creations by Sanatan Dinda at his Hatibagan Pujas. Reproduced courtesy of the visual archive of the CSSSC.
a (left) Durga in the style of a Pala-period black schist sculpture, 2002.
b (right) Durga in the style of Tibetan Buddhist bronze sculpture, 2006.

Figure 2.18a Two Durga creations by Bhabatosh Sutar: Durga in the style of Bankura terracotta statuary, Barisha Shrishti Puja, 2002.

Figure 2.18b Durga as a primeval animistic force rising out of fire, Naktala Udayan Sangha Puja, 2009. Both reproduced courtesy of the visual archive of the CSSSC.

Figure 2.19 A Tantrik-style unclothed Durga being worshipped at Selimpur Pally Puja, 2006. Reproduced courtesy of the visual archive of the CSSSC.

Notes

1   A longer version of this chapter was first written as a plenary lecture for a conference titled 'Deus (e)x Historia', organized by the History, Theory and Criticism programme of the Department of Art and Architecture, MIT, USA, in April 2007. The main concern of the conference was with the 'return' of religion as a critical factor in global affairs and the profound challenges this has posed to the secularized practices of intellectual and artistic productions. It has subsequently been presented at seminars at the Centre for Studies in Social Sciences, Calcutta; at the Center for South Asian Studies, University of California, Los Angeles; and at TRAIN (Centre for Transnational Studies in Art, Identity and Nation), London. I am grateful for the comments and questions received at each of these presentations.

2   The text of the Delhi High Court judgement, along with a selection of recent newspaper editorials and petitions in support of Husain, has been published in a booklet, *Maqbool Fida Husain … Petitioner* (New Delhi: Sahmat, 2008).

3   Somini Sengupta, 'An Artist in Exile Tests India's Democratic Ideals', *New York Times*, 8 November 2008. The current state and predicament of the artist is discussed in my essay, 'Fault-lines in a National Edifice: On the Right and Offences of Contemporary Indian Art' and several other essays in Sumathi Ramaswamy, ed., *Barefoot Across the Nation: Maqbool Fida Husain and the Idea of India* (forthcoming, New Delhi: Routledge, 2010).

4   The categorical distinction between the two is taken for granted in all Western theories of art, from antiquity to the Enlightenment. See, for example, Moshe Barasch, *Theories of Art: From Plato to Winckelmann* (New York: New York University Press, 1985). On the art museum as the main institutional site for the production and perpetuation of this distinction, see, for example, Carol Duncan, *Civilizing Rituals: Inside Public Art Museums* (London and New York: Routledge, 1995), or David Carrier, *Museum Skepticism: A History of the Display of Art in Public Galleries* (Durham: Duke University Press, 2006).

5   I have elaborated on this theme in some of the essays in my book, *Monuments, Objects, Histories: Institutions of Art in Colonial and Postcolonial India* (New York: Columbia University Press, 2004)

6   Ever since its outburst, the 'Husain affair' has been the subject of a lot of journalistic and academic writing. Among the latter, are Monica Juneja, 'Reclaiming the Public Sphere: Husain's Portrayals of Saraswati and Draupadi', in *Economic and Political Weekly*, 25–31 January 1997; Karin Zitzewitz, 'On Signature and Citizenship: Further Notes on the Husain Affair', in Parul Dave-Mukerji, Deepta Achar and Shivaji Panikkar, eds, *Towards a New Art History: Studies in Indian Art* (New Delhi; D. K. Printworld, 2002); and my two essays, 'Clothing the Goddess: The Modern Contest over the Representations of the *Devi*', in Vidya Dehejia, ed., *Devi: The Great Goddess, Female Divinity in South Asian Art* (Washington DC: Sackler Gallery, 1999) and 'Art History and the Nude: On Art, Obscenity and Sexuality in Contemporary India' in *Monuments, Objects, Histories*.

7   The number of books written on Husain has been in proportion to the celebrity stature of the artist. Richard Bartholomew and Shiv S. Kapur, ed., *Maqbool Fida Husain* (New York: Harry N. Abrams, 1972); Geeta Kapur, 'Maqbool Fida Husain: Folklore and Fiesta' in *Contemporary Indian Painters* (New Delhi: Vikas, 1978); Dnyaneshwar Nadkarni, *Husain: Riding the Lightning* (Mumbai: Popular Prakashan, 1996); Rashda Siddiqui, *In Conversation with Husain Paintings* (New Delhi: Books Today, 2001); and K. Bikram Singha, *Maqbool Fida Husain* (New Delhi: Rahul & Art, 2008) provide a good sample, over time, of the field of writing on the artist.

8 Juneja, 'Reclaiming the Public Sphere', and Zitzewitz, 'On Signature and Citizenship'.

9 Md. Shahid Pervez, 'Why Sunderlal Patwa went for Husain's jugular', report from Bhopal, *The Statesman*, 15 October 1996.

10 Guha-Thakurta, 'Art History and the Nude', pp. 245–8.

11 Charges stated in the first criminal case brought against the artist by the Jamshedpur unit of the VHP, quoted in *The Telegraph*, 5 October 1996.

12 'M. F. Husain disrobes even our beloved Bharat mata! See with your own eyes the rogue painter's anti-national act' – Petition circulated by the Hindu Janjagruti Samiti 'to Protect the Pride of the Motherland' on Monday, 6 February 2006. Website: *Viveka-Jyoti* – 'Contributing our bit to Awaken, Unite and Strengthen Hindu Society'.

13 On the legal history of prosecutions of art, and the definitions in law about what constitutes 'crimes by art' as distinct from 'crimes against art', see Rajeev Dhavan, 'Censorship and Intolerance in India' and Akhil Sibal (the young lawyer defending Husain), 'Freedom of Speech and Expression: Constitutional and Legal Provisions' in *Iconography Now* (New Delhi: Sahmat, 2006); also, Lawrence Liang, 'Sense and Censoribility', Lead Essay, *The Art News Magazine of India*, Issue on Censorship, vol. xii, issue iii, no. iii, 2007.

14 One of the strongest expressions of this was carried in the cover story, 'In Defence of Freedom in Art: Against the *Hindutva* attack on M. F. Husain', *Frontline*, Chennai, 15 November 1996, pp. 4–13.

15 Ibid., pp. 11–12. Citation from an interview with M. F. Husain in London, carried in *Frontline*, Chennai, 17 October 1996.

16 Guha-Thakurta, 'Art History and the Nude'.

17 Lynda Nead, *The Female Nude: Art, Obscenity and Sexuality* (London and New York: Routledge, 1992), p. 25.

18 Anthony Julius, *Transgressions: The Offences of Art* (Chicago: University of Chicago Press, 2002) delves into transgressions as a constitutive feature of the identity of modernist art, ever since Flaubert and Manet, in an age that he marks as the 'Origins of the Transgressive Period'. Working out a complex typology of transgressions and its charges of offences, the book ends with its own provocative 'Coda: Every Work of Art is an Uncommitted Crime'.

19 Juneja, 'Reclaiming the Public Sphere', p. 157.

20 Gayatri Sinha, 'Masses of Maqbool', *The Telegraph*, Arts & Ideas, Calcutta, 24 November 1995.

21 This section on Durga Puja in contemporary Calcutta is based on a collaborative research project, undertaken between 2002 and 2008, with my colleague, Dr Anjan Ghosh. It has drawn on the large archive of interviews, newspaper writings, publicity material, and photographs housed in the archive of the Centre for Studies in Social Sciences, Calcutta. The prime focus of my study has been on the changing visual culture and artistic profile of the festival.

22 Some of my main formulations about the new 'artistic' identity of the contemporary festival phenomenon in Calcutta are laid out in my article, 'From Spectacle to Art', *Art India, The Art News Magazine of India*, vol. ix, issue iii, quarter iii, 2004.

23 For a brief history of the changing social and civic character of the festival in nineteenth-century Calcutta, see Tithi Bhattacharya, 'Tracking the Goddess: Religion, Community and Identity in the Durga Puja Ceremonies in Nineteenth-Century Calcutta', *Journal of Asian Studies*, vol. 66, no. 4, November 2007.

24 My research has closely tracked the careers and changing forms of Puja productions of Sanatan Dinda and Bhabatosh Sutar, along with those of other Puja
   'artists' in different neighbourhoods of Calcutta, from 2002 to 2008. While
   Sanatan Dinda ceased working on Durga Pujas in 2007, after ten years in this
   field, to graduate to a new identity as a painter and a Puja judge, Bhabatosh
   Sutar continues to be one of the topmost, award-winning Puja designers.

25 Even the most successful of Durga Puja designers, Bhabatosh Sutar, stands
   disillusioned about the prospects of his Puja productions (on which he invests
   immense expense, labour and time) finding their deserved place in art collections or corporate spaces. He is also disappointed by the lack of adequate
   attention and care given to his terracotta Durga Puja ensemble from 2003 that
   stands largely ignored behind glittering wedding party tableaux on the plush
   lawns of the ITC Sonar Bangla Hotel in Calcutta.

26 This theme of 'risk' and 'exile' entangling Husain's life and art is powerfully
   explored by Sumathi Ramaswamy in her Introduction, 'Barefoot across India;
   An Artist and his Country' in *Barefoot Across the Nation*.

3 Ray, ventriloquism and illusion

Robert J. C. Young

In Satyajit Ray's Fellini-esque film *Nayak* (1966), a train journey to Delhi becomes the stage for searching self-introspection for Arindam, the famous film star. As he seems gradually to lose control of himself, Arindam becomes racked by disturbing memories. In a chilling flashback, his mind reverts to the moment when, as a young actor, he was originally tempted by an offer to go into films and give up the theatre. The scene shows Shankarda, his mentor, a somewhat overbearing theatre director, warning him that if he goes into film, he will lose his self and fall into the power of cinema's abstract machine, becoming a mere puppet on the screen. As always in Indian cinema, English is used to make a point emphatically:

> *Shankarda*: [In Bengali] I know this for certain – I've done a detailed study of it. [In English] A film actor is nothing but a puppet. [Switch again to Bengali] A doll. A puppet in the hands of the director, a puppet in the hands of the cameraman, and the sound recordist. Then there's the man who cuts the film and sticks it together again – a puppet in his hands too.

Nayak, troubled by this ominous advice, says nothing. It turns out that the egotistical manipulative star has achieved his fame by allowing himself, in turn, to be manipulated. Film, Ray is suggesting, is all about these shifts of power relation, starting with the way that a director has to submit to and ventriloquize through the inanimate machine of the camera, and ending in the way that an audience, in going to see a film, allows itself to be subjected to the manipulative power of its illusion.

A short story by Ray called 'Bhuto' concerns a young man, Naveen, who is completely entranced when he goes to a performance of the famous ventriloquist, Akrur Babu. Akrur Chowdhury is the only person present on the stage but the effect of his performance is to make it seem as if he is 'conversing with someone invisible, hidden somewhere near the ceiling in the middle of the hall'.[1] When a reply comes to his questions, his lips don't move at all, and it is impossible to tell that he is actually answering his own enquiries. 'Naveen was astounded. He had to learn this art. Life would not be worth living if he did not. Could Akrur Chowdhury not be persuaded to teach him?' (66). He duly takes the train to Calcutta the next day and throws himself at Chowdhury's feet as his newly adopted guru. But Akrur Chowdhury coldly rejects him: 'This kind of art is not for all and sundry. You have to be extremely diligent. No one taught me this art. Go and try to learn it by yourself, if you can' (67). After being dismissed a second time, Naveen decides that he will learn the art of ventriloquism by himself and slowly begins to succeed. He decides to follow the more modern fashion of using a dummy rather than a voice projected from the middle of the hall, and in an inspired moment of revenge for his rejection, has the dummy, which he calls Bhuto, made to look just like Akrur Chowdhury. 'Akrur Babu would become a mere puppet in his hands! What a wonderful way to get his own back!' (68). Naveen hopes that Akrur Babu will come to one of his shows. Instead, however, he arrives on his doorstep, extremely displeased, tells him that he is not prepared to tolerate his impertinence and warns him that he has other magical powers. Soon after, Naveen notices that his puppet seems to have started to grow some grey hairs, like the real Akrur Babu. Worse still, when Naveen begins his next perform-ance, the puppet starts to say things that were never in the script, and even begins to use obscure English words the meaning of which he hardly knows. In his conversations with Bhuto, he finds himself saying words that he had never consciously intended. Bhuto even starts coughing at night, and then, during a performance, his voice comes out so hoarse that the audience can't hear him. Naveen has to stop the performance. That night, he realizes that Bhuto is breathing – 'Bhuto!' he calls out, to which he receives the reply, 'This is not Bhuto. I am Akrur Chowdhury!' (74). The puppet has come to life. Soon though, the breathing becomes fainter and stops. The puppet lapses into a *rigor mortis*. Next morning, Naveen hears that Akrur Chowdhury died overnight.

'Bhuto' is a very typical Satyajit Ray short story. Those who associate him above all with cinematic realism are surprised at first to discover that many of Ray's stories concern the supernatural, or the classic inverted form of supernatural gothic fiction, the detective story. The stories, we might say, offer a kind of unresolved magic realism very far from the neo-realist mode with which Ray's cinema is often associated. Among the ninety-nine films that Ray saw during his film-watching marathon in London in 1950, he may well have caught the wonderful cult Ealing Studios portmanteau horror thriller *The Dead of Night* (1945), best known for the 'ventriloquist's dummy' episode in which Michael Redgrave plays a demented ventriloquist who comes to believe that his amoral demonic dummy Hugo is alive – so much so that Hugo eggs Redgrave on to murder a rival ventriloquist. Ray's story of Naveen and Bhuto stages the same kind of reversal: at first Naveen speaks through Bhuto and controls him but he eventually finds himself being spoken through and controlled by a Bhuto who has become a real person. Ventriloquism always manages to maintain its ancient uncanny links with possession by the inanimate.[2] Many of Ray's stories in fact concern the idea of dolls or robotic machines of various kinds coming to life, often in conjunction with shifting, unstable and illusory identities.

The camera is another such robot, a kind of chameleon that turns out an exact but illusory image of its surroundings freed from the conditions of time and space. Photography, as André Bazin puts it, satisfies 'our appetite for illusion by a mechanical reproduction in the making of which man plays no part'.[3] In the age of mechanical reproduction, the production of the image of the human is transferred to the machine: cinema is produced through an inanimate machine that becomes animate by means of a second machine, the projector, that produces the effect of animation. In many ways the speaking machine of the cinema, the 'talking picture', as Steven Connor remarks in his book *Dumbstruck* (2000), is itself quite close to ventriloquism, an illusory projection of voices and images into the hall of the cinema that produces the effect of the real upon the audience.[4] 'Bhuto' shows the narrator captivated by someone who produces illusions, who projects the real into a scenario which the audience knows is not real but which they nevertheless enjoy as real, particularly because at another level they know that it is real. Ventriloquism, like cinema, suspends the difference between illusion and the real – for the ventriloquist's voices are themselves real enough – they are after all actual voices. The illusion only comes with respect to where or whom the listening audience projects as their source. Ventriloquism provides an illusion that at the same time is real, so that the real and the illusion become one and the same thing, or move into ambiguous, shifting relations with each other.

In cinema, it is the image which is ventriloquized, so that the audience sees an image of the real displaced onto the screen, seeing it represented somewhere other than its actual source, which was both staged and real at the same time. This quality of producing an effect of the real through a staging of it is one way in which cinema in general differs from photography, where the projection onto the paper or the screen is always a truthful inscription of what was actually there before the camera at a particular moment, 'an image that is a reality of nature, namely, an hallucination that is also a fact'.[5] The machine produces this hallucination by transforming and reducing the real, producing the illusion of three dimensions in two. This reduction of three dimensions to two itself contributes to the way in which some moments in Ray's films come across as a kind of visual ventriloquism, where he throws images onto the screen without giving the viewer any indication of where or how they are situated. As the camera takes us without interruption through different visual realms, in what might be called the concealed or seamless montage technique, we constantly have to resituate our sense of where the image is coming from. Take for example the wonderful sequence from *Apur Sansar* that Moinak Biswas characterizes as the 'frame trick', where the camera moves subtly and without interruption from a shot of Apu teaching Aparna the English alphabet to a stormy sequence that we gradually realize is a film that Apu and Aparna are watching in the cinema. The exploding fiery lights of the film then slip into a maelstrom of lights that, as the camera pans back, is revealed as the dancing night lights of the city seen through the small window, its frame identically sized to the cinema screen that we have just been viewing, at the back of the taxicab as Apu and Aparna drive home together.[6] In his films, Ray is not interested in reminding us how the illusion of cinema is always constructed. What he prefers to emphasize is the reverse: that cinema is in some ways no more or less illusory than other visual effects that we encounter daily in our lives, as in the *Apur Sansar* sequence. The rear window of the taxicab frames the real into a two-dimensional image in no more illusory a way than the camera does.

What Ray thus prefers to suggest is the idea that the everyday world is cinematic, full of reflections and framing devices. The world that is constantly being framed into forms of real illusion or an illusory real is self-consciously played upon in Ray's films through the frequent use of mirrors, such as the scene in *Pather Panchali* (1955) when Apu looks at himself in the mirror using two leaves to make a moustache. Many of the other shots in the film make use of reflections, such as the scene where we see the children follow the sweet-seller by watching their reflected images moving across the lake below them, or of natural framing devices, such as when Durga opens a large pot to look at the kittens inside. Instead of seeing her peering in, we suddenly see her face from below, framed by the round opening of the pot into which she is peering. Or, more formally, Ray frames the characters by means of the architecture of the buildings that they inhabit, however humble, as when Durga or her mother are seen standing right inside the small brick arch in their house wall, or from a view that is sometimes taken through another arch from outside the house so that you can see the characters standing inside and outside at the same time (figure 3.1), or in shots taken through doorways, or windows, as when Apu's mother leans through the bars of the window from outside to wake him up, or when Nayak is seen through his car window or his rear-view mirror. Ray and Mitra frequently use deep focus shots that articulate different modalities of space and perform the illusion or magic of photography by turning three dimensions into two before our eyes, such as the scene in *Pather Panchali* where the father is lying on his bed and we see the mother through the doorway, sitting at the far end of the room behind while they talk to each other. This self-conscious reduction of the three dimensional is particularly powerful in those shots in which we see two people at the same time mediated via a reflection that doubles them onto the same plane, such as the wonderful café scene, shot in the Neera Restaurant, in *Mahanagar* (1963) where Arati the ambitious working wife talks flirtatiously with her male friend while Subrata her husband is seen sitting behind a pillar overhearing them.[7] The camera then moves forward so that we see all three – the back of Arati's head as she talks, the smiling face of her male friend and the horrified look of the husband – on the two sides of a glass pillar, a technique that is used again in *Nayak* in a scene that reverses the dynamics of the first, where the advertising man, Pritish Sarkar, and his wife Molly converse fretfully when she refuses to help him by making up to the rich businessman. She is turned away with her back to him as he sits beside her but we see both faces together side by side, reduced to the intimacy of the same plane in their reflection in the train window.

Cinema, like fiction and photography, is predicated on the paradox that it will produce the real without itself being that real, which it presents by excluding its own reality, the reality of filmmaking and the production of film, from the reality that the film displays. Cinema is, as Benvenistian-minded theorists would say, a split subject, in which the subject of the enunciation will be always necessarily separated from that which is being enounced. At the same time, as an event that produces effect, in its own way, cinema can be seen as a machine that produces an illusion that also produces the real in the audience. For the emotional effect of cinema's illusory real is real enough. This is why, for fifty years, the audiences that have watched Ray's films have found them such powerful experiences.

But what is special about the illusion that his films produce? I want to argue that there is something different about the photography in Ray's films, and that thinking about the relation of the ventriloquist to his dummy, the director to his camera, helps us to understand the distinctiveness of the illusion that is created. What is the mediating role of the animating machine? I first found myself asking this question when I saw the absolutely mesmerizing opening title shot of *Mahanagar* which, like the famous three-minute-and-thirty-second tracking shot which opens Orson Welles' *Touch of Evil* (1958), seems to go on interminably, lasting a full two minutes. The focus of the hand-held camera on the spring-loaded trolley wheel or 'skate' running along the electric wire at the top of the trolley pole identifies the film very clearly in an Indian context with Calcutta, the first and the last Indian city to have trams. As we watch, fascinated with the continuing focus of the slightly jerky hand-held camera on the bird-beaked top of the trolley pole, the camera always seems to be about to let it slide out of the frame but in fact never losing sight of this animated object, half-bird half-machine, which slides tensely along the overhead wire, chirping, hissing and sparking with a flash at each contact with the pulley on the supporting girders. The image brings to life a wonderful visual metaphor of conformity and tension, of something about to slide out of its containing frame, or off the straight and narrow of the electric wire, that anticipates the whole narrative of the film – which immediately switches straight from the sliding trolley pole to the anxious face of Subrata, the vulnerable husband riding in the tram beneath.

If photography provides a form of illusion, there is a particular quality to that illusion in Ray that a generic reference to the influence of Italian neo-realism does not wholly comprehend. Much is also made of Ray's encounter with Jean Renoir, though in film terms, Ray's involvement with the influential avant-garde London film journal *Sequence*, edited by Lindsay Anderson, Gavin Lambert and Karel Reisz, which was to form the basis of the British Free Cinema movement, was probably at least as important as his brief encounter with the founder of French poetic realism. Ray's provocative 1948 essay, 'What is Wrong with Indian Films?', makes it clear that his thinking at that time was of a piece with many of the cutting edge ideas espoused by the French and Italian neo-realists and the British Free Cinema movement, particularly regarding location shooting and the use of non-professional actors. In terms of his ideas about cinema, Ray was very much a product of his time, the post-war era when there was a sustained desire to transform social and cultural life – the difference, of course, was that he was based in Bengal rather than in Europe, but this was also the mood that accompanied the independence movements. At the same time, in many other ways Ray's films were not like those of Renoir, De Sica or Rossellini. What is different is the visual style of the real that his camera projects, very different from the newsreel style of De Sica or Rossellini. Ray had been planning *Pather Panchali* since he had produced illustrations for the shortened children's version of the novel that had been published in 1945. Though he had no script for the film, he had already sketched out the scenes shot by shot. So the scenes had been strongly visualized twice already. Added to this, the film itself was shot by a photographer – and I want to argue that what makes *Pather Panchali* particularly special was that the film was in many ways not shot as film at all, but as a series of photographs.

Certain films come together for particular reasons – the fact that almost all the actors in *Casablanca* (1942), for example, were actual European refugees is one reason why it was an unrepeatable performance. It is accepted that one of the things that helped to make *Pather Panchali* and even the rest of the Apu trilogy special was that they were improvised films made by a bunch of enthusiastic amateurs. Famously, only Bansi Chandragupta, whom Jean Renoir had hired as an art director on his film *The River*, shot partly on location in India in 1949, had had any professional experience. It was not just that they lacked experience, however, but that Ray himself deliberately chose to surround himself with actors and technicians who had no experience. He had clear ideas about how a film should be made, and avoided using any local professionals because he wanted to break their rules. In particular, he writes that he did not want to use a professional cameraman. In the event, the cameraman that he got was even less experienced than he had anticipated, since Ray's originally intended cameraman was away filming in Madras by the time *Pather Panchali* began to be made. So instead, the young man who had been designated his assistant, Subrata Mitra, was promoted to be in charge of the camera.

> I started with one cameraman, Subrata Mitra, who was a beginner. He was 21 when he shot his first film; never handled a movie camera before in his life. But I had to have a new cameraman, because all the professionals said you can't shoot in the rain, and you can't shoot out of doors, that the light keeps changing, that the sun goes down too fast, and so forth. I got a new cameraman, and we decided on certain basic things. We believed in available light. We aimed at simulating available light in the studio by using bounced lights.[8]

So the extraordinary fact was that Mitra, a science student, and a photographer, had never been behind a movie camera in his life before the filming of *Pather Panchali*.[9] His only qualification was that he had studied Claude Renoir's methods from a distance while Claude was filming Jean Renoir's *The River*. Despite the opportunity and his intense desire to be a cameraman on Ray's film, Mitra was hesitant.[10] But Ray was confident in his potential. 'He kept explaining to me that film photography was only photography in movement and I would be able to manage', Mitra later reported.[11] As it turned out, apart from the very first trial session in which they used a borrowed 16mm Bolex movie camera, the camerawork turned out better than anyone could have anticipated.[12] The first question we might ask, though, is why was Ray so confident that Mitra would be able to manage? And second, why did it turn out so well?

Why was Ray so confident? Aside from his general belief in his friend's abilities as a still photographer – and it was of course from portrait photography that Mitra derived the idea of bounce lighting – Ray's confidence can also be related to the ideas currently circulating among avant-garde filmmakers and photographers, that seeing was more important than technique. In suggesting that 'film photography was only photography in movement', we can surmise that Ray was relying on the resources of the new ideas of neo-realism, as articulated most notably by André Bazin. It was Bazin who saw film through the medium of photography, through its privileged relation to the real, and the primacy of recording the real in its own time and space rather than the director inserting himself, via montage or the use of zoom for example, in order to interpret it for the audience.[13] Cinema, for Bazin, was a form of photography in time – 'an imprint of the duration of the object'. So film was simply a form of still photography – no montage, no zoom, just deep focus and close-ups – hence Ray's confidence.

Why did it turn out so well? First of all, because like the alternating relations between the ventriloquist and his dummy, from the first moment of filming *Pather Panchali*, the camera itself took charge. Ray writes:

> Then the problems of film making began to fade into the background, and you found yourself belittling the importance of the camera. After all, it was merely an instrument. The important thing was the truth. Get at it and you had your great masterpieces. But how wrong we were! The moment you are on the set, this three-legged instrument took charge. Problems came thick and fast. Where to place the camera? High or low, near or far, on the dolly or on the ground? Was the thirty-five okay? Would you rather move back and use the fifty?[14]

The filmmaker ventriloquist's struggle with the camera that appeared at times to have a mind of its own was, I am arguing, an important part of the secret of the film's success. The main camera that they used encouraged, indeed enforced, a certain stasis and monumentality in the way that it was filmed – it became, as it were, the dummy that controlled the visualization of the film. After the Bolex, they experimented with an imported Wall newsreel camera, then switching to a hand-held Eyemo newsreel camera with only one 2.5 mm wide-angle lens, before settling for a Mitchell, the Hollywood standard with which most of *Pather Panchali* was filmed. But a Mitchell of that era was basically designed for studio shots, it was a beast of a camera that as Ray himself remarks, was completely unsuitable for location shooting (figure 3.2). In the photograph, you can see, underneath the cloth protecting it from the heat, that the huge ungainly Mitchell that they used was an old pre-war model, with a separate parallax viewfinder, which predated the BNC Reflex version that became the standard camera used in Hollywood in the 1950s. This meant that they were unable actually to see the exact image that the camera was filming. Ray writes:

> In *Pather Panchali* we had mainly used a Mitchell camera, which was a giant instrument, and being heavy and cumbersome was more suited for studio work than location where it had to be carried on the shoulder of a coolie from shot to shot. For *Aparajito* Subroto suggested that we buy a German camera called Arriflex, which had just come into the market ... Arriflex was supposed to be a very versatile camera and was specially suited for outdoor work.[15]

Indeed Arriflex then became the Indian film industry standard, and most of the iconic photographs of Ray and Mitra at work shooting, show one of them with his eye to an Arriflex camera (figure 3.3). Rather as contemporary photographers such as Simon Norfolk are reutilizing unwieldy box cameras to achieve a different kind of monumentality to their images, the effect of using the cumbersome Mitchell on location was to give *Pather Panchali* a particular kind of static or still photographic effect. The unyielding camera, the heavy almost unmovable materiality of the machine, the film-ventriloquist's dummy, took charge. And that is why the film is so visually stunning.

One of the things that you notice about Ray's early films that makes them different is the quality of the stills – which is why his films themselves are often associated with particular images, such as the famous image from *Aparajito* (1956) (figure 3.4). For the most part, in film criticism, when individual stills are shown to illustrate a critical essay, they look flat and dull, and this is usually implicitly acknowledged in that they are reproduced in very small sizes. In general, no one actually looks at a film still as an interesting image in itself: it is a token to remind one of what happens at a particular point in a film. In Ray's case, this is altogether different. Almost each still that we see, works completely as a powerfully composed photograph that stands formally in its own right (figures 3.5 and 3.6). So, an important but often neglected part of the power of the film comes from the visual impact of the way the images are *composed* on the screen, the result of Mitra being a still photographer, and Ray himself, another photographer, also being an illustrator and draughtsman. It is noticeable that even when Ray describes his encounter with Jean Renoir, he writes of him as if he were a painter as much as a film director:

> what really fascinated me was his way of looking at things – land-scapes, people, houses and a hut, clustering bananas by a pond with water hyacinths in them. The 'aahs' and 'oohs' that punctuated his words were always something seen with a great painter's eye.[16]

Part of the power of *Pather Panchali* also comes from the fact that Ray had already conceived the story through a draughtsman's eye. Some of his illustrations for the book, such as the children sheltering under the tree in the storm (figure 3.7), are echoed directly and dramatically in the film (figure 3.8). The painterly aspect of Ray's cinema always continued, though it is rarely as explicitly visible in the films themselves as in the way Ray's 1941 brush drawing of his future wife (figure 3.9) is directly echoed in *Pather Panchali* (figure 3.10).

Ray's enthusiasm for photography meanwhile had long been conducted according to what he described as his 'unswerving allegiance'[17] to the photography of a man, Henri Cartier-Bresson, who emphasized the continuities between photography and drawing,[18] and had also worked as Jean Renoir's assistant director on many of his films including *La règle du jeu* (1939). In his preface to Cartier-Bresson's collection of photographs of India, Ray writes that the first Cartier-Bresson photographs that he saw were his images of Mexico in the 1930s, and, as with De Sica's *Bicycle Thieves* (1948), it was clearly the lived social realism of Cartier-Bresson's images to which Ray responded. But it was doubtless also the extraordinary formal compositional qualities of the images that affected Ray. Later in the early 1940s, Ray came across a catalogue of Cartier-Bresson's photographs. He writes

> The photographs had the same compelling, mysterious and memorable quality, as distinctive and as instantly recognizable as the work of any great painter. Here was a new way of looking at things – the eye seeking the subject matter and, at the same time, its most expressive disposition in geometrical terms within the conventional rectangle of the photographic space.[19]

Photography for Cartier-Bresson involved the fixing of 'the precise and transitory instant', the momentary impression of the real, but one in which the eye had sought out a powerful aesthetic arrangement. For Cartier-Bresson, just as for Ray, it must never be theatrical, and the actual 'available light' must always be respected.[20] Like Ray, Cartier-Bresson's credo was that the camera was merely an instrument and that the important thing was the truth of the real,[21] and therefore that reality must never be manipulated, even to the extent of cropping or manipulating the result in the darkroom – Cartier-Bresson's aesthetic is the very opposite to the elaborate post-production manipulations of today's Sebastião Salgado.[22] In Cartier-Bresson's formulation, photography is simply 'at one and the same time the recognition of a fact in a fraction of a second and the rigorous arrangement of the forms visually perceived which give the fact expression and significance'.[23] The photograph seizes upon the moment, but the art of photography is to capture that particular 'one moment in which the elements in motion are in balance'.[24]

Here we might compare Ray's images not only with Cartier-Bresson but also with another photographer of Mexico, Tina Modotti. Compare, for example, the image of the grandmother eating in *Pather Panchali* (figure 3.11) with Modotti's 'Hands Washing' (figure 3.12), or the image of the telegraph wire by the railway line in the railway sequence (figure 3.13) with Tina Modotti's 'Telegraph Wires' (1925–8) (figure 3.14). The concept of photographic composition, of articulating the interrelationships of the geometric pattern in the image, can also be found at the centre of the visuality of Ray's early films in which, as we have seen, the shots are all composed with the aesthetic geometry of the photograph.

One of the factors that makes Ray's cinema so compelling is his use of the particular dynamics of the photograph as Cartier-Bresson describes it: capturing the surrealist's 'fugitive moment', together with the geometrical arrangement of form within each image that the visual instinct of the photographer has apprehended. The description that Ray gives of Cartier-Bresson could very well describe the visual appeal of his own cinema. Ray's cinematic photographs at the same time give the viewer the film's subject matter but each image is also composed in 'its most expressive disposition in geometrical terms within the conventional rectangle of the photographic or cinemagraphic space'. This is particularly noticeable in the early black and white films, for, as Cartier-Bresson observed, 'black and white photography is a deformation, that is to say, an abstraction. In it, all the values are transposed'. In black and white images, photography transposes the real into a moment of formal abstraction that is at once real and illusory. A distinctive quality of Ray's film images is their constant tendency towards abstraction in which casual everyday things, such as plants growing through the surface of a pond, clothes on a washing line, the bottom of an old wooden door, books heaped in a pile, are derealized and transformed into images of extraordinary formal beauty (figure 3.15).

As a photojournalist, Cartier-Bresson's photography not only caught the real in an instant of time, but gave a temporal dimension to photography as well: 'photography', he argued, 'implies the recognition of a rhythm in the world of real things' (32). Cartier-Bresson reveals how his own particular form of photojournalism, 'photographic reportage, a picture story' (23), in which the photographer would take a sequence of images about a subject or an event, a sequence of actuality to be published across a two- or three-page spread in a magazine like *Life*, was itself in part inspired, as well as technically facilitated, by the experience of cinema: 'From some of the great films', he wrote, 'I learned to look, and to see' (20). Ray's storyboards in which he planned his films visually long in advance as a series of shots, are an artistic-cinematic equivalent of Cartier-Bresson's 'picture story' form of photojournalism (figure 3.16).

The series of stills on the storyboard were then reinforced as individual images because Ray used a photographer as his cameraman. Even the opening credits of Ray's films credit Subrata Mitra not as cinematographer or cameraman, but as 'photographer'. While the English subtitle says 'photographed by', the Bengali says 'Aalok-chitro-shilpi', which literally means 'light painting artist', the Bengali term for 'photographer'. After he had fallen out with Mitra, later Ray films, such as *The Chess Players* (1977), are generally more conventionally and, at times, crudely filmed from a visual point of view, particularly with respect to the amateurish use of zoom, or moments where you can see the microphones at the top edge of the picture as in *Ghare Bhaire* (1984). He also switched to the

conventional credit line of 'camera'.[25] Despite the general acknowledgement that Mitra was perhaps the finest camera operator in Indian film
history, Ray gave him very little credit in the making of the early films,
nor indeed the assistant cameraman, Soumendu Roy, who subsequently
took over. This is compounded by the tendency to project Ray as a master
of everything, so that on the website satyajitray.org, for example, we are
told that 'Ray wrote all the screenplays of his films, operated the camera
and composed music for most of the films and many of his films are
based on his own stories'. Auteur theory has here become complete, total
'rayification'.

To list the cameraman as 'photographer' was in fact standard practice
of the European neo-realist filmmakers by whom Ray was so influenced.[26]
Calling the cameraman the photographer, rather than the preferred
Hollywood designation of 'Director of Photography' (e.g. in *Casablanca*)
or simply 'Camera', suggests the degree to which neo-realist cinema,
filmed largely on location, saw itself as filming the real in the manner of
photography. Cinema, in Bazin's words, was merely a photograph with
movement. However, the camerawork on Ray's early films is, in fact,
nothing like that in *Bicycle Thieves* or *Rome: Open City* (1945), films that
present themselves in newsreel style, with the camera shifting quickly and
following the action, moving seamlessly with the movement of the plot.
Ray/Mitra's style of filming in the *Apu Trilogy*, particularly the use of low-
angled shots, the child's eye view, comes closer at times to film noir, even
to another contemporary film almost entirely filmed on location, Carol
Reed's *The Third Man* (1949) (though there is no suggestion of Reed's
famous angled shots).

Ray's style, no doubt partly enforced by the Mitchell camera, which sits
motionless or at most slowly pans across from left to right or from right
to left from a single fixed pivot point, is to film the narrative almost as a
series of stills, with the camera offering a single view into which subjects
walk in and out. Instead of moving back and forth with the actors as
he would later do, for example at the opening of *Charulata* (1964), Ray
allows them to move across or in and out of the shot. The motionless
camera takes us back to *Citizen Kane* (1941), but we might also recall here
the great last scene of *The Third Man*, which lasts for about a minute and
a half in which the camera does not move at all but we watch mesmerized
as Anna Schmidt walks towards the camera down the long avenue of bare
trees, past Holly Martin (who has killed her lover Harry Lime) and the
camera without acknowledgement. In *Pather Panchali*, Ray constructs an
extraordinary sequence in which the camera remains rooted to the spot
for the entire scene when Harihar, the father, returns home not knowing
about Durga's death and encounters the desolate cottage. In the film, with
a truly Bengali slowness, he walks into the image, turns round, walks out
of the image, you then hear the gate opening, after which there is a long

silent pause, until finally he reappears (figures 3.17–3.20). This movement within and across the image is often accentuated by the striking way
in which the camera gives us views which include barriers that prevent us
at times from seeing the character. In Ray's later films, his camera reverts
to the more typical all-seeing eye that gives the viewer complete unmediated access to every scene. But in the early films, the camera does not
assume any kind of primacy, and has to deal with all the obstructions of
natural objects that exist in the real and that get in the way – trees, posts,
door frames, parts of buildings.

The particular power of *Pather Panchali*, then, is partly because there
was no professional cameraman, and that it was filmed on a completely
unsuitable camera, that came to control the kind of photography that
Ray and Mitra were able to do. One way of looking at the trajectory of
Ray's films would be to see him trying to free himself from the control
of the camera, so as to turn it into a mere instrument with no agency of
its own. However, that freedom in the late films came at a cost. Perhaps
the most telling response to *Pather Panchali* in the context of my argument about the power of its illusion of the real being constructed through
the aesthetics of another illusion, that of photography, came with the
film's premiere, which Ray, ever well connected, contrived to have at
the Museum of Modern Art in New York. After the showing, the MOMA
director, Monroe Wheeler, sent Ray a telegram, which simply read: 'a
triumph of sensitive photography'. Ray writes, 'I handed over the cable
to Subrata Mitra, giving him a pat on the back'.[27] Here, for once at least,
Ray gave his great photographer, Subrata Mitra, his due.

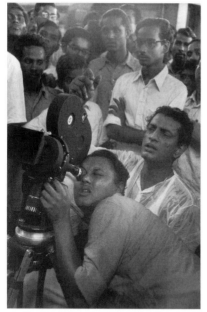

Figure 3.1 Pather Panchali (1955). Durga (Uma Dasgupta) and Sarbajaya (Karuna Banerjee). Courtesy of the Ray Foundation archive.

Figure 3.2 Ray and Mitra with the Mitchell camera shooting *Pather Panchali*. Courtesy of the Ray Foundation archive.

Figure 3.3 Mitra and Ray shooting *Aparajito* (1956) with the much smaller Arriflex. Photographer: Marc Riboud. Courtesy of Magnum Photos.

Figure 3.4 Apu (Pinaki Sengupta) in *Aparajito* (1956). Courtesy of the Ray Foundation archive.

Figure 3.5 Pather Panchali (1955) Apu (Subir Banerjee) drinking up his milk. Courtesy of the Ray Foundation archive.

Figure 3.6 Pather Panchali (1955) Durga (Uma Dasgupta) in the rain scene. Courtesy of the Ray Foundation archive.

Figure 3.7 Ray's illustration of children sheltering under the tree in the storm. Courtesy of the Ray Foundation archive.

Figure 3.8 Pather Panchali (1955). The children sheltering under the tree. Courtesy of the Ray Foundation Archive.

Figure 3.9 Ray, 1941 brush drawing of Bijoya Das, his future wife. Courtesy of the Ray Foundation archive.

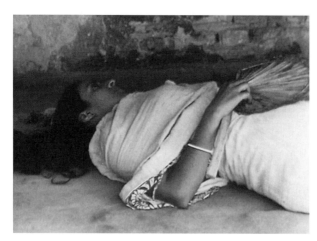

Figure 3.10 Pather Panchali (1955) Sarbajaya (Karuna Banerjee) lying on her back during the rain sequence. Courtesy of the Ray Foundation archive.

Figure 3.11 Pather Panchali (1955) Indir Thakrun (Chunibala Devi) eating. Courtesy of the Ray Foundation archive.

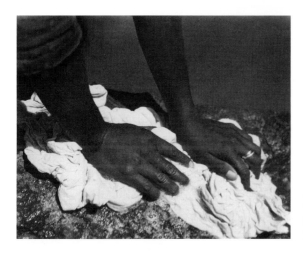

Figure 3.12 Tina Modotti: 'Hands Washing' (1925). Courtesy of Art Resource Inc.

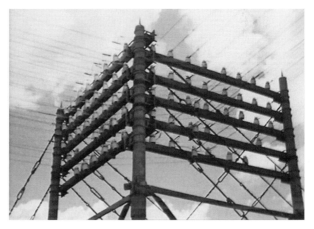

Figure 3.13 Pather Panchali (1955). Telegraph wires in the railway sequence. Courtesy of the Ray Foundation archive.

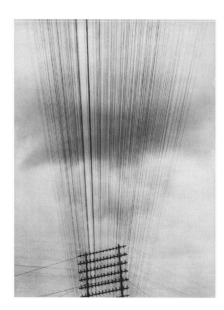

Figure 3.14 Tina Modotti, 'Telegraph Wires' (1925–8). Source: Artnet. Courtesy of Art Resource Inc.

Figure 3.15 Pather Panchali (1955). Washing line. Courtesy of the Ray Foundation archive.

Figure 3.16 Ray story-board for *Pather Panchali* (1955). Courtesy of the Ray Foundation archive.

Figure 3.17–3.20   Pather Panchali (1955). Harihar (Kanu Banerjee) returns home after Durga's death. Courtesy of the Ray Foundation archive.

Notes

1   Satyajit Ray, 'Bhuto', in *Twenty Stories*, trans. Gopa Majumdar (New Delhi: Penguin Books, 1992), 66. Further references will be cited in the text.
2   Steven Connor, *Dumbstruck: A Cultural History of Ventriloquism* (Oxford: Oxford University Press, 2000), 315.
3   André Bazin, *What is Cinema?* trans Hugh Gray. Two vols. (Berkeley: University of California Press, 1967–71), I, 12.
4   Connor, *Dumbstruck*, 411.
5   Bazin, *What is Cinema?* I, 16.
6   Moinak Biswas, 'Early Films: The Novel and Other Horizons', in *Apu and After: Re-Visiting Ray's Cinema*, ed. Moinak Biswas (Chicago: University of Chicago Press, 2005), 37.
7   Plate XLVIII in Marie Seton, *Portrait of a Director: Satyajit Ray* (London: Dobson, 1971) shows Mitra behind the camera shooting the café scene with the double image in *Mahanagar* (1963), with Ray behind analysing the shot with a cupped hand. It is Seton who reports that the location, the Neera restaurant, was chosen because it had not been done up since the 1950s (265).
8   Satyajit Ray *et al.*, *Satyajit Ray: An Anthology of Statements on Ray and by Ray* (New Delhi: Directorate of Film Festivals, Ministry of Information and Broadcasting, Government of India, 1981), 124.
9   Ray himself was also a photographer before a filmmaker, using a Leica and modelling himself on the photographic ethos of Cartier-Bresson (see Ray, *My Years with Apu: A Memoir* (New Delhi: Penguin Books, 1996), 36).
10 Seton, *Portrait of a Director*, remarks: 'There was also Subrata Mitra, who had been an observer of Renoir's direction of *The River*, especially watching the camerawork of Claude Renoir. Mitra, by nature a cautious soul, slow to be carried away by enthusiasm, and often easily reduced to despondency, had an intense desire to be a cameraman on Satyajit Ray's projected film' (89).
11 Seton, *Portrait of a Director*, 100. See also Ray, *My Years with Apu*, 37, for Ray's description of this moment.
12 Ray, *My Years with Apu*, 37.
13 Cf. Ray's comment on Cartier-Bresson in Satyajit Ray, *Our Films Their Films* (Hyderabad: Orient Longman, 1976), 11.
14 Ray, *My Years with Apu*, 54–5.
15 Ray, *My Years with Apu*, 102–3.
16 Ray, *My Years with Apu*, 17.
17 Ray, *Our Films Their Films*, 11.
18 Henri Cartier-Bresson, *The Mind's Eye. Writings on Photography and Photographs*, trans. Diana C. Stoll (New York: Aperture, 1999), 45.
19 Satyajit Ray, 'Foreword' to Henry Cartier-Bresson, *In India* (London: Thames & Hudson, 1987), 5.
20 Cartier-Bresson, *The Mind's Eye*, 27–8.
21 Ray, *My Years with Apu*, 55.
22 Cartier-Bresson, *The Mind's Eye*, 27, 34.
23 Ray, Foreword to Cartier-Bresson, *In India*, 5.
24 Cartier-Bresson, *The Mind's Eye*, 33. Further references will be placed in the text.
25 Ray himself often plays down the role of photography, according to the ethos of *auteur* theory. 'There is no such thing as good photography *per se*. It is either right for a certain kind of film, and therefore good; or wrong – however lush, well-composed, meticulous – and therefore bad' (Ray, *Our Films Their Films*, 68).

26 We can find this distinction in other neo-realist films – *Bicycle Thieves* (1948), for example, lists on its credits 'Fotografia Carlo Montuori, Operatore Mario Montuori', or Roberto Rossellini's iconic *Roma: Citta aperta* (1945) lists among its credits 'Fotografia do Ubaldo Arata', while his second neo-realist film *Paisà* (1946) announces 'Fotografia Otello Martelli'.

27 Ray, *My Years with Apu*, 83.

4 Fan bhakti and subaltern sovereignty

Enthusiasm as a political factor

M. Madhava Prasad

The problem of popular sovereignty has to be investigated beyond the confines of the republican institutions themselves, in fields where supplementary, virtual formations of sovereignty create community effects that compensate for their lack in the political structure proper. In this chapter, the emergence of sovereignty formations around film stars is discussed with particular reference to Rajnikanth, in the context of the challenge posed to such formations by a newly triumphant commodity logic. Far from solving the problem of sovereignty, however, the corrosive power of the economic logic may be expected to create new political crises.

The release of Tamil superstar Rajnikanth's film, *Sivaji*, in 2007 was heralded by an unprecedented coverage of the star and his fans on national television channels. For more than a week all the major English language news channels aired special programmes with feeds from Tamil Nadu and other parts of India as well as several foreign cities showing Rajni fans, first in excited anticipation and then in exuberant celebration as the film finally hit the screens. The most memorable of the images was surely the one of fans performing *palabhishekam*, a Hindu temple ritual of washing the idol with milk, on a gigantic Rajni cut-out.

It was a strange case of the missing moral lesson. News anchors usually cue the audience to the right response to any news item not only by their choice of words and parenthetical remarks but also through subtle changes of facial expression. On this occasion, compared to previous instances of such coverage that one can recall, the anchors showed few signs of cultural anxiety. On the contrary, when they reached the Rajni segment (which they did several times a day for more than a week), their faces would invariably light up with a practised show of excitement usually reserved for an Indian cricket victory or the stock index hitting a round figure. The accompanying words too were upbeat. None of the usual expressions of civilized worry about the irrational passions of the masses could be heard (although these were, of course, given due representation among the experts called in for the discussions). What accounts for this sudden and positive interest shown by the national media in the Rajni phenomenon?

We will return to this mystery in due course, after we have considered the figure at the centre of it. Rajnikanth started out playing small bad-man roles in the 1970s, first in K. Balachander's middle class melodramas. Even in these brief appearances, he impressed audiences with his signature gestures such as throwing a cigarette into his mouth from a distance, lighting it with a stylish flick of the hands, etc. The 1970s were a time of change for film industries in India. The transition to colour had just taken off and the painted faces of the black-and-white era were starting to look (un)really pink. For reasons that remain to be explored, it was only with the advent of colour that dark-skinned actors – notably Amitabh Bachchan, Shatrughan Sinha and Rajnikanth – began to appear in prominent roles in Indian popular cinema. Rajni was the Tamil cinema's first unabashedly black-skinned star, a rude eruption of reality into an industry dominated by painted faces. Like his predecessor, M. G. Ramachandran, Rajni was an outsider, a Maharashtrian from Bangalore who had worked as a bus conductor before joining the acting course in the Madras Film Institute where he was spotted by the director Balachander (who is also credited with introducing Kamalahasan).

Rajni (as he is referred to by fans) quickly rose to the heights of stardom and soon he and Kamalahasan were occupying the same parallel positions of star power that M. G. Ramachandran and Sivaji Ganesan had occupied a generation before, positions that can be described, in the language of the industry, as those of 'mass hero' and 'class hero'. This broad division which also prevails in other film industries of south India can also be read as a distinction between political representation (mass hero) and cultural-economic representation (class hero). The prevalence of this equation of the mass hero with political representation and power in the film industries of the south has been noticed and studied before (Forrester 1976; Hardgrave Jr 1979; Sivathamby 1981; Venkat Narayan 1983; Pandian 1992; Dickey 1993).

My own work in this area up to now has covered the singular phenomenon of south Indian film stars turning into politicians or functioning in regional cultures as surrogate political icons. This development has usually been attributed either to the gullibility of the illiterate, religiously inclined masses, or to the cinema's power of manipulation. My attempt in previous work has been to show that the rise of one film star each in three southern states to a position of absolutist authority needs to be investigated as a historical event in the evolution of Indian political ideologies. Thus all three film stars in question, M. G. Ramachandran (MGR), N. T. Rama Rao (NTR) and Rajkumar, who dominated their respective film industries for three to four decades each, share certain attributes and historical circumstances. They came to the cinema from the popular commercial theatre, they were associated in the popular mind with stunt and costume films, rather than middle-class narratives, they were the first big stars to feature in the revamped 'social' films of the 1950s, which got rid of, or relativized, the joint family scenario to foreground the romantic relationship between the lead pair, and they were also among the first set of stars to sport a modern, short-cropped hairstyle and clothing. In addition, there is the important historical factor, that their transformation into national icons for these southern nationalities, occurred in the wake of the linguistic reorganization of states, and partly as a strategy to expand and consolidate the language cinema markets (Prasad 1999, 2003, 2004a).

In this chapter I deal with the next generation of stars, focusing in particular on Rajnikanth, who is undoubtedly Ramachandran's successor, with the aim of approaching a better understanding of the relation between fan bhakti and the political problem of what I am calling enthusiasm and subaltern sovereignty. By this I mean to suggest that a congenital crisis of sovereignty in the Indian republic gives rise to various phenomena, including the political power of film stars. I begin by introducing a few films of Rajnikanth from the 1990s, before proceeding to a discussion of the political significance of star worship and its relation to religious practices. In order to historicize the question of the subaltern spectator as a figure forged in the colonial imaginary and endowed with an essential piety, and his relation to the contemporary Rajni fan, we will take a detour through the 1927–8 Film Inquiry Committee proceedings before arriving at a distinction between religious and political sites of enthusiasm.

Some Rajni films

Annamalai (1992, Suresh Krissna) is a film of Rajnikanth's that may be considered typical of his oeuvre. He plays the title role of Annamalai, a fatherless boy who lives with his mother and sister, and runs a small dairy on a plot of land in the heart of Chennai. Ashok, a motherless rich boy and Annamalai meet and, after a quarrel, become close friends. As is usual with such subaltern narratives, Annamalai's mother is partial to Ashok, and soon Annamalai himself joins her by assuming for himself the role of unquestioning loyalty to his rich friend. The family defines this friendship in terms of a primal bond that falls outside of any contractual relationships, practically identical to a blood relationship. Ashok's father disapproves of the friendship, but fails to influence his son. Annamalai is described as a prince by his friend, inducing in the heroine (Khushboo) fantasies of being romanced by royalty. In Rajni's films such false statements are usually made by a sympathetic associate. His image cannot accommodate even brief bouts of playful immorality or dishonesty. When an MLA takes over a part of Rajni's land to build huts for his own people, Rajni retaliates by taking his cattle into the MLA's bungalow, where he delivers a lecture on politics. The rest of the plot concerns the attempts of Ashok's father and his goons to capture Annamalai's land for a five-star hotel, and Ashok's temporary betrayal of friendship. Annamalai, reduced to penury, procures a loan and rises to the heights of industry, overtaking Ashok's family and reducing them to bankruptcy before setting things right.

In *Annamalai* we can already see a feature that distinguishes Rajnikanth's films from those of other big stars: the social context in *Annamalai* crucially includes the politician, the community is imagined as one that includes the MLA as a figure of power and authority. Here Annamalai is not only the moral prince that a hero usually is, but also someone with a political message. The moral world of popular films remains immanent to the present social context, an order within an order, one that is rarely conscious of its location within a political order. Occasional references to politics, corruption, etc, do not change this in any significant way. In Rajnikanth's films, the moral and political orders may not coincide, but they meet in the figure of Rajnikanth, who transcends the moral order and locates himself on the political plane not concretely as MLA or MP, but as the political consciousness of the people. This gives the Rajni persona a transcendent, superhuman quality that lesser stars can never aspire to. In another film, *Yajaman*, the political role is more pronounced: 38 villages boycott the election, all of them owing allegiance to the Yajaman (Rajni). The candidate is perplexed: it turns out that the people, who had been paid to vote, have donated this money for developmental works, under the leadership of Rajni, who is their traditional landlord-master. Confronted on this, Rajni gives a long speech about the unfulfilled promises from past elections and the need for alternative plans for development. *Yajaman* is an AVM Studios film that tries to harness the Rajni persona to a conservative political agenda: the Rajni persona is not endowed with a clear political perspective, only a symbolic political function.

Basha, one of Rajni's biggest hits, has him playing an auto (rickshaw) driver. The film begins with two situations of economic hardship saved by the timely arrival of help, sent by 'Manickam' (Rajni). He has another name, Basha, which he has taken on after the death of his friend of the same name, with whom he had tried to combat crime in Bombay, eventually turning into a fierce gangster himself. Here the Govinda-style moral plot is employed, and the political messages are anchored to it. The film begins with photographs of Annadurai, Jayalalithaa and Ramachandran, with Rajni himself shown bowing to the last one. The first appearance – always a dramatic one – is as a rickshaw driver, singing a song eulogizing the good qualities of rickshaw drivers on the day of Ayudha Pooja. In Madras, Manickam is living in exile, his past as a gangster unknown to the locals. In order to keep his disguise as a peace-loving and meek man, Rajni has to suffer many insults, resulting in scenes that add to a mounting anticipation of the moment when the mask will come off. Meanwhile, the moral subplot has him living as an orphan in a family to whose welfare he has committed himself: he fulfils his promises to the dead father of the children (to whom he is like an elder brother): getting one a job, another admission to medical college, and getting the third one married off, each time reporting to the garlanded photo of the father that one of his wishes has been fulfilled.

What distinguishes Rajni's films from popular films in general is the supplementary horizon of political power that they seem to incorporate. As a fictional prince of the virtual domain unfolding on the screen, Rajni's kingdom seems to spill over into the real world, his sovereignty value seems to reside in his own person and determine the shape of his films to an overwhelming degree. While there are references to Tamil nationalism in Rajni's films – in *Annamalai* he recites a little verse that goes: 'Gandhi drank goat's milk, I sell cow's milk. I was brought up on mother's milk, and survive on Tamil milk'; and in *Yajaman*, when a government officer speaks in English in front of a village crowd, Rajni asks him in English to speak in the people's language, Tamil – his sovereignty appears less tied to the Tamil nation and the realities of state politics than Ramachandran's.

The cultural logic of indirect rule: profiling the spectator of cinema

The cinema is a 'poor man's entertainment', says Colonel Crawford, member of the Indian Cinematograph Committee of 1927 to Lala Lajpat Rai, the Indian nationalist leader; and the latter readily agrees (ICC, *Evidence*, vol. 3, p. 210).[1] It is a rare moment during his extended oral testimony to the committee, for until then Lajpat Rai had been vigorously opposing point by point every one of the propositions put forth to him. It is also a rare moment throughout the committee's proceedings, because most of the time, it is precisely the poor man's interest in the cinema that seems to be a source of worry for members of the committee as well as the witnesses giving evidence before it. There was apprehension here of a cultural problem peculiar to the colonial order and in excess of the problems generally associated with cinema as a leisure-time entertainment for the working masses in the industrialized countries in the early decades of the twentieth century. Latika Basu, Indian representative of the Bengal Presidency Council of Women, addressing the committee, provides a clue to the source of the problem.

> The cinema first came to the country for the English audiences here and then Indians began going there, because they could not get cinemas of their own. Look at the Empire Theatre. A few Indians go there, but if you look at the theatres where Indian dramas are shown, you see Indians flocking to them. If we had our own cinemas representing our own life, we would prefer to go there. But because we do

not have them in large numbers we are forced to go to the Western pictures (ICC, *Evidence*, vol. 2, p. 926).

Unlike the masses in the industrialized countries of the West, the ethnic and religious identities of the Indian masses were a source of concern to the governmental machinery since preservation of these identities was a structural feature of colonial rule, the basis on which the indigenous elite extended its support to the colonial regime. Thus, while nationalists invoked the figure of the people in the modern sense and underplayed the importance of religious, ethnic and caste differences, various community leaders and other sections of the Indian and European elite highlighted the threat posed by cinema to the social order based on the coexistence of discrete communities under the paternal eye of the Empire. Historians of British India distinguish between territories directly under British control and those 'princely states' where ruling dynasties were allowed to maintain a notional autonomy, described as a form of 'indirect rule'. However, in an important sense all of India was under indirect rule. The only difference is that while in the territories of indirect rule proper, the defining feature was the presence of a king, elsewhere the social covenant entailed the mediation of community leaders. In other words, there were two forms of indirect rule, one ostensibly political in character, the other concealed under the appearance of social givenness. In effect, the British ruled over communities, not individuals: some of these communities were political in character (the princely states), while others were religious, ethnic or caste. The communities in turn were ruled by leaders whose legitimacy derived as much from the recognition accorded by the colonial administration as it did from that of the community itself.

Such was the social context in which the profile of the subaltern spectator of Indian popular cinema was cast as early as the 1920s. Like many aspects of colonial rule that survived into and determined the character of independent India, this profile too has remained with us until recently. The context was provided by the widespread concern, expressed by sections of the colonial administration and civil society, as well as British members of parliament and public, over the ill-effects of cinema, American films in particular, on native 'social hygiene'. The spectator who is the source of concern is variously described as illiterate, uneducated, rural people, the ignorant, the uninformed, the working classes, the lower classes, adolescents, youth, etc. As far as youths or adolescents were concerned, the problem could be seen as developmental in nature, related to the susceptibility of young minds to strong stimulation. That leaves us with the uneducated, ignorant, the rural people and the working class. The 'working class' posed problems of governance and its leisure time was a matter of concern to all governments. Film industries elsewhere had indeed recommended themselves to governments by pointing to the benefits to society of leisure spent away from the streets, in the confines of movie halls. But although the term working class is frequently encountered in the proceedings, it is not employed in this strong sense, but as a synonym for the other terms (uneducated), serving to make an overall bipolar distinction (working classes v educated classes) to indicate a new class specific to modern society. Judging by the evidence, two qualities were salient to the profile of this class. One, the spectator was figured as a peasant, or if located in a city, as an uprooted peasant. Two, the spectator's primary identity was assumed to derive from his/her membership of one of the many communities of which Indian society was thought to be composed. The educated Indian urban middle class posed no problems to the governing elite and with some adjustments they could easily be assimilated to the third category, that of the white or 'European' community in India who were assumed to be the naturally intended audience for this modern amusement.[2]

But among the respondents to the committee's summons, there was also a group of nationalists who were either thorough modernists or strategically adopted a modern-progressive line of argument with the aim of frustrating British designs to impose imperial preference in the film trade, which would mean reducing or completely banning import of American films, increasing the circulation of British films, restricting or preventing the screening of foreign films to uneducated audiences, etc. In their arguments, the profile of the subaltern spectator is also suitably modified. Some of them emphasize cinema's importance as a modern amusement for working masses in the strong sense; others, while agreeing that the ordinary spectators were illiterates and peasants, refute the claim that they need to be protected from the 'evil influence' of the American cinema. They flatly deny that the masses are gullible and defenceless against the immoral lure of American culture. Here we must distinguish the nationalists, who were committed to modernization, unification and independence, from conservative Indian public opinion which was increasingly forced to acknowledge the demands of nationalism but was intent upon minimizing its social consequences. The national movement, of course, consisted of both these sectors. The government of independent India, its progressive leadership notwithstanding, nervously embraced conservative opinion in matters of popular culture when it found that its own position in the power set-up was barely distinguishable from the one the British had lately vacated. In any case, the net result was that while on the one hand, the defence of cinema against conservative efforts was reasonably successful in that, apart from censorship, no drastic measures were taken to restrict circulation of American films; on the other hand, the divide between the educated and the illiterate – which united the educated and rich among the colonized with the colonizer against the rest of the population – became entrenched in the colonial common sense and affected cultural policy. India's political freedom has always been undergirded by this social constraint, which has so far proved intractable. Thus, it is not surprising that free India's policy as regards cinema was an extension and reinforcement of colonial policy. The ghost of the emperor continued to preside over the republic long after the demise of empire.

An interesting difference between these debates and similar ones going on in Britain, the US and other nations around the same time is that while in the latter, the focus is on the films themselves and the possible ill-effects they may have on people, in colonial India attention was focused on the existence of a problematic category of spectators and the difficulties created thereby. It is as if these people were watching movies without the necessary qualifications for doing so! The films were considered likely to have a bad influence on them not only because of what they showed, but also because of who they were, culturally, educationally, and by occupation. One can see the culturalist argument in formation here, the idea that cultural consumption deracinates if the consumed products are not of the consumers' own making and continuous with their cultural pasts. The proponents of this deracination thesis are those who are concerned to maintain community boundaries, to perpetuate the idea that the subcontinent is composed of caste and religious communities each with its own organic leadership. Cinema was seen as drawing people out of their loyalty to community, into a space of unsanctioned consumption, a social space devoid of community demarcations. The conservatives had nightmares of social disorder, of the dissolution of traditional ties which were essential to the maintenance of the colonial social order. Cinema could be made to serve this order only if films could be made that would reinforce people's cultural and religious traditions. Films based on Indian themes, and especially mythological ones, were seen as a solution, where spectatorship would be indistinguishable from acts of piety and would constitute an extension of traditional life rather than a disruption of it.

The proceedings of the committee are throughout marked by a symptomatic ambivalence, a two-sided diagnosis of the nature of the problem which reflected the irresolvable contradictions of colonial rule. The ambivalence arises in relation to the supposed victim of the evil influence of the cinema: on the one hand, it is sought to be projected that the illiterate masses are the victims, they are liable to be uprooted from their authentic lives by exposure to the alien imagery put into circulation by American cinema. 'I do not think it is fair to offend the Indian standard of etiquette by showing Western films which may do so', avers Mrs Coulson, an English member of the Bengal Women's Council (ICC, *Evidence*, vol. 2, p. 926). On the other hand, it is asserted that it is the British who are the ultimate victims, for it is their image in the eyes of the natives that will suffer when the illiterate masses are exposed to American cinema's irreverent portrayal of white people, with its lack of concern for the delicate position of the 'European race' running an empire far away from home. The source of this duplicity is the rule of colonial difference that encounters in the cinema an industry of metaphors that threatens to disrupt the carefully maintained borders between communities and castes. This fear of metaphoric play, of the dissimulative power of the cinematic image is most clearly expressed by a respondent of British origin who objects to white actresses playing roles of Hindu women in Indian films. Questioned repeatedly he stubbornly reiterates his point: he objects not only to the representation of interracial exchanges on screen, but to the concealment of racial origins behind fictive role-playing (ICC, *Evidence*, vol. 1, pp. 306–20). This is no doubt a somewhat extreme position, but it is in keeping with the overall logic governing the rescue operation mounted against the flood of American images. Suddenly, the cinema's images force the British to identify themselves with the European race (i.e. to give themselves an ethnic community identity to match those that prevail among the natives: these include Hindu and Muslim, but also Bengali, Madrasi, Punjabi and so on, as well as caste identities) and to fear such identification by the masses, which will lead to equating, say, images of white American women from the films, with real white, British women living in the colony.

As for the dualism of the diagnosis, it no doubt served a concrete purpose. It helped to shift the problem from the political axis to the social field. To present it as a question of white people's or women's public image alone would be to acknowledge the political order's reliance upon the myth of white superiority. Deflecting the problem onto the masses as members of discrete communities and sanctified identities made it possible to project the dissolution of communities as the ultimate and common social threat to be jointly addressed by the rulers and the (leaders of the) ruled. In the process, the British too were prepared, if not compelled, to project themselves as one community among many. Indeed conservative European representatives are found to be speaking exactly like the community leaders of various religious or caste groups, claiming that as a distinct race of people, they are entitled to protection from the public gaze, that they should be able to determine what kind of images of white people are fit for the consumption of the natives, that 'their women' are being exposed to native ridicule by the American cinema, etc. A European claim to the right of purdah was being put forward in the face of Hollywood.[3]

This anxiety about the subaltern gaze continued to determine policy as Indian popular cinema expanded rapidly with the advent of the talkies. Cultural policy in this domain remained largely unaffected by the installation of indigenous rule and popular cinema continued to be treated as a hopelessly anarchic and culturally degraded form of mass entertainment frequently equated with drinking, gambling and prostitution as a social evil. Although statistically the middle class consumer was a decisive factor in the success of popular cinema, the illiterate masses continued to figure centrally in debates about it. On the one hand, the state perpetuated mass illiteracy and gave nativist fantasy a longer lease of life to indulge in the pleasures of counter-posing India's unique indigenous culture to the deracinating and deracinated modern. On the other hand, the cinema that catered to this illiterate population was condemned as an abomination and subjected to arbitrary and irrational policing.

The profiling of the subaltern spectator as a figure with special cultural needs was one of the lasting results of these deliberations that stretched across the teens and twenties of the twentieth century and beyond. Films based on mythologies were widely declared to be the best way to fulfil this need. In this, the participants in the debate were only pointing to what already existed, for Indian cinema itself had begun, as the story is told, with the filming of mythological themes.

A new bhakti movement?

Against this background, let us now turn to a consideration of the relation of the subaltern spectator to the image on the screen. The early popularity of the 'mythological' or *pouranic* genre, of which D. G. Phalke is the acknowledged pioneer, already brings into view the spectator as a member of an organic community who extends to the godly image on screen, without any inflection or change of stance, the same devotion that is naturally addressed to 'real' gods. Of course, we know that Phalke and others contributed their mite to encourage this extension by figuring the devotee on screen as a spectator of miraculous events.[4] Thus in the extant fragment of Phalke's *Kaliya Mardan*, the child Krishna's trouncing of the snake is witnessed from the banks of the river by the people whose position on screen duplicates that of the spectators in the cinema hall. Within the diegetic frame, the devotee is figured as a spectator so that from outside it, the spectator might identify with the devotee.

Thus in the mythological, the body of the actor is supplemented by the spirit of the deity. No doubt such a possibility is predicated on a feature of Hindu worship whereby any image of a deity can be rendered sacred by the very act of worship. What Marcel Duchamp did when he demonstrated that there is a 'space of art', is paralleled in converse by what the Hindu worshipper does when s/he produces a 'space of worship' around any suitable image, however produced. It is not that they fall victim to an illusion, mistaking the actor dressed up as Krishna for the real Krishna (this would imply a difference between the 'real' Krishna and some other kind) but that they are able to replicate the performance of worship at any site and around any suitable image.

Let us say that in mythological/devotional films, there are moments of frontal address when the sacred spirit is called into presence by the body of the actor. The actor's presence is temporarily effaced in order to enable the spirit to inhabit the body-image. There is then a manifestation of *bhakti* (devotion).

In India, the adoration of film stars by fans has also been described as a form of bhakti. The spectator who identifies with a screen persona beyond the requirements of narrative intelligibility is the fan, who used to be known in common parlance as a 'bhakta' (usually translated as devotee) in many Indian languages (e.g. Tamil, Telugu, Kannada, Bengali) until the emergence of an organized sector in fandom, after which suitably more classical names, like *abhimani*, *rasikar*, etc. were introduced.

The question of translation is of vital importance here, since we are in the historically unique position, in India, of conducting scholarly research in a language which is radically discontinuous with the languages prevalent in the field of research and because there are conventions of translation/ interpretation that this situation gives rise to – of whose practical consequences we remain inadequately aware. Thus the use of the term 'bhakta' to refer to a film star's fan may prompt us to equate religious devotion and star worship and to take seriously the idea that to the Indian mind, no great gap separates exemplary human beings from divine figures. This would constitute a mode of etymology-based interpretation proper to Indological studies. At its heart is the idea, jointly elaborated by Western orientalists and Indian nationalists, that continuity of tradition is a feature of Indian civilization that distinguishes it from the West. On the other hand, we might take a more modern approach that is attentive to shifts in meaning effected by such extensions of terms to new areas. Thus in a modern dictionary free from Indological assumptions one would expect it to be noted (confining ourselves to this instance), that the term 'bhakta' has at least (the above) two meanings. The etymological continuity would remain but the lexicographer would not impose upon these two instances of usage an interpretation that treats them as fundamentally one. We know from practical instances of such extended usage that there is not always any connotation of religiosity present in them. Thus in Satyajit Ray's *Nayak*, the film star protagonist's co-passenger tells him that her daughter is his 'bhakto'. Nothing remotely religious is implied in this usage. Thus, there is a need to displace the diachronic unity of Indian culture and civilization, a constitutive assumption for Indian nationalism and for orientalist scholarship, by breaking up the historicist continuum and treating the synchronic dispersal as valid in itself, as the truth of our contemporaneity.

Sites of enthusiasm

Bhakti is a form of enthusiasm[5] that unites the community of the faithful. This community does not pre-exist the act of bhakti but is constituted by it. Thus we can distinguish the two forms of bhakti at issue here by reference to this community-forging power of bhakti. The Indological assumption is based on the fallacy that the place of the spirit is fixed, and survives independently of the acts of bhakti addressed to it. From this it is a short step to the conclusion that when a film star comes to occupy this space, it is because he is being equated with the gods. Contrary to this, we propose that enthusiastic communities can form around a variety of entities, and that the nature of the community thus formed will have to be inferred from the nature of the entity, the nature of the acts of bhakti addressed to it, the nature of the satisfactions derived from these acts, etc. We must avoid assuming that the elements that make the performance of bhakti are in themselves embodiments of a fixed idea of religious worship. Thus, when Rajnikanth's fans poured milk over the cut-outs of the star, they were clearly borrowing a practice of consecration of the icon from temple culture. An obvious conclusion offers itself. But we must learn to see the practice of star worship as an independent site of enthusiasm which derives elements of its own culture of worship from other sources but is not therefore reducible to these latter. What we need to explain is why stars become a focus of enthusiastic communities.

In star worship, the body of the actor seems to be inhabited by a spirit, as in the previous instance, but here this spirit is not that of some pre-given divine entity, but as it were some essence that underlies the actor's appearances. In the case of a god, it matters little who is playing the role in any particular film, piety is aroused by the iconic presentation of body-images in a frontal mode that evokes the scene of worship. In the case of the star, a spirit is produced by acts of abstraction from all the particular appearances. The actor's body is endowed with his own sublimated spirit returned back to it as a henceforth-imperishable feature. There is something here that is deemed to survive all particular manifestations, but this has to be produced out of these manifestations themselves and must be constantly renewed by fresh manifestations. It is a supplement generated from the entity itself.

As the language cinemas expanded and developed their own star systems, the phenomenon of fan bhakti began to grow, spurred by the encouragement of the industry, and the example set by American cinema. In time, a split in the community of bhaktas takes place with far-reaching effects. While the phenomenon of informal fan identification and adulation of celebrity continued to prevail, the rise of organized fan clubs created a new segment where fan devotion took on more durable forms and began to involve an array of activities.[6] Hero worship reached new heights of intensity. Meanwhile, as mass following of stars increased mani-fold, occasional reports of fans building temples to their favourite stars seemed to confirm the suspicion that fan devotion was indistinguishable from religious devotion, that the fan was equating the star with gods. When magazines like *Stardust* or *Star and Style* cater to readers' interest in celebrity lives, they are catering largely to a star-craze comparable to the kind that is probably prevalent in most large film industries, notably Hollywood. However, the organized fan clubs and the magazines (usually in the regional languages) that cater to their members' interests, take a different approach. Here there seems to be a stronger belief in the star's superhuman powers, a willingness to believe that the star is an exceptional figure. There is also a certain effect of reciprocity that is established between star and fan. The fan has a sense of belonging, a claim over his favourite star, which is expressed in, say, the intolerance of any role that is not true to type (i.e. losing a fight, indulging in immoral acts like rape and murder, or dying at the climax). In effect, the star is put under the compulsion of adopting a fictive identity composed of the idealist elements of the characters he plays. When the real individual thus adopts a fictive identity, the fictive ideal thereby becomes reality. However – and this is the crucial point of divergence between fan cultures in general and this particular instance of it – fans seldom expect any continuity at the level of the *imaginary*; it is not a question of *keeping up appearances*, but of sustaining a moral-political order, in the form of a community whose members gain symbolic sustenance from participation in it.

Here we must guard against the illusion of an illusion. It is a virtual game into which the fan invites the star. Of course once he enters, it is going to be very difficult for the star to get out, because the virtual reality that comes into being is a durable one. The 'reality' that is thereby produced is neither a cultural illusion nor a religious belief; it is a virtual political space.

What I want to bring into focus here is the effective creation of a relatively closed community whose identity is anchored to the star. There are degrees of closure, to be sure, and this must be kept in mind in analysing the sovereignty effect of star-based communities. But the important thing is that fans subject themselves to the star in what seems to be a political act of loyalty, rather than an expression of identification at the level of the imaginary. If the Indian political scene features an array of 'fragmented sovereignties' (Hansen 2005) and we were to include these fan-formations among them, then there would be one vital difference between them and the others discussed by Hansen. The fan communities would appear to have been constituted at least nominally upon the initiative of the people, rather than of the putative sovereigns. These are kings chosen and anointed by the people: kings of democracy![7]

In Hindu political institutions the link between the divine and the sovereign has a long history. Bhakti represents, in this context, an attempt to wrest the divine away from kingly dominion, to constitute communities of the faithful that have their own models for kingly virtue. The star-worshipping cults of southern India effect a similar transformation in the political field, wresting sovereignty from those who inherited it from the British and bestowing it upon monarchs of their own choice, thus demonstrating the subcontinent's continued dependence upon the logic of indirect rule.

Sovereignty

The linguistic reorganization of states, which was forced upon the central government by the linguistic nationalities, particularly in the south, resulted in a watered down form of the multinational federation that India had envisaged before Independence. After Independence, the Indian State adopted a policy of cultural conservatism that served the Congress regime well, depending as it did upon the continued loyalty of a paternalist social class that delivered the votes of its traditional subordinate classes – the lower castes in particular – to the party. In addition, the Congress increasingly defined Indian nationalism as a substantive and distinctive thing in itself, rather than as the sum of a complex of nationalities. The nationalist aspirations of the major linguistic regions were thus sought to be subsumed under an overarching Indian nationalism, and towards this end, the central leadership hoped to adopt an approach where the administrative units of the new republic ought not to coincide with linguistically homogeneous territories, in the interests of the unity of the whole. But the unrest around this question could not be ignored and finally in the mid-1950s, linguistic reorganization was reluctantly granted. The dismantling of the presidencies – administrative units of the colonial regime that developed their own distinctive cultural features – and the re-centring of popular consciousness around new linguistic-national identities has continued to unfold in the last 50 years, and still remains an active process.

The presidencies were culturally dominated by the landed aristocracy, the colonial bureaucracy and the nationalists, who together constituted a literate social elite whose cultural aspirations were predominantly expressed in literature. Before Independence, the elite were divided between conservative and national-modern approaches to the imagining of a modern India. Post-Independence, the uncertainties and anxieties of the time led to the triumph of conservative cultural policy, which continued to treat the masses paternalistically as a kind of 'cultural reserve' that needed to be protected from the deracinating effects of modern popular culture. With the advent of the linguistic states, however, the ground was laid for the development of film cultures in the southern states, which soon overtook literature as the site of elaboration of national identities. Cinema suddenly proved itself to be an effective means of integration of populations previously scattered across different presidencies and princely states into one linguistic nationality. For the film producers, initially, this was no more than a marketing strategy, what they were aiming for was a national market for a cultural product that spoke in a particular language. But it soon became clear that cinema was a more productive institution that would quickly become the emblematic supplement to national identities that were restricted to cultural self-expression. The literary class soon recognized this potential and began to take an active part in the film industry.

The Indian national/metropolitan elite has always underestimated the place of language in people's lives, and has remained stubbornly optimistic in the evaluation of its own programmes of social engineering, treating differences of language as a 'divisive factor' that would be eliminated by development and patriotism. Substantive Indian nationalism is a historically anomalous project born of the Indological-colonial imagination. The fashionable raiments of nationalism were and still remain ill-suited to the body of an ageing civilization which has stunted the growth of its children – the linguistic nationalities – in order to reserve for itself the pleasures of modern nation-statehood. This turn of events in the subcontinent's history has not been without its disastrous consequences. For can we not discern, behind the convulsions engendered by *Hindutva*, the impotent rage of a civilizational fantasy unable to secure for itself a permanent field of play?

That, however, is the topic for another project. For the moment we are concerned with how, beneath the skein of Indian nationalism, and the political project of Indian democracy, various collective identities are being forged in the virtual domain of the cinema. Here, I am more concerned with the cultural politics of popular sovereignty which may or may not be tied to linguistic national identities, but which certainly involves the question of political subjectivity.

The ideology of popular sovereignty has it that in modern democracies, the monarch is divested of the sovereignty vested in him, which is then fragmented and distributed equally among the people of the republic to constitute them as sovereign citizens. If we then assume that the Indian republic was constituted by wresting sovereignty from the imperial power, the question is: did the people receive their rightful share of the spoils of independence? Even if we take into account the insight that the sovereignty of the modern state is a factor of international relations, and not the mirror image of the collective sovereignty of the people, we are still left with the question whether the interior has been subjected to a morphological overhaul – the constitution of new subjectivities, new modes of association, new contractual relations, etc. – to bring it in line with the substantive idea of a republican polity.

I think the answer to that question is no. Or at best some might prefer to say that the process is underway, that the revolution is in progress. Recent essays in political theory have suggested, however, that rather than being in transition to some finished state of republican constitution, India might have arrived at a qualitatively different, singular state of political being, marked by an internal structural division between, to cite an influential and useful nomenclature, civil and political society. Partha Chatterjee, the author of this distinction, does not clarify whether political society is a sociological category (a class among classes in an established social structure), or a historical one (a kind of Lukácsian agent of history engaged in a political project that promises unexpected results). We, however, may regard political society as the domain of a range of cultural activities that bear witness to acts of meaning making, of imagining political futures, utopias that may remain within the horizon of the republic or transcend it. If, following this line of thinking, we treat India as an inorganic cultural compound, rather than an organic, internally homogeneous cultural formation, we are faced with the task of describing and analysing the different elements of the concrete reality that we inhabit. In particular, here I want to point to the way popular cultural texts propose orders of sovereignty, which are at odds with the theory of sovereign citizenship, and may point us towards a better understanding of the play of political passions in contemporary India. Political commentators assume that when we vote in an election, we are exercising citizenly sovereignty. The election becomes the proof of existence of such sovereignty, rather than a consequence of it. Cultural texts, however, show that other forms of collective sovereignty continue to attract political passions, indicating that the general election may often be a new avenue for expression of old or non-democratic modes of sovereignty.

Recently, Thomas Blom Hansen has drawn attention to the multiple and fragmentary sovereignties that dominate the Indian political scene. According to this reading, communities, big men, nationalities, caste groups and other formations effectively enjoy sovereignty over parts of the Indian social body. Supplementing Hansen's description with an ideological approach, we would be able to locate film stars within this field of fragmented sovereignties, functioning in a supplementary capacity. For the difference between film stars and the actually existing big men is that the former are, at least in principle, beholden to the fans that bring them to power. Another difference is that they are located in the space of the universal, rather than being in an adversarial or complementary relation to it. They differ from politicians too. For unlike them, the stars have charismatic authority, they retain the attributes of the king, who is a more familiar figure of sovereignty than any other available. In India sovereignty has had a strange history. The jettisoning of princely sovereignties in the moment of independence was not accompanied by any force that would render the people sovereign. Popular sovereignty thus remained a textbook ideal whose realization the state has left to the forces of history, if not nature. This is what explains the resurgence of the ineluctable logic of indirect rule in an unreconstructed polity. The survival of old sovereignties or the production of new ones, however, takes place not in isolation or in a horizontal field of multiple sovereignties, but in a field over-determined by the republication institutions. The universal was proposed, it was in the air. But the empowerment of the people had not happened. The people felt remote from the representatives whom they sent to Delhi, it did not seem as if anybody was in control the way a king is in control. The king's control has something indisputable about it. The monarch binds the political passions of his subjects. However, in independent India, these passions, reduced to objectless enthusiasms, for want of a magnet, roamed aimlessly. Where film stars became available, they were able to quickly draw around themselves a fan following that functioned very much like a king's personal bodyguard and military force.

Film stars everywhere bring to the film text a bloc of ready-made meaning, a range of associations that contribute to narrative economy as well as extra-narrative value. It is in this sense that while the actor earns wages for his/her labour, the star body/persona earns a sort of rent by being a new kind of scarce commodity. Unlike other non-renewable commodities that command rent, like land, the star persona is manufactured by the industry and endowed with scarcity value, so that it can then be inducted into the product film. The industry wants such ready-made value, but individual firms also risk being deprived of it, or having to pay a high price, once the stars recognize their rent-value and begin to charge scarcity prices for it.

Unlike other film stars, however, some Indian stars develop personae that, instead of simply adding value to a product, become supreme values in themselves, and reduce the film text to the status of an occasional event in the life of the star persona. A resplendent scarce commodity occasionally shows itself to the public; the release of a Rajnikanth film is thus not all that different from a monarch's public appearance on the palace balcony. In other words, what has happened in the case of some Indian film stars is that the scarcity value of a commodity (an economic fact), and the singularity of kingly sovereignty (a political fact), have fused together into one unique politico-cultural phenomenon. Political sovereignty's intimate link with (economic) value, even in its democratic manifestation (think of all the qualifications that the citizen was required to have: property, male gender, education, etc.), is here expressed in a direct form: star value is the basis of sovereignty explaining and giving legitimacy to the position of unquestioned power that the characters, played by the star, enjoy in the film text. With such a star, the spectator relates, not as one sovereign to another, but as one element in a collective whose identity depends upon the presence of the sovereign star at the apex. There could be no clearer evidence than is offered by these films for the fact that the majority of Indians do not occupy the substantive subject position of citizenship.

Their subalternity takes the form of a dependence on such exemplary entities for any chance of a share in collective sovereignty. It would be a mistake to think of this as simply a variant of group psychology; it is much more durable and systematic than that. Nor is it merely a question of identification with star personae, as happens with other stars. It is not that a subject uses a star persona as an anchor for his own self-image, by imitation or adulation. There is no such instrumentality at work in this dynamic relationship between star and fan. It is more akin to a virtual socio-political order within which subjects feel securely located. Even at the level of spectatorial engagement with on-screen narrative events, this relation of symbolic identification is maintained.

The citizen is a figure whose political passions may be assumed to have been committed, channelled into the republican order. If the citizen displays other passions – sexual, spiritual, in general pathological – these do not affect the prior commitment of political passions to the new democratic regime. If we examine the Indian cultural field with this in mind, we cannot help noting the existence of multiple popular enthusiasms that cannot be defined as pathological (non-political), since they seem to be mixed. The enthusiasms of today are the demobilized passions of past political orders: unbound to monarchy, they have not undergone a rebinding to the new order (i e. the republic of popular sovereignty, which remains an inert element of the compound rather than an actively transformative one). They continue to seek, and to find, modes of investment that resemble the premodern monarchic forms from which they have been cut off.

Cinema's alienness, however, remains a central feature of its popularity. The screen, as a space of representation, retained its separateness, and it is this that then enables the idea of a star as a representative who occupies that space on our behalf. This inflection of star discourse is what distinguishes fan bhakti from the more routine forms of star worship. The spectator is aware of the screen as a universal. Unlike other cultural objects, the cinema turns out to be not a synthetic whole that will remain permanently alien, but one in which images can be replaced by other images. It is this universality that Phalke noted when he realized that you can replace images of Jesus with images of Krishna. A theatre of exchange, where background is a void space ready to receive all representations, which unlike the drama stage, is visibly present before us as an emptiness. The drama stage, being a three dimensional space, did not quite project its own separateness in this fashion because it simply merged into the space around it, returned to its physical nature. The screen, however, remained intact, a space that, between projects, remains solidly white and empty, as if awaiting its next image. Political passions are directed at selected figures that appear on this screen, to force them to abide with the community beyond the transient experience of a screening.

To return to *Sivaji*, Rajnikanth's latest release: the director of this film is Sankar, who is most strongly associated with the post-modern style of recent Tamil cinema addressed to youth. The coming together of the absolutist power of Rajni and the global-capitalist digital-age style of Sankar is an event in itself, comparable to the meeting of the *Titanic* and the iceberg. The result is a film in which Rajni's sovereignty has been turned into capital, losing the political surplus, the virtual community, built upon its scarcity value. Here he does not get to speak to the community of the faithful in the old way. The Rajnikanth brand has been managed in recent years by the star's wife, a businesswoman who, a couple of releases ago, was rumoured to be exploring the possibility of patenting Rajni's signature gestures; and lately by his daughter, who is producing animation films featuring her father as hero. Absolute star power has been resistant to commodification but the new capitalist spirit has overcome this obstacle as it has others in its way. Amitabh Bachchan is the prime example of an eventually successfully re-deployed scarce resource. With *Sivaji*, it appears that Rajni, too, has been converted into a commodity. The political surplus, which was the property of the fans, the foundation of their sovereignty, has been converted into an investible economic surplus. Will the fans go along with this dissolution of their cherished virtual monarchy? It is hard to predict, but we can certainly now explain the triumphalism of the media in reporting 'Rajnimania'. It was a celebration of the triumph of profit over rent, the trumping of politics by economics, which is the Indian media's favourite news item.

Notes

An early version of this chapter was first presented at a conference on 'The Subaltern and the Popular' at the University of California at Santa Barbara in 2003. I thank the participants for their valuable comments. This chapter also previously appeared in *Economic and Political Weekly*, 44(29) (18 July 2009), pp. 68–76.

1   The report and the four volumes of *Evidence*, originally published by the government of India in 1928, is now available in digital format from several sources, including the Roja Muthaiah Research Library in Chennai and the Centre for the Study of Culture and Society in Bangalore. The original publication is available at the National Film Archive of India Library in Pune. The evidence consists of the written and oral testimony of a wide selection of people from politics, the film industry, civil society, the military, the police, the press and the universities. Sittings of the committee were held in all major cities of British India, including those in present day Pakistan and Burma.

2   The educated among the Indians knew very well, the argument went, that the 'European culture' was different from their own and were unlikely to get the wrong idea about Western society when they saw men and women

dancing together and kissing. But the uneducated would judge the Europeans according to their own moral standards and find their behaviour unbecoming. Some of the Indian members of the committee and witnesses would seize the opportunity to embarrass their British counterparts by pointing out that it was members of their own race who were producing these immoral pictures, that it was not the native's fault if they were incapable of producing better films, and so on. The main purpose behind these jibes appears to have been to demolish the pretence that it was a concern for the native's moral health rather than the declining mystique of the white race that was prompting all this activity.

3 For a more detailed discussion of this unusual turn of events occasioned by American cinema, see M. Madhava Prasad (2004b).

4 Phalke was a proponent of *swadeshi*. While in other sectors of industry this merely implied native ownership of industry, in the case of cinema we have to consider the possibility that to be truly *swadeshi*, a film company's products too would have to be of local origin. The *swadeshi* industrialist could produce a 'foreign' product like a clock, but would a film made by a native and modelled on American silent movies have qualified as *swadeshi*? Phalke's choice of mythological topics must be seen, in any case, not as a response to latent demand, but a conscious political act. By extension, the popularity of the mythological does not demonstrate anything other than the fact that early Indian filmmakers were aligning themselves with the *swadeshi* spirit.

5 'Enthusiasm is an emotion of the ethical part of the soul' remarks Aristotle in *The Politics*. Locke, in the *Essay on Human Understanding*, contrasts enthusiasm with both revelation and reason, as a sort of eruption of the irrational. 'This I take to be properly enthusiasm, which, though founded neither on reason nor divine revelation, but rising from the conceits of a warmed or overweening brain, works yet, where it once gets footing, more powerfully on the persuasions and actions of men than either of those two, or both together: men being most forwardly obedient to the impulses they receive from themselves; and the whole man is sure to act more vigorously where the whole man is carried by a natural motion' (Book IV, Ch. 19.7). Enthusiasts demonstrate 'great independence of devotion' whereas the superstitious are 'favourable to priestly power' observes David Hume ('On Superstition and Enthusiasm'). Kant speaks of enthusiasm as a glow of anticipation on the faces of onlookers near and far at a time of revolutionary change. There is a European history of enthusiasm spread over the fields of politics, religion and poetry. I borrow the term from the Slovenian Lacanian philosophers, who have revived discussion of the term, but my usage may not entirely coincide with or be in agreement with theirs. It seems that in our own context, the exploration of the historical meanings of bhakti has been blocked by the problems arising from the separation of the field of study from the languages and methods of study (the translation problem discussed above). The translation problem still remains and the above historical survey by no means exhausts the meanings of the term, but it has seemed to me profitable, so long as we have to conduct such inquiries in English, to explore possibilities of translation in all directions, rather than insist on a resistance to translation as a hallmark of our cultural distinction, a position that is characterized by a stubborn resistance to self-understanding.

6 See S. V. Srinivas (1996 and 1997) for a detailed study of fan clubs to which this account is indebted.

7 The phrase is Francois Furet's.

References

Dickey, Sara (1993) *Cinema and the Urban Poor in South India* (Cambridge: Cambridge University Press).

Forrester, Duncan (1976) 'Factions and Filmstars: Tamil Nadu Politics since 1971', *Asian Survey*, 16(3): 283–96.

Hansen, Thomas Blom (2005) 'Sovereigns beyond the State: On Legality and Public Authority in India', in Ravinder Kaur (ed.), *Religion, Violence and Political Mobilization in South Asia* (New Delhi: Sage), pp. 109–44.

Hardgrave Jr, Robert L. (1979) 'When Stars Displace the Gods: The Folk Culture of Cinema in Tamil Nadu', in *Essays in the Political Sociology of South India* (New Delhi: Usha Publications).

Indian Cinematograph Committee (ICC) (1927–8) Report plus four volumes of *Evidence* (Calcutta: Government of India Central Publication Branch).

Narayan, S. Venkat (1983) *NTR: A Biography* (New Delhi: Vikas).

Pandian, M. S. S. (1992) *The Image Trap: M. G. Ramachandran in Film and Politics* (New Delhi: Sage).

Prasad, M. Madhava (1999) 'Cine-politics: On the Political Significance of Cinema in South India', *Journal of the Moving Image*, Issue no. 1.

—— (2003) 'Cinema as a Site of National Identity Politics in Karnataka' in *Journal of Karnataka Studies*, 1: 60–85.

—— (2004a) 'Reigning Stars: The Political Career of South Indian Cinema', in Lucy Fischer and Marcia Landy (ed.), *Stars, the Film Reader* (New York, London: Routledge), pp. 97–114.

—— (2004b) 'The Natives are Looking: Cinema and Censorship in Colonial India', in Leslie Moran *et al.* (eds), *Law's Moving Image* (London: Cavendish/Glasshouse Press).

Sivathamby, Karthigesu (1981) *The Tamil Film as a Medium of Political Communication* (Madras: New Century Book House).

Srinivas, S. V. (1996) 'Devotion and Defiance in Fan Activity', *Journal of Arts and Ideas*, 29, January: 67–83.

—— (1997): 'Fans and Stars, Production, Reception and Circulation of the Moving Image', PhD dissertation, University of Hyderabad.

Part II

Translating cultural traditions

Introduction

Elleke Boehmer and Rosinka Chaudhuri

A. K. Ramanujan, pre-eminent among Indian postcolonial theorists of translation, once referred to the impossibility of what John Dryden had called, in 1680, the *metaphrase*, the method of 'turning an author word by word, and line by line, from one language into another'.[1] Ramanujan's theories of 'outer' and 'inner' poetic form, the *akam* and the *puram*, are too well known to bear repetition. Instead, it is to his belief that the production of discourse results from the 'infinite use of finite means', ensuring a text's resistance to translatability, that postcolonial theories of the poetics of translation bear a resemblance in their ideological and theoretical operations.[2] Translation studies has, for some time now, insisted upon the difference between the activity called 'translating' and the wider circumference of the complexities of 'translation' or 'translation studies'. Postcolonial theories are imbricated with the latter field in common conceptual and textual grids that reconstruct the way in which cultures inhabit reality and representation.

In postcolonial studies, the problematic of translating other cultural traditions becomes an important marker for raising questions of representation, power and historicity. The asymmetric relationships between colonizer and colonized result in contesting accounts of relations between languages, races and peoples, and this then invites an examination of the technologies or practices of power/knowledge as they operate through the coercive machinery of the state within multiple discursive sites, one of which is translation. Translation then proceeds as 'strategies of containment' that occlude the violence accompanying the constitution of the colonial subject – a hegemony that circulates through various discourses in several registers to produce the status of the colonized as 'objects without history'.[3] The argument is derived from Edward Said's demonstration of the manner in which translation became part of the colonial discourse of Orientalism in a meta-narrative constituted of various genres of writing, all implicated in the reinforcement and perpetuation of colonial rule. That thesis has acquired, if anything, a greater urgency in postcolonial studies today, given its importance for rethinking the postcolonial subject's neo-colonial situationality.

Among the chapters included in this section, the figure of Said is most prominently featured in Aamir R. Mufti's deliberations upon his notion of 'secular criticism', which Mufti reads through the lens of minority culture, invoking, in the process, the powerful yet liminal form of Auerbach in Istanbul during the writing of *Mimesis*, a repetitive image in Said that has also left a lasting legacy in analyses of his work. Said never named his critical practice 'postcolonial criticism', preferring, rather, the term 'secular criticism', Mufti maintains, to denote his engagement with practices of reading imbued with a notion of minority-ness (where minority is a fundamental 'condition of possibility' of the 'secular'). Debates about secularism in the postcolonial world, then, may take from Saidian criticism the means for overcoming some of the impasses generated by the polarized debates around postcolonial culture, canon or community. The importance of Auerbach's Jewishness, which configures him as a member of a minority above all else for Said, is emphasized by Mufti in order to reinforce the problematic of culture and dignity that recurrently occasions the crisis of post-Enlightenment secularism for the modern critic. The model of exile provided for a Palestinian such as Said by the person of Auerbach or, later, Adorno, is resonant with the experience of minority existence in modernity that relates also to the globalized strategies of reading provided by postcolonial critics. Secular criticism thus makes an ethical imperative of loss and displacement, insisting upon the possibility of emancipation even while recognizing that all universal claims are particular in nature. Undeniably, the fate of secularism is now being forged in postcolonial contexts, and Mufti proceeds to examine the postcolonial criticism of those such as Ashis Nandy, who have argued that secularism is an idea that falls under the rubric of an 'imperialism of categories', an argument that might superficially seem to be derived from Said's critique of Orientalism, but is actually, Mufti suggests, quite the opposite. His critical engagement with the scholarship of Partha Chatterjee interrogates the notion of the minority in Chatterjee's writings, pointing towards a failure to think beyond the boundaries of the postcolonial state and thus to think 'from the position of a minority group', which is one of Said's procedures of secular criticism.

While it might seem that Vinayak Chaturvedi's individualist chapter on the secret origins of the name he shares with one of the ideologues of right-wing Hindu politics in colonial India, Vinayak Savarkar, occupies the opposite pole to the minority question invoked by Mufti, focusing as it does on the majority question, if it may be called that, both are in fact concerned with similar issues. The wider cluster of problems associated with the construction of an aggressive nationalist politics of the majority community in postcolonial India is refracted through the prism of the personal name and its politics in Chaturvedi's chapter, where he tries to make sense of the disturbance created in him by the revelation that he was named at the suggestion of a man who helped the men who shot the Father of the Nation, Mahatma Gandhi. The paradoxical tension between this original act of patricide and the deliberate seeding of a great many boys named Vinayak to carry forward Savarkar's majoritarian ideology in postcolonial India by the overly masculine Dr Parchure, is uncovered through the complexities that construct oral narratives, where 'hidden transcripts' and silences often have a history of their own. Making the personal the political, Chaturvedi in this chapter explores the gaps and fissures latent in any narrative of representation or translation where fidelity is never arrived at because people of flesh and blood in concrete situations with certain aims in mind impose the rules that govern the decoding or reformulation of the actual situation. The fragments and collages that make up the structure of remembrance are markers that are played off against each other until the reader or interpreter is faced as much with a problem of translation as with one of composition, riddled as these are with discrepancies in conceptual and textual languages of representation. Questions about the historical nature of family life and nationalist politics in central and western India are themes central to the arguments discussed in this chapter, which is located in a very particular place and time but nevertheless points toward a richer theorizing of the relation between personal memory and nationalist politics in postcolonial India.

Belatedness as possibility is the theme of Dipesh Chakrabarty's ruminations on the historical and political significance of the idea of arriving late. The notion of late arrival in the context of India is sparked by the theme of an exhibition in Chicago in 2007 on contemporary art from India, which has become truly contemporary only now, with the arrival of India on the stage of world economy. The chapter militates against commonplace statements such as that present in the art catalogue: 'Like Modernism, feminist art came to India later than to the West'. Chakrabarty has been writing against such teleological, developmental and historicist overviews for some time now. It is only recently, however, that critiques such as his have had any impact in the Western mainstream media, if at all. A year after the Chicago exhibition witnessed by Chakrabarty, in an article in the *New York Times*, art critic Holand Cotter shared a similar insight with his readers. Reviewing a show called 'Rhythms of India: The Art of Nandalal Bose (1882–1966)' at the Philadelphia Museum of Art in 2008, he wrote: 'Along with detailed information about one artist's life and times, the show delivers a significant piece of news, or what is still probably news to many people: that modernism wasn't a purely Western product sent out like so many CARE packages to a hungry and waiting world. It was a phenomenon that unfolded everywhere, in different forms, at different speeds, for different reasons, under different pressures, but always under pressure'.[4] At the end of his retrospection on the modern art of Nandalal Bose, and on the bed of modern Indian culture from which it sprang, Cotter concludes with a sentiment attuned to postcolonial critical practice, 'that every Museum of Modern Art in the United States and Europe should be required, in the spirit of truth in advertising, to change its name to Museum of Western Modernism until it has earned the right to do otherwise'.[5]

The questions raised by the place of Indian art in modern history are rephrased by Chakrabarty in the context of the Subaltern Studies project, with which he has long been associated. Speaking of how the world is constituted when belatedness is converted into possibility, he focuses on the problem of repetition and recognition in history. Rephrasing Bhabha, he asks, 'How do we know what is new in what seems like repetition?' Two paradoxical propositions, of displacement and disguise, provide some part of the answer for him as he interrogates these Deleuzian notions through the example of Subaltern Studies. Western categories have to be continually processed, Chakrabarty suggests, in order to displace them from the locus of their original signification, making them valid for usage in the rest of the world. The theme of disguise, on the other hand, inheres in our capacity to name the new; in categorizations of the political in the non-West that have not yet been named. The new is born as a challenge to judgement and law in the figures of both poetry and politics, yet needs to be contemplated in our time through repetition and belatedness.

Situated directly in the field of translation studies within postcolonial theory, Aniket Jaaware's chapter invokes demons, angels and historical humans in order to address questions related to issues of translation in what he calls 'our fuzzy postcolonialism'. By considering the socio-historical contexts of other kinds of translation activity apart from those related to literature and language, it might be possible to render this field complex in another way. The history of translation in Europe, for instance, has been typically Eurocentric in foregrounding the translation of the Bible into modern European languages, neglecting entirely the socio-historical context of translations of the Bible into several non-European languages in a colonial context, where local demands change the shape, in one example, of the notion of the Trinity. Using Benjamin's notion of translation as the afterlife of a work, he suggests that this after-life exists in two modes, the angelic and the demonic, one in which the positive potentials of a work are revealed, and the other in which the demonic aspects – always a little more interesting – hold sway. His argument is thickly peopled with examples from a Marathi translation of Nietzsche, a nineteenth-century travelogue, and the English translation of a letter by a sepoy in the Native British Army, which uphold his ultimate contention that the issue of alternative modernities in postcolonial societies has implications for our understanding of postcoloniality as a social – as distinct from a theoretical – practice, an aspect often under-represented in postcolonial studies.

Notes

1   Cited in Vinay Dharwadker, 'A. K. Ramanujan's theory and practice of transla-tion' in Susan Bassnett and Harish Trivedi (ed.) *Post-Colonial Translation: Theory and Practice* (1999), p. 116.
2   See A. K. Ramanujan, *Poems of Love and War: From the Eight Anthologies and the Ten Long Poems of Classical Tamil* (1985); *Folktales from India: A Selection of Oral Tales from Twenty-two Languages* (1991).
3   Tejaswini Niranjana, *Siting Translation: History, Post-Structuralism, and the Colonial Context* (Berkeley: University of California Press, 1992), p. 3.
4   H. Cotter, 'Indian Modernism via an Eclectic and Elusive Artist', *New York Times*, 19 August, 2008.
5   For a further discussion, see Rosinka Chaudhuri, 'Reading Bharatchandra: Literary Language and the Figuration of Modernity in Bengal (1822–1858)' in *Interventions*, 11(3), 2009.

5 Auerbach in Istanbul

Edward Said, secular criticism, and the question of minority culture

Aamir R. Mufti

Edward Said has never left any doubt as to the significance he attaches to what he calls secular criticism. It is by this term, not *postcolonial criticism*, that he identifies his critical practice as a whole. The meaning of this term is a theme he has returned to repeatedly since first elaborating it at length in the introduction to *The World, the Text, and the Critic*. But this facet of the Saidian project has received nothing like the attention that, for instance, has been lavished upon the concept of Orientalism or the strategy of what he calls contrapuntal reading. Nor does it seem to have been productive for younger scholars in quite the same way as these two latter conceptual constellations. There may even appear to be something odd about the persistence of this concern in Said's work, at least within the context of the Anglo-American academy. Could all this conceptual and rhetorical energy and all this ethical seriousness really be directed at literary readings of the Bible or at works concerning the traditions of Judeo-Christian hermeneutics, as a few stray comments towards the end of *The World, the Text, and the Critic* might lead one to believe?

Interpreters have often shied away from this aspect of Saidian criticism, despite its undeniable importance in the corpus of his work. There are, of course, exceptions, the most notable from my point of view being Bruce Robbins. But in Robbins's work, too, one senses an extraordinary effort at interpretation and a dislodging of the term *secular* from its usual meanings. *Secular*, Robbins argues, stands in opposition not to religious concerns or beliefs per se but to the nation and nationalism as belief system.[1] It is, I think, an ingenious suggestion, one that I would like to hold on to for the moment in order later to expand upon it and also perhaps to recontextualize and partially to displace it.

I would like to begin mapping out the meaning of secular criticism by arguing that a concern with minority culture and existence occupies a central place within it. This is not, I shall argue, an accidental concern, such as one might expect from any progressive critical practice. It is, rather, a fundamental and constitutive concern, a condition of possibility of the critical practice itself. Furthermore, it is my view that careful attention to this subtext will help clear up some fundamental and widely held misconceptions about Saidian criticism, in particular concerning the concepts of culture, canon and community that it deploys. The Saidian critical position implies, I shall argue, not a contentless cosmopolitanism but a secularism imbued with the experience of minority – a secularism for which *minority* is not simply the name of a crisis. Such a rethinking of the meaning of Saidian criticism is, of course, an enormous project. I can only hint here at one possible direction this rereading might take. I shall focus on the repeated appearance in Said's writings of Erich Auerbach, a figure I consider to be a locus both for the minority problematic I am speaking of and for the misunderstandings to which I have already alluded. Said's turn to Auerbach will serve as a starting point or *Ansatzpunkt* – in the sense in which Said, following Auerbach, himself uses that term – from which I shall approach and enter the field of secular criticism.[2] Along the way I shall argue that Saidian criticism carries certain definite implications for debates about secularism in the postcolonial world, that it offers the means for overcoming many impasses generated by these debates, and that these latter cultural and political contexts provide some of the impulse for the critical notions themselves.

There are scattered references to Auerbach and his works throughout Said's major critical writings from *Beginnings* onwards – to the tradition of German romance scholarship of which he was a representative, to the breadth of philological knowledge that scholars such as he and Ernst Curtius brought to their work, to the importance of Vico for his conception of comparative scholarship, to Auerbach himself as a figure of exile. Like the notion of secular criticism – and for related reasons, as I shall try to show – the meaning and function of this figure for Said have also proved difficult to interpret. One possibility has been to read Said's interest in Auerbach as an instance of his interest in philology – his treatments of Ernest Renan, Louis Massignon, and Raymond Schwab being among the other instances. Tim Brennan, for example, has made an interesting case for what appears to him to be the paradoxical importance of the European philological tradition for Said's critical practice. Said's relationship to philology is indispensable, Brennan argues, for his success as 'TV celebrity', adding that 'philology is what has helped Said matter to political life in this country in a way that many Left theorists and academic Marxists do not'.[3] Brennan has read Said's references to Auerbach within this larger argument.[4] I shall follow a somewhat different direction here and argue that Said's concern with Auerbach as philologue is inseparable from his interest in the latter as a figure of exile. Auerbach in Turkish exile appears at length in the essay on secular criticism and returns repeatedly in later works, including *Culture and Imperialism*.

The importance of Auerbach for Said was noted in earlier responses to his work as well. In his well-known review of *Orientalism*, for instance,

James Clifford pointed to the famous passage from Hugo of St Victor about the loss of home and strength of consciousness. Cited by Auerbach at the end of his late essay, 'Philology and *Weltliteratur*' (1952), an essay Said himself co-translated in 1969, the passage appears repeatedly in Said's writings (on four occasions, by my count):

> It is, therefore, a source of great virtue for the practised mind to learn, bit by bit, first to change about invisible and transitory things, so that afterwards it may be able to leave them behind altogether. The man who finds his homeland sweet is still a tender beginner; he to whom every soil is as his native one is already strong; but he is perfect to whom the entire world is as a foreign land. The tender soul has fixed his love on one spot in the world; the strong man has extended his love to all places; the perfect man has extinguished his.[5]

Said has used this passage in a number of related ways. In his essay on exile, it becomes a means for arguing that exile consists not in rejecting ties to the home but rather in *'working through'* them: 'What is true of all exile is not that home and love of home are lost, but that loss is inherent in the very existence of both' (Said 1984, p. 171). The ethical imperative of exile is to cultivate a 'scrupulous' subjectivity, one that will not undermine a keen recognition of its own tentativeness and fragility by seeking 'satisfaction from substitutes furnished by illusion or dogma' (Said 1984, pp. 170, 171). Exile must therefore be seen 'not as a privilege, but as an *alternative* to the mass institutions that dominate modern life' (Said 1984, p. 170). At the conclusion of *Culture and Imperialism*, the passage from Hugo stands as the credo of a politicized cosmopolitanism equally wary of an imperial universalism and the beleaguered solace of tribal identities.

Clifford offers a peculiar gloss on Said's citing of this passage in *Orientalism*. It appears to him to signal Said's endorsement of the 'anthropological commonplace' about 'participant-observer' immersion in distant cultures: 'The anthropologist as outsider and participant-observer (existential shorthand for the hermeneutical circle) is a familiar modern *topos*. Its wisdom – and authority – is expressed with a disturbing beauty by Hugo of St Victor'.[6] The casualness of this series of equations is startling: anthropological fieldwork as exile; Said as a closet anthropologist; participant-observation as an instance of the hermeneutic circle; and, perhaps strangest of all, the twelfth-century monk as a kind of precursor of Malinowski. But the upshot of all this for Clifford is that Auerbach marks Said's continued adherence to 'humanist perspectives' and the failure of these perspectives to 'harmonize with his use of methods derived from Foucault' (Clifford 1988, p. 264). Clifford is wrong, as Brennan has noted, to see *Orientalism* as merely an attempt 'to extend Foucault's conception of a discourse into the area of cultural constructions of the exotic' – Raymond Williams, Antonio Gramsci, and Auerbach himself being equally potent sources (Clifford 1988, p. 264).[7] But my point is also that Auerbach becomes a sign for Clifford (as for Brennan) of a liberal-traditional and *affirmative* conception of culture and therefore of Said's elite cosmopolitanism.[8]

Auerbach also plays an important role in Aijaz Ahmad's infamous polemic against Said. To begin with, he too, like Clifford before him, makes a great deal of the Foucault–Auerbach opposition, even appearing disingenuously as a sort of defender of the rigours of Foucauldian 'Discourse Theory', as he puts it, against the purported eclecticism of Said's work, in particular of *Orientalism*.[9] Where he does in fact diverge from Clifford is in making Auerbach the site of a psychological melodrama for Said.

> Said denounces with Foucauldian vitriol what he loves with Auerbachian passion, so that the reader soon begins to detect a very *personal* kind of drama being enacted in Said's procedure of alternately debunking and praising to the skies and again debunking the same book, as if he had been betrayed by the objects of his passion. (Ahmad 1992, p. 168)

This passage exemplifies the somewhat blustery view of literary and cultural criticism that informs Ahmad's entire book; for him it is all a matter of praise or denunciation, *either* praise *or* denunciation.[10] And this soap-opera vision of Said as a battleground for a never ending struggle between Foucault (standing in for 'anti-humanism') and Auerbach (standing in for 'High Humanism', the canon, 'Tory' orientations) forms the basis of Ahmad's entire critique of Said (Ahmad 1992, pp. 164, 162, 162). But Ahmad goes further, arguing that *Orientalism* is in every point of detail a riposte to *Mimesis*.

> The particular texture of *Orientalism*, its emphasis on the canonical text, its privileging of literature and philology in the constitution of 'Orientalist' knowledge and indeed the human sciences generally, its will to portray a 'West' which has been the same from the dawn of history up to the present, and its will to traverse all the main languages of Europe – all this, and more, in *Orientalism* derives from the ambition to write a counter-history that could be posed against *Mimesis*, Auerbach's magisterial account of the seamless genesis of European realism and rationalism from Greek Antiquity to the modernist moment. (Ahmad 1992, p. 163)

From my present perspective, it is this characterization of *Mimesis* as an 'account of the seamless genesis of European realism and rationalism from Greek Antiquity to the modernist moment' that constitutes the most interesting failure of critical imagination in Ahmad's discussion of Said, for it reveals what he takes the intellectual and ethical meaning of Auerbach for Said to be.

First of all, *Mimesis* cannot appear to even the casual reader as a 'continuous' or 'seamless' account of anything. It is in at least one important sense a fragmentary work, literally, consisting of a series of close readings of small fragments of texts with no overall argument or theoretical perspective. (I am not suggesting that the work lacks unity, merely an explicit frame or argument.) It begins, as Vassilis Lambropoulos has noted, *in medias res*, without any introductory statement of overall method and purpose. Furthermore, its entry into the analysis of the problem announced in the subtitle, *The Representation of Reality in Western Literature*, is 'surreptitious' rather than systematic, as it is only several pages into the first chapter, 'Odysseus' Scar', that it becomes apparent that the purpose is not to analyse the Homeric text as such but rather to contrast two texts and modes of description, the Homeric and the biblical – the analytical and the interpretive – and that the former is to be approached not on its own terms but *through* the latter.[11] Auerbach himself also speaks, in his later book, *Literary Language and Its Public in Late Latin Antiquity and in the Middle Ages*, of the constitutive gaps in the structure of *Mimesis* and in fact refers to the later work as a 'supplement' to the earlier one.[12] He mentions in particular one type of discontinuity, the jump roughly from AD 600 to 1100, a gap he blames on his Turkish exile, an interesting matter to which I shall return shortly. But my real point here is that Ahmad, like Clifford before him, has fundamentally misread the significance of Auerbach for Said, for whom *Mimesis*, far from being a triumphalist text, is inscribed through and through with pathos, dignity, and the ethical. I shall therefore now turn to Said's writing in an effort to interpret the meaning for him of Auerbach in exile.

What voices are colliding in the Saidian text? What happens to Auerbach in his appearance on this stage? What sense can we make of the fact that Said turns to this figure again and again? The first thing we should note in this connection is that even as early as *Orientalism* we find Said counterposing Auerbach's critical practice to the procedures of Orientalist discourse. Both Orientalism and the comparative literary imagination share, Said argues, the tendency to interpret literature synthetically, '*as a whole*'.[13] And while they also both emphasize a certain estrangement from the object of scholarly inquiry, they diverge sharply as to the meaning and consequences of this distancing. Where Auerbach's notion of estrangement – as expressed in his use of the passage from Hugo of St Victor – implies a generosity of spirit, an interpretive 'magnanimity', as he had put it in his late essay on Vico, for the Orientalists, 'their estrangement from Islam simply intensified their feelings of superiority about European culture' (Said 1978, p. 260).[14] Furthermore, if the synthesizing ambition in philology (as conceived by Auerbach or Curtius) was to lead to an enlargement of the scholar's awareness, of his sense of the brotherhood of man, of the universality of certain principles of human behavior, in Islamic Orientalism synthesis led to a sharpened sense of difference between Orient and Occident as reflected in Islam. (Said 1978, p. 261)

In the introduction to their 1969 translation of Auerbach's essay on philology, Said and his co-translator had already emphasized that for Auerbach 'philology treats contingent, historical truths', that it proceeds 'dialectically, not statically'.[15]

But Said's most sustained treatment of Auerbach to date is in the essay on secular criticism in *The World, the Text, and the Critic*, which serves as an introduction to that work. He becomes a central point of reference and resource in the elaboration of the key terms of the essay, *filiation* and *affiliation*, and it is through him that Said tries to recall and to recuperate for the present what he considers to have been 'the destiny of critical consciousness in the recent past'.[16] Said begins his discussion of Auerbach immediately with *Mimesis* and the occasion of its composition. Auerbach's own comments on this location come in the last passages of *Mimesis* itself, almost as an afterthought, in the brief methodological epilogue to the work. Commenting on the many gaps in content as necessary and unavoidable in a work of this scope, Auerbach adds:

> I may also mention that the book was written during the war and at Istanbul, where the libraries are not well equipped for European studies. International communications were impeded; I had to dispense with almost all periodicals, with almost all the more recent investigations, and in some cases with reliable critical editions of my texts. Hence it is possible and even probable that I overlooked things which I ought to have considered and that I occasionally assert something which modern research has disproved or modified. ... On the other hand it is quite possible that the book owes its existence to just this lack of a rich and specialized library. If it had been possible for me to acquaint myself with all the work that has been done on so many subjects, I might never have reached the point of writing.[17]

Said notes 'the drama of this little bit of modesty' and points to the pathos and dignity of the passage and to the multiple ironies of Auerbach's situation (Said 1983, p. 6): that Auerbach, the German Jewish refugee from European fascism, writes from outside the European homeland what has perhaps become the definitive interpretation of European literary history, the dates of composition of *Mimesis* – 1942 to 1945 – roughly corresponding to the peak of the Holocaust; that this act of cultural survival, of survival through culture, of the reclaiming of culture, is performed at the height of the modern self-conflagration of the culture of the West; and, finally, that the place of this exile, the place of refuge that enables and even requires Europe to be apprehended as a whole perhaps for the last time, is none other than Turkey, historically the site of Europe's other, the Terrible Turk.

> Throughout the classical period of European culture Turkey was the Orient, Islam its most redoubtable and aggressive representative. This was not all, though. The Orient and Islam also stood for the ultimate alienation from and opposition to Europe, the European tradition of Christian Latinity, as well as to the putative authority of ecclesia, humanistic learning, and cultural community. For centuries Turkey and Islam hung over Europe like a gigantic composite monster, seeming to threaten Europe with destruction. To have been an exile in Istanbul at that time of fascism in Europe was a deeply resonating and intense form of exile from Europe. (Said 1983, p. 6)

Abdul JanMohamed has discounted the importance Said accords to the place of Auerbach's exile on the grounds that there is no evidence in *Mimesis* that this location – Turkey, the Middle East, Islam – exerts any cultural 'influence' on the content of the work.[18] Said's point, I think, is rather that the relevance of this location, or, more precisely, this dislocation, lies in the light it throws on the relationship between the critical consciousness and its object of study – Western Literature.

For what really draws Said to this passage in Auerbach is the latter's own assertion that his non-Occidental exile was the *condition of possibility* of the work itself.

> At this point, then, Auerbach's epilogue to *Mimesis* suddenly becomes clear: 'it is quite possible that the book owes its existence to just this lack of a rich and specialized library'. In other words, the book owed its existence to the very fact of Oriental, non-Occidental exile and homelessness. And if this is so, then *Mimesis* itself is not, as it has so frequently been taken to be, only a massive reaffirmation of the Western cultural tradition, but also a work built upon a critically important alienation from it, a work whose conditions and circumstances of existence are not immediately derived from the culture it describes with such extraordinary insight and brilliance but built rather on an agonizing distance from it. (Said 1983, pp. 7–8)[19]

Said therefore reads Auerbach's exile, and the composition of *Mimesis* during that exile, as questioning received notions of 'nation, home, community, and belonging' (Said 1983, p. 12). The point of Said's reading is that Auerbach's relationship to 'the Western cultural tradition' is *already* one of exile, a condition tragically dramatized by the literal displacement to Istanbul – the preeminent site of non-Europe – an exile brought about by the rise of genocidal fascism in the European home itself.

In other words, Said reads Auerbach in a rigorous sense as a Jewish figure, as a member of a minority, of *the* minority par excellence, partly in the political sense in which Hannah Arendt uses that term. For Arendt, minority, as exemplified by the Jews of Europe, is a condition doubly determined: it is marked by specific forms of alienation vis-à-vis state and society. The Jews, she argues, remained as a group outside the class structure of society that emerged from the destruction of the *ancien régime*. And what made them 'the *minorité par excellence*' in the years after the peace treaties of 1919–20 was the fact that no state could be relied upon to protect their rights. The predicament of the stateless in the twentieth century, Arendt argues, is not 'the loss of specific rights, then, but the loss of a community willing and able to guarantee any rights whatsoever'.[20] The right they are denied is the right to *have* rights. In other words, what the stateless are stripped of is human dignity, that quality of the subject that has been encoded since the eighteenth century in the language of the Rights of Man.

A remarkably compelling image of this dynamic of 'dignity' in the literature of the modern West is Peter Schlemiel, the protagonist and narrator of Adelbert von Chamisso's 1814 novella of the same name. A man of humble means, Peter is convinced by another man to sell his shadow in exchange for a purse that contains boundless wealth. Although he is now rich, because he lacks a shadow Peter is turned instantly into a homeless pariah – taunted by children wherever he goes, avoiding sunny places, subject to the scorn of 'those well-dressed burghers who themselves cast such a broad and imposing shadow'.[21] This narrative from the early years of the modern era allows us to see that the right and the ability to, as it were, throw a 'broad and imposing shadow' is distributed unequally among the members of modern state and society. Or, rather, that the universalism of the category of citizen is itself brought to crisis by this maldistribution of 'dignity'. And it is hardly surprising that Chamisso finds a figure for this distinctly modern form of haplessness in the Jewish schlemiel. For Arendt, the philosophical significance of the modern phenomenon of statelessness, as exemplified in the Jewish minorities of Europe at mid-century, is that it represents the denial to human beings of those basic attributes of humanness that come to us coded as dignity. The philosophical lesson that the death factories force us to learn is therefore the following: 'The world found nothing sacred in the abstract nakedness of being human' (Arendt 1979, p. 299).

For Said, the resonance of Jewishness-minority for the modern critical temperament lies in this problematic of culture and dignity. The political dimension of this problematic for Arendt is that the Jew is a person who is perennially on the verge of becoming a stateless refugee. That for a Palestinian the resonance of such a political experience should be enormous and complex is not surprising, and I shall return to that question at the end of the present chapter. But what interests Said more directly here is the history of Jewishness-minority as the recurring occasion for crisis and control in post-Enlightenment secularism, and the possibilities it opens up for the distinctly modern vocation of critique. The German Jewish critic in ('Oriental') exile becomes for Said the paradigmatic figure for modern criticism, an object lesson in what it means to have a critical consciousness: 'The intellectual's *social identity* should involve something more than strengthening those aspects of the culture that require mere affirmation and orthodox compliancy from its members' (Said 1983, p. 24; emphasis added). It is, in other words, highly significant that it is Auerbach – and, in Said's more recent work, Adorno – who provides him the model for exile, and not, say, Joyce and his contemporaries, let alone Nabokov, Solzhenitsyn, or Brodsky.[22] The victims of fascism represent for Said the paradigmatic instance of the 'social identity' called exile. Through the figure of the Jewish exile, Said makes direct links between the experience of minority existence in modernity and the problematic of exile in social, political and cultural terms.

In a brief but remarkable essay on the ethos of comparative literary scholarship in the post-war US, Emily Apter has argued that the discipline Auerbach, Curtius, Leo Spitzer, and others founded (or reformulated) on their arrival in the US was structured in fundamental ways around the experience of exile and displacement. The globalized strategies of reading proposed by 'postcolonial' critics, she argues, therefore do not constitute the kind of break with comparatist traditions that their so-called traditionalist opponents often characterize them to be.

> One could say that new-wave postcolonial literacy bears certain distinct resemblances to its European antecedents imbued as it often is with echoes of melancholia, *Heimlosigkeit*, cultural ambivalence, consciousness of linguistic loss, confusion induced by 'worlding' or global transference, amnesia of origins, fractured subjectivity, border trauma, the desire to belong to 'narration' as a substitute 'nation', the experience of a politics of linguistic and cultural usurpation.[23]

The form of cultural 'literacy' that Said calls secular criticism makes an ethical imperative of loss and displacement. It holds, with Adorno, that 'it is part of morality not to be at home in one's home'.[24] It sees minority as a permanent condition of exile and requires that in our affiliative efforts at critical community and comprehension we assume the posture of minority. The implications of such a critical project for, among other things, secularism in the postcolonial world are enormous and have not even begun to be explored. The significance of the exiled German Jewish author of *Mimesis* for such a project, therefore, lies in the fact that 'we have in Auerbach an instance both of filiation with his natal culture and, because of exile, *affiliation* with it through critical consciousness and scholarly work' (Said 1983, p. 16).

This problematic of the displacement of culture and authority, which Apter and Said rightly emphasize in their interpretation of Auerbach, becomes explicit in 'Philology and *Weltliteratur*', Auerbach's late reflections on the method and significance of comparative literary scholarship. Auerbach proposes a method for the contemporary philologist that is almost an antimethod. The work of philology, he insists, is still the large synthesis, a comprehension of the whole – ultimately of human experience or world history as such. But such synthesis can proceed only by means that appear limited, partial, and local: 'in order to accomplish a major work of synthesis it is imperative to locate a point of departure [*Ansatzpunkt*], a handle, as it were, by which the subject can be seized'. This point of departure, itself concrete and well circumscribed, must have a 'radiating power' that brings a larger problematic within the philologist's purview. The whole, in other words, is to be comprehended not on the basis of its most general or, strictly speaking, universal principle, but rather *contingently*, from one possible location within it or trajectory through it. For the choice of *Ansatzphänomen* is not subject to a strict method. It emerges out of the particular experience and location of the researcher, her 'intuition', which itself is the sediment of the larger social processes at whose intersection the individual is located (Auerbach 1969, pp. 13–14, 15, 11). What is proposed here is a synthesis that nevertheless does not depend on pre-existing categories or at least is not a mere rearrangement of them. The point of such synthesis is precisely not to reify the whole. It is this aspect of the notion of *Ansatzpunkt* that Said turns to in elaborating his own concept of beginnings, which he deems 'eminently secular', as opposed to 'origins', concern with which is the sign of a state of mind that is 'theological'.[25] In other words, critics who read Said's turn to Auerbach as evidence of traditional and affirmative notions of culture and authority make the mistake of those readers who, in Said's own words, 'will assume that [Spitzer and Auerbach] were rather old-fashioned versions of Brooks or Warren' (Said 1983, p. 149).[26] They fail to recognize that what Said invokes here is precisely the possibility of rupture in the purportedly continuous and seamless text of liberal culture.

What Said cites, therefore, is not so much the Auerbachian text, the text whose author-function bears the name of Auerbach, but rather Auerbach *as* text. It is a 'worlding' of Auerbach and must not be confused with a confronting of text with context. Said's reading disrupts the economy of attribution and location within which the mutual relationships of text, context and author are produced. That this 'worlded' Auerbach should become in Said's work the source and the icon of a secular critical practice is therefore far from paradoxical. It is unquestionably true, as Robbins has noted, that the word *secular* has a long history of serving 'as a figure for the authority of a putatively universal reason, or (narratively speaking) as the ideal end-point of progress in the intellectual domain'.[27] Hence its association with elitism and its rejection, in the present atmosphere of the critique of Eurocentrism, by scholars as diverse as Ashis Nandy and Brennan.[28] But to speak of secularism in general in this manner is to treat all secularisms as formally equivalent, leading Robbins, for instance, in this important essay, to frame his defence of Saidian secularism within apologies for its supposed privilege and elitism. Such formalism does not equip us to perceive the distinctness of what I am here identifying as secularist arguments enunciated from *minority* positions. We need only pursue Robbins's own useful insight that Said most often opposes the term *secular* not to religion per se but to nationalism, in order to clarify what I mean. *Secular* implies for Said a critique of nationalism as an ideology of hearth and home, of collective *Gemütlichkeit*; a critique of the 'assurance', 'confidence', and 'majority sense' that claims on behalf of national culture always imply; a critique of 'the entire matrix of meanings we associate with "home", belonging and community' (Said 1983, p. 11). It contains the charge that the organicism of national belonging, its mobilization of the filiative metaphors of kinship and regeneration, obscures its exclusionary nature; that it can be achieved only by rendering *certain* cultural practices, *certain* institutions, *certain* ethical positions representative of 'the people' as such. Secular criticism seeks continually to make it perceptible that the experience of being at home can only be produced by rendering some other homeless.

Said's use of the word *secular* is therefore catachrestic, in the sense that Gayatri Chakravorty Spivak has given to the term – that is, it is a meaningful and productive *mis*use. It is an invitation to rethink, from within the postcolonial present, the narrative of progress that underlies the very notion of secularization. It carries the insight that nationalism does not represent a mere transcending of religious difference, as Benedict Anderson, among others, has argued, but rather its reorientation and reinscription along national lines.[29] Secular criticism is aimed at the mutual determinations of the religious and the national, at the unequal division of the field of national experience into domains marked by religious difference. Said's insistence on the critical imperative of the secular can appear elitist and hence paradoxical only if we fail to recognize this minority and exilic thrust in his work, if we forget the haunting figure of Auerbach in Turkish exile that he repeatedly invokes. It is in this sense that we must read Said when he himself speaks of exile not as 'privilege' but as permanent critique of 'the mass institutions that dominate modern life'. Saidian secular criticism points insistently to the dilemmas and the terrors, but also, above all, to the ethical possibilities, of minority existence in modernity.

This concern with minority-exile cannot be understood outside the tradition, now well over a century old, of the Arab Christian contribution to the elaboration of a secular Arab culture, in which Levantine Christians, in particular, have played a prominent role. In his classic study, *Arabic Thought in the Liberal Age, 1789–1939*, Albert Hourani carefully distinguishes between the Islamic reformisms of the late nineteenth century and the varieties of secularism propagated by a wide range of Arab Christian thinkers and public figures, reading in the latter not just an echo of European precursors but rather 'the expression of an active political consciousness among the Arab Christians'. For instance, when Farah Antun, the Syrian Christian thinker and polemicist, calls for a secular state – as an Ottoman subject in Egyptian exile, we might add – he is doing more, Hourani argues, than demanding religious tolerance: 'He is calling for a community in which [Christians] can take an active part, for a sphere of political responsibility'. Antun's is, according to Hourani, 'an eastern Christian consciousness', anxious to distance itself from both 'the Western missionaries, and still more from the European Powers who use religion for political purposes'.[30] We may find traces of such a minority consciousness in Said's quest for a secular criticism, a critical consciousness constantly alert to the terms of experience of majority culture, a consciousness both assertive and on the defensive, both vocal and alert to its own quiet vulnerabilities.

A great deal of this critical positioning becomes visible in Said's writings concerning what is variously called the Islamic revival, Islamism, or Islamic fundamentalism. His journalistic writings around the Rushdie affair are a case in point.[31] But there is a particularly revealing moment in the essay that is Said's contribution to *After the Last Sky*. The occasion is a photograph by Jean Mohr that shows a number of young Palestinian men in a classroom situation, sitting on two rows of desk chairs, with a large book lying open in front of each student. They are wearing warm clothing for the winter and socks but no shoes. The caption reads: 'Jerusalem, 1984, Koranic studies within the walls of the Mosque of Omar'. In turning to the photograph Said has the following to say:

> To look at the perhaps plodding efforts of a group of Islamic school students in Jerusalem is therefore to feel some satisfaction at how their unexceptional attention to the Koran – I speak from an essentially non-religious viewpoint – furnishes a counterweight to all the sophisticated methods employed to wish them away. I do not by any means refer to the so-called Islamic resurgence, which is what every resistance to Israel is converted to these days (as if 'the Shi'ite

fundamentalists' of South Lebanon, or 'the Arab terrorists' on the West Bank, did not have the same antioccupation drive as any other *Maquis* in history). What I do mean, however, is that the local attentions of Palestinians – to their work, families, teachers and friends – are in fact so many potential breaks in the seamless text, the unendingly unbroken narrative of US/Israeli power.[32]

Who is the addressee of this passage? The polemical drive here is directed, first of all, at the metropolitan public sphere, highlighting the neo-Orientalist turning of resistance into terrorism that characterizes the appearance of the Arab world within it. Said points to the impressive ability of the foreign policy establishment – think tanks, the State Department, the news media – to assimilate any act of self-assertion on the part of the victims of Israeli violence to the text of subversion and terror. But what is Said's relationship to 'the so-called Islamic resurgence', which he mentions only to say that it is not what he refers to? Is Said denying the emergence, in Palestine and in Lebanon, of political formations and cultural identities that may properly be spoken of as Islamist? What is the meaning of this reference that disavows itself?

I suggest that we read in this text the presence of a second addressee, that we read it as directed simultaneously at the inhabitants of postcolonial space. This double movement, I would argue, characterizes Said's work as early as *Orientalism*, a fact Said touches upon in the introduction to that work:

> For the general reader, this study deals with matters that always compel attention, all of them connected not only with Western conceptions and treatments of the Other but also with the singularly important role played by Western culture in what Vico called the world of nations. Lastly, for readers in the so-called Third World, this study proposes itself as a step towards an understanding not so much of Western politics and of the non-Western world in those politics as of the *strength* of Western cultural discourse, a strength too often mistaken as merely decorative or 'superstructural'. My hope is to illustrate the formidable structure of cultural domination and, specifically for formerly colonized peoples, *the dangers and temptations of employing this structure upon themselves or upon others.* (Said 1978, pp. 24–25; emphasis added)

'Themselves' and 'others' here obviously carry multiple references. But the dialectic of self and other in the contemporary 'non-Western world' cannot be understood without reference to the determinations of majority and minority domains, as the postcolonial histories of any number of societies – including Ireland, India-Pakistan-Bangladesh,

Egypt, Malaysia-Singapore, Lebanon, and, more recently, South Africa – amply demonstrate.

One of the few places in his published works where Said himself explicitly makes this connection is in an interview with Michael Sprinker and Jennifer Wicke, at the point where he begins to talk about the 'fetishization' of national identity.

> It must be possible to interpret ... history in secular terms, under which religions are seen, you might say as a token of submerged feelings of identity, of tribal solidarity.... But religion has its limits in the secular world. Possibilities are extremely curtailed by the presence of other communities. ... One identity is always going to infringe on others that also exist in the same or continuous spaces. For me the symbol of that, in the Arab world, is the problem that has been postponed from generation to generation: the problem of the national minorities.

Shortly thereafter, as if anticipating the charge of elitism, Said goes on:

> Obviously I'm not suggesting that everybody has to become a literary critic; that's a silly idea. But one does have to give a certain attention to the rather dense fabric of secular life, which can't be herded under the rubric of national identity or can't be made entirely to respond to this phony idea of a paranoid frontier separating 'us' from 'them' – which is a repetition of the old sort of orientalist model where you say that all Orientals are the same.[33]

This, then, is the connection in Said's critical practice between secular criticism and the critique of Orientalism: the critical and ethical imperative invoked here requires a scrupulous recognition of the '*strength* of Western cultural discourse', of the conflicting identities it produces, of the 'dangers and temptations' that Orientalism in the broadest sense poses to our postcolonial modernity – temptations that are dangerous precisely because they are *temptations* and not merely external injunctions. A major impulse behind the critique of Orientalism is therefore the possibility, the danger, that Orientalist descriptions take hold and repeat themselves in the very societies that they take as their objects.

Thus, far from denying its existence, the comments on Mohr's photograph have Islamism as their second addressee, as the latest expression of majoritarian culture. In the image, all the students seem absorbed in their 'plodding efforts' and 'unexceptional attention to the Koran' – all, that is, save one. Along the right edge of the photograph, a man has turned his head to look to his left, directly at the photographer, resting his head on his hand and leaning slightly forward, as if trying to enter the frame. Mohr's photograph is a rich and complex text – a group of young Palestinian men engaged in the performance of Islamic identity, with one lone individual cautiously returning the gaze of the Western photographer who observes and records the scene. That the caption identifies the location of this scene as the Mosque of Omar, that is, as al-Haram al-Sharif/ Temple Mount, is also highly significant.[34] For it points to the ease of appropriation of the secular symbolism and frameworks of nationalism and state by emergent forms of Islamist politics. It draws our attention to the terrifying doubling of neo-Orientalist discourse within the nation-space itself, the national struggle for sovereignty and self-determination now increasingly framed in religious terms as a struggle over the fate of places and meanings that predate the nation.

Said's text raises important questions about the intellectual 'in exile', a subject-position from which this scene can be described as cause for 'satisfaction'. I have suggested that we give this subject-position, this location that here allows the critic to gloss religious-political piety as a species of the 'local attentions' with which Palestinians combat their dispersed condition, the name *minority*. The secularism that is implicit in Said's comments must be clearly distinguished from a merely sociological one, one that seeks to explain the rise of Islamic political identity by placing it within a sociopolitical history – of the failures of secular nationalism, of the continuance of colonial occupation, of the hurdles in the way of bourgeois modernization. Its priority is ethical engagement rather than historical explanation. It is also not the species of postcolonial secularism – irreverent, transgressive and voluble – whose most visible international icon since 1989 has been Salman Rushdie. It seeks to place the historic turn towards Islamic identity in majority culture within a larger framework – the 'local attentions' of *all* Palestinians to their lives – that allows the insertion of other, minority experiences into the realm of national experience, thus displacing fundamentalism's sense of itself as a counter-universal.

We may begin clarifying what it means in Saidian terms to *affiliate* with, to adopt the critical posture of, minority by noting that when he is asked to explain the meaning of secular criticism Said often uses language reminiscent of Bacon and sometimes even invokes the latter explicitly, as in the interview with Wicke and Sprinker: 'The national identity becomes not only a fetish, but is also turned into a kind of idol, in the Baconian sense – an idol of the cave, and of the tribe'.[35] What draws Said to Bacon in this context is the image of critical activity as the breaking of idols. But this critical posture must not be confused with a naive trust in the traditions of Enlightenment as demystification. The relationship of Said's critical practice to Enlightenment is dialectical – as expressed in his account of the dialectic of filiation and affiliation in modern consciousness. This relationship is routinely misread in poststructuralist readings of his work as the sign of a lingering 'humanism'.[36] Said speaks of

a 'three-part pattern' in modern consciousness, in which the perception of the failure or impossibility of 'natural' or filiative regeneration is
followed by a 'pressure' to produce alternative, affiliative human relationships, with this 'compensatory' affiliative order then itself becoming the
basis for a new 'hierarchy', a new legitimation (Said 1983, pp. 16, 17, 19,
24). The challenge for the critic, broadly conceived – and here Said is
really speaking of the intellectual vocation as such – is to avoid playing
a merely affirmative role in this process, to avoid becoming its 'midwife'
(Said 1983, p. 24). What the secular critical consciousness seeks continually to make visible is this 'cooperation between filiation and affiliation',
this 'transfer of legitimacy' from the former to the latter (Said 1983, pp.
16, 24).[37] This is a form of critical engagement for which an obvious philosophical source is Adorno and Horkheimer's perception of the route by
which Enlightenment becomes its opposite, mystification.[38] It insists upon
the possibility of emancipation even as it expresses profound scepticism
about the transparency of all such claims. Secular criticism does not imply
the rejection of universalism per se. It implies a scrupulous recognition
that all claims of a universal nature are particular claims. Furthermore,
and most importantly, it means rescuing the marginalized perspective
of the minority as one from which to rethink and remake universalist
(ethical, political, cultural) claims, thus displacing its assignation as the
site of the local. Said's critique of nationalism is not made in the interest
of an elitist (and empty) cosmopolitanism. It is made in the interest, and
from the perspective, of all those who would be minoritized in the name of
a uniform 'national' culture – 'the homeless, in short' (Said 1983, p. 11).
Therefore, to the extent that it implies a 'cosmopolitanism' – that is, to
the extent that it calls for a community of interpretation not based on the
accidents of birth and always points, albeit asymptotically, towards the
world as horizon – this is a cosmopolitanism of 'stepchildren', and not
of 'the ruling kind', to use terms that Anita Desai has made meaningful
in this context in *Baumgartner's Bombay*, her remarkable novel of Jewish
exile and postcolonial affiliations.[39] But if the community of criticism
implied by Said is not formed under the intact and triumphalist sign of
the universal, neither can it be conceived of as a sort of rainbow coalition
of already existing (minority) identities. It requires the 'secularization'
of minority itself as a position within the social process to which may be
imputed, in the Lukácsian sense, a consciousness of the social *in medias
res*. For Said, minority *is* criticism, a fact that is obfuscated whenever and
wherever actually existing minorities succumb to the 'temptations' of
'Orientalism'. For Said, therefore, the significance of minority for modern
consciousness has nothing to do with the possibilities for separate existence of empirical minorities. His is a critique of minority separatism, the
mode of political and cultural behaviour that corresponds to the minority's desire to become a majority. The true meaning of minority for him

lies in the vantage it allows on majority itself, the critique it makes possible of all forms of living based upon notions of being '*at home*' and '*in place*' (Said 1983, p. 8).

In the two decades since the Iranian revolution, it has become an increasingly common perception – vague and general for the most part, but occasionally unnerving in its clarity – that the fate of the great secularization project of eighteenth-century Europe is being determined in the contemporary postcolonial world. It is a historical situation of enormous complexity – one producing, as Spivak has noted, distinctive forms of inversion and alienation, 'asymmetrical reflections, as in a cracked mirror', and the dislodging of meanings from their 'proper' domains.[40] The articulation between the process of global expansion of a regional (that is, European) bourgeoisie and the 'sublation' of Christianity into secular ethics and politics is, she argues, a contingent one, but is routinely misread as the unfolding of (modern) society's 'Law of Motion', the process of merely *extending* the fully formed European project of modernity to non-European spaces (Spivak 1993, pp. 239, 240). Marx and Engels already noted in the *Manifesto* that the European bourgeoisie is forced, by the nature of the production process in which it engages, to draw 'all, even the most barbarian, nations into civilization. ... It compels all nations, on pain of extinction, to adopt the bourgeois mode of production; it compels them to introduce *what it calls civilization* into their midst, *i.e.* to become bourgeois themselves'. What they could not fully conceive of, but a conception of which is nevertheless compatible with the contingency that they ascribe to modern 'civilization', is the possibility that this attempt to create 'a world after its own image' transforms the original itself.[41] As an ever increasing body of scholarship has demonstrated in recent years, the Western bourgeois subject is caught from its very inception between an impulse to reproduce sameness and a postulation of (colonial) difference. Sameness, articulated in the figure and the speech of the other, is displaced and made other than itself.[42] The failure to grasp this, whether in the name of the universalism of Western 'values' and the end of history or in the defence of native 'tradition', results in the erroneous presupposition that, as Spivak writes, 'Reason itself is European' (Spivak 1993, p. 240).

It is therefore not surprising that one of the salient dimensions of the contemporary crisis of postcolonial societies is expressed in debates about the purportedly European provenance of secularism.[43] One increasingly visible critical tendency has come to rely upon what I shall call, dislodging Adorno's formulation from its own 'proper' domain, the jargon of authenticity. In a famous argument about the meaning of secularism in modern Indian life, Nandy, for instance, has subsumed the Indian trajectory of this 'idea' under the rubric of 'imperialism of categories' (Nandy 1992, pp. 71, 69). Secularism, argues Nandy, is an 'import' from nineteenth-century

Europe into Indian society and furthermore is the cultural banner of the dominant elite, so that to 'accept the ideology of secularism is to accept the ideologies of progress and modernity as the new justifications of domination' (Nandy 1992, pp. 71, 90). While it may appear at first that such a view is derived from the critique of Orientalism that Said has inaugurated, nothing could in fact be further from the truth, and it is a critical task of the utmost importance that we distinguish carefully between them.

Nandy critiques secularism in the name of Indian traditions of tolerance, for whose embodiment he often turns to the figure of Gandhi, conceiving of him naïvely as a sort of Archimedean point outside Indian modernity. He relies on a false dichotomy of religion as 'faith' and as 'ideology' and locates in the former a resistance to the modernizing juggernaut of the nation-state, which 'always prefers to deal with religious ideologies rather than with faiths'. By 'faith' Nandy means 'religion as a way of life, a tradition which is definitionally non-monolithic and operationally plural' (Nandy 1992, p. 70). Nandy's formulation is based, first of all, on a failure to recognize that the resources of 'faith' itself in colonial and postcolonial modernity have come to be appropriated, shaped and saturated by the political. The manner in which Islamic fundamentalist movements can mobilize, for their own political ends, social groupings whose religious life is judged in fundamentalist theology to be heterodox and even un-Islamic is a case in point. And the forces of *Hindutva* are quite capable of attracting to their *kar sevas*, or religio-political mobilizations, and of persuading to vote for the BJP (Bharatiya Janata Party) individuals who at other times quite unselfconsciously seek benediction at the shrine of the thirteenth-century Sufi saint Hazrat Nizamuddin.

Secondly, Nandy's elevation of 'faith' over what he considers modern, ideological religion is based on a nostalgic notion of the syncretic nature of traditional Indian religious life, a syncretism that is then understood as the basis for indigenous forms of religious tolerance and coexistence. The first difficulty with syncretistic notions like Nandy's 'faith' is that the practices that are described by the observer as syncretic are typically not conceived as such by their practitioners, as Gauri Viswanathan has noted.[44] The logics of cultural difference proper to them remain, by definition, invisible to the syncretism-invoking modern observer. Hence the circularity inherent in accounts of a syncretic premodern: all they say about the past is that it was not like the present. Furthermore, syncretism as a concept is by no means incompatible with secularism, including (and especially) the official variety. Facts such as that '200,000 Indians' declared themselves to be 'Mohammedan Hindus in Gujarat in the census of 1911' are not themselves transparent. If they can be marshalled by Nandy as part of his 'anti-secularist manifesto', they can equally serve the opposite end: to shore up arguments about the popular basis for secularism itself. Jawaharlal Nehru, icon of Indian state-secularism and the bête noire of

Nandy's argument, routinely turns to this image of the syncretism of popular life in order to condemn Muslim separatism as inherently elitist. 'There is nothing in Indian history', Nehru writes, 'to compare with the bitter religious feuds and persecutions that prevailed in Europe. So we did not have to go abroad for ideas of religious and cultural toleration; these were inherent in Indian life'.[45] The only difference here is that while Nandy wants to protect, preserve, and extend this syncretism, as the basis for a form of tolerance that is religious and not secular, Nehru wants to see it transcended and sublated into a modern, rationalist secularism.[46] And, finally, whether or not it is historically accurate to describe premodern cultural life as syncretic, the problem of how to address religious and cultural difference under the conditions of *modern* life still remains. Within a nation-state composed of 'equal' citizens, majority and minority are fundamental (and paradoxical) categories of political and cultural life. To propose the syncretic as a solution to the crisis of cultural difference under such conditions is both to ignore this basic fact and to take these categories for granted. From the perspective of cultural practices that are deemed minor, such a solution cannot but take the form of being subsumed within the majority domain. It is difficult to see how such a fate is preferable to the one promised by official, liberal secularism – being merely 'tolerated'. But my main point here is the following: no amount of talk of the plurality of 'traditions' on Indian soil can erase the fact that these traditions have come to us in modernity differently located within the nation-space and, hence, differently and unequally authorized. The conceptual consequences of ignoring this are in fact on display in Nandy's own search for traditions of tolerance in Indian society. For despite gestures towards 'everyday' forms of 'Islam', what emerges from this search is an identification of national culture as *Indic*, an identification that, of course, has a long history in the conflict, now over a century and a half old, over the meaning of modern nation and community in South Asia (Nandy 1992, p. 86; see also p. 74).[47] Precisely because Nandy's critique of the secular nation-state is based on a gesture of disavowal – secularism as a Western ideology, to be countered by the recuperation of truly indigenous lived traditions – it ends up reproducing the metaphysical gesture at the heart of cultural nationalism itself: the translation of the problem of cultural discontinuity in the modern conjuncture into a narrative of the transmission of a cultural essence. The syncretistic critique of state-secularism inhabits the same conceptual terrain as this secularism itself.

To put it somewhat differently, Nandy's critique remains inescapably *majoritarian* in nature, seeing the crisis over secularism as a struggle entirely within the majority realm – between a tiny, Westernized, and modernizing elite, on the one hand, and the masses of 'non-modern Indians (i.e. Indians who would have brought Professor Max Weber to tears)', on the other (Nandy 1992, p. 74). And it subsumes secularism entirely within the life of the state. While it is perceptive about the manner in which the postcolonial secular state manipulates religious identity for its own ends, it is incapable of seeing minority itself as a means of disrupting the majoritarian definitions of nation and state, as a site for the possible enunciation of secular claims upon state and society. A mere denunciation of Nehruvian secularism is not a critical position within contemporary Indian society, for the denunciation merely replicates and affirms the self-representations of *Hindutva* as a popular rejection of an elitist secularism. This charge of elitism directed at secularism, which implies that *Hindutva* is a spontaneous resurgence of the subaltern, is bogus. At one level, all that the rise of (Islamic or Hindu) fundamentalism in South Asia means in social terms is that the ongoing bourgeois integration of society, together with the integration of the national economy into the global imperium, has reached a stage where it can no longer be conducted in terms of the culture of the bourgeoisie itself but requires an appropriation of a petty bourgeois idiom for its cultural slogans. Nandy himself betrays a half consciousness of this fact when he says that he has 'come to believe that the ideology and politics of secularism have more or less *exhausted their possibilities*', not that they have always been irrelevant to Indian modernity (Nandy 1992, p. 73; emphasis added). And he himself attributes this exhaustion of usefulness to the successes of bourgeois-liberal democracy itself, which has produced conditions such that 'India's ultra-elites can no longer informally screen decision-makers the way they once used to' (Nandy 1992, p. 79). The danger inherent in the populism of Nandy's argument is that it reinforces and naturalizes, in the name of a numerical (that is, quantitative) majority of abstract citizens – as against the tiny minority that is the national elite – the privileges of a *cultural* (that is, qualitative) majority. In this sense as well, its procedures are no different from those of official secularism itself, which declares a formal equality of all citizens but at the same time normalizes certain cultural practices as representative of 'the people' as such. The syncretistic critique of state-secularism is *internal* to the majoritarian terrain marked out by the state.

The (Saidian) critical imperative here is continuously to put 'Hindu' and 'Muslim' (and 'Indian' and 'Pakistani') in question, to make visible the dialectic of majority and minority within which they are produced, which constitutes the larger part of the movement of Indian modernity itself. The terms of Nehruvian secularism itself have to be turned against it with the demand that it 'secularize' itself. A critique of state and society in contemporary South Asia that does not simply replicate the frozen categories of majority and minority must take as its basic premise the insight that the (Muslim) minority problematic continues to play itself out on a *subcontinental* scale, within and between three postcolonial nation-states. This fact is brought jarringly into focus at key historical moments, like the aftermath of the destruction of the mosque at Ayodhya, when in the rapid spread of the fires of communal violence a new map of the subcontinent seemed momentarily to have emerged, one in which the borders implemented over forty years earlier through the Partition of British India had been erased. Such a critique implies not proceeding as if Partition never took place but rather rigorously examining what precisely it *means*. The arrival of Indian nationalism at the nation-state, which it viewed as its self-realization and the fulfilment of a historical destiny, required a partitioning of the society it had claimed to encompass and to represent. The problematic of Muslim identity in colonial India exceeded the categories within which nationalism sought to contain it. And this normalization of the categories of nationalist thought by the apparatus of a nation-state could not take place until this excess had been excised. Before 'Muslim' could become 'minority', the majority of the Muslims of India had to be turned into non-Indians. This paradox is always lingering in the background whenever secularism and its terms are invoked, whether in avowal or disavowal, in postcolonial India.

That Partition is not an accidental event in the life-history of Indian nationalism; that the division of the country is the only solution to the Muslim question with which it can live, has not been dealt with rigorously by even radical scholarship, for instance by Partha Chatterjee in his monumental work *Nationalist Thought and the Colonial World*. This radical scholarship, of which Chatterjee is a founding figure and for which his work continues to be a major resource, has sought to redefine the relationship of the intellectual to the truth-claims of nationalism as a critical rather than a merely affirmative one. But in one important sense it continues to replicate the autobiographical assumptions of the postcolonial nation-state: it assumes an essential continuity of 'Indian' polity from pre- to post-Partition times – an indefensible premise and point of departure. Chatterjee's work on nationalism represents nothing short of a revolution in our understanding of the forms of culture and politics that emerged in India in colonial times. It represents an attempt to break with the projects of the nation-state and to make visible the disjunctures and displacements, the twists and turns, that the state naturalizes within a narrative of linear development as it writes 'its own life-history'.[48] The view of minority I am attempting to delineate here is possible only because of the successes of Chatterjee's work and takes these as its own condition of possibility. But it is also a partially critical engagement to the extent that Chatterjee's work reproduces the categorical structure that historically it has been the aim of the nation-state to normalize. The crisis over Muslim identity, which produced the division of the country amidst a communal holocaust of unprecedented proportions, and which continues to resurface today in newer and more baffling forms, appears in Chatterjee's book as a marginal event in the life of nationalism, a placing of the 'Muslim', person and problematic, at the margins of the nation.

The task of critical scholarship is to make possible a conceptual framework for a rethinking of 'India' in which 'Muslim' does not function as the name of minority. The obverse of this critical imperative is that Pakistan itself has to be scrupulously recognized, in the Saidian sense of that word, as an *Indian* – and not simply South Asian – polity and society. (This is a matter of more than mere terminology. Or, rather, it is entirely a question of terminology, and, in this case at least, terminology is everything. For it is precisely in the language of geopolitics and regionalism that the nation-state seeks to normalize the Partition of 1947, translating the religio-communal conflict of colonial India into the 'secular' and hence *acceptable* antagonism of mutually hostile nation-states.) No attempt to think critically about and beyond the present impasse can bypass a genealogy of postcolonial citizenship. The abstract, 'secular' citizen of postcolonial India has its *Entstehung*, its moment of emergence, in a violent redistribution of religious identities and populations.[49] Even as we are forced to use the antinomies normalized by the state – Hindu and Muslim, majority and minority, Indian and Pakistani, citizen and alien – our task is to make visible the work of this normalization, to reveal its unfinished nature.

In an important recent essay, 'Religious Minorities and the Secular State', Chatterjee proposes that we rethink minority cultural rights as including the right to refuse to give reasons for one's difference. To declare oneself unreasonable in the face of the purportedly reasonable demands of the state is to refuse to enter 'that deliberative or discursive space where the technologies of governmentality operate', thus staking a claim for the irreducibility of a cultural difference.[50] This right cannot be recognized as such by liberal theory, argues Chatterjee, because it undermines the universalism of the categories of liberal thought or, rather, introduces contradictions within them. Once such a right is granted – and Chatterjee here turns to Foucault and governmentality in order to move beyond the impasse of liberalism – what the cultural difference actually is could be negotiated entirely within the minority community itself. Chatterjee thus opens up the possibility of a distinct politics of minority, within which claims of representativeness could be fought out and tested. To the minority itself this offers the advantage of (relative) cultural autonomy and the (probable) democratization of its own institutions. For the rest of society, Chatterjee hopes, such a formulation holds out the attraction that it opens up the question of minority rights to a *strategic* politics, thus freeing it from the frozen frames of the faltered liberal attempts at a solution.

Chatterjee's essay represents an important attempt to think beyond the present impasse. Particularly clarifying is its understanding of the politics of its own location; Chatterjee insists that the critical task is not 'arguing from the position of the state' but rather exploring the conditions of a strategic politics 'in which a minority group, or *one who is prepared to think from the position of a minority group*, can engage in India today' – a perception that is unavailable to Nandy's critique of secularism (Chatterjee 1995, p. 34; emphasis added). But in the figure of the *unreasonable* subject of the sovereign we may sense a replication of the relative positions of majority and minority that characterize the postcolonial status quo. For the minority subject's refusal to give reasons for his or her difference in no way alters the structure within which the minority is cast as the site of unreason, and reason subsumed entirely within the life of the state. It also leaves intact the *externality* of minority to the nation-state. Chatterjee's critique of the state's claim that it embodies a universal principle thus remains apologetic; the 'minority group', he proposes we argue, 'is an actually existing category of Indian citizenship' (Chatterjee 1995, p. 36). Give the minorities the *right* to a separate existence, he seems to be telling his potential critics, and it will give them a stake in the liberal state. But the larger problem in this essay is the same as the one in *Nationalist Thought and the Colonial World*, namely, that the contours of nation and state are taken for granted. The notion that what we are faced with is a problem internal to the Indian state continues to operate. The desire to defuse the charge – increasingly common and acceptable in Indian public life today – that Indian Muslims constitute a fifth column loyal to a so-called foreign power (namely, Pakistan) must not be allowed to produce a failure to think beyond the boundaries of the postcolonial state, a failure to rigorously question the foreignness of Pakistan (and, of course, Bangladesh). That the Muslim 'problem' of the Indian state cannot be thought, let alone solved, without reference to Pakistani (and Bangladeshi) state and society remains in Chatterjee's article, literally, unthinkable.

The procedures of Saidian secularism are, as I have already noted, dialectical. In Saidian terms, to adopt the posture of minority – 'to think from the position of a minority group' (Chatterjee's words) – is first of all to renounce one's sense of comfort in one's own (national) home, that 'quasi-religious authority of being comfortably at home among one's people' (Said 1983, p. 16). It is not simply to demand a separate existence for minorities – a demand not so incompatible with the classic liberal paradigm for tolerance as is sometimes assumed – but rather to engage in a permanent and immanent critique of the structures of identity and thought in which the relative positions of majority and minority are produced. It is, I believe, with such a view of minority in mind that Homi Bhabha has spoken of 'minority discourse' as that which 'acknowledges the status of national culture – and the people – as a contentious, performative space'.[51] The critique of nationalism from the position of minority participates in the modes of critique that David Lloyd has ascribed to minority discourse in general: it undermines from within the narrative resolutions through which the representative self is produced.[52] To turn minority into the language and gesture of an affiliative community is to critique the filiative claims of majority; it is to interrupt the *narratives* of filiation through which the meanings of majority and minority are determined, fixed, and internalized. Said shares the perception, common to every radical critique of liberal society since Marx's early writings on the subject, that the crisis over the Jews constitutes an irreducible feature of Western modernity, that minority is a fundamental category of liberal secular society. Saidian secularism is based upon a scrupulous recognition that not only does minority not disappear when we make it subject to a critique from the point of view of the universal but it is precisely universalist categories that require its existence as the site of the local. Said demands that we critique this marginalized, threatened (and threatening) existence precisely by inhabiting it, that we make it the position from which to enunciate claims of an ethical, cultural and political nature. Saidian secular criticism implies an 'ethics of coexistence', as Bhabha has put it in a different context, whose basis lies in the sharing of social space with 'others', a 'subaltern secularism' for which 'solidarity is not simply based on similarity but on the recognition of difference'.[53] In other words, Said allows for the claims of secularism in the postcolonial world to be formulated in terms of the *contingent* demands of peace and justice, rather than as the imperative of a putatively universal Reason. In order to be authentically critical today, research and speculative thought must turn their attention to the urgent task of elaborating the bases of this formulation and the contours of this contingency, rather than succumbing to an undialectical rejection of Enlightenment as (colonial) domination.

As an outsider to the Palestinian–Israeli conflict, one is often led to wonder how the life of a Palestinian intellectual can be anything but an exercise in daily confrontation with the whole history and legacy of the Jewish question in European modernity. Said himself is of course exemplary in the detail of attention, the ironic imagination, and the Auerbachian critical 'magnanimity' he has brought to the entangled histories of Palestinians and European Jews over the last century. In *The Question of Palestine* – a profound exercise in historical, cultural, and moral criticism that is too often read as a merely topical and polemical work – Said turns repeatedly to an exploration of what it means to be the victims of the paradigmatic victims of twentieth-century terror, what moral ground such an experience can come to occupy, and what it implies for the meaning of 'Jew' and 'Palestinian' in the latter decades of the twentieth century. The book's magnificent second chapter is an examination not so much of historical Zionism itself as of that entanglement – the colonial provenance of Zionism's emancipatory ideals; the baffling displacements and inversions of the roles of oppressor and victim, militarist and refugee; and the continuing and undiminished resonance of Jewish suffering for any project of social criticism.

Said traces what he calls the self-consciousness of Palestinian experience to the first Zionist settlements of the 1880s, thus refusing to base
his case for Palestinian rights in a metaphysics of national essence and
autonomous selfhood. Throughout this modern Palestinian experience,
he argues, 'is the strand formed by Zionism'. The goal of the book, Said
writes, is therefore to describe the process by which Palestinian experience
has become 'an important and concrete part of history'.[54] So powerful are
the moral consequences of the Holocaust that the mere existence of the
Palestinians, which puts the narratives of Zionist settlement and redemp-
tion in question, becomes a sign of perversion, of terror, of anti-Semitism
itself. The solution of the Jewish question – and here Said cites Arendt's
famous conclusion in *The Origins of Totalitarianism* – 'solved neither the
problem of minorities nor the stateless. On the contrary, like virtually all
other events of our century, the solution of the Jewish question merely
produced a new category of refugees, the Arabs, thereby increasing the
number of the stateless by another 700,000 to 800,000 people' (Arendt
1979, p. 290; quoted in Said 1979, p. xiii). For Arendt, the significance
of the Palestinian–Israeli conflict in world-historical terms is that the
'problem' of the quintessential European stateless has been 'solved' by
the creation of 'a new category' of stateless person, this time non-European. The state of statelessness has merely been displaced from (and by)
a European onto a Third World people. But Arendt goes even further,
in the sentence immediately following the passage cited by Said: 'And
what happened in Palestine within the smallest territory and in terms
of hundreds of thousands was then repeated in India on a large scale
involving many millions of people'. While her primary focus throughout
this chapter is of course on the plight of European minorities and stateless refugees in the first half of this century, Arendt reveals here a keen
and prophetic sense of the manner in which the crisis of minority and
statelessness has repeated itself in 'all the newly established states on earth
which were created in the image of the nation-state' (Arendt 1979, p. 290).
But Said reverses the trajectory embodied in *The Origins of Totalitarianism*,
for it is now imperialized Palestine that provides the starting point for an
intellectual and ethical journey that leads back to the history of European
anti-Semitism and its devastating consequences.

If in the decades leading up to the Second World War the Jews of
Europe had been thrust into the foreground repeatedly as the site for
crisis and control and at the end of that era had become the ultimate
modern symbol of the stateless and dispossessed, whose physical extermination marked the crashing of the Euro-centred world, in the era
of decolonization it is the Palestinians whose terrifying fate it is to be
beyond even oppression, to paraphrase Arendt's comments regarding
the Jews. For the global culture of decolonization, it is the figure of the
stateless Palestinian – wasting in prison without recourse, on the move

ahead of yet another invasion, pleading at the border – that constitutes something like the reproach that the Jewish victim of fascism represents for Western liberal culture.[55] Fascism's Jewish victims confront liberalism with the terrifying possibility that genocide is not a sign of its incompleteness or failure, but part and parcel of its success, that the successful bourgeois integration of Western Europe – the sanitized Europe of the EU – required the extermination of its Jewish-minority cultures and populations. Similarly, the meaning of Palestinian experience for the culture of decolonization is not simply that it reminds us that decolonization is still ongoing and incomplete, that there are societies that are yet to acquire postcolonial sovereignty. Rather, the figure of the disenfranchised Palestinian, repeatedly brutalized with international impunity, holds up a mirror to this sovereignty itself, revealing to us its limited, formal and ultimately farcical nature.

It is often remarked in the West that there is something arbitrary about the resonance of the Palestinian experience for Third World intellectuals, given the proliferation of oppressed and disenfranchised peoples around the world. Apologists for Israeli terror routinely dismiss this resonance as evidence of a new anti-Semitism. The meaning of the Palestinian experience is indeed inseparable from the fact that the immediate oppressor is the Jewish state, and not a classic imperial power such as France or Britain. But the crisis here is precisely that this is liberalism at its best. In its support for the rights of the Jews of Europe – that is, in its most inclusive and universalist moment – liberalism trips on its own categories and can conceive of nothing but a colonial solution, a solution 'by means of a colonized and then conquered territory', to quote Arendt's damning judgement (Arendt 1979, p. 290). At the very dawn of the era of decolonization, the crisis of Jewishness at the heart of post-Enlightenment European culture and society is finally laid to rest by the 'normalization' of the Jews as a colonizing people. What the Israeli–Palestinian conflict makes visible is that the problematic of European modernity has *always* unfolded within a field of global, colonial dimensions. It is Said's accomplishment to have demonstrated that it is an entangled history that escapes the traditional, national and continental, moulds in which official accounts seek to contain it. A comprehension of its immense ethical and intellectual implications requires, he writes, 'an ironic double vision', a vision capable of simultaneously comprehending the enormity of the Jewish experience in Europe and the disaster visited upon a people in the Middle East (Said 1979, p. xiii).

This complex awareness is equally evident in the invocations of Auerbach in Said's writings. In 'Philology and *Weltliteratur*' speaking from this side of the defeat of fascism and the normalization of European culture and society, Auerbach had asserted, as Lévi-Strauss would in *Tristes Tropiques* (1955), that the fate of culture in the new world to emerge from the war was 'imposed uniformity'. But this standardization of culture did not mean for him a world at peace with itself. The paradox of culture a century and a half after the age of Goethe was that while 'national wills' were everywhere 'stronger and louder than ever', each nevertheless promoted 'the same standards and forms for modern life' (Auerbach 1969, p. 2). Auerbach thus distinguished the concept of *Weltliteratur* he was proposing from the earlier notion that was derived from Goethe. While the present formulation was 'no less human, no less humanistic, than its antecedent' had been (Auerbach 1969, p. 7), it was distinct from that earlier notion in one important respect: 'There is no more talk now – as there had been – of a spiritual exchange between peoples, of the refinement of customs and of a reconciliation of races' (Auerbach 1969, p. 6). In the light of twentieth-century events, it had become clear that, although 'small groups of highly cultivated men' had always enjoyed 'an organized cultural exchange', such cultural activity had 'little effect on culture or on the reconciliation of peoples' (Auerbach 1969, p. 6). In an age when the 'antitheses' of national identity are 'not being resolved except, paradoxically, through ordeals of sheer strength', the ethical ideal of *Weltliteratur* must come to be imbued with a sense of its own fragility and must also 'help to make us accept our fate with more equanimity so that we will not hate whoever opposes us – even when we are forced into a posture of antagonism' (Auerbach 1969, p. 7). The vocation of philology was therefore now tied to the crisis of Europe. Said's reading of Auerbach is alert to the final irony that this ethically complex sense of the fate of culture in the modern world is undermined by a sense of fear and loss at the displacement of Europe in the new world that emerged from the war. 'When Auerbach ... takes note of how many "other" literary languages and literatures seemed to have emerged (as if from nowhere: he makes no mention of either colonialism or decolonization)', Said argues, 'he expresses more anguish and fear than pleasure at the prospect of what he seems so reluctant to acknowledge. Romania is under threat'.[56] Said records his own sadness at Auerbach's barely suppressed terror of the non-European world and its emergence on the modern historical stage. This fear compromises the ethical ideal of *Weltliteratur* in its very formulation, even as it highlights the necessity with which any conception of world literature (or culture) must now confront the legacy of colonialism. Where Adorno once insisted that in the wake of Auschwitz speculative thought could no longer take the form of traditional philosophical system building, Said is relentless in pointing out the manner in which the concepts of culture, canon and value must be inflected in the aftermath of the classical colonial empires. The question that Auerbach finally poses for Said is a version of the same underlying question that emerges from his consideration of historical Zionism: how is it possible that a conception of culture meant to embody the dignity of the victims of fascism could be at the same time ethnocentric and, in fact, fearful of the coming challenge to European cultural supremacy?

The presence of Auerbach in the Saidian text is far from the unproblematic citation of liberal cultural authority it is so often thought to be. The full meaning of this figure emerges only out of a series of historical ironies and inversions. It marks the critic's exilic-minor relation to both metropolitan and indigenous-national culture, first of all. But, with haunting irony, it also points to the exiled state of the Palestinian people, their history now inextricably intertwined with that earlier European history of minoritization, dispersal and persecution.

Notes

This chapter previously appeared in *Critical Inquiry*, Vol. 25, No. 1 (Autumn, 1998), 95–125.

For Mazen Arafat.

An earlier version of this chapter was presented as an essay at 'After Orientalism', a conference to honour the work and life of Edward Said, organized at his home institution, Columbia University, by his present and former students, and held in October of 1996. I am deeply grateful to the organizing committee and to its ringleader, Qadri Ismail, in particular, for inviting me to participate in what proved to be an experience of a lifetime and an opportunity to begin to acknowledge an unrepayable debt. I am also indebted to Val Daniel for inviting me to present related work at the Program in the Comparative Study of Social Transformation at the University of Michigan, Ann Arbor. For their encouragement at various stages, I must especially thank Kamran Asdar Ali, Jean Howard, Tejaswini Niranjana, Edward Said, Milind Wakankar, and Cornel West. My thanks also to the editors of *Critical Inquiry*, and to Homi Bhabha in particular, for the carefulness of their responses and suggestions. The chapter has benefited enormously from the close reading of Mazen Arafat, Qadri Ismail, and Gyan Prakash. It is really an episode in an ongoing conversation with Mazen.

1   See Bruce Robbins, 'Secularism, Elitism, Progress, and Other Transgressions: On Edward Said's "Voyage In"', *Social Text*, no. 40 (Fall 1994): 26.
2   See Edward W. Said, *Beginnings: Intention and Method* (New York, 1975), p. 68. See also Erich Auerbach, 'Philology and *Weltliteratur*', trans. Maire and Edward W. Said, *Centennial Review* 13 (Winter 1969): 11.
3   Tim Brennan, 'Places of Mind, Occupied Lands: Edward Said and Philology', in *Edward Said: A Critical Reader*, (ed.) Michael Sprinker (Oxford, 1992), pp. 81, 92.
4   See ibid., p. 80.
5   Quoted in Said, 'Reflections on Exile', *Granta* 13 (Autumn 1984): 171. Auerbach leaves out the last sentence.

6 James Clifford, 'On *Orientalism*', in *The Predicament of Culture: Twentieth-Century Ethnography, Literature, and Art* (Cambridge, MA, 1988), pp. 263–64.

7 See Brennan, 'Places of Mind, Occupied Lands', p. 77.

8 Brennan, of course, points to the strategic value of that elitism within the US public sphere.

9 Aijaz Ahmad, *In Theory: Classes, Nations, Literatures* (London, 1992), p. 164.

10 On the characteristic 'hairshirt attitudinizing' tone of Ahmad's book, see Marjorie Levinson, 'News from Nowhere: The Discontents of Aijaz Ahmad', *Public Culture* 6 (Fall 1993): 101. Levinson's is by far the most astute and ambitious essay in this special issue on Ahmad's book.

11 Vassilis Lambropoulos, *The Rise of Eurocentrism: Anatomy of Interpretation* (Princeton, NJ, 1993), p. 4; see also pp. 3, 5. I am grateful to Stathis Gourgouris for first pointing me to this work.

12 Auerbach, *Literary Language and Its Public in Late Latin Antiquity and in the Middle Ages*, trans. Ralph Manheim (New York, 1965), p. 22; see also p. 24.

13 Said, *Orientalism* (New York, 1978), p. 258.

14 Auerbach, 'Vico's Contribution to Literary Criticism', in *Studia Philologica et Litteraria in Honorem L. Spitzer*, (ed.) A. G. Hatcher and K. L. Selig (Bern, 1958), p. 34.

15 Said and Said, introduction to Auerbach 1969, p. 2.

16 Said, *The World, the Text, and the Critic* (London, 1983), p. 5.

17 Auerbach, *Mimesis: The Representation of Reality in Western Literature*, trans. Willard R. Trask (Princeton, NJ, 1953), p. 557.

18 Abdul R. JanMohamed, 'Worldliness-without-World, Homelessness-as-Home: Toward a Definition of the Specular Border Intellectual', in *Edward Said*, pp. 98–99.

19 Lambropoulos misconstrues Said's meaning entirely when he extracts from this final sentence only the phrase 'a massive reaffirmation of the Western cultural tradition' and presents it as Said's characterization of *Mimesis* (quoted in Lambropoulos, *The Rise of Eurocentrism*, p. 6).

20 Hannah Arendt, *The Origins of Totalitarianism*, rev. edn (San Diego, CA, 1979), pp. 289, 297.

21 Adelbert von Chamisso, *Peter Schlemiel: The Man Who Sold His Shadow*, trans. Peter Wortsman (New York, 1993), p. 14.

22 Works on Joyce and exile are, of course, legion. But I have in mind the kind of paradigmatic status he has for a number of French critics, such as Hélène Cixous, *The Exile of James Joyce*, trans. Sally A. J. Purcell (New York, 1972).

23 Emily Apter, 'Comparative Exile: Competing Margins in the History of Comparative Literature', in *Comparative Literature in the Age of Multiculturalism*, (ed.) Charles Bernheimer (Baltimore, 1995), p. 90.

24 Theodor Adorno, *Minima Moralia: Reflections from Damaged Life*, trans. E. F. N. Jephcott (London, 1974), p. 39; quoted in Said 1984, p. 170.

25 Said, *Beginnings*, pp. 372–73.

26 I assume that Said means Cleanth Brooks. However, it is not clear from Said's text if he means Robert Penn or Austin Warren – I suspect the former – although from my present perspective the meaning here would remain substantially the same in either case.

27 Robbins, 'Secularism, Elitism, Progress, and Other Transgressions', p. 27.

28 'The banner of "secularism" has for more than a century been the standard of a Westernized elite' (Brennan, *Salman Rushdie and the Third World: Myths of the Nation* [New York, 1989], p. 144). See also Ashis Nandy, 'The Politics of Secularism and the Recovery of Religious Tolerance', in *Mirrors of Violence:*

Communities, Riots, and Survivors in South Asia, (ed.) Veena Das (Delhi, 1992), pp. 69–93, to which I shall return at length below. The antisecularist gesture has also proved a temptation, surprisingly, in subaltern studies; see Dipesh Chakrabarty, 'Radical Histories and Question of Enlightenment Rationalism: Some Recent Critiques of *Subaltern Studies*', *Economic and Political Weekly*, 8 April 1995, pp. 751–59.

29 See Benedict Anderson, *Imagined Communities: Reflections on the Origin and Spread of Nationalism* (London, 1983), p. 19.

30 Albert Hourani, *Arabic Thought in the Liberal Age, 1789–1939* (New York, 1962), p. 259. See also Hourani's classic study of the minority question within the Arab successor states to the Ottoman empire, *Minorities in the Arab World* (1947; New York, 1982).

31 See, for instance, *The Rushdie File*, (ed.) Lisa Appignanesi and Sara Maitland (Syracuse, NY, 1990), pp. 164–66.

32 Said and Jean Mohr, *After the Last Sky: Palestinian Lives* (New York, 1986), pp. 142–44.

33 Said, interview by Jennifer Wicke and Sprinker, in *Edward Said*, pp. 232, 233.

34 I am grateful to Shai Ginsburg for this valuable suggestion.

35 Said, interview by Wicke and Sprinker, p. 232.

36 In this sense not only Clifford's but also Ahmad's reading of Said may be spoken of as poststructuralist.

37 According to Said, an important instance of this process, whereby a critique of second nature itself becomes the basis of a new acquiescence to it, is the institutionalization of Theory in the North American literary academy.

38 'We are wholly convinced – and therein lies our *petitio principii* – that social freedom is inseparable from enlightened thought. Nevertheless, we believe that we have just as clearly recognized that the notion of this very way of thinking, no less than the actual historic forms – the social institutions – with which it is interwoven, already contains the seed of the reversal universally apparent today' (Max Horkheimer and Adorno, *Dialectic of Enlightenment*, trans. John Cumming [New York, 1972], p. xiii).

39 Anita Desai, *Baumgartner's Bombay* (New York, 1989), pp. 51, 104.

40 Gayatri Chakravorty Spivak, 'Reading the *Satanic Verses*', *Outside in the Teaching Machine* (New York, 1993), p. 239. See also ibid., p. 217, and Spivak, 'Marginality in the Teaching Machine', *Outside in the Teaching Machine*, p. 60.

41 Karl Marx and Friedrich Engels, *Manifesto of the Communist Party*, in *The Marx-Engels Reader*, 2nd edn, (ed.) Robert C. Tucker (New York, 1978), p. 477; emphasis added.

42 See Gyan Prakash, 'After Colonialism', introduction to *After Colonialism: Imperial Histories and Postcolonial Displacements*, (ed.) Prakash (Princeton, NJ, 1995), p. 3. In the present context, see the excellent contributions to this volume by Joan Dayan, Anthony Pagden, Emily Apter, and Homi Bhabha.

43 Elsewhere, I have analysed the interplay of these forces in what is perhaps one of their most dramatic enactments in recent decades, namely, the Rushdie affair. See my 'Reading the Rushdie Affair: "Islam", Cultural Politics, Form', in *The Administration of Aesthetics: Censorship, Political Criticism, and the Public Sphere*, (ed.) Richard Burt (Minneapolis, 1994), pp. 307–39.

44 See Gauri Viswanathan, 'Beyond Orientalism: Syncretism and the Politics of Knowledge', *Stanford Humanities Review* 5, no. 1 (1995): 18–32.

45 Jawaharlal Nehru, *The Discovery of India* (Delhi, 1989), p. 382.

46 That syncretism has a *Western* history, that is to say, that it has played a prominent role in Western projects for negotiating cultural difference, has been

amply demonstrated by Peter van der Veer, 'Syncretism, Multiculturalism, and the Discourse of Tolerance', in *Syncretism/Anti-Syncretism: The Politics of Religious Synthesis*, (ed.) Charles Stewart and Rosalind Shaw (London, 1994), pp. 196–211.

47 I have discussed this problem with respect to Nehruvian nationalism in my 'Secularism and Minority: Elements of a Critique', *Social Text*, no. 45 (Winter 1995): 75–96.

48 Partha Chatterjee, *Nationalist Thought and the Colonial World: A Derivative Discourse* (Minneapolis, 1993), p. 51.

49 The particular conception of genealogy I am invoking here is due to Foucault's influential reading of Nietzsche; see Michel Foucault, 'Nietzsche, Genealogy, History', in *Language, Counter-Memory, Practice: Selected Essays and Interviews*, trans. Donald F. Bouchard and Sherry Simon, (ed.) Bouchard (Ithaca, NY, 1977), pp. 139–64.

50 Chatterjee, 'Religious Minorities and the Secular State: Reflections on an Indian Impasse', *Public Culture* 8 (Fall 1995): 33; see also p. 32.

51 Homi K. Bhabha, 'DissemiNation: Time, narrative, and the margins of the modern nation', *The Location of Culture* (London, 1994), p. 157.

52 It will be clear throughout, I hope, that my debt to Lloyd's work on minority discourse is too comprehensive to be fully acknowledged through individual citations; see, for instance, David Lloyd, 'Genet's Genealogy: European Minorities and the Ends of the Canon', *Cultural Critique* 6 (Spring 1987): 161–85; and 'Violence and the Constitution of the Novel', *Anomalous States: Irish Writing and the Post-Colonial Moment* (Durham, NC, 1993), pp. 125–62.

53 Bhabha, 'Unpacking My Library … Again', in *The Post-Colonial Question: Common Skies, Divided Horizons*, (eds) Iain Chambers and Lidia Curti (London, 1996), p. 211.

54 Said, *The Question of Palestine* (New York, 1979), pp. xv, xiii.

55 The most influential literary representation of this Palestinian figure is still Ghassan Kanafani's novella *Men in the Sun*; see Ghassan Kanafani, '*Men in the Sun' and Other Palestinian Stories*, trans. Hilary Kilpatrick (Washington, DC, 1983), pp. 9–56.

56 Said, *Culture and Imperialism* (New York, 1993), p. 45.

6 Vinayak and me

Hindutva and the politics of naming

Vinayak Chaturvedi

During the spring of 1969, my grandmother Bai had taken me to Dr Dattatrey Sadashiv Parchure for a physical examination. Apparently, as an infant I had been quite ill and Bai had given up on standard remedies prescribed by my paediatrician. She had convinced my parents that a consultation with Dr Parchure might reveal alternative therapies for my illness, as he specialized in Ayurvedic medicine and had acquired a prominent reputation as a local healer in the central Indian city of Gwalior. After a brief examination, as I am told, Dr Parchure queried my grandmother about my name when he was filling out a prescription for some medication. Bai replied that the family had not given an official first name as yet, but that I had an informal household name. Dr Parchure asked if it would be possible for him to give me the name Vinayak, and my grandmother accepted the doctor's request.

Unfortunately, Bai passed away before I could speak to her about the interaction with Dr Parchure. In a recent conversation, my mother stated that Bai was initially resistant to the idea of giving me any official name, Vinayak or otherwise, but she only agreed out of respect for Dr Parchure. It is common practice in India for families to wait several years before giving formal names to children: some argue this has to do with wanting to give a name that matches a child's personality; others say these are the cultural practices of a society that has high infant mortality rates.[1] In my case, I suspect that Bai was concerned about the latter, especially as I was regularly ill.

Throughout my childhood, aunts and uncles had often recounted the story of my name and I had grown accustomed to the idea that it had somewhat of an unusual origin. Relatives also had reminded me that Vinayak was another name of the elephant-headed god Ganesh, who was an auspicious deity celebrated as the remover of obstacles.[2] It was a common name among some communities in western and southern India, but certainly not within my clan in north India. I had long accepted that Dr Parchure, as a Marashtrian Deshastha brahmin, probably had favoured the popular Ganesh and felt the need to give the name Vinayak to sick children who needed many obstacles to be removed: after all, it had been an age-old practice to name children after Hindu deities. The story of my name could have ended here and I often wish it had. But those who are more familiar with the complexities of studying oral narratives will know that 'hidden transcripts' and silences often have a history of their own: this was especially true in the uncovering of the secret origins of my name. At some point in the mid-1980s, one of my aunts revealed a piece of information about Dr Parchure's past that had never been voiced to me before, even though it was clear that the entire family was well aware of its significance: Dr Parchure had been arrested and convicted as a conspirator in the 1948 murder of Mohandas K. Gandhi – the Mahatma.

From that day, I began to wonder if Dr Parchure's desire to name male children Vinayak had anything to do with his involvement in Gandhi's murder. I remember quickly searching through my books for any information about the murder and the trial. I was looking for a clue that would satisfy my curiosity, when I came across a copy of a book I had kept from my first undergraduate course in modern Indian history – *Freedom at Midnight* by Larry Collins and Dominique LaPierre. I recalled that somewhere within the text were the names of the men tried for killing Gandhi: Nathuram Vinayak Godse, Gopal Vinayak Godse, Vinayak Damodar Savarkar, Narayan Apte, Vishnu Karkare, Digamber Badge, Madan Lal, Shankar Kisayya, and Dattatrey S. Parchure. As I read over the names of the accused, I began to see how the story of my name may have had less to do with the god Ganesh, and more to do with a legacy of the Mahatma's murder. Yet, at the same time, I also felt that my suspicion may have been unfounded; after all, Savarkar was the only one with the name Vinayak, and the Godse brothers had inherited their father's first name following a practice common in western India. Additional conversations with my parents and relatives about the links between Parchure, the accused, and the naming issue left me dissatisfied with no additional information. However, for reasons that continue to evade me, I had decided not to investigate further into this story.

In April 2001, I returned to Gwalior after a long interval. I cannot remember how Uma Bua – my father's sister – and I began speaking of Dr Parchure one afternoon, but it must have had something to do with recounting stories about Bai. Uma Bua, as a secular, life-long supporter of the Congress Party, had regularly condemned the rise of the Hindu nationalist Bharatiya Janata Party (BJP), and for her the conspirators to Gandhi's assassination were some of the earlier 'trouble-makers' in a lineage leading up to today's right-wing leadership.[3] She argued that Dr Parchure's politics were fundamentally problematic, if not completely corrupt, especially as he had supplied the automatic pistol used by Nathuram Godse to kill Gandhi. As much as I had chosen to avoid the subject of my name, I now felt that it was impossible to do so. I wanted to meet Dr Parchure: I wanted to ask him about the significance of naming: I wanted to know why the name Vinayak was so important: I wanted to know who was Vinayak.

Unfortunately, I had waited too long: Dr Parchure was dead. In fact, he passed away in 1985, a couple of years before I first discovered his links to Gandhi's murder. Uma Bua suggested that I could speak to one of his two sons who still lived in Gwalior. I contacted Upendra Dattatrey Parchure: he was trained as an Ayurvedic doctor, like the senior Dr Parchure, and continued to practise in his father's office. I wanted to retrace Bai's steps and return to the location where the story of my name began. This seemed like the obvious place to start. Initially, I was apprehensive about how to introduce myself and explain why I was interested in speaking about Dr Parchure. There were important problems to be considered prior to the meeting: some intellectual, some political, some ethical, and some personal. An interview to secure oral testimony about the past is generally a difficult, complex process in itself, but in this case, the nature of the problem was linked to some desire to come to terms with my own subjectivity: that is, not only a subjectivity of an oral historian, but also that I was somehow the passive subject of some historical and ideological processes intertwined with the life-story of Dr Parchure.[4]

My first meeting with Upendra Parchure was brief, barely lasting ten minutes. I introduced myself as someone whom his father had named Vinayak; I narrated how my grandmother had consulted his father when I was ill; I explained that I was hoping to have a conversation about his father. I also made clear that I was researching modern Indian history and that I was interested in writing about the intellectual development of Hindu nationalism. The doctor's first question was whether my parents had decided to keep the name Vinayak, or replace it with another. I assured him that my grandmother had promised his father back in 1969 that the family would not change the name, and that my formal first name was Vinayak. He was obviously pleased, but now wanted to know my surname. For those who are familiar with the legacies of India's multicultural politics will know that family names often reveal a great deal about one's background: caste, language, region, and even class.[5] I was aware that my Chaturvedi kinship-affiliation would identify me as an educated, middle-class, local, Hindi-speaking brahmin, but I was also acutely cognizant of the fact that in this situation, my position of social privilege would be welcomed by Upendra Parchure, who came from a similar, but Marashtrian background. After a few additional questions about my father and grandfather, establishing a patriarchal genealogy, the doctor asked if it would be possible for us to meet in his home where we could speak privately and at length; he stated that the kinds of things I wanted to know were best discussed outside the purview of his patients and staff. We agreed to meet the following week.

From the onset of the second meeting, I realized that Upendra Parchure was uncertain about the nature of the interview. He repeated his questions from our first meeting, and wanted to know what I intended to do with the information about his father. I stated that I was interested in knowing more about his father for two primary reasons: first, I had long wondered about the origins of my name; and, second, I wanted to write about his father's political activities in the locality as part of a research study on Hindu nationalist intellectuals. Apparently satisfied with my explanation, Upendra Parchure pursued an in-depth conversation about his father's public and private life for the next three hours. It began with a narrative of some major events in the senior Dr Parchure's life.

Upendra Parchure wanted me to know that, more than anything else, his father, who was born in 1902, was a strong man, a strong nationalist, and a strong Hindu. He described his father with awe and pointed out that he was a big, powerful man with broad shoulders, thick thighs, and large arms.[6] His physical strength and martial prowess was also illustrated by the fact that he was a skilled wrestler, winning the Gwalior State title in his late teens. Although specific details of Dr Parchure's training were not discussed, what can be inferred is that the process of becoming a local, or regional wrestling champion, would have involved years of regimented and disciplined training with a guru and a cohort throughout childhood.[7] The Indian wrestler is typically dedicated to a distinct ideology that is centred on somatic principles, and requires an acceptance to an ethos of wrestling as a way of life.[8] Initially, I was unclear why Upendra Parchure emphasized his father's masculinity, until later in the conversation it occurred to me this was a consistent theme of how Dr Parchure was remembered in his personal and public life. This point was further clarified when Upendra Parchure celebrated the values and ethics his father learned while training as a wrestler, linking them to the development of his politics as a nationalist. It is not clear whether Dr Parchure intended to make this connection himself, or this is how his son remembers him. However, recent scholarship suggests that central to Hindu nationalism from the 1920s has been the need to set political agendas which rely upon power, masculinity, and strength, both discursively and institutionally.[9] Dr Parchure's political career may have had a beginning during his teens in ideologies of 'wrestling nationalism',[10] but according to his son, the application of some of these strategies later in his life translated into brutal forms of violence, at home and in the public sphere. At another level, as I was soon to discover, the assertion of masculinity was also at the centre of naming male children Vinayak.

In 1935, Dr Parchure founded the Gwalior Branch of the All-India Hindu Mahasabha (literally, the Great Hindu Association), an organization first established in 1915 to defend and protect Hindu interests. The idea of creating the national-level Hindu Mahasabha, however, emerged out of a regional collective known as the Punjab Hindu Sabha, which originally had incorporated a wide range of ideas of high-caste Hindu thinkers on the themes of nationalism and patriotism.[11] By the 1920s, the All-India Hindu Mahasabha had transformed its image to a 'hard-line' organization, marginalizing the moderate Hindu leadership from within. This marked an important conjuncture in nationalist politics of the early twentieth century, as the development of Hindu nationalism was firmly established, incorporating the idea of creating a powerful and militant Hinduism that was both anti-British and anti-Muslim.[12] For Upendra Parchure, his father ranked among a group of elite Hindu nationalists in India during this period, arguing that Dr Parchure had established himself as president of the local branch of the organization for the purpose of promoting an independent Hindu nation. He led a grass-roots movement travelling to villages and small towns in central India – between Gwalior, Bhind, Sheopur and Guna – with the aim of 'injecting a pure Hindu spirit' and creating a pan-Hindu *jati*, including both high and low castes. It occurred to me during the conversation that the ideas expressed about Dr Parchure's politics appeared consistent with those articulated by Vinayak Savarkar. And, it came as little surprise when Upendra Parchure described his father as a 'true Savarkarite', who had for many years followed Savarkar's writings on revolutionary politics, Hindutva and anti-colonial nationalism. I felt that the mystery of my name had finally been solved: Dr Parchure was evoking Vinayak Savarkar when naming male children. I wanted to know more about the naming issue, but Upendra Parchure continued on more important themes: his father's place within an emergent Hindu nationalism and his connections with Savarkar, Nathuram Godse, and Gandhi's murder. I remained silent and listened.

Dr Parchure had trained as a medical student and received his MBBS from Grant Medical College in Bombay during the 1920s. According to Upendra Parchure, his father continued to practise medicine in Bombay until 1935, when he was dismissed for insubordination from the Jamsetjee Jeejeebhoy Hospital. By 1937, he became disillusioned with the methods of 'Western' medicine and began a study of Ayurvedic medicine, specializing in paediatrics.[13] The narrative of Dr Parchure's professional life appeared rather fragmented, and little else was discussed about the significance of the events around being fired, or why Ayurveda acquired such an important role. However, it may be worth saying something about the relationship between the medical profession and nationalism as a way to further contextualize the development of Dr Parchure's politics in the mid-1930s.[14]

The decades of the late nineteenth century were marked by the 'return of Hindu science', particularly in reviving the fields of 'indigenous' medicine, especially Ayurveda.[15] It has been argued that this revivalist movement in medicine was predominantly a 'corollary' to the emergence of Hindu nationalism in the 1890s.[16] At one level, Ayurveda represented a type of 'authentic' response to colonial intervention in medicine, especially in a period when state policies to control epidemic diseases, like the bubonic plague, were popularly considered coercive and draconian.[17] Ayurvedic medicine was viewed as a legitimate replacement to the Western system which had come to dominate with British colonial expansion in India. However, at another level, Ayurveda also provided a complementary direction to the development of Western medicine that could rely upon Indian contributions to the making of the modern science.[18] Indian nationalists, like Bal Gangadhar Tilak and M. K. Gandhi, had engaged in public debates on the importance of medical profession in India, but neither wholeheartedly accepted the claim of the 'revivalists' who sought to replace Western medical practices with the 'indigenous' Ayurveda.[19] However, there were doctors trained in Western medicine who were inspired by the Ayurvedic revivalism and sought to professionalize and modernize the 'indigenous' tradition by publishing textbooks, and opening colleges, hospitals and clinics, while also participating in the 'Freedom Movement'.[20] It has been suggested that the presence of these doctors in formal nationalist politics acquired prominence after 1920, especially in the inter-war period.[21] According to Upendra Parchure, his father's decision to take up Ayurveda after abandoning Western medicine occurred in this period, a time when medical politics became increasingly significant in public debates throughout India. Dr Parchure's decision to study Ayurvedic medicine was in consonance with the practices of other doctors throughout India, most of whom were also inspired by the ideology of Hindu revivalism, a key component of the emergent Hindu nationalism.

In 1939, Dr Parchure met Vinayak Savarkar for the first time at a Hindu Mahasabha conference. According to Upendra Parchure, the meeting was an important moment for his father, who, by this point, considered himself a 'disciple' of Savarkar. Dr Parchure, like many other Indian nationalists, had followed Savarkar's illustrious political career as 'freedom-fighter' against the British Raj. Biographical accounts of Savarkar posit that he had participated in underground revolutionary activities from a young age, in organizations like the Mitra Mela and the Abhinava Bharat Society (ABS), for the purpose of politicizing Hindus for nationalist aims.[22] Savarkar remained active in the ABS as a law student in Bombay, and became a prolific writer during his college years. In 1906, Savarkar arrived in London for an advanced law degree, and here his collaboration with his patron Shyam Krishnavarma furthered Savarkar's involvement in underground activities against British rule.[23] Intellectually, Savarkar had developed an interest in the revolutionary ideas of the Italian thinker Giuseppe Mazzini, and published a Marathi translation of his autobiography in 1907. In fact, it has been suggested that the ABS was modelled after Mazzini's group Young Italy and underground organizations in Russia.[24] The following year, Savarkar completed his opus titled *Indian War of Independence, 1857*, a text with a polemical flair adopted from Mazzini's writings on Italy in the nineteenth century, and combined with claims of a universal Hindu identity for India's past in the form of *swaraj* and *swadharma*.[25] The British government banned the book, but, nevertheless, it achieved wide circulation among revolutionaries in India.

Savarkar was finally arrested in London on 13 March 1910 on five separate charges, ranging from 'delivering seditious speeches', 'procuring and distributing arms', to 'waging war against the King Emperor of India'.[26] Savarkar was extradited to India, and convicted of seditious activities for which he was sentenced to fifty years in the infamous penal settlement in Port Blair located in the Andaman Islands.[27] In 1922, Savarkar was transferred to a prison in Ratnagiri due to ill health, and in 1937 he was finally released after 27 years. However, during his term of incarceration, Savarkar had continued to write extensively on the issues which had initially landed him in trouble with the British authorities.[28] Savarkar's prison writings were centrally informed by debates in European social theory, especially the literature on German ethnic nationalism.[29] Yet, his claim for independence from colonial rule was at the centre of his work, as was the articulation of resurrecting a powerful Hindu nationalism that lay dormant for centuries. Savarkar had acquired an important public reputation throughout India, especially within the Hindu Mahasabha, for his nationalist and anti-Muslim writings, for his patriotic actions in India and Britain, and for having spent the bulk of his adult life as a political prisoner. Shortly after Savarkar's release from prison, he officially joined the All-India Hindu Mahasabha and served as its president between 1937 and 1944.[30] Savarkar was promulgated into power on a platform that certainly had appealed to Dr Parchure and the entire Hindu Mahasabha: 'Hinduize Politics and Militarize Hindudom'.[31]

Although, Upendra Parchure emphasized his father's dedication to Savarkar's principles, there was very little discussion about the specific details of these ideas. He may have believed that the intellectual connections with Savarkar were too obvious to discuss with me, or simply chose not to explain them. However, for me, this point marked an important transition in the interview. Upendra Parchure had thus far celebrated his father's accomplishments, but now the nature and tone of the conversation changed as it moved towards the topic of violence. In 1939, Dr Parchure formed a paramilitary-style organization in Gwalior known as the Hindu Rashtra Sena (literally, Hindu National Army), which boasted a cadre of three thousand volunteers.[32] The development of this organization probably had something to do with the meeting with Savarkar in the same year, but according to Upendra Parchure, his father specifically had grown tired of what he believed to be Muslim persecution of Hindus in Hyderabad State, and felt that a local retaliation was necessary. In fact, the Hindu Mahasabha, under Savarkar's leadership, had been agitating against the Nizam of Hyderabad in southern India between October 1938 and July 1939 to secure demands for Hindus, arguing that a Muslim ruler was suppressing their 'civil liberties' and 'culture'.[33] Dr Parchure, as the president of the Hindu Rashtra Sena, subsequently began organizing Hindu attacks on Muslim localities,[34] and, in the process, acquired the notoriety of being 'the most controversial political figure in Gwalior'.[35]

Nathuram Godse was a frequent visitor to the Parchure family home in Gwalior. These may have been long-standing ties, but during the interview I was unable to establish the origins of Dr Parchure's relationship with Godse. However, a brief examination of Godse's activities reveals important parallels relevant to the discussion here. Sometime during the early 1930s, Nathuram Godse joined the Poona branch of the Hindu Mahasabha and a paramilitary unit known as the National Volunteer Association, or Rashtriya Swayamsevak Sangh (RSS).[36] It has been suggested that for Godse, and the argument can be expanded to include Dr Parchure, participation in these organizations represented a 'Hindu search for self-esteem' and 'political potency' through the use of power and violence.[37] Godse abandoned the RSS after some years, claiming that it lacked proper levels of militancy, and co-founded the Hindu Rashtra Dal (Hindu National Party) – an organization whose name and objectives closely matched Dr Parchure's Hindu Rashtra Sena.[38] In 1942, Savarkar had promoted the idea of establishing the Dal as a secret volunteer organization among a small group of disciples in the Poona Hindu Mahasabha, who, like Godse, shared similar opinions about the RSS.[39] Savarkar required volunteers to take an oath of loyalty to him and perform underground activities that could not be sanctioned by the Mahasabha.[40] The group's primary objective was to propagate 'Savarkarism' as a way to 'protect Hindudom and render help to every Hindu institution in their attempt to oppose encroachment on their rights and religion'.[41] Training camps were set up throughout western and central India, advocating villagers to take up arms, teaching individuals 'Indian games, physical exercises, [and] shooting exercises', in addition to spreading Savarkar's ideology.[42]

Dr Parchure and Naturam Godse are said to have met on several occasions to discuss the activities of the Hindu Mahasabha.[43] In fact, it has been argued that Dr Parchure, while on a political lecture tour in Poona, approached Godse with the aim of merging the Sena and the Dal. The deliberations failed, but both agreed to proceed with their respective, yet intimately connected projects. Further links between Dr Parchure's Hindu Rastra Sena and the Dal remain unclear, especially in understanding the exact nature of the collaboration between Dr Parchure, Savarkar and Godse. I asked Upendra Parchure if his father had kept any personal letters, diaries, or writings about the activities in this period, especially related to his interactions with Godse and Savarkar; he argued that Dr Parchure did not believe in keeping any evidence that could potentially incriminate him, and, more importantly, the government had confiscated all the documents in the house when his father was arrested in 1948. However, it still may be suggested that there were important intellectual and personal ties that were forged in this period. An individual by the name of Panna Lal Chaube told government officials that Dr Parchure and Nathuram Godse were travelling companions, who arrived in Alwar, located in Rajasthan, around October 1947 for the specific purpose of acquiring a handgun from comrades in the local Hindu Mahasabha.[44] Chaube claimed to have met Dr Parchure and Godse, and discussed the plan to murder Gandhi with them. According to Chaube, Dr Parchure argued that 'it was not in the interest of the country that the Mahatma should live and that Godse alone could assassinate Gandhi'.[45] The two left Alwar dissatisfied with the quality of pistols offered to them.

On 2 December 1947, Dr Parchure returned to Poona as the main speaker at a Hindu Mahasabha meeting in the Tilak Samarak Mandir,[46] where Godse and Savarkar were certainly present. An official report of Dr Parchure's speech provides further insight into his position:

> He was described as a second Savarkar and that so great was his influence that on every mosque in Gwalior flew the Bhagwa flag. In his speech Dr Parchure, after referring to the state of affairs in Gwalior, advocated the use of force to achieve whatever they wanted. He also said that Gwalior Army was full of Muslims who were in a majority and that the State was increasing the Muslim elements ... The trend of the speech was anti-Congress and extremely anti-Muslim. He criticized Pandit Nehru's policy as regards Kashmir and pointed out the quiescence of Hindus in the face of Mohammedan aggressiveness. In the end he made a significant remark, the importance of which was perhaps not then appreciated, that *Gandhiji and Nehru would surely reap the fruits of their sins in a short time.*[47]

Dr Parchure appears to have achieved a prominent status within the inner circle of the organization by this point, especially as he was now being compared with Savarkar. His anti-Muslim and anti-Congress positions were consistent with those advocated by Savarkar and the Hindu Mahasabha, even though Savarkar had by then resigned from the presidency of the organization. However, Dr Parchure's other intellectual and political connections with the Mahasabha, Sena, or Dal are not as apparent in this period. Nevertheless, Dr Parchure acquired an enormous public profile when he was convicted for helping Nathuram Godse to arrange for the handgun that was used to assassinate Gandhi.

Upendra Parchure shifted the discussion away from his father's public life at this point in the conversation and began talking about some personal details. The separation between public/private sphere, or the spiritual/material domain, has been a topic of much debate in the scholarship about how to think about Indian politics within this framework.[48] At the time the debates had little to offer as I was faced with a dilemma of interpreting the private details within the context of Dr Parchure's public life, as President of the Gwalior Hindu Mahasabha and Hindu Rashtra Sena. Moreover, as my questions never even broached the subject of Dr Parchure's private life, I was surprised when Upendra Parchure openly narrated an incident about family abuse. Dr Parchure spent three-quarters of his income from his medical practice to fund his two organizations. One day Upendra Parchure's mother Sushilabai required some money to purchase items for the family.[49] Dr Parchure was apparently unavailable, and the mother decided to take a few rupees from his organizational fund. Upon realizing that Sushilabai had taken the money, Dr Parchure proceeded to beat his wife until she was unconscious. Upendra Parchure stated, 'It is only by the grace of God that my mother did not die that day'.

This was the only time his mother was mentioned in the conversation, but it was clear that this was not an isolated incident. The conversation appeared to have triggered a son's memory about his parents' conflictual relationship that often resulted in violence against the mother. I questioned myself as to why Upendra Parchure wanted to ensure that his father's abuse was included in the narrative of Dr Parchure's politics. There are at least two ideas which can be offered as explanations. First, Upendra Parchure wanted to establish a continuity between his father's activities in the public sphere and his violence at home. And second, the discussion of attacks against innocent Muslims and his mother was one way to prevent the construction of a hagiographical account of his father's life, especially as he knew I was conducting an interview for the purpose of writing about Dr Parchure.

At another level, Hindu nationalists in western India had already developed discourses on the themes of domesticity, 'the home', and family life by the end of the nineteenth century.[50] Inscribed within the debates was a view that the 'domestic sphere' was central for the preservation of Hindu spiritual values, and a necessary space for 'respectable women' to serve their duty as 'devoted wives' and 'enlightened mothers' in the making of the nation.[51] It has been suggested that these processes were corollaries to the re-emergence of Maharashtrian *brahmans* in the nineteenth century, when forms of brahmanic Hinduism became important determinants for social behaviour, especially on the 'woman's question'.[52] Tilak and other conservatives, writing in the 1880s, argued against the education of Hindu women on grounds that reading was likely to encourage 'immorality' and 'insubordination', and, thereby, challenge Hindu traditions and religion.[53] Savarkar later contributed to these debates in an essay titled 'Woman's Beauty and Duty', arguing that 'the primary duty of a woman is to the home, children, and the nation'.[54] Although, Savarkar was not against formal education for women, he felt that they should be trained in areas suited to their 'temperament': that is, women primarily needed to be educated as mothers to create a new generation of patriots for the betterment of the nation.[55] For example, in a speech given in 1937, he encouraged women 'to be mothers of fine, healthy progeny', while the 'kitchen and children were the main duties of women'.[56] However, any woman who digressed from her duty in the domestic sphere, as prescribed by Savarkar, was declared 'morally guilty of a breach of trust'.[57] Public debates on the topic of female improprieties that violated the emergent Hindu norms within the domestic sphere often concluded with harsh resolutions, like advocating the use of violence against 'weak' and 'wicked' women.[58] Were Sushilabai's actions of taking a few rupees from Dr Parchure's organizational fund an immoral act and a transgression from her duty as a devoted wife? Unfortunately, Upendra Parchure did not have an answer to this question.

The conversation next turned to Mahatma Gandhi's murder. The leadership of the Hindu Mahasabha and its affiliates had declared the partition of India and the creation of Pakistan a failure. It had been condemned by Savarkar, for example, on the grounds that the 'vivisection of the Motherland' was an insult to all Hindus, and the idea of a Pakistan was a threat to the making of a Hindu nation in the aftermath of the British Raj.[59] For Savarkar's followers, like Godse and Dr Parchure, Mahatma Gandhi and the Congress Party were to blame for the turn in political developments leading up to the partition 1947, a period in which it was argued that the rights of Hindus were not being protected. Godse echoed Savarkar's claims by arguing:

> Gandhiji failed in his duty as the Father of the Nation. He has proved to be the Father of Pakistan. It was for this reason alone that I as a dutiful son of Mother India thought it my duty to put an end to the life of the so-called Father of the Nation who had played a very prominent part in bringing about vivisection of the country – our Motherland.[60]

According to Upendra Parchure, Nathuram Godse and Narayan Apte travelled from Delhi to Gwalior by train on 28 January 1948.[61] They arrived at the Parchure family home for the purpose of securing a gun, which was to be used to assassinate Gandhi. Godse was unhappy about the gun he already had in his possession because it was not an automatic and it frequently locked up without firing a round. Upendra Parchure remembers his father showing a pistol to Godse, and says that he even saw

Godse firing it outside. The pistol was said to have originated in Europe, and only came to Gwalior when one Mr Deshmukh, a military officer in the Gwalior State Army, acquired it while on a training exercise in Germany.[62] The connection between Dr Parchure and Deshmukh remains unclear in this narrative. Upendra Parchure's only other comment about Godse was that he was someone who was shy and afraid of being in the presence of women. Although, this point has been made by scholars studying Godse's life, it is unclear why the comment was inserted at this point in the conversation, except as a way to highlight some seeming tension or paradox within Godse's personality.[63] On 29 January Godse and Apte left Gwalior for Delhi, and on the following evening Nathuram Godse walked up to Mahatma Gandhi and fired three rounds from the automatic pistol into his body.

Dr Parchure reportedly celebrated Gandhi's death by distributing sweets in Gwalior.[64] On 3 February, Dr Parchure was detained by the police, and then formally arrested for conspiracy to commit murder two weeks later.[65] He confessed to his role in Gandhi's murder on 18 February while being interrogated by R. B. Atal, the First Class Magistrate of Gwalior,[66] but later retracted his confession arguing that it was 'untrue' and forcefully extracted.[67] Dr Parchure, along with five others, were found guilty of the conspiracy to murder Mahatma Gandhi and sentenced to 'transportation for life'.[68] Nathuram Godse and Narayan Apte were determined to be the primary perpetrators, and were ordered to be executed, while Savarkar was acquitted of all charges with no direct evidence linking him to the murder. Digamber Badge became the official 'approver' in the case and was released after the trial. Dr Parchure filed an appeal in the Punjab High Court arguing that he had no role in the conspiracy, even though, he had met Godse and Apte prior to the murder.[69] He stated that the two had arrived in Gwalior to recruit volunteers from the Hindu Rashtra Sena for some demonstrations in Delhi. Apte and Godse corroborated with Dr Parchure's testimony during the trial, and Nathuram argued that the automatic pistol used to kill Gandhi was purchased through an arms dealer in a Delhi refugee camp.[70] The High Court accepted Dr Parchure's claim that coercion was used to extract his initial confession, and that there was enough doubt about the exact nature of his interactions with Godse and Apte to warrant an acquittal of all charges.[71] According to Upendra Parchure, his father was banned from Gwalior for two years following his release from prison, but he finally returned in 1952 on the condition that he would no longer participate in public politics.[72] He re-established his medical practice and continued to live in Gwalior till his death in 1985.

Upendra Parchure did not mention that there was a controversy about his father's involvement in Gandhi's murder. Officially, Dr Parchure was acquitted of all charges, but within the family he has continued to be celebrated as one of the conspirators. Dr Parchure's original confession described how he had instructed an individual by the name Dandavate to purchase a gun from one Jagdishprasad Goel.[73] Dandavate returned to Dr Parchure's house with a 9-millimetre Beretta automatic and about ten rounds of ammunition. Nathuram Godse tested the weapon in Dr Parchure's yard, and agreed to purchase it for 300 rupees. Upendra Parchure's narrative of events generally appears to be consistent with his father's original confession, except that there is no discussion of Dandavate and Goel, but there is an addition of one Mr Deshmukh (who was not mentioned by Dr Parchure). Yet Dr Parchure's exact role remains unresolved today, but it is popularly accepted that he assisted Godse with the purchase of the gun. 'The Official Mahatma Gandhi eArchive' even has a brief history of the murder weapon titled 'The Gun: a 9mm Beretta Automatic' and states that Dr Parchure had organized Godse's acquisition of the weapon.[74] In a recent interview, Gopal Godse claims that Dr Parchure did help his brother, but was not part of the inner circle who plotted Gandhi's murder: 'Nathuram managed to get an automatic pistol from Dr Dattatrey Parchure from Gwalior, though he was not a part of the conspiracy, and was later released by the High Court'.[75]

Upendra Parchure finally turned to the question of naming children. He argued that his father probably had named 'dozens upon dozens of children Vinayak' if not 'hundreds upon hundreds'. He stated he personally knew seven Vinayaks presently living in Gwalior who had acquired the name as patients in his father's clinic; I happened to be number eight. Upendra Parchure was very clear that his father's desire to name boys Vinayak was in honour of Savarkar. Dr Parchure had spent his adult life promoting the ideologies of his guru, initially through the Hindu Mahasabha and the Hindu Rashtra Sena, and then later in his life, when forced out of public politics, he adopted alternate strategies to promote Savarkarism. Upendra Parchure argued that I should feel very proud to have been named after such a strong, powerful nationalist who spent his entire life fighting for Hindu rights, and stated, 'the spirit of Savarkar now lives through you'.

Since that moment in the interview, I began questioning why my family decided to keep the name Vinayak, especially as they knew Dr Parchure's background. Were they aware of his hidden agenda that was directly tied to Savarkar? I have repeatedly asked my parents about this topic over the past few months, but the answers fail to explain the intricate details that interest me. My mother states that I was named after Ganesh, the decision was not political, and she was unaware that Dr Parchure had an agenda. She reminds me that Bai was not interested in giving me any name; I was too ill. In one conversation, she stated that Dr Parchure told Bai that my health would improve, and because it did, the family decided to keep the name. My father repeats my mother's explanation, but reminds me that he was not even living in Gwalior when I was named. I find it difficult to probe my parents any further about my name, not least because they have grown frustrated with my questions. I certainly get a sense that my illness was very serious, my recovery was a tremendous relief for a family that had already lost one child to an illness, and Dr Parchure was thanked for his medical advice and honoured by naming me Vinayak. Needless to say, Savarkar does not emerge anywhere in their narratives.

Dr Parchure's strategy of naming children as a way to promote Savarkarism initially appeared rather innocuous, especially for someone who had achieved national-level notoriety for his public politics. It is not clear when Dr Parchure began giving the name Vinayak, but it may be suggested that the process began after Savarkar's death in 1966. However, it is important to note that Dr Parchure was not the first to take up the idea of using the name Vinayak for political purposes. In fact, he may have been following a pattern set by other disciples of Savarkar, namely, Nathuram Godse and the conspirators to Gandhi's murder. In the months leading up to the assassination, these individuals regularly used a half-dozen or so aliases when travelling, mostly centring on the name Vinayak in honour of Savarkar.[76] Dr Parchure, who in 1947 was described as a 'second Savarkar', would have been well-versed in his guru's writings, especially the seminal text *Hindutva: Who is a Hindu?* Since its first publication in 1923, *Hindutva* has acquired a reputation as a defining treatise for the development of Hindu nationalism in the twentieth century. The editor's introduction to the fifth edition of *Hindutva* furthers this point by arguing that 'the concept of Hindutva is Savarkar's own ... [that] the Hindus are tied together by bonds of a common fatherland, ties of blood, a common culture and civilization, common heroes, common history and above all, the will to remain united as a nation'.[77] Savarkar intended to use the text to clarify divergent opinions on how to define 'Hindu', 'Hinduism', and 'Hindutva' by establishing a history of the term 'Hindu', demonstrating links between territoriality and Hindu identity, and answering the question 'who is a Hindu?'. His main focus in the text, nevertheless, was to argue that the conceptualization of Indian national identity, must, at its foundation, be based within the political philosophy of Hindutva.[78]

I would suggest that Dr Parchure's desire to give names was a return to the basic principles outlined by Savarkar in *Hindutva*, especially when considering the first section of the book begins with the title 'What is in a name?', and others following include 'Names older still', 'Other names', and 'How Names are Given'.[79] In *Hindutva*, there does not appear to be a specific prescription of naming individuals; instead, the focus is on the importance of naming a society and a nation.[80] Savarkar, of course, was focusing on these issues as a way to identify the etymology of 'Hindu' and 'Hindustan', and to establish a genealogy of names connecting Hindus and Hindustan with India and Indians. However, an examination of Savarkar's argument for 'what is in a name' provides a clue to Dr Parchure's tactics.

> For, things do matter more than their names, especially when you have to choose one only of the two, or when the association between them is either new or simple. The very fact that a thing is indicated by a dozen names in a dozen human tongues disarms the suspicion that there is an invariable connection or natural concomitance between sound and the meaning it conveys. Yet, as the association of the word with the thing it signifies grows stronger and lasts long, so does the channel which connects the two states of consciousness then to allow an easy flow of thoughts from one to the other, till at last it seems almost impossible to separate them. And when in addition to this a number of secondary thoughts or feelings that are generally roused by the thing get mystically entwined with the word that signifies it, *the name seems to matter as much as the thing itself.*[81]

Upon reading this passage, I was reminded of Upendra Parchure's vivid declaration that 'the spirit of Savarkar' was now living through me, and by extension, through the dozens or hundreds of other Vinayaks. It certainly may be argued that Dr Parchure held the belief that inscribed within the name Vinayak was a signifying system tied to Savarkar and the principles of Hindutva. For those versed in semiotics would suggest that Dr Parchure was aware of the power of the name-sign, and by naming children, he had hoped to evoke a mental image of Savarkar as an icon in everyday life.[82] Indeed, the name Vinayak has become more popular in India over the past generation than in previous ones, but at the same time, it would be incorrect to assume that all the links go back to Savarkar. My own parents say that they had no clue about Dr Parchure's interest in naming boys, and I wonder if other parents whose sons are named Vinayak also have remained oblivious to the information over the years and think that the origins of the name are only tied to Ganesh. But, here too, there is a 'hidden transcript' with a history intertwined with the ideological development of Hindu nationalism.

It may be worth saying something more about the long-term significance of Ganesh, as every conversation about the name Vinayak usually begins here. The worship of Ganesh in western India began as early as the sixth or seventh century, although primarily limited to Maharashtrian Brahmins, the Deshastha and Konkanastha.[83] By the eighteenth century, Ganesh was popularized in temples and festivals around Pune through the patronage of the Maharatta Peshwas, but there was a significant decline with the subsidence of Peshwa power after 1818 and the arrival of the British in the area.[84] In the 1890s, Ganesh's popularity had a resurgence under the leadership of Bal Gangadhar Tilak, who began mobilizing large numbers of Hindus from upper and lower castes around an annual Ganesh festival.[85] Tilak was concerned about harnessing mass support against colonial rule, while simultaneously using the symbol of Ganesh to articulate a political agenda linking 'Hindu revivalism' with Indian nationalism. It was considered an 'extremist' form of nationalism for its celebration of Maharashtrian 'martial prowess'[86] and for its militant anti-Muslim character.[87] In fact, it has been argued that Tilak's invention of a Ganesh tradition was primarily in response to, and corresponded with, the annual Muslim festival of Muhharam.[88] This point is generally obscured in today's popular memory of the Ganesh festival's origins, especially as it has achieved national appeal throughout India, moving beyond the local and regional centres in Maharashtra. Tilak's role is also important in this discussion for another reason: namely, that Dr Parchure, Savarkar, and the others in the Hindu Mahasabha and its affiliated organizations were heavily influenced by his nationalist politics.[89]

The fact that over the years neither my parents nor I were cognizant of Dr Parchure's naming practice is irrelevant for the politics of Hindutva. It may be argued that for Dr Parchure, the celebration of Vinayak as Ganesh, or as Savarkar, was equally powerful, because inscribed in both were the legacies and inspirations of Hindu nationalism. As I write this chapter, I sit in a room with a dozen or so idols of Ganesh – recent gifts I have received from friends and family, each of whom stated that they purchased the idol because of my name. I often wonder how many other Vinayaks are out there who share a similar story, but part of me simply does not want to meet a Vinayak who actually embodies the myriad of characteristics which would make Dr Parchure proud.[90] For Savarkar and his contemporary disciples, the creation of a Hindu nation was a long, multi-generational process which could not be achieved in their lifetime. Savarkar was keenly aware of the risks and limitations of his political strategies, but advocated that his followers promote the ideals of a Hindu nation, even in minute ways, for the benefit of future generations:

> The seed of the banyan tree is so trivial as to be smaller than the mustard seed. But it holds within itself the rich promise of a luxuriant expanse. If we are to live with honour and dignity as a Hindu Nation ... that nation must emerge under the Hindu flag. This my dream shall come true – if not in this generation, at least in the next. If it remains an empty dream, I shall prove a fool. If it comes true, I shall prove a prophet.[91]

Savarkar's principles of Hindutva are very much alive today, and the new generation of Hindu nationalists have been openly working towards the goal of creating a Hindu fatherland by following Savarkar's prescription:

> The nation that has no consciousness of its past has no future. Equally true it is that a nation must develop its capacity not only for claiming a past but also for knowing how to use it for the furtherance of its future.[92]

In India, there are many who have been inspired by the writings and activities of Savarkar and his disciples. And, one does not need to look very hard to find these individuals and groups, especially as their public presence cannot be avoided in everyday life. The discursive project of Hindutva, led by the Bharatiya Janata Party (BJP) and its subsidiaries, for example, promotes the changing of names in consonance with Savarkar's ideals.[93] In November 1995 the Maharashtrian state government led by the Shiv Sena (Shivaji's Army) changed the official name of Bombay to Mumbai.[94] The Shiv Sena, as a nativist organization, had been demanding the vernacularization of the city's name since its founding in 1966, but could only change it once it had secured the patronage of the BJP government at the centre.[95] The process was extended to replacing the names of streets, buildings, railway stations, neighbourhoods, and anything deemed necessary to rid the city of its Portuguese and British titles, and as a way to re-inscribe a Hindu identity into the city. Institutionally, the project has played an important role in targeting Muslims, Christians, and other minorities: the incarnations of the Hindu Rashtra Sena and the Hindu Rashtra Dal frequently make their presence felt, as in the case of the Bombay riots in 1992–3,[96] and most recently leading to the killing of an estimated 2000 Muslims in Gujarat.[97]

I asked Upendra Parchure about his views on the direction of today's Hindu nationalism, BJP-style. To my surprise, he was dissatisfied with the current leadership and their national programme. He argued that today's politicians were corrupt, and consequently, they did not live up to the ideals of creating a 'Hindu Nation' as articulated by Savarkar, his father, and the others involved in the Gandhi murder case. Upendra Parchure reiterated that the assassination was necessary for the betterment of the nation, to ensure that India could develop into a strong, powerful homeland for Hindus. For Upendra Parchure, I was part of the future generation his father and Savarkar had hoped would serve as the messengers of *Hindutva*. As Vinayak, I could embody the characteristics of power, strength, and masculinity inscribed in my name, and participate in the making of a Hindu Nation. As I stated from the onset, I wish the story of my name had ended many years ago, and did not require such a long, unsettling journey.

I thanked Upendra Parchure for his time and sharing memories of his father's life-story. My last request, however, was to see a photograph of Dr Parchure, whose image was the only one conspicuously missing among the numerous photographs of the group arrested in Gandhi's murder.

Upendra Parchure stated that he only had two photographs of his father in his house. I was taken into his bedroom where they were hanging: the first was a picture of Dr Parchure as a young wrestler, flexing his chest and arms; the second showed Dr Parchure with his wife, probably taken shortly after their wedding. As I was leaving, Upendra Parchure asked if I had noticed the third photograph in the room which had been carefully positioned above the door. I imagined that this was a reference to a picture of Ganesh, who is often placed in such a location as an auspicious symbol for all those who pass through the doorway. Instead, it was a large image of the assassin Nathuram Godse, who was being celebrated as an incarnation of Vinayak and the remover of obstacles.

Notes

This chapter previously appeared in *Social History* 28:2 (May 2003), pp. 155–73.

I would like to thank Dr Upendra Parchure for his generosity in narrating his father's life-story on two separate occasions in Gwalior, India, in April 2001 and May 2001. I have greatly benefited from advice and important comments from Tom Mertes, Bina Parekh, and David Washbrook. Warm thanks are due to Geoff Eley and Gina Morantz-Sanchez for a valuable reading of an earlier draft, and especially for suggesting that I develop the ideas in the chapter within a wider social historical context. Finally, I would like to thank my parents Yogeshwar and Kusum Chaturvedi for patiently answering my questions about the historical nature of family life and nationalist politics in central and western India: themes central to the arguments discussed in this chapter.

1   I thank Heidi Tinsman for reminding me of this point. Also, see Dipesh Chakrabarty, *Provincializing Europe: Postcolonial Thought and Historical Difference* (Princeton, 2000), 242.
2   For an etymology of the name Vinayak, see A. K. Narain, 'Gaṇeśa: A Protohistory of the Idea and the Icon', in Robert L. Brown (ed.), *Ganesh: Studies of an Asian God* (Albany, 1991), 21–5. Narain argues that by the fifth century AD Ganesh was popularly referred to as Vinayak, a name literally meaning 'a leader or guide for regulating, controlling or implementing order and discipline' (21–2). Ganesh also acquired additional names in this period, some based on the physical characteristics of an elephant, others determined by his position as the lord or leader of deities. In all, the literature on this topic suggests that Ganesh has 108 names. For a list of the names and definitions in English, Gujarati and Marathi, see www.rediff.com/gujarati/2002/feb/20ganesh.htm; www.esakal.com/ganeshutsav/names.htm; www.mantraonnet.com/108ganeshnames.html (accessed 15 January 2003). For a brief discussion on the significance of the number 108 within Hindu traditions, see www.zen-forum.com/a13/b2001/c12/d3/e783/z7 (accessed 15 January 2003). For a collection of Ganesh images and forms, see www.eprarthana.com/html/iganesh.asp; and, http://astrology.indiainfo.com/festivals/ganesh/ganesh-names.html (accessed 15 January 2003).

Also, see Paul B. Courtright, *Ganeśa: Lord of Obstacles, Lord of Beginnings* (New York, 1985).

3 See Bruce Graham, *Hindu Nationalism and Indian Politics: The origins and development of the Bharatiya Jana Sangh* (Cambridge, 1990).

4 On a similar theme, see Amitav Ghosh, *In an Antique Land: History in the Guise of a Traveler's Tale* (New York, 1994).

5 For a useful discussion on related themes, see James C. Scott, John Tehranian, and Jeremy Mathias, 'The Production of Legal Identities Proper to States: The Case of the Permanent Family Surname', *Comparative Studies in Society and History*, 44, 1 (2002), 4–44.

6 For a further physical description of Dr Parchure, see Manohar Malgonkar, *The Men Who Killed Gandhi* (Madras, 1978), 135.

7 See Joseph S. Alter, *The Wrestler's Body: Identity and Ideology in North India* (Berkeley, 1992), especially Chapter 7 on 'Wrestling Tournaments and the Body's Recreation'.

8 Ibid., 1. This point is also discussed in Nita Kumar, *The Artisans of Banaras: Popular Culture and Identity, 1880–1986* (Princeton, 1988), 111–24; John Rosselli, 'The Self-Image of Effeteness: Physical Education and Nationalism in Nineteenth-Century Bengal', *Past & Present*, 86 (1980), 121–48; Phillip B. Zarrili, 'Repositioning the Body, Practice, Power, and Self in an Indian Martial Art', in Carol A. Breckenridge (ed.), *Consuming Modernity: Public Culture in a South Asian World* (Minneapolis, 1995), 183–215.

9 See Tapan Basu, Pradip Datta, Sumit Sarkar, Tanika Sarkar, and Sambuddha Sen, *Khaki Shorts Saffron Flags: A Critique of the Hindu Right* (New Delhi, 1993); Ashis Nandy, 'Final Encounter: The Politics of the Assassination of Gandhi', in *At the Edge of Psychology* (Delhi, 1980), 70–98; Alter, op. cit., 237–55. Related themes outside the social context of India are also discussed in John Kasson, *Houdini, Tarzan, and the Perfect Man: The White Male Body and the Challenge of Modernity in America* (New York, 2001); Peter Filene, *Him/Her/Self: Gender Identities in Modern America* (Baltimore, 1998, third edition); Stephen Garton, 'The scales of suffering: love, death and Victorian masculinity', *Social History*, 27, 1 (2002), 40–58.

10 Alter, op. cit., 261–3. For a comparative perspective on the related themes of military aspects of national character and the construction of manliness, see, for example, Sam Pryke, 'The popularity of nationalism in the early British Boy Scout movement', *Social History*, 23, 3 (1998), 309–24; Robert Morell (ed.), *Changing Men in South Africa* (Pietermaritzburg, 2001); Jonathan Rutherford, *Forever England: Reflections on Race, Masculinity and Empire* (London, 1997); Michael Kimmel, *Manhood in America* (New York, 1996); Mrinali Sinha, *Colonial Masculinity: the 'manly Englishman' and the 'effeminate Bengali' in the late nineteenth century* (Manchester, 1995).

11 Christophe Jaffrelot, *The Hindu Nationalist Movement and Indian Politics 1925 to the 1990s* (London, 1996), 17–25; Stuart Corbridge and John Harriss, *Reinventing India: Liberalization, Hindu Nationalism and Popular Democracy* (Cambridge, 2000), 182–3.

12 See Gyanendra Pandey, 'Which of us are Hindus?', in Gyanendra Pandey (ed.), *Hindus and Others – The question of identity in India today* (New Delhi, 1993), 238–72.

13 The specialization of Ayurvedic paediatrics is called Kaumarabhritya. Its origins date back to the ancient text Artharvaveda, defining the branch of Ayurveda as 'the management of infants and advises ... to the means of rectifying the morbid conditions of milk of the wet-nurses and of curing various

diseases caused by unwholesome milk and planetary influence'. Cited in Girindranath Mukhopadhyaya, *History of Indian Medicine: From the Earliest Ages to the Present Time*, Volume 1 (New Delhi, 1974, second edition, original edition 1922), 3. Also, see Dr C. Chaturvedi, Dr Romesh Sharma, Prof. P. V. Tewari, *Advances in Ayurvedic Pediatrics* (Varanasi, 1988).

14 See David Arnold, *Colonizing the Body: State Medicine and Epidemic Disease in Nineteenth-Century India* (Berkeley, 1993); Roger Jeffery, 'Doctors and Congress: The Role of Medical Men and Medical Politics in Indian Nationalism', in Mike Shepperdson and Colin Simmons (eds), *The Indian National Congress and the Political Economy of India 1885–1985* (Aldershot, 1988), 160–73.

15 David Arnold, *Science, Technology and Medicine in Colonial India, The New Cambridge History of India*, III.5 (Cambridge, 2000), 169–210. I thank Douglas Haynes for this reference.

16 Ibid., 176. For a related discussion on the shifts in the field of medicine in Britain during the nineteenth century, see Robert Gray, 'Medical men, industrial labour and the state in Britain, 1830–50', *Social History*, 16, 1 (1991), 19–43.

17 See Vinayak Chaturvedi, 'Colonial Power and Agrarian Politics in Kheda District (Gujarat), c. 1890–1930' (PhD, University of Cambridge, 2001), 103–48; David Arnold, 'Touching the Body: Perspectives on the Indian Plague, 1896–1900', in Ranajit Guha (ed.), *Subaltern Studies V* (Delhi, 1985), 55–90.

18 Gyan Prakash, *Another Reason: Science and the Imagination of Modern India* (Princeton, 1999), 149–52; Arnold, *Science, Technology and Medicine*, op. cit., 169–70, 176–7. Also, see Charles Leslie, 'The Ambiguities of Medical Revivalism in Modern India', in Charles Leslie (ed.), *Asian Medical Systems: A comparative study* (Berkeley, 1976), 356–67. On related themes, see Ashis Nandy, *Alternative Sciences: Creativity and Authenticity in Two Indian Scientists* (Delhi, 1995).

19 In 1897, Tilak called for a 'judicious combination' of the two systems of medicine, while Gandhi remained altogether troubled with all fields of medicine. Arnold, *Colonizing the Body*, op. cit., 321, n.100. On the other hand, Gandhi condemned 'European medicine', arguing that 'the English have certainly effectively used the medical profession for holding us ... [and] for political gain', and 'to study European medicine is to deepen our slavery'. M. K. Gandhi, *Hind Swaraj or Indian Home Rule* (Ahmedabad, 1990, eighth edition), 52–4. Also, Partha Chatterjee, *Nationalist Thought and the Colonial World: A Derivative Discourse* (Minneapolis, 1993), 93.

20 Leslie, op. cit., 363.

21 Jeffery, op. cit., 166.

22 Dhanajay Keer, *Veer Savarkar* (Bombay, 1988), 23, 28–51. Also, see Lise McKean, *Divine Enterprise: Gurus and the Hindu Nationalist Movement* (Chicago, 1996), 71–96; Pandey, op. cit., 239–72; Jaffrelot, op. cit., 19–33; Amalendu Misra, 'Savarkar and the Discourse on Islam in Pre-Independent India', *Journal of Asian History*, 33, 2 (1999), 142–84; Vidya Sagar Anand, *Savarkar: A Study in the Evolution of Indian Nationalism* (London, 1967); Jyoti Trehan, *Veer Savarkar: Thought and Action of Vinayak Damodar Savarkar* (New Delhi, 1991); Chitra Gupta, *The Life of Barrister Savarkar* (New Delhi, 1939); Harindra Srivastava, *The Epic Sweep of V. D. Savarkar* (New Delhi, 1993).

23 See Harindra Srivastava, *Five Stormy Years: Savarkar in London, June 1906–June 1911* (New Delhi, 1983).

24 Keer, op. cit., 23.

25 See Vinayak Damodar Savarkar, *Indian War of Independence, 1857* (Delhi, 1986, tenth edition).

26 Keer, op. cit., 73.
27 See Satadru Sen, *Disciplining Punishment: Colonialism and Convict Society in the Andaman Islands* (Delhi, 2000).
28 S. S. Savarkar, 'Preface by the Publisher of Second Edition', in Vinayak Damodar Savarkar, *Hindutva: Who is a Hindu?* (Bombay, 1989, sixth edition), v–vi. Also, see *An Echo from Andamans: Letters Written by Br. Savarkar to his brother Dr Savarkar* (Nagpur, n.d.).
29 Jaffrelot., op. cit., 32. Jaffrelot cites Savarkar's *My Rransportation for Life* (Bombay, 1984), 271–2, where he argues that Johann Casper Bluntschli's *The Theory of the State* (Oxford, 1885) was influential in developing ideas of a Hindu nationalism.
30 See A. S. Bhide (ed.), *Veer Savarkar's 'Whirl-Wind Propaganda': Statements, Messages & Extracts from the President's Diary of his Propagandistic Tours, Interviews from December 1937 to October 1941* (Bombay, 1941); Keer, op. cit., 225, 230, 360.
31 Bhide, op. cit., v.
32 The size of the Sena is given in Manohar Malgonkar, *The Men Who Killed Gandhi* (Madras, 1978), 136.
33 Nathuram Godse, *May It Please Your Honour* (Pune, 1977), 23, 93, 100; Bhide, op. cit., 57–88, 101–14, 180–1; Keer, op. cit., 240–5.
34 Gopal Godse, 'Events and Accused', in Godse, op. cit., xv. M. K. Gandhi is reported to have received a telegram from 'some Muslims in the Gwalior State' stating, 'The Hindus attacked our village and beat us, destroying our houses and crops and the State authorities take no notice in spite of requests'. The date of the telegram is not given, but the incident appears to correspond with the activities of the Hindu Rashtra Sena. Full details are given in Government of India, *Report of the Commission of Inquiry into Conspiracy to Murder Mahatma Gandhi*, Part II, Vol. IV, 72 (henceforth, *RCI*).
35 Malgonkar, op. cit., 135.
36 Godse, op. cit., 15–16; Nandy, 'Final Encounter', op. cit., 81. On the development of the RSS's politics, see Basu, Datta, Sarkar, Sarkar, and Sen, op. cit.; Jaffrelot, op. cit.; Sumit Sarkar, 'Fascism of the Sangh Parivar', *Economic and Political Weekly*, 28, 5 (1993), 163–7; Sumit Sarkar, 'Indian Nationalism and the Politics of Hindutva', in David Ludden (ed.), *Contesting the Nation: Religion, Community, and the Politics of Democracy in India* (Philadelphia, 1996), 270–93.
37 Nandy, 'Final Encounter', op. cit., 81.
38 Godse, op. cit., 18, 37.
39 *RCI*, Part II, Vol. IV, 66–7.
40 Ibid., 67.
41 Ibid., 67.
42 Ibid., 67; *RCI* , Part I, Vol. III, 263.
43 The discussion of the interaction between Dr Parchure and Nathuram Godse is given in Malgonkar, op. cit., 135–6.
44 Evidence of Panna Lal Chaube, Witness Number 47, *RCI*, Part I, Vol. II, 239–41.
45 Ibid., 239.
46 *RCI*, Part I, Vol. III, 265.
47 Ibid., 265. (Italics in original.)
48 Here I am thinking of Partha Chatterjee's argument in *The Nation and Its Fragments* (Princeton, 1993).
49 For a brief discussion about Sushilabai Parchure, see P. L. Inamdar, *The Story of the Red Fort Trial 1948–49* (Bombay, 1979).

50 See Rosalind O'Hanlon, *A Comparison between Women and Men: Tarabai Shinde and the Critique of Gender Relations in Colonial India* (Delhi, 1994). The literature on this theme is extensive for India, especially in the context of Bengal, see Antoinette Burton, 'House/Daughter/Nation: Interiority, Architecture, and Historical Imagination in Janaki Majumdar's "Family History"', *Journal of Asian Studies*, 56, 4 (1997), 921–46; Antoinette Burton, 'Thinking beyond the boundaries: empire, feminism and the domains of history', *Social History*, 26, 1 (2001), 60–71; Tanika Sarkar, 'The Hindu Wife and the Hindu Nation: Domesticity and Nationalism in Nineteenth-Century Bengal', *Studies in History*, 8, 2 (1992), 213–34; Judith E. Walsh, 'What women learned when men gave them advice: Rewriting patriarchy in late-nineteenth century Bengal', *Journal of Asian Studies*, 56, 2 (1997), 371–90; Mary Hancock, 'Home Science and the Nationalization of Domesticity in Colonial India', *Modern Asian Studies*, 35, 4 (2001), 871–903; Pradip Kumar Bose, 'Sons of the Nation: Child Rearing in the New Family', in Partha Chatterjee (ed.), *Texts of Power: Emerging Disciplines in Colonial Bengal* (Calcutta, 1996), 118–44; Uma Chakravarti, 'Whatever Happened to the Vedic *Dasi*? Orientalism, Nationalism, and a Script for the Past'; and Partha Chatterjee, 'The Nationalist Resolution of the Woman's Question', in Kumkum Sangari and Sudesh Vaid (eds), *Recasting Women: Essays in Indian Colonial History* (New Brunswick, 1990), 27–87, 233–53. Also, see Kamala Visweswaran, 'Small Speeches, Subaltern Gender: Nationalist Ideology and Its Historiography', in Shahid Amin and Dipesh Chakrabarty (eds), *Subaltern Studies IX* (Delhi, 1996), 83–125; Gayatri Chakravorty Spivak, 'The New Subaltern: A Silent Interview', in Vinayak Chaturvedi (ed.), *Mapping Subaltern Studies and the Postcolonial* (London, 2000), 324–8; Partha Chatterjee and Pradeep Jeganathan (eds), *Subaltern Studies XI: Community, Gender and Violence* (Delhi, 2000); and Pandey, op. cit., 260–2.

51 O'Hanlon, op. cit., 51.

52 Ibid., 10.

53 Ibid., 16.

54 Keer, op. cit., 210, 213.

55 Ibid., 213–14. For examples of comparative perspectives on related debates outside of the Indian case, see the discussion on the relationship between nationalist politics and motherhood in Argentina in Daniel James, *Doña María's Story: Life, History, Memory, and Political Identity* (Durham, 2000), 241. I thank Heidi Tinsman for this reference. On the themes of nationalism and the female body, Marcelo Bergman and Mónica Szurmuk, 'Gender, Citizenship, and Social Protest: The New Social Movements in Argentina', in Ileana Rodríguez (ed.), *The Latin American Subaltern Studies Reader* (Durham, 2001), 383–401; Elsa Barkley Brown, 'Negotiating and Transforming the Public Sphere: African American Political Life in the Transition from Slavery to Freedom', in The Black Public Sphere Collective (ed.), *The Black Public Sphere* (Chicago, 1995), 111–50. Joan B. Landes, *Women and the Public Sphere in the Age of the French Revolution* (Ithaca, 1988) is also relevant for a discussion of the above themes. I thank Sharon Block for this reference. Also, see the following contributions in Craig Calhoun (ed.), *Habermas and the Public Sphere* (Cambridge, 1996): Nancy Fraser, 'Rethinking the Public Sphere: A Contribution to the Critique of Actually Existing Democracy', 109–42; Mary P. Ryan, 'Gender and Public Access: Women's Politics in Nineteenth Century America', 259–88; and, Geoff Eley, 'Nations, Publics, and Political Cultures: Placing Habermas in the Nineteenth Century', 289–339.

56 Keer, op. cit., 230. Also, see Lise, op. cit., 86–7; Pandey, op. cit., 260–1.

57 Ibid., 214.

58 O'Hanlon, op. cit., 36–8.

59 Keer, op. cit., 386–7.

60 Gopal Godse, *Gandhihatya ani Mee* (Poona, 1967), 306. Originally cited in Nandy, 'Final Encounter', op. cit., 83.

61 For the official narrative of events relevant to Gandhi's assassination, see *RCI*, Part I, Vol. I. Also, see Inamdar, op. cit.; Malgaonkar, op. cit.; Ghosh, op. cit.

62 Malgaonkar suggests that the gun was manufactured in Italy in 1934, and was in the possession of an officer in Mussolini's army. An officer in the 4th Gwalior State Infantry, fighting in Abyssinia, acquired the gun when his Italian counterpart had surrendered. Malgaonkar, op. cit., 137.

63 See Nandy, 'Final Encounter', op. cit., for further development on this theme.

64 Tapan Ghosh, *The Gandhi Murder Trial* (New York, 1973), 100.

65 *RCI*, Part I, Vol. I, 57.

66 Ghosh, op. cit.,115.

67 Ibid.,119.

68 *RCI*, Part I, Vol. I, 60.

69 For a full discussion on Dr Parchure's case and subsequent appeal, see the reflections on the trial by his lawyer in Inamdar, op. cit.

70 Godse, op. cit., 7, 13–14.

71 See Inamdar, op. cit.

72 Inamdar suggests that Dr Parchure's period of absence was set at six months through an 'order of Externment from the Gwalior division of the state of Madhya Bharat'. ibid., 220

73 See *RCI*, Part I, Vol., I.

74 See 'Dr Dattatraya Sadashiv Parchure' and 'The Gun' available online at www.mahatma.org.in/conspirators (accessed 15 January 2003).

75 'The Men Who Killed Gandhi', *Asian Age Online* (18 August 2001), available online at www.hclinfinet.com/2001/AUG/WEEK3/7/AOSCS2frame.jsp (accessed 15 January 2003).

76 Nandy, 'Final Encounter', op. cit., 96–7, n.36. For example, Nathuram Godse used the aliases Vinayakrao and N. Vinayak Rao. *RCI* , Part I, Vol. I, 59, 78. Also, see Malgonkar, op. cit., 115; Ghosh, op. cit., 90.

77 G. M. Joshi, 'Introduction', in Savarkar, *Hindutva*, op. cit., xi.

78 Savarkar articulates this point in *Hindutva*, op. cit., 3; He states: 'The ideas and ideals, the systems and societies, the thoughts and sentiments which have centered round this name are so varied and rich, so powerful and so subtle, so elusive and yet so vivid that the term Hindutva defies all attempts at analysis … Hindutva is not a word but a history. Not only the spiritual or religious history of our people as at times it is mistaken to be by being confounded with the other cognate term Hinduism, but a history in full. Hinduism is only a derivative, a fraction, a part of Hindutva'.

79 Savarkar, *Hindutva*, op. cit., 1–16.

80 See Lise, op. cit., 79–80; Pandey, op. cit., 247–9. The literature on the politics of naming is extensive; for a comparative perspective, see Dietz Bering, *The Stigma of Names: Antisemitism in German Daily Life*, Neville Plaice (trans), (Cambridge, 1992); bell hooks, *Yearning: Race, Gender, and Cultural Politics* (Boston, 1990); and, Malcolm X, *The Autobiography of Malcolm X*, with the assistance of Alex Haley (New York, 1988, edition).

81 Savarkar, op. cit., *Hindutva*, 1–2. Emphasis mine.

82 For example, see Anna Makolkin, *Name, Hero, Icon: Semiotics of Nationalism through Heroic Biography* (Berlin, 1992).

83 Paul B. Courtright, 'The Ganesh Festival in Maharashtra: Some Observations', in Eleanor Zelliot and Maxine Berntsen (eds), *The Experience of Hinduism* (Albany, 1988), 76–7.

84 Courtright, *Ganeśa*, op. cit., 226.

85 See Richard Cashman, 'The Political Recruitment of God Ganapati', *Indian Economic and Social History Review*, 7 (1970), 347–73.

86 C. A. Bayly, *Origins of Nationality in South Asia: Patriotism and Ethical Governance in the Making of Modern India* (Delhi, 1998), 108–9.

87 S. Tejani, 'A Pre-History of Indian Secularism: Categories of Nationalism and Communalism in Emerging Definitions of India, Bombay Presidency, c.1893–1932' (PhD., Columbia University, 2002), especially Chapter 1, 'Cow Protection and Tilak's Ganpati'; Thomas Blom Hansen, *Wages of Violence: Naming and Identity in Postcolonial Bombay* (Princeton, 2001), 29–30.

88 Tejani, op. cit., 113–26.

89 Gopal Godse, 'Events and Accused', in Godse, op. cit., xii. Also, see Richard Cashman, *The myth of the Lokamanya: Tilak and mass politics in Maharashtra* (Berkeley, 1975); Dhananjay Keer, *Lokamanya Tilak, father of the Indian freedom struggle* (Bombay, 1969); Ram Gopal, *Lokamanya Tilak: a biography* (New York, 1965); T. V. Parvate, *Bal Gangadhar Tilak: a narrative and interpretive review of his life, career and contemporary events* (Ahmedabad, 1958); Dattatraya Parashuram Karmarkar, *Bal Gangadhar Tilak: a study* (Bombay, 1956); Theodore Shay, *The legacy of the Lokamanya: the political philosophy of Bal Gangadhar Tilak* (Bombay, 1956); D. V. Tahmankar, *Lokamanya Tilak: Father of Indian Unrest and Maker of Modern India* (London, 1956); Stanley Wolpert, *Tilak and Gokhale: Revolution and Reform in the Making of Modern India* (Berkeley, 1961).

90 Savarkar develops this idea in *Hindutva* under the heading 'How Names are Given'. He states: 'A name by its nature is determined not so much by what one likes to call oneself but generally by what others like to do. In fact a name is called into existence for this purpose. Self is known to itself immutable and without a name or even without a form. But when it comes in contact or conflict with a non-self then alone it stands in need of a name if it wants to communicate with others or if others persist in communicating with it. It is a game that requires two to play at. If the name chosen by the world for us is not directly against our liking then it is yet more likely to shadow all other names. But if the world hits upon the word by which they would know us as one redolent of our glory or our early love then that word is certain not only to shadow but to survive every other name we may have.' Savarkar, *Hindutva*, op. cit., 15–16.

91 Vinayak Damodar Savarkar, 'This My Legacy', cited in *Savarkar Darshan Pratishthan, Savarkar: Commemoration Volume* (26 February 1989), 3.

92 Vinayak Damodar Savarkar, *Samagra Savarkar Vangmaya*, vol. V (Poona, 1987), 1. Originally cited in Misra, op. cit., 142.

93 On the theme of 'naming like a state', see Scott, Tehranian, and Mathias, op. cit.

94 Hansen, op. cit., 1. Also, see Pauline Rohatgi, Pheroza Godrej, and Rahul Mehrotra (eds), *Bombay to Mumbai: changing perspectives* (Mumbai, 1997); Meera Kosambi, 'British Bombay and Marathi Mumbai: Some Nineteenth Century Perceptions', in Sujata Patel and Alice Thorner (eds), *Bombay: Mosaic of Modern Culture* (Bombay, 1995), 3–24.

95 See Mary Fainsod Katzenstein, Uday Singh Mehta, and Usha Thakker, 'The Rebirth of the Shiv Sena: The Symbiosis of Discursive and Organizational

Power', *Journal of Asian Studies*, 56, 2 (1997), 371–90; Mary Fainsod Katzenstein, *Ethnicity and Equality: the Shiv Sena Party and Preferential Policies in Bombay* (Ithaca, 1979); Vaibhav Purandare, *The Sena Story* (Mumbai, 1999); Sikata Banerjee, *Warriors in Politics: Hindu nationalism, violence, and the Shiv Sena in India* (Boulder, 2000); Shripad Amrit Dange, *Shiv Sena and the Bombay Riots* (New Delhi, 1969); Dipankar Gupta, *Nativism in a Metropolis: the Shiv Sena in Bombay* (New Delhi, 1982). Also, see Arjun Appadurai, 'Spectral Housing and Urban Cleansing: Notes on Millennial Mumbai', *Public Culture*, 12, 3 (2000); Satish Deshpande, 'Communalising the Nation-Space: notes on spatial strategies of Hindutva', *Economic and Political Weekly*, 30, 50 (1995), 3220–7.

96 See The Indian People's Human Rights Commission, *The People's Verdict. An inquiry into the December 1992 & January 1993 riots in Bombay by the Indian People's Human Rights Tribunal Conducted by Justice S. M. Daud & Justice H. Suresh* (Bombay, 1993).

97 A large number of journals in India have devoted special issues to the Gujarat riots of 2002. For example, see 'Genocide. Gujarat 2002', *Communalism Combat*, 8, 77–8 (2002); and, 'In Bad Faith', *The Little Magazine*, 3, 2 (2002). Also, see *A Joint Fact Finding Team Report. A Continuing Crime: The relief and rehabilitation measures, the attitude of the judiciary and police investigation and arrests with regard to the genocide in Gujarat* (Mumbai, 2002).

7 Belatedness as possibility

Subaltern histories, once again

Dipesh Chakrabarty

Even though I will be discussing historiography, not art, in the main body of this chapter, I have to acknowledge that the chapter owes its title to the accident of an invitation I received recently from the noted historian of visual culture in South Asia, Professor Christopher Pinney, to speak at a conference on art history he had organized at the Northwestern University in Chicago in May 2008. The topic of belatedness was being discussed at the conference, and the invitation made me remember that my most recent encounter with the theme of belatedness was at an exhibition of Indian art held in Chicago in 2007.

A marvellous exhibition of 'contemporary art from India' was held at the Chicago Cultural Center that year. The art works of Gulammohammed Sheikh, Nalini Malani, Subodh Gupta, Vivan Sundaram and others were impressive and brilliant in their own right. But the catalogue of the exhibition, *New Narratives: Contemporary Art from India* made it clear what the sense of time was that underwrote words like 'new' or 'contemporary'.

Indian art could be 'contemporary' because, as the curator, Betty Seid,[1] put it in her introduction to the volume, it 'reflect[ed] her [India's] world recognition as a major player in the new millennium'. American museums had avoided purchasing or exhibiting contemporary Indian art until it became truly contemporary, something that had moved from being 'stuck in an ethnographic mode of self-comparison' to a state where 'contemporary artists from India *of the world* happen to be living and working in India'.[2] So 'Western curators of contemporary art' are now 'beginning to catch on about India' but it is easy to see why: they are catching on because Indian artists are, at long last, catching up!

Has the curse of belatedness ever been lifted from India, I wondered? The same catalogue goes on to speak of the history of modernism and feminist art in India thus: 'Like Modernism, feminist art came to India later than to the West'.[3] Indian art does not become 'global' or of 'the world' until it arrives at the point that is recognized in the West as 'contemporary' – a point at which the West presumably has always been, at least long before Indian art got there. 'The communication capabilities of our electronic age have provided global cognition of the art-making world that was unavailable to many mid-twentieth century artists of India', the catalogue essay explains, and continues:

> Before independence in 1947, Western modern art was virtually unknown in India. Indian artists had not been exposed to the gradual evolution of modern art history. Rather, they were bombarded with the entirety of it, with exhibitions in India and with newly available opportunities to study and travel abroad.[4]

I felt honoured by Professor Pinney's invitation but, for me, it spoke to the issue of belatedness in ways both formal and personal. I was, first of all, a belated choice for the conference. Their second keynote speaker absented himself at the last moment and I was parachuted into the conference to fill the gap. I felt that I was in a situation somewhat similar to what the All India Radio once used to describe as being 'in the place of the scheduled artiste'. I was invited most cordially but belatedly – not anybody's fault; but that was how it worked out. Besides, some of the themes adumbrated in the conference-statement Professor Pinney had circulated also spoke to the idea of belatedness. The conference, the statement said, was meant to be a window into 'the logic of a certain sort of historiographic practice'. Certain modes of art production are disqualified from the canons of art history by being seen as 'belated' – modernism in India would be an example, I presumed. 'Is there a single temporality at stake?' the statement asked. In fact, it was issued in a spirit of rebellion against any such judgement: 'Is the putatively universalizing space of the white cube itself only a Euro-American fantasy … ? Would a global practice dictate a heterogeneity which eschewed the possibility of the "global"? … Can territories be abandoned in favor of "flows"?' And it also met the question of judgement head on: 'How can the attributions of value occur in unfamiliar aesthetic worlds? … Are such attributions … necessary to a World Art?'[5]

So in agreeing to speak belatedly about belatedness, I was reminded of a joke in my hometown of Calcutta. Bengali senior citizens are often addressed by adding a respectful 'da' at the end of their names: thus Ashisda for Ashis Nandy, or Ranajitda for Ranajit Guha. When Derrida visited the city a few years ago to inaugurate and speak at a book fair, people ignorant of foreign ways assumed that he was probably an older Bengali man whose real name was 'Deri', a word that in Bangla quite appropriately means 'delay', and that it was as a mark of respect that he was called 'Deri-da'. So when it was clear that I could be at the conference only in somebody else's place, the chain of association to the noted philosopher led me to one of the thoughts that I will be elaborating in this chapter – the relationship between belatedness and displacement, for

I do think that it is through that connection that belatedness becomes an opportunity, or a 'possibility', an association I gesture towards in the title of this chapter.

The questions raised by Professor Pinney in his conference statement reverberate in the halls of subaltern histories that I frequent in the course of my work as a historian. The theme of belatedness and a certain spirit of rebellion against it were written all over *Subaltern Studies*. That discussion was a critical part of the process through which *Subaltern Studies*, a series that we could once think of only ever as an *Indian* project, became a part of global or world-history. So while Professor Pinney's conference bracketed the word 'world' in the expression '(World) Art', let me speak of the world as it is constituted when we convert belatedness into possibilities. You will see that the same problem of judgement that occurs in art history when the trope of belatedness is used occurs in political historiography as well: how do we evaluate developments in subaltern history as that history becomes part of an emergent global formation?

II

Right from the moment of its birth, *Subaltern Studies* was greeted by several commentators as a 'belated' project, carrying out in the subcontinent what British 'history from below' had accomplished a long time ago. Arif Dirlik was one of the better known of these critics. Belatedness in history was not a new problem as such. Alexander Gerschenkron, the reputed Harvard historian who wrote a book in the early 1960s, *Economic Backwardness in Historical Perspective*, saw the problem of Russian modernization through the prism of belatedness and the politics of having to 'catch up' with the more 'modern' nations.[6] The Indian Prime Minister Nehru would often say after independence that India had to accomplish in decades what the Americans had achieved over a few hundred years. 'Belatedness', as I tried to argue in *Provincializing Europe*, was an integral part of a certain kind of historicist outlook that was born in the nineteenth century. As my quotations from the catalogue volume of last year's exhibition in Chicago will have shown, the outlook still informs discussions of art history in the public realm.

The problem of belatedness speaks to a problem of repetition and recognition in history. If something happens that resembles something else within a field that is conceptually structured by before–after relationships, then that which comes later is seen as belated. This in turn raises a question that Homi Bhabha once asked, using Rushdie's words with some sense of urgency: How does newness enter the world?[7] How do we know what is new in what seems like repetition?

I want to submit to you two propositions that may seem a little paradoxical. My first proposition is that newness enters the world through acts of displacement. My second proposition is that newness confounds judgement because judgement tends to see the new as repetition and therefore deficient. Newness is hard to distinguish from a simulacrum, a fake that is neither a copy nor original. To be open to the new is to engage in a Heideggerian struggle: to hear that which I do not already understand. Judgement, and in my case I mean political judgement, makes this a very difficult task. In the rest of this chapter I will elaborate and explain my propositions by using *Subaltern Studies* as an example.

Before I do so, however, it may be helpful to take a page out of Gilles Deleuze, surely someone who has in our times thought more than most about some of these questions. Deleuze makes a primary distinction between 'repetition' and 'generality' in order to make a further distinction between 'repetition' and 'resemblance'. 'Repetition is not generality', he says and adds: 'repetition and resemblances are different in kind – extremely so'. Generality, according to Deleuze, 'presents two major orders: the qualitative order of resemblances and the quantitative order or equivalences. Cycles and equalities are their respective symbols'. Repetition, on the other hand, refers to 'non-exchangeable and non-substitutable singularities'. To repeat 'is to behave in a certain manner, but in relation to something unique or singular that has no equal or equivalent'.[8]

> If exchange is the criterion of generality, theft and gift are those of repetition. … This is the apparent paradox of festivals: they repeat an 'unrepeatable'. They do not add a second or third time to the first, but carry the first time to the 'nth' power … [I]t is not the Federation Day which commemorates or represents the fall of the Bastille, but the fall of the Bastille which celebrates and repeats in advance all the Federation Days; or Monet's first water lily which repeats all the others. Generality, as generality of the particular, thus stands opposed to repetition as universality of the singular. The repetition of a work of art is like singularity without a concept, and it is not by chance that a poem must be learned by heart.[9]

The distinction hinted at in this passage between law and poetry, history and memory, is what gives repetition its power to transgress. 'The theatre of repetition is opposed to the theatre of representation, just as movement is opposed to the concept and to representation which refers it back to the concept'.[10] Deleuze makes it clear that repetition is how newness enters the world but it does so in disguise and through displacement – 'disguise no less than displacement forms part of repetition' – for repetition (this is Deleuze's reading of Kierkegaard and Nietzsche) is 'the double condemnation of habit and memory' both of which, as we shall see, underlie political judgement.[11] Repetition thus constitutes a crisis of political judgement.

III

Now I want to elaborate the themes of displacement and disguise, the two aspects of Deleuzian repetition, through the example of *Subaltern Studies*. First, let me document the theme of displacement and then I will turn to the more difficult question of disguise.

Subaltern Studies, the series with which I have been associated since 1982, was an instance of politically motivated historiography. Political judgement was central to this project. It came out of a Marxist tradition of history writing in South Asia and was markedly indebted to Mao and Gramsci in the initial formulations that guided the series. The tradition of history writing on the Left in India was deeply, though perhaps unsurprisingly, influenced by English Marxist or socialist historiography, the so-called 'history from below' tradition pioneered by the likes of Edward P. Thompson, Eric Hobsbawm, Christopher Hill, George Rudé, and others. Thompson's work on English popular history was predicated on the question: what contributions did the lower orders of society make to the history of English democracy? Historians in the *Subaltern Studies* series begin by asking a similar question: What contributions did the subaltern classes make on their own to the politics of nationalism in India, and hence to Indian democracy as well?[12] But here the similarity ended. English Marxist narratives of popular histories were moulded on a developmental idea of time: the peasant, in that story, either became extinct or was superseded to give rise to the worker who, through machine breaking, Chartism, and other struggles for rights, one day metamorphosed into the figure of the citizen or the revolutionary proletariat. The peasant or tribal of the third world who – as if through a process of telescoping of the centuries – suddenly had the colonial state and its modern bureaucratic and repressive apparatus thrust in his face, was, in this mode of thinking, a 'pre-political' person. He or she was someone who did not understand, as it were, the operative languages of modern, governing institutions while having to deal with them. In terms of the English 'history from below' propositions, it was only over time, and by undergoing a process of intellectual development, that the subaltern classes could mature into a modern political force.

Subaltern Studies began by repudiating this developmental idea of 'becoming political'. The peasant or the subaltern, it was claimed, was *political* from the very instant they rose up in rebellion against the institutions of the Raj.[13] Their actions were political in the sense that they responded to and impacted on the institutional bases of colonial governance: the Raj, the moneylender, and the landlord. We did not then think much about the implications of our claim that the subaltern could be political without undergoing a process of 'political development'. Yet the implications of that claim were writ large on our historiography.

I should explain that the legacies of both imperialism and anti-colonialism speak to each other in this implicit debate about whether the subaltern became political over time (through some kind of pedagogic practice) or whether the figure of the subaltern was constitutionally political. Developmental time, or the sense of time underlying a stadial view of history, was indeed a legacy bequeathed by imperial rule in India. This is the time of the 'not yet' as I called it in *Provincializing Europe*. European political thinkers such as Mill (or even Marx) employed this temporal structure in the way they thought history. Nationalists and anti-colonialists, on the other hand, repudiated this imagination of time in the twentieth century in asking for self-rule to be granted right away, without a period of waiting or preparation, without delay, 'now'. What replaced the structure of the 'not yet' in their imagination was the horizon of the 'now'.[14]

The British argued against giving self-rule to educated Indians in the nineteenth century by saying that they were not representative of the larger masses of the Indian 'people'. The answer came from Gandhi who, following his entry into Indian politics during the First World War, made the main nationalist party, the Indian National Congress, into a 'mass' organization. He did so by enlisting peasants as ordinary, so-called 'four-anna' members with voting rights within the party. The 'mass base' of the Congress enabled its leaders to claim the status of being 'representative' of the nation even if the poor and the non-literate formally did not have any electoral power under the Raj. The educational gap that separated the peasant from the educated leaders was never considered a problem in this idea of representation. The peasant, it was assumed, was fully capable of making citizenly choices that colonial rule withheld from him or her. From the very beginning of the 1920s, Gandhi spoke in favour of universal adult franchise in a future, independent India. The peasant would thus be made a citizen overnight (at least with respect to voting) without having to live out the developmental time of formal or informal education – that was the 'now' the nationalists demanded. In the constitutional debates that took place in the Constituent Assembly right after independence, the philosopher, and later statesman, Radhakrishnan argued for a republican form of government by claiming that thousands of years of civilization had – even if formal education was absent – already prepared the peasant for such a state.[15]

What underwrote this anti-colonial but populist faith in the modern-political capacity of the masses was another European inheritance, a certain kind of poetics of history: romanticism. It is, of course, true that the middle-class leaders of anti-colonial movements involving peasants and workers never quite abandoned the idea of developmental time and a pedagogical project of educating the peasant. Gandhi's writings and those of other nationalist leaders often express a fear of the lawless mob and see education as a solution to the problem.[16] But this fear was qualified by its opposite, a political faith in the masses. In the 1920s and the 30s, this romanticism marked Indian nationalism generally – many nationalists who were not Communist or of the Left, for instance, would express this faith. Francesca Orsini, who works on Hindi literature, recently excavated a body of evidence documenting this tendency. To take but stray examples from her selection, here is Ganesh Shankar Vidyarthi (1890–1931), the editor of the Hindi paper *Pratap*, editorializing on 31 May 1915:

> The much-despised peasants are our true bread-givers [*annadata*], not those who consider themselves special and look down upon the people who must live in toil and poverty as lowly beings.[17]

Or Vidyarthi again on 11 January 1915:

> Now the time has come for our political ideology and our movement not [to] be restricted to the English-educated and to spread among the common people [*samanya janta*], and for Indian public opinion [*lokmat*] to be not the opinion of those few educated individuals but to mirror the thoughts of all the classes of the country ... democratic rule is actually the rule of public opinion.[18]

One should note that this romantic-political faith in the masses was populist as well in a classical sense of the term. Like Russian populism of the late nineteenth century, this mode of thought not only sought a 'good' political quality in the peasant, but also, by that step, worked to convert the so-called 'backwardness' of the peasant into an historical advantage. The peasant, 'uncorrupted' by the self-tending individualism of the bourgeois and oriented to the needs of his or her community, was imagined as already endowed with the capacity to usher in a modernity different and more communitarian than what was prevalent in the West.[19] The contradiction entailed in the very restricted nature of franchise under colonial rule and the simultaneous induction of the peasant and the urban poor into the nationalist movement had one important consequence. The very restrictions put on constitutional politics then meant that the field, the factory, the bazaar, the fair and the street became major arenas for the struggle for independence and self-rule. And it is in these arenas that subaltern subjects with their characteristic modes of collective mobilization (that included practices of public violence) entered public life.

The inauguration of the age of mass-politics in India was thus enabled by ideologies that displayed some of the key global characteristics of populist thought. There was, firstly, the tendency to see a certain political goodness in the peasant or in the masses. In addition, there was the tendency also to see historical advantage where, by colonial judgement, there was only backwardness and disadvantage. To see 'advantage' in 'backward-ness' – that is, to see belatedness as an opportunity – was also to challenge the time that was assumed by stadial views about history, it was to twist the time of the colonial 'not yet' into the structure of the democratic and anti-colonial 'now'.

I give this potted history of the romantic-populist origins of Indian democratic thought – though not of Indian democracy as such and the distinction is important – to suggest a point fundamental to my exposition. The insistence, in the early volumes of *Subaltern Studies* (first published in 1982) and in Ranajit Guha's *Elementary Aspects of Peasant Insurgency in Colonial India* (1983), that the peasant or the subaltern was always-already political – and not 'pre-political' in any developmentalist sense – was in some ways a recapitulation of a populist premise that was implicit in any case in the anti-colonial mass movements in British India.[20] But there was, in my sense, a displacement as well, of this term. The populism in *Subaltern Studies* was more intense and explicit. There was, first of all, no 'fear of the masses' in *Subaltern Studies* analysis. Absent also – and this went against the grain of classically Marxist or Leninist analysis – was any discussion of the need for organization or a party. Guha and his colleagues drew inspiration from Mao (particularly his 1927 report on the peasant move-ment in the Hunan district) and Gramsci (mainly his *Prison Notebooks*). But their use of Mao and Gramsci speaks of the times when *Subaltern Studies* was born. This was, after all, the seventies: a period of global Maoism that Althusser and others had made respectable. Excerpts from Gramsci's notebooks had come out in English in 1971. Both Gramsci and Mao were celebrated as a way out of Stalinist or Soviet Marxism after Czechoslovakia of 1968. Many of the historians in *Subaltern Studies* were participants in or sympathizers of the Maoist movement that shook parts of India between 1969 and 1971.[21]

Yet, significantly, neither Mao's references to the need for 'leadership of the Party' nor Gramsci's strictures against 'spontaneity' featured with any degree of prominence in what we wrote. Guha's focus in his *Elementary Aspects of Peasant Insurgency* remained firmly on understanding how rebel-lious peasants mobilized themselves in nineteenth-century British India, that is to say, before the age of Gandhian 'mass nationalism'. Guha sought to comprehend the peasant as a collective author of these uprisings by doing a structuralist analysis of the space- and time-creating practices of mobilization, communication, and public violence that constituted rebel-lion (and thus, for Guha, a subaltern domain of politics). There were limi-tations, from Guha's socialist point of view, to what the peasants could achieve on their own but these limitations did not call for the mediation of a party. A cult of rebellion marked the early efforts of *Subaltern Studies*, reminiscent of one of Mao's sayings that was popular during the Cultural Revolution: 'to rebel is justified'. Rebellion was not a technique for achieving something; it was its own end. Indeed, from a global perspective, one might say that *Subaltern Studies* was the last – or the latest – instance of a long global history of the Left: the romantic-popular search for a non-industrial revolutionary subject that was initiated in Russia, among other places, in the nineteenth century. This romantic populism shaped much of Maoism in the twentieth century, and left its imprint on the antinomies and ambiguities of Antonio Gramsci's thoughts on the Party as the Modern Prince.

The once-global and inherently romantic search for a revolutionary subject outside of the industrialized West has thus had a long history, travelling from Russia in the late nineteenth century to the colonial and semi-colonial (to use a Maoist expression) 'third' world in the twentieth century. The political potential of this romanticism is exhausted today. But looking back one can see what plagued this history of a search for a revolutionary subject in the relatively non-industrialized countries of the world. Such a subject by definition could not be the proletariat. Yet it was difficult to define a world-historical subject that would take the place of the industrial working classes that did not exist, not in great numbers anyway, in the peasant-based economies drawn into the gravitational pull of the capitalist world. Would the revolution, as Trotsky said, be an act of substitutionism? Would the Party stand in for the working classes? Could the peasantry, under the guidance of the party, be the revolutionary class? Would it be the category 'subaltern' or Fanon's 'the wretched of the earth'?

When the young, left-Hegelian Marx thought up the category of the proletariat as the new revolutionary subject of history that would replace the bourgeoisie – and he did this before Engels wrote his book on the Manchester working class in 1844 – there was a philosophical precision to the category. It also seemed to find a sociological correlate in working classes born of the industrial revolution. But names like 'peasants' (Mao), 'subaltern' (Gramsci) 'the wretched of the earth' (Fanon), 'the party as the subject' (Lenin/Lukács) have neither philosophical nor sociological precision. It was as if the search for a revolutionary subject that was *not-the-proletariat* (in the absence of a large working class) was an exercise in a series of displacements of the original term, the proletariat. A telling case in point is Fanon himself. The expression 'the wretched of the earth', as Fanon's biographer David Macey has pointed out, alluded to words of the Communist Internationale, in the song – '"Debout, les damnés de la terre"/ Arise, ye wretched of the earth' – where it clearly referred to the proletariat. Yet Fanon used it to mean something else, something other than the proletariat. This other subject he could not quite define but he was clear that in the colony it could not be the proletariat. One only has to recall how, quite early on in his book, he cautioned: 'Marxist analysis should always be slightly stretched every time we have to deal with the colonial problem'.[22]

A collective subject with no proper name, a subject who can be named only through a series of displacements of the original European term 'the proletariat' – this is a condition both of failure and of a new beginning. The failure is easy to see. It lies in the lack of specificity or definition. Where is the beginning? First of all, the very imprecision is a pointer to the inadequacy of Eurocentric thought in the context of a global striving for a socialist transformation of the world. Outside of the industrialized countries, the revolutionary subject was even theoretically undefined. The history of this imprecision amounts to the acknowledgment that if we want to understand the nature of popular political practices globally with names of subjects invented in Europe, we can only resort to a series of stand-ins (never mind the fact that original may have been a simu- lacrum as well). Why? Because we are working at and on the limits of European political thought even as we admit an affiliation to nineteenth- century European revolutionary romanticism. Recognizing the stand-in nature of categories like 'the masses', 'the subaltern' or 'the peasant' is, I suggest, the first step towards writing histories of democracies that have emerged through the mass-politics of anticolonial nationalism. There is a mass-subject here, no doubt. But it can only be apprehended by consciously working through the limits of European thought. A straight- forward search for a revolutionary world-historical subject only leads to stand-ins. The global and theoretical failure to find a proper name for the revolutionary subject that is not-the-proletariat thus inaugurates the need for new thought and research outside the West, resulting in a series of displacements of the once-European category, the proletariat.

IV

To sum up, then, much socialist political thought has been made possible outside of the West by a continual process of working through European categories in order to displace them from the locus of their original signifi- cation. So much for the theme of displacement that, as Deleuze reminded us, was a critical part of the transgressive power of repetition. But what about the theme of disguise?

The theme of disguise pertains to our capacity to name and recognize the new. It is here that the tension (to speak with Deleuze) between gener- ality and repetition, between law and poetry, between history/sociology and memory, reveals itself at its most intense and demonstrates how polit- ical judgement seeks to tame the new.

Consider once again the foundational text of *Subaltern Studies*, Ranajit Guha's *Elementary Aspects of Peasant Insurgency in Colonial India*. What is the status of the category 'political' in Guha's (and our) polemic with Hobsbawm that the peasants and the tribals were not 'pre-political', that they were in fact as political as the British or the middle classes?[23] The status is ambiguous: the peasants were political in the already-understood sense of the terms – in that they dealt with the institutions of colonial rule – but they were also 'political' in some other sense about which we were not clear at all. The political claim that nineteenth-century peasant rebellions were political could only be made on the assumption – and this remains an assumption – that we already knew completely what 'being political' meant. What was new about peasant resistance in nineteenth-century India could only be expressed in the guise of the old category: 'politics'.

Something very similar happens – to cite a distant example that will show that the problem is more than historiographical or merely Indian – in the Australian historian Henry Reynold's path-breaking work on Aboriginal resistance to White occupation in nineteenth-century Australia. Take his book, *Fate of a Free People*, analysing Aboriginal resistance in nine-teenth-century Tasmania. Reynolds is aware of the European roots of the modern idea of the political. He writes how some European settlers were astonished to find among Aboriginals 'ideas of their natural rights' which Reynolds regards, rightly, as European attempts at interpreting 'in European terms' the world-making they encountered among the Aboriginals. Yet, in resisting histories written by earlier White historians and chroniclers, Reynolds, much like Guha, insists on the applicability of the category 'political' in describing Aboriginal resistance. He challenges 'the clear assumption that the Tasmanians were incapable of taking polit-ical action' and deliberately describes the nineteenth-century Aboriginal leader, Walter Arthur, as 'the first Aboriginal nationalist', tearing the idea of 'nationalism' from all its anchorage in the history of modern institu-tions.[24] Clearly, 'politics' and 'nationalism' are under-determined, part-sociological and part-rhetorical categories here, not completely open to the demand for clarification. And it is in their rhetorical imprecision that the disguising of the new happens.

Or take Partha Chatterjee's category of 'the governed' – again, a term in the series of displacements of the revolutionary subject that I have already traced before. Having documented the struggle for survival (including the stealing of electricity) – within which lessons are indeed learned by subaltern and other groups – that goes on every day in the city of Calcutta, he suddenly, towards the end of his lectures on the theme, makes 'the governed' the creators of something that even Aristotle might recognize: democracy. 'What I have tried to show', he writes, 'is that along-side the abstract promise of popular sovereignty, people in most of the world are devising new ways in which they can choose how they should be governed'. He recognizes that 'many of the forms of the political society' and their unlawful activities that he describes perhaps would not have met with 'Aristotle's approval'. Yet he believes that the 'wise Greek', if he could see Chatterjee's evidence, might actually recognize an 'ethical justification' for democracy in popular action that he might otherwise have disapproved of.[25] My point is, again, the ambiguity of this move, the claim that while popular action in everyday Calcutta does not always look democratic, it still heralds a democracy to come. It is, of course, entirely possible that everyday life in Calcutta looks forward to a future for which we just do not have a category yet. But in Chatterjee's prose, it is, once again, in the ambiguity of old and new uses of the word 'democracy' that the actual 'newness' of what goes on in Calcutta both shows and hides itself. Now we see it, now we don't.

My last example of disguise of the new is Hardt and Negri's well-known category of the 'multitude', once again a candidate for inclusion in my list of terms that displace the original revolutionary subject of Europe. The disguise is ironical for a book that, in its first half, struggles – in a Deleuzian vein – to capture that which is about domination in the world: Empire. Yet their revolutionary agency 'the multitude', while conceived of as immanent in a Spinozist way, has to acquire an 'adequate consciousness' (resonances of Hegel–Marx here) in order to be political. 'How can the actions of the multitude become political?' they ask. Their answer: 'The only response we can give … is that the action of the multitude becomes primarily political when it begins to confront directly and with *an adequate consciousness* the central repressive operations of Empire'.[26]

I am then left to ask my final question: why does displacement combine with disguise to create the very structure of repetition? It goes back, I think, to a problem that Marx referred to a long time ago. Newness enters the world as a challenge to judgement and law. That is why Deleuze refers to it through the figure of poetry. Political judgement is tied to the old. It is salutary to remember that even Homi Bhabha, whose generative mediations on the postcolonial condition would not have much to say about the conditions for the struggle for socialism (as conventionally understood), began his journey as a postcolonial theorist with a gesture towards connecting with socialist politics as it was known in Britain in the 1980s.[27] I think Marx, in a moment of reflection on the problem of repetition and resemblance in history – and thus on the figure of the belated – put his finger on the necessary disguise of the new. The lines are very well known indeed but may bear repetition in the context of this discussion. Let me give Marx the final word with one minor qualification:

> Men make their own history, but they do not make it just as they please … The tradition of all the dead generations weighs like a nightmare on the brain of the living. And just when they seem … engaged in creating something that has never yet existed … they anxiously conjure up the spirits of the past to their service and borrow from them names, battle cries and costumes in order to present the new scene of world history in this time-honoured disguise and this borrowed language.

Marx expects this process to have a happy Hegelian ending. He, as you know, compares this process to a person's experience of learning a new language:

> a beginner who has learnt a new language always translates it back into his mother tongue, but he has assimilated the spirit of the new language and can freely express himself in it only when he finds his way in it without recalling the old and forgets his native tongue in the use of the new.[28]

We are rightly suspicious of such happy endings. We remain interested in remainders and failures of translation that always come back to haunt and trouble what translation achieves. This is indeed where we may have to part with Marx and his progenies in contemplating the problem of repetition and belatedness in our time.

Notes

Thanks are due to the editors of this volume for their editorial suggestions.

1 Betty Seid, *New Narratives: Contemporary Art from India* (Ahmedabad and Ocean Township, NJ: Mapin, Grantha, 2007).
2 *New Narratives*, p. 13.
3 *New Narratives*, p. 15.
4 *New Narratives*, p. 19.
5 Conference statement, '(World) Art: Art History and Global Practice', Northwestern University, 23–24 May 2008.
6 Alexander Gerschenkron, *Economic Backwardness in Historical Perspective – A Book of Essays* (Cambridge, MA: Belknap Harvard, 1962).
7 Homi Bhabha, 'How Newness Enters the World: Postmodern Space, Postcolonial Times and the Trials of Cultural Translation' in his *The Location of Culture* (London: Routledge, 1994).
8 Gilles Deleuze, *Difference and Repetition*, trans. Paul Patton (New York: Columbia University Press, 1994), p. 1.
9 Deleuze, *Difference*, pp. 1–2.
10 Deleuze, *Difference*, p. 10.
11 Deleuze, *Difference*, pp. xvi, 7.
12 See E. P. Thompson, *Whigs and Hunters* (Harmondsworth: Penguin Books, 1977).
13 I discuss this in some detail in my essay 'A Small History of *Subaltern Studies*' in my *Habitations of Modernity: Essays in the Wake of Subaltern Studies* (Chicago: The University of Chicago Press, 2002), Ch. 1.
14 See the discussion in the Introduction to my book *Provincializing Europe: Postcolonial Thought and Historical Difference* (Princeton, New Jersey: Princeton University Press, 2000).
15 See *Provinicializing Europe*, 'Introduction' for details.
16 See Gyanendra Pandey's essay on the topic in Ranajit Guha and Gayatri Chakravorty Spivak (eds), *Selected Subaltern Studies* (New York: Oxford University Press, 1988).

17 Francesca Orsini, 'The Hindi Public Sphere and Political Discourse in the Twentieth Century', unpublished paper presented at a conference on 'The Sites of the Political in South Asia', Berlin, October 2003.
18 Ibid.
19 For an excellent discussion of this point, see Andrzej Walicki, *The Controversy over Capitalism: Studies in the Social Philosophy of the Russian Populists* (Notre Dame, Indiana: University of Notre Dame Press, 1989), Chapters 1 and 2, in particular the section of 'The Privilege of Backwardness'.
20 Ranajit Guha, *Elementary Aspects of Peasant Insurgency in Colonial India* (Delhi: Oxford University Press, 1983), Chapter 1.
21 Shahid Amin, 'De-Ghettoising the Histories of the non-West'; Gyan Prakash, 'The Location of Scholarship'; in my 'Globalization, Democracy, and the Evacuation of History?' in Jackie Assayag and Veronique Benei (eds), *At Home in Diaspora: South Asian Scholars and the West* (Bloomington, Indiana: Indiana University Press, 2003).
22 Frantz Fanon, *The Wretched of the Earth*, trans., Constance Farrington (New York: Grove Press, 1963), p. 40.
23 Ranajit Guha, *Elementary Aspects of Peasant Insurgency in Colonial India* (Delhi: Oxford University Press, 1983), Chapter 1.
24 Henry Reynolds, *Fate of a Free People* (Ringwood, Victoria: Penguin, 1995), pp. 11, 23, 69.
25 Partha Chatterjee, *The Politics of the Governed: Reflections on Popular Politics in Most of the World* (New York: Columbia University Press, 2004), pp. 77–8.
26 Michael Hardt and Antonio Negri, *Empire* (Cambridge, MA: Harvard University Press, 2000), p. 399.
27 Bhabha, 'The Commitment to Theory'.
28 Karl Marx, 'The Eighteenth Brumaire of Louis Bonaparte', in Karl Marx and Frederick Engels, *Selected Works*, vol. 1 (Moscow: Progress Publishers, 1969), p. 398.

8   Of demons and angels and historical humans

Some events and questions in translation and postcolonial theory

Aniket Jaaware

In what follows, I attempt to show that a look at some curious examples of translation from European texts makes us think about issues in translation theory and postcolonial theory from a slightly different angle. The metaphor of translation can very well be employed for understanding the relation between European texts and some texts and social and political practices in India in the colonial period, and this in turn helps us look critically at what I shall call our fuzzy postcolonialism. I also argue that Walter Benjamin's metaphor of translation as the afterlife of a work can be extended to posit two basic modes of afterlife.[1]

I

It is more than clearly evident in the field of translation theory that the most significant developments have come out of a consideration of literary translations. Viewing literature mainly as a special linguistic and cultural activity with exceptional ontological and pragmatic features, these considerations tend to focus on two questions: (1) is the literary and cultural value of the 'original' work properly and proportionately demonstrated in the translation; and (2) following upon this, is the work of 'equivalence' and/ or 'untranslatability' properly and convincingly done in the use of words, phrases, sentences and larger linguistic patterns in the translation? More often than not, a discussion of translation tends to be reduced to a discussion of equivalence between works of the interacting languages, as in the theoretical works by J. C. Catford, Eugene A. Nida and, to a certain extent, Edwin Gentzler and Susan Bassnett.[2] Equally often, equivalence between words of these different languages is measured and judged by referring to the sameness of the object to which the words are supposed to refer. The sameness of the object, in turn, is measured in ontological or pragmatic terms – in terms of what the object is, or in terms of the function that a given object may have in a specific culture, and the equivalent, or untranslatable object in the other culture. It is the absence of a specific object within the other culture that makes a word, or a sentence, 'untranslatable'.

This is not to suggest that these contributions have not helped us understand and theorize translation activity and saved us from all the ill-thought discussions of translation, but merely that complex notions of literature and language have operated in the field of translation theory. The complexity of the relations that literature has with life and the objects and effects which it is supposed to include is inherited by translation theory. One cannot claim to render the field simple, but it might be possible to render this field complex in another way, by considering the socio-historical contexts of other kinds of translation activity. Several contributions already contain hints that it is possible, indeed necessary to do so. Neither a linguistic, nor a literary consideration of translation can in fact do without paying attention to the socio-historical contexts of translation.

A socio-historical consideration can also not carve itself into parts, or manageable portions, by thinking in terms of national or cultural independence or autonomy as if there were no historical interactions across nations or cultures. I shall not discuss here the nexus between translation theory and nationalism and nationalistic delimitations of culture since this is minor. The history of translation in Europe cannot be rendered independent of translations, for example, of the Bible into Marathi or Bangla, merely two of the languages used in the South Asian subcontinent; or any of the languages used in Africa. Several European scholars have believed otherwise, in spite of the fact that quite a lot of European thought on translation has centred on the translation of the Bible. In their own, possibly forgivable Eurocentric manner, they have thought of Bible translation in terms of the relation between the classical languages and more modern *European* languages, tending to neglect, if not ignore, the socio-historical context of translations of the Bible into several non-European languages. One of the instances that could have been considered, for example, is that of a very early rendering of the life of Jesus in Marathi,[3] and this example could be juxtaposed with the legend of the Septuagint Bible.[4] This writing on the life of Jesus is not, strictly speaking, a translation, but a definite carrying across takes place in the very conception and production of the text. This was written in Marathi by a priest, Father Stephens. The point is that even though this is not a translation in the sense of rendering one text into another language, this 'original' Marathi text cannot be produced without an antecedent 'translation' of some European text. The scope of the meaning of the word 'translation' would have to be enlarged to enable us to use this text in order to understand what happens. Thus, on the one hand, in the legend around the Septuagint, we come across this notion of the absolute translatability and sameness of the Word of God, and on the other hand, in the case of the *Khrista-puraana*, we have Father Stephens attempting to get across the notion of the Christian

Trinity by using a word that reminds the reader of the Hindu trinity, but at the same time differs from it in meaning.[5] The Christian notion of the trinity is partly being accommodated to local Marathi demands in this case.

Also, like the printing press, translation can become an agent of social change. This is more than clearly evident in the colonial period in South Asia. Various European ideas were 'translated', and the circulation of these ideas, through the various educational institutions, presses and conversations, resulted in social change. It would seem, therefore, that it would be counter-productive to restrict the meaning of translation to linguistic, or even cultural equivalence, because such a restriction of meaning disallows a fuller consideration of social change. Moreover, it is important to remember that quite a lot of specifically non-English texts were read by the intelligentsia in English translation, and these were subsequently abridged, summarized and translated, as for instance, into Marathi. The scope of the word 'translation' can be enlarged in yet another way, by considering the kinds of translations that are not normally considered within translation theory. It is interesting to consider the Marathi novel from this angle. Traditionally, the Marathi novel is said to be modelled on, copied from or borrowed from the English literary tradition. However, even a passing acquaintance with the early novels in Marathi tells us that they are curiously different from the English novel, and the model of simple mimesis cannot be used to understand them. It is possible to argue that the Marathi novel is a translation of the English novel – it is the *genre* itself that gets translated, *not* individual novels as such, nor the chapters, sentences or words of individual novels. There is, in translation theory, considerable discussion of what should or should not be the unit of translation, with the word serving as the smallest unit (even for Walter Benjamin). The word is *not* the smallest unit of translation. I am suggesting that units larger than paragraphs or chapters can quite easily be imagined, and that the genre itself could serve as a unit. It is evident that we need not stop at the level of the genre either, since a whole discourse too could be translated, and this is how translation can be made to relate to social change. Thus, if we look at the function of the Marathi novel in society and how the discourse of the novel functioned and was generated, we find that the novel is only slightly different from the novel in Europe. There was some debate over this in Marathi, in the nineteenth and twentieth centuries. It should be evident that a simple notion of imitation, copying or even plagiarism is less helpful than the notion of translation. It is necessary, in fact, to consider the possibility of translating not an individual book, but a *genre* itself. The metaphor of transplantation, already apposite to the metaphor of translation, is applicable here. It also has a certain affinity with the metaphor of afterlife.

II

I think it can be demonstrated that translation, as the afterlife of a work, lives in two basic modes, which we might call angelic and demonic. An angelic afterlife is one in which the positive potentials of a work are revealed, and possibly emancipatory social change begins to take place. This is what happened with the 'translations' into Marathi of Western authors who discussed ideas of equality, fraternity and liberty. It should be appreciated that in none of the Hindu scriptures is it asserted that human beings are equal at the level of lived, material reality. The only equality asserted there is at the spiritual level, before God. Thus various British authors – and arguments advocating equality – were translated, abridged and summarized into Marathi in a variety of ways, applicable to the various debates on widow-remarriage, age of consent, education, politics as well as innumerable others issues relating to culture, women, and caste. This aspect of the history of translation is rather well known and we need not spend time in asserting its positivity. It can be seen that there is a kind of 'actualization' of translated ideas taking place in these debates and that translation in the limited linguistic sense is only one phase in this larger translation of ideas in the sense of actualizing them in socially lived reality. Neither should we forget in our postcolonial interests that nineteenth-century Marathi readers did find the ideas of John Stuart Mill or Herbert Spencer, or even Bentham, liberating and that some emancipatory change did take place through the agency of British authors, British education and the translations of British and European writings. This is not to suggest that 'liberal' or 'utilitarian' ideology should be supported today, but only to acknowledge a certain social and historical debt. Without the ideas of equality, fraternity and liberty, the anti-caste struggles and the feminist struggles, for example, would not have begun in the nineteenth century. This is what the term 'angelic' is also meant to include.

The demonic aspects – as always – are a little more interesting, and I shall give a few examples here. The first is a translation of Nietzsche's *The Anti-Christ*, done around 1931[6] by a *brahman* Vedic scholar, Shankar Raamchandra Raajwaade, otherwise known for his commentaries on some scriptural texts, for the generally eccentric and rather extreme views he held, and the odd positions he took on politics and culture. This translation also makes us see how a very good translator may, in his or her practice, reveal aspects of not merely the work, but also the *socio-historical situation* into which the work is being translated, things which otherwise would be invisible without the translation, and how strange affinities and resonances might come about, in this case, between Nazi appropriations of Nietzsche and Raajwaade's appropriation of Nietzsche.

Ahitaagni Raajwaade was a staunch Vedic *brahman*, more orthodox, in many ways, than contemporary *brahmans*. For him, modern Hinduism is already a degenerate, 'decadent' form of religiosity and virtue, or rather *virtu* in all its meanings. It is from this position that he finds an affinity with Nietzsche's *The Anti-Christ*. In Nietzsche's book he finds a vindication of *Aryan* values, which also means *Vedic* values, since these two are synonymous for him. It is a remarkable and frightening truth that the translation as such is very good, in the sense that Raajwaade is very resourceful with the language that he uses to make visible, present or give an echo of Nietzsche's work.[7]

In the commentary, Raajwaade attempts to summarize *all* of Nietzsche's thought, and also gives an account of the kind of person Nietzsche was, drawing upon Elisabeth Förster-Nietzsche. In the process, he also manages to speak about himself in the manner of Nietzsche, placing himself not merely *above*, but *beyond* all contemporary thinkers and teachers of philosophy and several public figures, political and literary. What is striking in this translation is, in the final analysis, its *contemporaneity* with the Nazi appropriation, and with Nazism itself. Considering that the book was published around 1931 – the date is a little imprecise because the book gives the date according to the Hindu calendar – and considering the amount of writing in the book, Raajwaade could have been working on the book a year before it was published, that would give the date of composition as 1930, or perhaps even a few months into late 1929; it seems uncannily contemporary.

What would seem to be a matter *internal* to European history and philosophy, Nietzsche's works reveals certain affinities that are interesting from a historical and social angle. While it is true that Nietzsche's work never explicitly supports Nazi ideology, the fact that it can be appropriated for quasi-fascist purposes needs attention. It is here that the notion of the demonic aspect of the afterlife of a work might be useful. This is what Raajwaade says in his preface to the book:

> *Khristaantak* is a book written by a modern European sage (*mahaamuni*) of a *brahman* temperament and nature (*vrutti*), in the German language. This Marathi version has been prepared for the Marathi readers. In this version, the whole meaning in the original author's mind, along with his style, has been rendered into Marathi. Every son of an Aryan, and especially the followers of the Vedic religion and practice and classical followers of culture should read this with serious attention. Because in it he will easily find the basic principle and root of the natural superior mentality that he is born with, but which is diminishing in the hostile circumstances around him. Every thinker who is willing to read with care and devotion cannot but see that this book will prove to be a block in the path of the modern

degeneration of Aryans, and will make him think, and sustain him. In this part, the original *Khristaantak* has been rendered complete, and of the proposed three-volume explication and commentary, the first is here included. The remaining parts will eventually be presented.[8]

The 'commentary' on Nietzsche's book is a rather long invective, containing attacks on contemporary 'Hindu' religious practices, contemporary political leaders, and so on. It reveals how a retrograde classicism can pretend to be a modernism, how it can claim an affinity with Nietzsche's 'revaluation of all values'. It is easy to see how present day right-wing criticisms of Western modernity will find such retrograde, classicist 'revaluation' particularly attractive. This complex nexus throws up the possibility that there can be two kinds of voluntary or inadvertent criticisms of colonialism. One is that which is more familiar to us, associated with names like Spivak, Bhabha and several others. We might call the other, less familiar criticism of colonialism a classicist anti-colonialism which seeks to reject egalitarian and emancipatory social change in the name of being anti-colonial, or anti-Western. In this sense, this translation predicts later trends in Indian culture and politics: contemporary political groups such as 'Vande Mataram' in Pune (who have adopted the Nazi swastika as their sign and do not see themselves as fascistic but entirely in the service of a Hindu nation), or the various young readers of Hitler's autobiography in English and Marathi, and who think, as it were, 'here was a man'. Raajwaade feels the power of Nietzsche's writing, but fails to see, translator in a specific socio-historical condition that he is, the *modern* irony in the style as such. He measures the Greenblattean resonance between himself and Nietzsche with the tuning fork of classicism, and not modernism.

What is *not* demonical here is the always present possibility that someone's writings can be misunderstood or misused, but the *similarity* is two different misunderstandings and misuses, one the context of the language and social circumstance in which it is written (about to become fascist Germany), the other while translating into a *different* language and society (about to become free India). However, in retrospect, one wants to ask, does not the fact that it *could* be misunderstood in a *similar* manner mean that there was an incipient quasi-fascism already present in India in the 1930s? I think this question is more important than the other possible question, 'if this is true, then must not there be something in Nietzsche's writing itself which makes for such appropriation?'. I am emphasizing the conditions of the translation, not of the original. This example of translation is more literary than social; however, in the next example it *is* beyond doubt a question of 'mere transmission' of the same content into another language. Perhaps not surprisingly, but ironically, it is *not* with literary translations but with socially functional translations that the activity of translation is rendered *merely* linguistic. This is a more or less inconsequential event in the narrative of a *brahman* from near Pune, Godse Bhatji, of his travels across north India during the truly turbulent year of 1857, an early example of the genre of travelogue and autobiography in Marathi:

> At that time, the district was new. Travelling on the road, we went to the town. But then the *chaukidar* (guard) sat us down at the *chauki* (the town centre, also administrative office), and later took us to the *saaheb* (boss, officer). We went to the bungalow in the morning hour. We sat there for some time, then the *saaheb* came down and placing [himself in] a chair, commenced inquiries about us. In these, we proved to be pure, innocent *yaatri* (travellers/pilgrims), and [he] ascertained that we have no *dosh* (blame/fault) about the rebellion or anything else, and that we had a home in Pen under Bombay. Because that *saaheb* was a worker [had worked] in the Thane district for many years. Then *saaheb* told that, you are taking the *ganga kaavad* (a bamboo contraption for carrying water, used often to transport the waters of the Ganges over long distances), to your *desh* (place/area), but in all places, there is *bandobast* (law and order arrangements, verification of identity, deployment of state authority and police) for travellers. So I will write you a *sartipikit* (certificate), which [you should] keep with you and show to anyone who comes for inquiry. [He] having said thus, we said very fine, and took the certificate given by the *saaheb*. But that was *ingraji* (in English), so we told the *saaheb* that we do not understand *ingraji* (English) so [we asked that we] be given a Marathi *kapi* (copy). On this, on the other side of the same letter, the same matter was written out by a Marathi clerk, and we made *salaams* and went into the town to make arrangements for lodging etc.[9]

This is a minor, inconsequential example of translation, but a significant one, I hope, for translation theory. The ease with which the clerk seems to have done it indicates familiarity with both the languages (a pre-requisite for that job in any case), moreover, familiarity with the kind, or 'mode of meaning' that is to be 'merely' transmitted into another language. While travelling north, Godse Bhatji and his party had been given safe passage at Mahu by the rebelling soldiers. British governance had already set in, but a few months earlier, in the siege of Delhi and Lucknow, it had been touch-and-go. A few months later, the British were offering certificates to the Indian populace. No one found this remarkable: not the narrator, nor the British officer and certainly not the clerk who did the translation. This example epitomizes, in a certain sense, a shift in the authoritative function.

Let us now turn to two gruesome tales that have nothing to do, technically, with translation as such, but are related to issues of communication. This is still in 1857, just about the time when our previous author was beginning to think of returning from the north. Delhi has been captured by the 'rebelling' soldiers, and the charismatic John Nicholson, with the 52nd Light Infantry, is marching to 'rescue' it. As they march towards Delhi, they come to need bullocks. Reginald G. Wilberforce, the narrator, and one more person, are deputed to go to a nearby village and buy them. They have a problem in that they do not know the local language. They decide to get around this problem by asking those who know the language to give them the correct words, and then memorize the appropriate sounds of the appropriate sentences. They, however, are not well received in this village and barely manage to escape on horseback from a threatening mob of people led by the headman. On re-joining their forces, they report on what happened. This is what Reginald G. Wilberforce has to say: 'when we returned to camp, and told our story, a few Pathans succeeded where we had failed; their persuasions, however, were of such a pressing nature, that that particular headman ruled no more over the destinies of that village'.[10] An attempt to reconstruct the two scenes – Wilberforce's visit and the Pathans' visitation – shows a gruesome scene: because there was no translation possible, at least one 'headman' lost his life. This is the negative side of my previous example, in which translation had facilitated Godse Bhatji's journey.

Let us look at another example. This is an English translation of the memoirs of a soldier in the Native Army, Sita Ram Pande, who served 48 long years, and rose to become a *Subhedar*, a kind of officer. This is a translation very likely from an Avadhi (dialect of Hindi) source. The original is no longer available. However, it seems to me that the event that is narrated is far more significant than the fact that the 'original' is missing here, and we must imagine it as best we can, at least those of us who might know both English and Avadhi of the nineteenth century. This is how an interesting event in colonial history is narrated by a narrator who is part of the story, in fact the main character of the story:

> One day, in one of the enclosed buildings near Lucknow, a great number of prisoners were taken. They were nearly all *sepoys*. They were all brought in after the fight to the commanding officer of my regiment, and in the morning the order came that they were all to be shot. It happened that it was my turn to command the firing party. I asked the prisoners their names and their regiments. After hearing some five or six, one *sepoy* said he belonged to a certain regiment which was my son's. I naturally inquired whether he had known my son, Ananti Ram of the Light Company. He answered that that was his name. However, this is a very common name, and because I had

always imagined that my son must have died from the Sind fever, since I had never heard from him, it did not first strike me. But when he told me that he came from Tilowee [Sita Ram's place], my heart leapt in my mouth. Could he be my long lost son? There was no doubt about it, he gave my name as his father, and fell at my feet imploring pardon. He had mutinied with the rest of his regiment and gone to Lucknow. Once the deed had been done, what else could be done? Where would he have gone, even if he wanted to escape?

The prisoners were to be shot at four o'clock in the afternoon, and I must be my son's executioner! Such is fate! I went to the Major *sahib* and requested that I might be relieved of this duty as a very great favour. He was very angry and said he would bring me before a court-martial for trying to shirk my duty. He would not believe that I was a faithful servant of the British government – and he would not listen to me any further. At last my feelings as father got the better of me and I burst into floods of tears. I told him that I would shoot every one of the prisoners with my own hands if he ordered me but I confessed that one of them was my son. The Major declared that I was only making up an excuse ... but at last his heart seemed to be touched. He ordered my unfortunate son to be brought before him and questioned him very strictly.

I shall never forget this terrible scene. Not for one moment did I consider requesting that his life should be spared – that he did not deserve. Eventually the Major came to believe in the truth of my statement and ordered me to be relieved of this duty. I went to my tent bowed down with grief which was made worse by the gibes and taunts of the Sikhs who declared that I was a renegade. In a short time I heard a volley. My son had received the reward for mutiny! ... I would much rather that he had been killed in battle. Through the kindness of the Major I was allowed to perform the funeral rites over my misguided son. He was the only one over whom it was performed, for the remainder were thrown to jackals and vultures. The Major told me that he was much blamed by the other officers for allowing funeral rites to be performed on a rebel but if good deeds wipe away sins, and I believe some *sahibs* believe in this as we do, then *his* sins will be very white. Bad luck never waits upon the merciful! May my Major become a General![11]

The curious sentence here is 'Not for a moment did I consider requesting that his life should be spared – that he did not deserve', and goes a long way to show this soldier's feudal, 'pre-modern' loyalty to the British. The event is complex enough to epitomize a colonized consciousness in this curious conflict in the father's narrative: loyalty to the British (he does not beg for his son's life), religious-affective exigencies (the need to perform the last rites) and the enormity of having to shoot one's son, and the attempt to avoid participating in the shooting without trying to prevent it. The contradictory exigencies that he experiences are paralleled in what we might call a postcolonial consciousness, which is characterized by the need to criticize and work against colonialism, while also showing the historical and conceptual necessity of using ideas from the West, and a need to negotiate with the past for a better future.

III

When we – that is, all of us who have an interest in understanding post-coloniality – think of history, especially from our fuzzy 'postcolonial' point of view ('fuzzy' because though we are clear about our disagreements with each other, the areas of agreement over what is postcoloniality have fuzzy borders), we think of the period before colonization as the 'pre-colonial' period, thus obtaining the series 'pre-colonial, colonial, postcolonial'. A closer look at that series, however, shows us – ironically – that the word 'colonial' is the one that is *unmarked* and unqualified, a plain innocent word that is so natural and obvious that it can be what it is. This has several implications. I do not meant to suggest that the series has not been understood as filled with ruptures in society, culture, politics, and in our understanding of these as well. I mean to indicate, rather, the difficult relation that we have with we what call the 'pre-colonial' especially because it is often used to mean 'pre-modern'. When it comes to the terms 'colonial' and 'modern' there is less of a confusion between each other, and when it comes to the 'postcolonial' and 'post-modern' the difference is much clearer, and in fact has been discussed in other contexts.[12] I think similar difficulties are obtained in the series 'pre-modern, modern, postmodern'. The term 'pre-colonial' gives the impression that that long history, many times longer than the 'colonial period' was merely leading up to the colonial period, and it is here that the unconscious, if not surreptitious, complicity with Eurocentric historiography and modernity becomes clear.

It is also clear that we can take two views on the 'colonial' period itself. In one, we see it as a fundamental rupture in the continuity of history, an open gash in our consciousness, a time after which nothing was ever the same. But the difference it makes is at best ambivalent, for the simple reason that quite a lot of the changes that took place in this period were, in the final analysis, good. Without some of these social changes, the political and ethical issues of caste and gender would be impossible to raise. This is also the period in which capitalism established itself fully, and in a speeded up time. One can see varieties of capitalism co-existing in 'modern' South Asia, and also the period in which the Indian bourgeoisie seized the political sphere with that ubiquitous call for 'nationalism'.

IV

I need only to mention the vexed issue of modernity in postcolonial societies, or the issues of alternative modernities. Right-wing ideologues are seeking an alternative to modernity in the cultural sphere, valorizing, à la Raajwaade, 'ancient' values and claiming that this is merely an alternative modernity, not an alternative to modernity as such.

All this has implications for our understanding of postcoloniality, and its social practice in postcolonial societies, for the simple reason that while the most significant contributions have been made to 'theory', it must not be forgotten that postcoloniality is a social practice. It is found in the area of affects, as well as the area of concepts, and in the area of actions (and that includes speech acts and performatives) as well.

In the area of affects, one can find this double, often contradictory thing that is called the postcolonial consciousness, with its special investment in history, and historical methodology, on the one hand unable to endorse the past and its present effects, on the other hand, needing to maintain some of the effective elements of the past for present and future emancipation. This consciousness becomes postcolonial when the elements of the past belong to another culture, another people, one which was, in that self-same past, politically dominant. It is tempting to see here the reverse of Eurocentrism, which tended to see 'the Other' as something to be dominated, understood, digested, modified, written upon; whereas here we have an 'Other' that was, or is, dominating. However, it would be misleading to understand the issues on the model of the 'self and the Other', for here we are talking of whole societies, and it would be wrong to singularize these multiplicities into the pair self/Other. In fact, it would not be non-Eurocentric at all, since it is precisely the condensation or abstraction of many others into 'the Other' which was a typical procedure found in Eurocentric writing. Therefore, it is necessary to conceptualize these issues in terms of societies and social practices and their theories, before, or after, the facts of practices.

The other view is to state, or at least to suggest, that the 'colonial' period was a superficial 'foreign intervention' which was forced to retract and withdraw, and now we are free to re-assert the continuity of our own, 'authentic' national history. In Raajwaade's commentary some hint of this – that we can assert our own invented tradition in a more authentic, 'over-man' like manner – is already present. There is a trajectory of thought which traverses the difference between notions of authenticity and notions of identity within no time and space, and it allows the issues to be confused, especially in the realm of politics. On that trajectory it becomes possible to suggest that anything that looks Western is therefore not authentic Indian, it even becomes possible to suggest that any set of ideas that have Western elements in them cannot be authentically anti- or postcolonial. And finally, it becomes possible to reduce many of these issues to that of language. Nativists thus argue that Indian authors writing in English are, by that fact, unable to write about India, or have Indian characters in their fiction. While it is true that in 'Indian Writing in English', or that kind of writing which is known as 'post-colonial' in the West (mostly expatriate authors writing about India), many of the characters tend to be Westernized Indians, wealthy, highly educated, English-speaking and so on, the nativists base their arguments on the issue of language, rather than of specific interpretations of literary work, or the specific class-based sensibilities of the characters. It is possible to demonstrate that a large part of Marathi writing, for example, has the same tendency, since we should not forget that one can be Eurocentric in authentic Marathi as well. If it is possible to be Eurocentric in choicest, educated, resourceful Bengali, or Marathi, or Tamil, or any of the 'authentic Indian' languages, then presumably the question of complicity with Western notions cannot be made to rest on language. It is here that the metaphor of translation comes in useful, for this, I believe, is the crux of the issue: is it possible to conceive of translation outside of a concern with language? There is reason to believe that in India, in the present social formation, what we have is an interpretive attempt to translate traditional caste hierarchies into capitalistic class differences and distinctions, and to translate capitalistic social formations into caste hierarchies. There can be little doubt that both the forms will adjust to each other to produce a different hierarchical form. There is an attempt to translate symbolic capital into economic capital, and vice versa. The coming years of a further opening of Indian markets, further 'globalization', will show us all the results of that translation. One can only hope that that translation is postcolonial, rather than a translation which valorizes colonial, or 'pre-colonial' values.

Jotirao Phule, working and writing in late nineteenth-century India, had already had an inkling of this, as is evident in the fact that he criticizes the *brahmans not* for their exploitation of others in the realm of symbolic capital, but for exploiting the lower castes economically, *through* the deployment of symbolic capital.[13] The *notion* of material equality was a gift that the British and, by extension, the European Enlightenment gave us pre-colonials, who have managed to translate ourselves into colonials and later postcolonials. I think that is the bottom line.

Notes

This chapter previously appeared in *The European Legacy* 7.6 (2002) pp. 735–45.

1   Walter Benjamin, 'The Task of the Translator: an Introduction to the Translation of Charles Baudelaire's *Tableaux Parisiens*', in *Illuminations*, translated by Harry Zohn (London: Jonathan Cape, 1970). For what is perhaps a

better translation, see 'The Task of the Translator', translated by James Hynd and E. M. Valk, *Delos* 2 (1968): pp. 76–99.

2 For example, J. C. Catford, *A Linguistic Theory of Translation: An Essay on Applied Linguistics* (London: CUP, 1969), Eugene A. Nida, *Toward a Science of Translating* (Leiden: E. J. Brill, 1969) and *Translating Meaning* (San Dimas, CA: English Language Institute, 1982). For more recent surveys, see Susan Bassnett and Harish Trivedi (eds), *Post-colonial Translation: Theory and Practice* (London: Routledge, 1999); and Edwin Gentzler, *Contemporary Translation Theories*, revised second edition (Clevedon: Multilingual Matters Ltd, 2001).

3 This translation of the life of Jesus attempts to belong to the local Marathi/ Indian tradition of *Puraanas* and is, interestingly, called the *Khrista-puraana*. There are several linguistic innovations in it. Father Thomas Stephens, Father Drago (ed.) (Mumbai: Popular Prakashan, 1996). This was first printed in Roman script in 1616. I have transcribed the Marathi words such that *kh* renders the very strong aspirated Marathi /kha/. The /n/ has two values, which are sensible only to speakers of Sanskrit derived languages.

4 The legend is that 72 translators were commissioned to translate the Bible, were then isolated into presumably 72 monastic cells and when they had all completed the translation and came out of their cells, the translations were identical.

5 There is a kind of trinity, the *trimuurti* in the Hindu tradition, but Father Stephens naturally wished to distinguish between the Hindu trinity and the Christian Trinity, so he devised a new word for the notion, *traikya*, which could roughly be translated back into a European language as 'oneness of three'. In the Hindu trinity, each of the three godheads or aspects might be worshipped separately.

6 Shanker Raamchandra Raajwaade, *Neetshechaa Khristaantak aani Khristaantak Neetshe* (Pune: Raajwaade, c. 1931). Raajwaade published the book himself. The book contains the translation of Nietzsche's *The Anti-Christ* and a commentary on it (longer than the translation itself). The title translates roughly as *Nietzsche's Anti-Christ and the Anti-Christ Nietzsche*, where *Khristaantak* literally means 'the annihilator of Christianity'. Referred to in all subsequent references as *Khristaantak*.

7 I give an example here, though it would be more useful to someone who knows both English and Marathi. The translation of 're-valuation of all values' in Raajwaade is '*sarva arthaanche arthaantarikaran*'. This is resourceful, because the word 'value' does not have an exact equivalent in Marathi, which would normally render it in a way that takes away the valencies of that word in English, rendering it as '*mahatva*' (importance, value; literally, in its Sanskritic origins, largeness, similar to 'mega'), or as a '*muulya*' (price, value). The word that Raajwaade uses is '*artha*', which has at least two meanings in Marathi, *meaning* and, in the context of economy and politics, it can even mean *money*. Economics, for example, is called *arthashaastra*, the science of *artha*. 'Revaluation' is rendered in a complex way: *artha-antari-karan*. Literally, this would mean 'rendering *artha* differently'.

8 Raajwaade, *Khristaantak*, pp. 7–8. The other parts were never published. Translations of all Marathi texts are mine.

9 *Veda Shaastra Sampanna* Vishnubhat Godse, *Maazaa Pravaas: 1857 cyaa bandaaci hakikat* (ed.), *Mahaamahopadhyaaya Saahityavaachaspati* Datto Vaman Potdar (Pune: Venus Prakashan, 1974), pp. 172–3.

10 Reginald G. Wilberforce, *An Unrecorded Chapter of the Indian Mutiny, Being the Personal Reminiscences of Reginald G. Wilberforce, Late 52nd Infantry, compiled from*

a Diary and Letters Written on the Spot (London: John Murray, 1884; facsimile reprint Gurgaon: The Academic Press, 1976), pp. 86–7.

11 *From Sepoy to Subedar, Being the Life and Adventures of Subedar Sita Ram, a Native Officer of the Bengal Native Army, Written and Related by Himself*, translated by Lieutenant-Colonel Norgate, ed. James Lunt (Delhi: Vikas Publications, 1970; first published, Bengal Staff Corps, Lahore, 1873), pp. 167–9. G. C. Spivak discusses another example of the shifting functions of authority in her essay 'Three Women's Texts and a Critique of Colonialism', in *The Feminist Reader: Essays in Gender and the Politics of Literary Criticism* (ed.) Catherine Belsey and Jane Moore (London: Macmillan, 1989).

12 Kwame Anthony Appiah, 'Is the Post- in Postmodernism the Post- in Postcolonialism?' in *Contemporary Postcolonial Theory: A Reader* (ed.), Padmini Mongia (London: Arnold, 1996), pp. 55–71.

13 This is evident in almost all of Phule's writings, some which are available in *Selected Writings of Jotirao Phule* (ed.) G. P. Deshpande (New Delhi: Leftword, 2002). It is interesting to note that Pierre Bourdieu's notion of symbolic capital is commonly used for describing the *acquisition*, rarely the *deployment*, or the results of that deployment.

Part III

The ethical text

Introduction

Elleke Boehmer and Rosinka Chaudhuri

A telling development in postcolonial studies worldwide across the first decade of the twenty-first century, was the shift away from issues of political resistance and overcoming per se, towards a greater concern with the ethical dimensions of inter-cultural contact and exchange, even while such criticism remained vigilant about the ongoing imperial project. This ethical shift bore the imprint of the newly ascendant critical discourses growing up in response to the changing crises and questions of the decade – trauma theory and holocaust studies (in response to Bosnia and Rwanda in particular), environmental debates, and related eco-critical discussions of the importance of inter-species relationality and interdependence, as well as a growing involvement on the part of postcolonial critics with the ideas of Jacques Derrida and Emmanuel Levinas on the absolute demands of the other upon the self. In particular, postcolonial critics explored the invitation of the postcolonial text to think as other, or to submit to the difference of the other's ideational world.

The following section, 'The ethical text', brings four well-known postcolonial practitioners into dialogue, who in their different chapters test and try out ethical questions as these have been expressed in Indian contexts, though not exclusively so. An interesting point of connection between the chapters is the emphasis that is placed on literary reading and writing as inciting or producing an ethical engagement, or on the ethical approach as a response that emerges from close engagement with a text. Reading for Spivak, to cite one instance, is sacred in so far as it offers a 'taste' of 'the impossible status of being figured as an object in the web of the other'. There is, relatedly, a noticeable sense of how productive the detachment of the ethical view from the political can be, combined with a palpable interest on the part of all the critical thinkers which is directed to the grainy and embedded Indian dimensions of the ethical questions they raise and discuss – 'the outer reaches of rural West Bengal' in one case, late nineteenth-century Christianized Kerala in another.

Gayatri Chakravorty Spivak begins the section by asserting, via Kant and then Levinas, that 'the discontinuities between the ethical and the epistemological and political fields can be staged by means of the play of logic and rhetoric in fiction'. She draws on the writing of Nobel prize-winners Tagore and Coetzee to consider how the 'I' is projected as object in their work, in particular through invocations of abjection and disgrace, and how important it is to come to terms with such objectification in order to carry out political work. In many ways, the status of both Tagore and Coetzee as twentieth-century world writers is incidental to the chapter. What connects them in Spivak's deft intertextual reading is their figuration or 'dis-figuration' of the object that subtends all knowing, or, in other words, of the disgraceful state which levels all equally, to which any community must be reduced before it can emerge renewed. The second half of the chapter speaks up first for literature's capacity for teaching the singular and the unverifiable, and then for the importance in any situation where democracy is to function, of the education of all equally (which would include an education in literature).

In a discussion of the body imaging of sages Sree Narayanan and Guru Kumaran Asan, Udaya Kumar's 'Self, body and inner sense' looks at the figuration of the self not so much through the other, in a philosophical sense, but through a somatic semiology, the sometimes controversial marking of the physical body with caste markers such as certain kinds of jewellery or the *melmundu* shawl for women, donned in order to aspire to greater spiritual status. On the premise that the spiritual self demands a representation of the worldly body, Kumar's reading of the late nineteenth-century Sree Narayanan and his disciple Kumaran Asan asserts a fluid identification on the part of the sage between individual body, community and human race. Different from Tagore or Coetzee in Spivak's interpretation, though not so different as to sever metonymic connections, for Kumar, 'the body functions as the model for conceiving collective effort'. It is also the prime site for social and spiritual redefinition.

Ringing further subtle changes on the ethical response as a channel towards developing a new polity, Rajeswari Sunder Rajan in her study of Gandhi's ethical imperatives, considers not only how Gandhi developed certain moral responses as a model for the conduct of political life but also, more specifically, how he himself introjected an ethics of giving and self-sacrifice in order to establish identification, to find ways of being one with the people. The bodies drawn into identification in this case are not of the pre-nation and the abjected body, as in Spivak, or of individual and community, as for Sree Narayanan, but of the voluntarily poor leader and the involuntarily poor mass. For such a leader, the rhetoric of moral rightness is established as a strategic means towards mass mobilization. Thus, Gandhi's chief concern was not so much with relating to a designated other as with losing his self in relating to the people, a goal he would share with Nehru, though their approaches towards it were divergent: Gandhi's 'absolute ethics' of giving without hope of return contrasted strongly with Nehru's more qualified ethics of responsibility to the people.

Finally, the famed Indian social psychologist Ashis Nandy in his ethical study of the limits of 'Humiliation' examines the different social and political gradients along which human degradation is experienced, both by those who humiliate and by the humiliated, in this way joining, with Spivak, an ongoing and genuinely transnational investigation of the ethical and psychological vocabularies for what Julia Kristeva in 1982 described as abjection.[1] He is especially interested in the controversial power the humiliated may be said to have over those who humiliate them and render them wretched, in so far as the humiliated must recognize their dishonour for it to be fully realized. Such concerns are especially acute in a globalized world, he claims, so neatly bridging over to the final section of the reader looking at global and cosmopolitan relations. This is because in such a world, he suggests, communities exist in closer and more frequent contact, melting-pot social relations are often assumed to obtain, and possibilities for insult multiply.

Nandy reaches beyond India's borders for illustrations with which to develop his case – citing, amongst other examples, Gandhi being insulted on the train in Pietermaritzburg, South Africa in the 1890s, and rape in Bosnia in the 1990s – yet the scenario of humiliation his argument repeatedly circles around is that of the Dalit–Savarna relationship in India, which is, he insists, endlessly iterable in any consideration of humiliation because it is both ineradicable and utterly dependent on the recognition of the humiliated – and hence a prime instance on which to rest his case. Indian social hierarchies depend on the ongoing and self-identified humiliation of the Dalit: the Dalit is in this sense indestructible, infinitely degradable, and yet indispensable.

Importantly for a *Critical Reader* exploring new inflections and adaptations of postcoloniality in India, Nandy specifically relates some of his questions in respect of human degradation to the post/colonial situation on the subcontinent. He asks if colonialism might be regarded as the ultimate situation of humiliation (with slavery as a further intensification), and queries as to whether colonialism might be said to have ended only when the former colonizers are more humiliated than the colonized by its mention. It is an interesting definition of postcoloniality, as is his suggestion that infantilization of the other is to colonialism, as the other's pathologization is to the postcolonial condition.

True to his reputation as a far-sighted postcolonial thinker, author of the influential theory of the 'intimate enemy' of colonized self-abnegation, Nandy concludes the chapter by taking on the once-controversial Hegelian theory of Octave Mannoni in *Psychologie du Colonialisme* (1950) concerning the colonized slave 'inviting' in some sense the colonial relationship with the master.[2] But he effectively sidesteps the problematic by proposing that in any master–servant relationship under colonialism, the servant internalizes both the master and the slave roles: s/he at one and the same time identifies with the aggressor and yet also refuses to identify, in that s/he sees that s/he as slave has ethical and cognitive superiority over the master.

Notes

1   See Julia Kristeva, *Power of Horror: An Essay on Abjection*, trans. Leon S. Roudiez (New York: Columbia University Press, 1982).
2   Ashis Nandy, *The Intimate Enemy: Loss and Recovery of Self under Colonialism* (London: Verso, 1983); Octave Mannoni, *Prospero and Caliban* (1950; Ann Arbor: University of Michigan Press, 2001).

9 Ethics and politics in Tagore, Coetzee and certain scenes of teaching[1]

Gayatri Chakravorty Spivak

It is practically persuasive that the eruption of the ethical interrupts and postpones the epistemological – the undertaking to construct the other as object of knowledge, an undertaking never to be given up. Lévinas is the generic name associated with such a position. This beautiful passage from *Otherwise than Being* lays it out, although neither interruption nor postponement is mentioned. That connection is made by Derrida.[2]

Here, then, is Lévinas, for whom Kant's critical perspectivization of the subject and the rigorous limits of pure theoretical reason seem to have been displaced by the structuralist hermeneutics of suspicion. For Lévinas, structuralism did not attend to what in Kant was the mechanism that interrupted the constrained and rigorous workings of pure reason: 'The interests that Kant discovered in theoretical reason itself, he subordinated to practical reason, become mere reason. It is just these interests that are contested by structuralism, which is perhaps to be defined by the primacy of theoretical reason'.[3]

The relationship between the postponement of the epistemological in Lévinas and the subordination of pure reason in Kant is a rich theme, beyond the scope of this chapter. Let us return to what Lévinas will perceive as a general contemporary hermeneutics of suspicion, related to the primacy of theoretical reason; 'The suspicions engendered by psychoanalysis, sociology and politics weigh on human identity such that we never know to whom we are speaking and what we are dealing with when we build our ideas on the basis of the human fact'.[4] The political calculus thematizes this suspicion into an entire code of strategy defined as varieties of game theory and rational choice. This can be verified across cultural difference, backwards through history, and in today's global academic discourse. Over against this Lévinas posits the ethical with astonishing humility: 'but we do not need this knowledge in the relationship in which the other is the one next to me [*le prochain*]'.

Kant thought that the ethical commonality of being (*gemeines Wesen* – repeatedly mistranslated as 'the ethical state') cannot form the basis of a state. Surprisingly, there is a clear line from the face-to-face of the ethical to the state in Lévinas.[5] It has long been my habit to scavenge and tinker in the field of practical philosophy. I will conserve from Kant the discontinuity between the ethical and the political, from Lévinas the discontinuity between the ethical and the epistemological. I will suggest that the discontinuities between the ethical and the epistemological and political fields can be staged by means of the play of logic and rhetoric in fiction.[6]

Enabled by such a suggestion, I can move to another bit of prose on that page in Lévinas: 'for reasons not at all transcendental but purely logical, the object-man must figure at the beginning of all knowing'.

The figure of the 'I' as object: this representation of the holy man in Lévinas does not match our colloquial and literal expectations. My general suggestion, that the procedure of fiction can give us a simulacrum of the discontinuities inhabiting (and operating?) the ethico-epistemic and the ethico-political, can, however, take such a figure on board. I will continue to want to say that fiction offers us an experience of the discontinuities that remain in place 'in real life'. That would be a description of fiction as an event – an indeterminate 'sharing' between writer and reader, where the effort of reading is to taste the impossible status of being figured as object in the web of the other. Reading, in this special sense, is sacred.

In this chapter I consider not only fiction as event but also fiction as task. I locate in Rabindranath Tagore (1861–1941) and J. M. Coetzee (1940–) representations of what may be read as versions of the 'I' figured as object and weave the representations together as a warning text for postcolonial political ambitions.[7] I am obviously using 'text' as 'web', coming from Latin *texere* – 'to weave'.

In the second part of the chapter I move into the field of education as a nation-building calculus. I examine planning as its logic and teaching as its rhetoric – in the strong sense of figuration.

On the cover of the first *Pratichi Education Report*, there is an artwork by Rabindranath Tagore, containing a poem, in English and Bengali, nestled in a tinted sketch, written and painted in Baghdad in 1932.[8] Here is the poem, in Tagore's own translation:

> The night has ended.
> Put out the light of the lamp of thine own narrow corner
>   smudged with smoke.
> The great morning which is for all appears in the East.
> Let its light reveal us to each other
> Who walk on the same path of pilgrimage.

The Bengali is slightly more active: *Nikhiler alo purba akashe jolilo punyodine / Ekshathe jara cholibe tahara shokolere nik chine.* The universe's light burns in the eastern sky on this blessed day/ Let those who'll walk together recognize each other. These lines resonate with what might be the mission statement of the moral entrepreneurship of the international civil society today, which, however laudable, is put together, not by democratic procedure, but largely by self-selection and networking. I am aware, of course, of the same forces at work in 'democracies'. But the presence of mechanisms of redress – electoral or constitutional – however remote, produces a faith in electoral education, which is useless if our faith is put entirely in self-selected international helpers.

'*Apoman*', the poem Tagore wrote more than twenty years before this, after reading Kshitimohan Sen's translations of Kabir, is much darker.[9] In this poem, Tagore uses the exact phrase 'human rights' – *manusher adhikar* – already at the beginning of the last century. What is to me more striking is that, instead of urging that human rights be immediately restored to the descendants of India's historical unfortunates, he makes a mysterious prediction, looking toward the historical future: '*apomane hote habe tahader shobar shoman*' – my unfortunate country, you will have to be equal in disgrace to each and every one of those you have disgraced millennially – a disgrace to which Kabir had responded.

How can this enigmatic sentence be understood? The idea of intertextuality, loosely defined, can be used to confront this question.

I will offer an anecdotal account of intertextuality. It will help us coast through Tagore's India, Coetzee's South Africa and the space of a tiny group of *adivasis*.[10]

In November 2002, Roald Hoffman, a Nobel Laureate chemist, gave a popular mini-lecture with slides in the basement of the Cornelia Street Café in New York. The topic was 'Movement in Constrained Spaces', by which Hoffman meant the incessant microscopic movement that goes on inside the human body to make it function. To prepare for his talk, he had asked a choreographer from neighbouring Princeton to choreograph a dance for the space of the stage, which is very small.[11] This is already intertextuality, where one text, Hoffman's, would make its point by weaving itself with another, the dance. A shot silk, as it were. Again, that venerable sense of text as in textile, and *texere* as weave.

The choreographer managed a pattern of exquisite and minute movements for two dancers, male and female, in that tiny space. But, at the back of the long and narrow bar, two singers, female and male, sang *La ci darem la mano* in full-throated ease. That wonderful aria from Mozart's *Don Giovanni*, sung with such force and skill, bought our choreographer the deep space of the bar, but also historical space – the space of an opera that has been heard and loved by millions for a few centuries. Yet her dancers gave something to Mozart as well. Full of lyric grace as a love song if heard by itself – a man telling his beloved the exquisite beauty of the place to which they will escape – *La ci darem* is, in context, a brutal seduction song of the most vicious class-fixed gendering, a gentleman seducing a confused farm girl only to fuck, and the audience sharing the joke. The two impish and acrobatic dancers on the diminutive stage, wittily partnering, gave the lie to the possibility of any such interpretation.

This is intertextuality, working both ways. Just as the chemist gave the dancer the lie, somewhat, for the movements *he* spoke of made the dance possible, so did the dancers give Mozart the lie by taking away his plot. Yet each gained something as well.

But in this case it did not work completely. Mozart is too elite for a radical New York audience. They did not catch the allusion. When the boring literary academic referred to it in a timid question, the choreographer melted in gratitude.

This *is* sometimes the task of the literary academic. To restore reference boringly in order that intertextuality may function; and to create intertextuality as well. In order to do a good job with the Tagore poem, I have to read Kabir carefully. And that will be another session with the fictive simulacrum of the helpless strength of the ethical.

J. M. Coetzee's novel *Disgrace* may be put in an intertextual relationship with Tagore's poem.[12] In representing *jare tumi niche felo she tomare bandhibe je niche* – the one you fling down will bind you down there – in rural South Africa, Coetzee offers an illustration of what that enigmatic prediction might mean: *'apomane hote hobe tahader shobar shoman'* – you will have to be equal in disgrace to all of them. Here too, intertextuality works two ways. Where Tagore alters his refrain in the last line: *mrityumajhe hobe tobe chitabhashshe shobar shoman* – you will then be equal to all of them in the ashes of death, thus predicting the death of a nation, Coetzee, writing an unsentimentally gendered narrative, makes his protagonist choose life. (I should add that Tagore's last stanza is somewhat more programmatic and asks for a call to all.)

Here is a plot summary of Coetzee's novel: David Lurie, a middle aged male professor, sentimental consumer of metropolitan sex-work, seduces a student, and is charged with sexual harassment by the appropriate committee. He refuses to utter the formulas that will get him off. He leaves the university and goes to his possibly lesbian daughter Lucy's flower farm. The daughter is raped and beaten by two young black men and he is himself beaten and badly burnt by them. The daughter is pregnant and decides to carry the child to term. One of the rapists turns up at the neighbouring farm and is apparently a relative of the owner. This farmer Petrus, already married, proposes a concubinage style marriage to Lucy. She accepts. The English Professor starts working for an outfit that puts unwanted dogs to sleep. He has a short liaison with the unattractive married woman who runs the outfit. He writes an operetta in a desultory way. He learns to love dogs and finally learns to give up the dog that he loves to the stipulated death.

These are some of the daughter Lucy's last words in the novel. Her father is ready to send his violated daughter back to her Dutch mother. Holland is the remote metropole for the Afrikaner:

> It is as if she has not heard him. 'Go back to Petrus', she says. 'Propose the following. Say I accept his protection. Say he can put out whatever story he likes about our relationship and I won't contradict him. If he wants me to be known as his third wife, so be it. As his concubine, ditto. But then the child becomes his too. The child becomes part of his family. As for the land, say I will sign the land over to him as long as the house remains mine. I will become a tenant on his land'. ... 'How humiliating', *he* says finally. ... 'yes, [she says] I agree, it is humiliating. But perhaps that is a good point to start from again. ... To start at ground level. With nothing. Not with nothing but. With nothing. No cards, no weapons, no property, no rights, no dignity'. (204–5; emphasis mine)

Apomane hote hobe tahader shobar shoman.

Insofar as *Disgrace* is a father–daughter story the intertextuality here is with *Lear*. If Lucy ends with nothing, Cordelia in the text of *King Lear* begins with the word 'nothing'. That word signifies the withholding of speech as an instrument for indicating socially inappropriate affective value. In Cordelia's understanding, to put love in the value-form – let me measure how much – is itself absurd.

Indeed, in the first impact of the word 'nothing' in the play, this protest is mimed in the clustering of silences in the short lines among the regular iambic pentameter lines. '*Cor.* Nothing, my lord. [six syllables of silence] / *Lear.* Nothing? [eight syllables of silence] / *Cor.* Nothing. [eight again] / *Lear.* Nothing will come of nothing: speak again' (1.1.87–90). The metre picks up and Cordelia speaks.

Now Cordelia shows that she is also a realist and knows that love in the value-form is what makes the world go around. She is made to chide her sisters for not thinking of the love due to their husbands: 'Why have my sisters husbands if they say/ They love you all?' (1.1.97–8).

Just as *Disgrace* is also a father–daughter story, so is *King Lear* also a play about dynastic succession in the absence of a son, not an unimportant topic in Jacobean England. It has been abundantly pointed out that the play's turnaround can be measured by the fact that 'the presence of Cordelia at the head of a French army ... marks the final horrific stage in the process by which Lear's division of the kingdom goes on turning the world upside down'.[13] Thus the love due to fathers bows to the love due to husbands and is then displaced, as it were. It is this story of fathers and husbands, and dynastic succession at the very inception of capitalist colonialism that *Disgrace* destabilizes, re-asking the question of the Enlightenment ('let those who will walk together get to know each other by the dawning universal *light*', says the cover of the *Pratichi Report*) with reference to the public sphere and the classed and gendered subject, when Lucy, 'perhaps' a lesbian, decides to carry the child of rape to term and agrees to 'marry' Petrus, who is not (one of) the biological father(s).

Lucy's 'nothing' is the same word but carries a different meaning from Cordelia's. It is not the withholding of speech protesting the casting of love in the value-form *and* giving it the wrong value. It is rather the casting aside of the affective value system attached to reproductive heteronormativity as it is accepted as the currency to measure human dignity. I do not think this is an acceptance of rape, but a refusal to be raped by instrumentalizing reproduction. Coetzee's Lucy is made to make clear that the 'nothing' is not to be itself measured as the absence of 'everything' by the old epistemico-affective value-form – the system of knowing-loving. It is not 'nothing but', Lucy insists. It is an originary 'nothing', a scary beginning. Why should we imagine that centuries of malpractice – *shotek shatabdir ashommanbhar* – can be conveniently undone by diversified committees, such as the one that 'tried' David Lurie for rape Enlightenment-style?[14]

'Unaccommodated man is no more but such a poor, bare, forked animal as thou art', Lear had said to Edgar's faked madness, erasing the place of the phallus: 'a poor, bare, *forked* animal'. What does it mean, in the detritus of colonialism, for one from the ruling race to call for interpella- tion as 'unaccommodated woman, a poor, bare, forked animal', and hold negotiating power without sentimentality in that very forkèdness? What if Lévinas's catachrestic holy man is a catachrestic holy woman, quite unlike the maternity that Lévinas embarrassingly places in the stomach in the passage from which I quoted? Is it a gendered special case, or can it claim generality, as making visible the difficulty of the postcolonial formula: a new nation. Neither *Lear* nor *Disgrace* is a blueprint for unmediated social policy. These are figures, asking for disfiguration, as figures must. And it is the representation of the 'I' as figured object – as woman relinquishing the child as property, as always, *and* as former colonizer in the ex-colony. This is how critique is operated through fictions.

I emphasize that it is not an equality in death – *mrityumajhe*. It is not the sort of equality that suicide bombing may bring. Suicidal resistance is a message inscribed in the body when no other means will get through. It is both execution and mourning, for both self and other, where you die with me for the same cause, no matter which side you are on, with the implica- tion that there is no dishonour in such shared and innocent death. That is an equality in disgrace brought about by the withholding of response, or a 'response' so disingenuously requiring duress as to be no response at all, as from Israel to Palestine.[15]

If Lucy is intertextual with *Lear*, Lurie is intertextual with Kafka's *The Trial*, a novel not about beginning with nothing, but ending like a dog when civil society crumbles.[16] Here is the end of *The Trial*, where Josef K.'s well-organized civil society gives way:

> Logic is no doubt unshakable, but it can't withstand a person who wants to live. Where was the judge he'd never seen? Where was the high court he'd never reached? He raised his hands and spread out all his fingers. But the hands of one man were right at K.'s throat, while the other thrust the knife into his heart and turned it there twice. With failing sight K. saw how the men drew near his face, leaning cheek-to-cheek to observe the verdict. 'Like a dog!' he said; it seemed as though the shame was to outlive him.

This is how Lurie understands Lucy's remarks about 'nothing but'. Not as a beginning in disgraceful equality but as the end of civil society (with the withdrawal of the colonizer?), where only shame is guaranteed continuity. This is a profound but typical misunderstanding. And this brings me to the second point about literature. The literary text gives rhetorical signals to the reader, which leads to activating the readerly imagination. Literature advocates in this special way. These are not the ways of expository prose. Literary reading has to be learned. Metaphor leans on concept and concept on metaphor, logic nestles in rhetoric, but they are not the same and one cannot be effaced in the other. If the social sciences describe the rules of the game, literary reading teaches how to play. One cannot be effaced in the other. This is too neat an opposition, of course. But for the moment, let it suffice as a rule of thumb.

What rhetorical signal does *Disgrace* give to the canny reader? It comes through the use of focalization, described by Mieke Bal as 'the relation between the vision and that which is "seen"'.[17] This term is deemed more useful than 'point of view' or 'perspective' because it emphasizes the fluidity of narrative – the impression of (con)sequence as well as the transactional nature of reading.

Disgrace is relentless in keeping the focalization confined to David Lurie. Indeed, this is the vehicle of the sympathetic portrayal of David Lurie. When Lucy is resolutely denied focalization, the reader is provoked, for he or she does not want to share in Lurie-the-chief-focalizer's inability to 'read' Lucy as patient and agent. No reader is content with acting out the failure of reading. This is the rhetorical signal to the active reader, to counterfocalize. This shuttle between focalization and the making of an alternative narrative as the reader's running commentary, as it were, used to be designated by the prim phrase 'dramatic irony' when I was an undergraduate. You will see immediately how much more effortful and active this counterfocalization is than what that older term can indicate.

This provocation into counterfocalization is the 'political' in political fiction – the transformation of a tendency into a crisis.[18]

When Lurie asks, after Lucy's impassioned speech, 'Like a dog?' Lucy simply agrees, 'Yes, like a dog'. She does not provide the explanation that the reader who can work the intertextuality will provide. *Lear* and *The Trial* are not esoteric texts. We can sense the deep contradiction of a split understanding of postcoloniality here: between the risk of beginning with nothing and the breakdown of civil societies. If not, we can at least see that Lurie literalizes her remark and learns to love dogs as the other of being-human, as a source, even, of ethical lessons of a special sort. He is staged as unable to touch either the racial or the gendered other. These may be Lucy's last words, but the novel continues, focalizing Lurie loving dogs, avoiding bathos only by his obvious race-gender illiteracy, as we counterfocalize the absent Lucy.

Literary reading teaches us to learn from the singular and the unverifiable. It is not that literary reading does not generalize. It is just that those generalizations are not on evidentiary ground. In this area, what is known is proved by *vyavahāra*, or setting-to-work. Martin Luther King, in his celebrated speech 'Beyond Vietnam', given on 4 April 1967 in Riverside Church, had tried to imagine the other again and again. In his own words, '[p]erhaps the more difficult but no less necessary task is to speak for those who have been designated as our enemies. ... Surely we must understand their feelings even if we do not condone their actions'.[19]

Here is a setting-to-work of what in the secular imagination is the literary impulse: to imagine the other who does not resemble the self. King, being a priest, had put it in terms of liberation theology, in the name of 'the one who loved his enemies so fully that he died for them'. For the secular imagination, that transcendental narrative is just that, a narrative, singular and unverifiable. When it is set to work, it enters the arena of the probable: King's imagination of the Viet Cong. I believe this is why Aristotle said *poiesis* or making-in-fiction was *philosophoteron* – a better instrument of knowledge – than *historia* – because it allowed us to produce the probable rather than account for that which has been possible.

In my words on suicide bombing, I was trying to follow Dr King's lead halfway, use the secular imagination as emancipatory instrument. When I was a graduate student, on the eve of the Vietnam War, I lived in the same house as Paul Wolfowitz, the ferocious Deputy Secretary of Defense who was the chief talking head for the war on Iraq. He was a Political Science undergraduate, disciple of Allan Bloom, the conservative political philosopher. As I have watched him on television lately, I have often thought that if he had had serious training in literary reading and/or the imagining of the enemy as human, his position on Iraq would not be so inflexible. This is not a verifiable conviction; but it is in view of such hopes that humanities teaching acts itself out.

To repeat: literature is not verifiable. The only way a reading establishes itself – without guarantees – is by sharing the steps of the reading. That is the experience of the impossible, ethical discontinuity shaken up in a simulacrum. Unless you take a step with me, there will be no interdisciplinarity, only the tedium of turf battles.

Insofar as Lucy is a figure that makes visible the rational kernel of the institution of marriage – rape, social security, property, human continuity – we can check her out with Herculine Barbin, the nineteenth-century hermaphrodite who committed suicide but left a memoir, which Foucault edited and made available.

Herculine Barbin was a scholar – a diligent student who became a schoolmistress. But when she was named a man by doctors she could not access the scholarly position – of writing and speaking to a general public – that Kant secures for the enlightened subject in 'What is Enlightenment?'.[20]

Let us look at Herculine/Abel's cautious elation at the moment of entry into the world of men:

> So, it was done [*C'en était donc fait*]. Civil status called me to belong henceforth to that half of the human race that is called the strong sex [*L'état civil m'appelait à faire partie désormais de cette moitié du genre humain, appelé le sexe fort*]. I, who had been raised until the age of twenty-one in religious houses, among shy [*timides*] female companions, was going to leave behind me a past entirely delightful [*tout un passé délicieux*], like Achilles, and enter the lists, armed with my weakness alone and my profound inexperience of men and things![21]

It is this hope – of entering the public sphere as the felicitous subject – that is dashed as the possibility of agency is annulled in suicide (98).

Barbin cannot articulate the relationship between the denial of agency and the incapability to reproduce. Yet, Tiresias-like, he offers a critical account of marriage:

> It has been given to me, as a man, the most intimate and deep knowledge of all the aptitudes, all the secrets, of the female character. I read in that heart, as in an open book. I count every beat of it. In a word, I have the secret of its strength and the measure of its weakness; and just for that reason I would make a detestable husband; I also feel that all my joys would be poisoned in marriage and that I would cruelly abuse, perhaps, the immense advantage that would be mine, an advantage that would turn against me (107; translation modified).

I presented 'Can the Subaltern Speak?' as a paper over twenty-five years ago. In that paper I suggested that the subaltern could not 'speak' because, in the absence of institutionally validated agency, there was no listening subject. My listening, separated by space and time, was perhaps an ethical impulse. But I am with Kant in thinking that such impulses do not lead to the political. There must be a presumed collectivity of listening and countersigning subjects and agents in the public sphere for the subaltern to 'speak'. Herculine Barbin wrote abundantly, presuming a reader repeatedly. And yet she could not speak. Her solution would be the normalization of the multi-sexed subject, a civil and agential rather than subjective solution. There would then be a listening public who could countersign her 'speech act'.

In the arrangement of counterfocalization within the validating institution of the novel in English, the second half of *Disgrace* makes the subaltern speak, but does not presume to give 'voice', either to Petrus or Lucy. This is not the novel's failure, but rather a politically fastidious awareness of the limits of its power. By the general dramatically ironic presentation of Lurie, he is shown to 'understand' Petrus by the neat reversal of the master–slave dialectic without sublation: 'Petrus needs him not for pipefitting or plumbing but to hold things, to pass him tools – to be his *handlanger*, in fact. The role is not one he objects to. Petrus is a good workman, it is an education to watch him. It is Petrus himself that he is beginning to dislike' (136–7). Once again, the novel and Lurie part company, precisely on the issue of reading, of control. This is a perfectly valid reading, as is the invocation of the end of Kafka's *The Trial* to describe the difficult birth of the new nation. And it is precisely this limited perfect validity of the liberal white ex-colonizer's understanding that *Disgrace* questions through the invitation to focalize the enigma of Lucy. Petrus's one-liner on Lucy shows more kinship with the novel's verdict: '"She is a forward-looking lady, not backward-looking"' (136). If we, like Lurie, ignore the enigma of Lucy, the novel, being fully focalized precisely by Lurie, can be made to say every racist thing.[22] Postcoloniality from below can then be reduced to the education of Pollux, the young rapist who is related to Petrus. Counterfocalized, it can be acknowledged as perhaps the first moment in Lucy's refusal of rape by generalizing it into all heteronormative sexual practice: '"When it comes to men and sex, David, nothing surprises me any more. … They spur each other on…." "And the third one, the boy?" "He was there to learn"' (158–9). The incipient bathos of Lurie's literalism ('like a dog' means love dogs; forgiveness from Melanie's parents means prostrating himself on the floor before them (173); loving dogs means letting one of them into the operetta (215); even the possibility that the last Christian scene of man giving up dog may slide into a rictus,[23] given the overarching narrative context) can be seen, in a reading that ignores the function of Lucy in the narrative, as the novel's failure, rather than part of its rhetorical web.

I want now to come to the second way in which Tagore's refrain can be understood: the failure of democracy.

The Pratichi Trust in India, to whose *Report* I have referred above, is doing astute work because it realizes that, if the largest sector of the electorate misses out on early education, democracy cannot function, for it then allows the worst of the upper sectors to flourish. Democracy sinks to that level and we are all equal in disgrace. When we read statistics on who wins and who loses the elections, the non-specialist located middle class as well as the rest of the world, if it cares, thinks it shows how the country thinks. No. In the largest and lowest sector of the electorate, there is a considerable supply of affect, good and bad; there is native sharpness and there is acquired cunning. But there is no rational choice. Election does not even pretend to be based on rational platforms. (This applies to the United States as well, in another way. But it would take me too far to develop that here.) Gendering must be understood simply here: female teachers are preferred, though they have less authority; gendering presuppositions must be changed through education, and so on.

There is little I can add to the Trust's magisterial work. After a general caution, that work in this sphere runs the risk of structural atrophy, like diversified committees in *Disgrace*, and therefore must be interrupted by the ethical, I will add a few codicils here and there.

Professor Sen, the founder of the Trust, supports the state in opposing 'the artificially generated need for private tuition', artificial because generated by careless non-teaching in the free primary schools.[24] While the state waits to implement this opposition legally, I have been trying to provide free collective 'private tuition' to supplement the defunct primary schools, to a tiny sector of the most disenfranchised. It is my hope that private tuition in this form can be nationalized and thus lose its definition. I will ask some questions in conclusion, which will make the direction of my thoughts clear. The one-on-one of 'private' tuition – at the moment in the service of rote learning that cannot relate to the nurturing of the ethical impulse – is the only way to undo the abdication of the politically planned 'public' education. 'Private tuition', therefore, is a relation to transform rather than prohibit. The tutorial system at the other end of the spectrum – the prestigious institutions of tertiary education in the Euro-US – is proof of this.

I must repeat that I am enthralled by the report and whatever I am adding is in the nature of a supplement from a literary person. The work of the Trust is largely structural. The humanities – training in literary reading in particular – is good at textural change. Each discipline has its own species of 'setting to work' – and the texture of the imagination belongs to the teacher of literary reading. All good work is imaginative, of course. But the humanities have little else.

There is a tiny exchange on page 69 of the book: 'On the day of our visit [to a school in Medinipur], we interviewed four children of Class 4 … Well, can you tell us something about what was taught? All four children were silent'.

Part of the silence rises from the very class apartheid that bad rural education perpetuates.[25] The relationship between the itinerant inspector and the child is, in addition, hardly ethical.

Training in literary reading can prepare one to work at these silences. I will submit an example which would be useless to translate here. It is lesson 5 from *Amader Itihash*, a Class 4 history book, specifically devoted to national liberation, one item, which is the story of Nelson Mandela. Let us overlook the implicit misrepresentation of Gandhi's role in Mandela's political victory in the lifting of apartheid, or the suggestive detail that the section on national liberation starts with George Washington. One cannot, however, overlook, if one is a reader of Bengali, the hopeless ornamentation of the prose, incomprehensible to teacher and student alike at the subaltern level, in the outer reaches of rural West Bengal. The point is not only to ask for 'a radically enhanced set of commitments' 'from the primary teachers', as the *Report* stresses. The real disgrace of rural primary education is that even the *good* teacher, with the best will in the world, has been so indoctrinated into rote learning that, even if s/he could understand the lugubrious prose and even if s/he had retained or imbibed enough general knowledge of the world – both doubtful propositions – the technique of emphasizing meaning is not what s/he would understand by teaching. Elsewhere I have emphasized this as the systematic difference in teaching between *baralok* and *chhotolok* – translated by Pratichi as high-born and low-born, brave attempts – *gatar khatano* and *matha khatano* – manual labour and intellectual labour does not quite translate the active sense of *khatano* – setting to work, then, of the body alone, and not of the mind as well – that keeps class apartheid alive. The common sight of a child of the rural poor trying to make the head engage in answer to a textbook question and failing is as vivid a figure of withholding humanity as anything in Tagore or Coetzee. The 'silence' is active with pain and resentment.

The solution is not to write new textbooks, the liberal intellectuals' favourite option. The teachers at this level do not know how to use a book, any book, however progressive. Many of the textbooks, for instance, have a list of pedagogic goals at the top of each lesson. The language of these lists is abstract, starting with the title: *shamortho*, capacity. Sometimes, for nine or ten lessons in a row, this abstract title is followed by the remark: 'see previous lesson'. No primary or non-formal teacher over the last 23 years has ever noticed this in my presence, and, when informed of the presence of this pedagogic machinery, been able to understand it, let alone implement it. Given the axiomatics of the so-called education within which the teacher has received what goes for training, it is foolish to expect implementation.

There are progressive textbooks that try to combine Bengali and arithmetic – the famous *Kajer Pata*. This combination causes nothing but confusion in student and teacher alike on this level. And frankly, it serves no specific purpose here. There are also books where some metropolitan liberal or a committee of them tries to engage what they think is a rural audience. I wish I had the time to recount the failure of their imagination case by case. There is no possibility of the emergence of the ethical when the writing subject's sense of superiority is rock solid. The useless coyness of these failed attempts would be amusing if the problem were not so disgraceful. Both Hindu and Muslim poets are included – communalism must be avoided at all costs, of course. The point is lost on these children – though a sort of equality is achieved. All poetry is equally opaque, occasions for memorization without comprehension, learning two-way meanings – what does *a* mean? *b*; and what is *b*? *a*, of course. The meaning of meaning is itself compromised for these children, these teachers. A new textbook drowns in that compromise.

Two girls, between eleven and fifteen years of age, show me what they are being taught in primary school. It is the piece about South Africa. I ask them some questions. They have absolutely no clue at all what the piece is about, as they don't about any piece in the book, about any piece in any book. To say 'they haven't understood this piece' would be to grant too much. The girls are not unintelligent. Indeed, one of them is, I think, strikingly intelligent. They tell me their teachers would go over the material again the next day.

The next day after school, we meet again. Did the teachers explain? 'Reading *poriyechhe*', is the answer – an untranslatable Bengali phrase for which there are equivalents in all the major Indian languages, no doubt. 'They made us read reading' would perhaps convey the absurdity? Any piece is a collection of discrete spelling exercises to be read in a high drone with little regard to punctuation. The scandal is that everyone knows this. It is embarrassing to put it in a writing about Tagore and Coetzee. It is better to present social scientific surveys in English. This too is a way of disgracing the disenfranchised.

To continue with the narrative: after the girls' answer begins the process of explaining. As I have already mentioned, the experience of a head attempting but failing to set itself to work is killingly painful. Most of us interrupt such silences with noise, speak up and create a version of explanation to break the experience. At that point we think we are teaching although no teaching is taking place. Sometimes we learn to resist this by excruciating self-control that often fails.

In *Foe*, another novel by J. M. Coetzee, there is a moment when a character called Friday (as in *Robinson Crusoe*), an abducted savage with his tongue cut out, resists the attempt of the white woman to teach him how to write.[26] Varieties of such resistance in the ground-level rural classroom can be read as the anger of the intelligent child not being able to work his or her head. Such readings are necessarily off the mark. But the literary critic is practised in learning from the unverifiable.

If the older girl was just frustrated by not grasping at all what I was trying to explain, the younger one, the strikingly intelligent one, faced me with that inexorably closed look, jaws firmly set, that reminds one of Friday, withholding. No response to repeated careful questions going over the same ground over and over again, simplifying the story of Nelson Mandela further at every go. These are students who have no concept or percept of the neighbouring districts, of their own state of West Bengal – because, as the *Pratichi Report* points out, they have arrived at Class 4 through neglect and no teaching. How will they catch the reference to Africa?

Into the second hour, sitting on the floor in that darkening room, I tried another tack. Forget Africa, try *shoman adhikar* – equal rights. It was impossible to explain rights in a place with no plumbing, pavement, electricity, stores, without doors and windows. Incidentally, do people really check – rather than interrupt the painful experience of having failed to teach – the long-term residue of so-called legal awareness seminars? What is learnt through repeated brushes with the usual brutality of the rural judiciary is not significantly changed by the conviction that the benevolent among the masters will help them litigate. What is it to develop the subject – the capital I – of human rights, rather than a feudal dispensation of human rights breeding dependency and litigious blackmail and provoking a trail of vendetta in those punishers punished remotely? Let us return to the schoolroom in gathering dusk.

It is common sense that children have short attention spans. I was so helpless in my inability to explain that I was tyrannizing the girls. At the time it seemed as if we were locked together in an effort to let response emerge and blossom with its own energy. The ethical as task rather than event is effortful. And perhaps an hour and a half into the struggle, I put my hand next to the bright one's purple-black hand to explain apartheid. Next to that rich colour this pasty brown hand seemed white. And to explain *shoman adhikar*, equal rights, Mandela's demand, a desperate formula presented itself to me: *ami ja, tumi ta* – what I, that you. Remember this is a student, not an asylum seeker in the metropole, in whose name many millions of dollars are moved around even as we speak.[27] This is just two students, accepting oppression as normality, understanding their designated textbook.

Response did emerge. Yesses and noes were now given; even, if I remember right, a few words uttered as answers to questions. In a bit I let them go.

The next morning I asked them to set down what they remembered of the previous day's lesson. The older one could call up nothing. The younger one, the more intelligent one, produced this: *'ami ja, tumi ta, raja here gachhe'* – what I, that you, the king was defeated. A tremendous achievement in context but, if one thinks of all the children studying under the West Bengal Board, including the best students from the best schools in Kolkata, with whom these girls are competing, this is a negligible result. I have no doubt that even this pitiful residue of the content of the lesson is now long lost and forgotten.

The incident took place about 10 years ago. The two girls would have been young women now, in high school. Speaking to them and their teachers in December, I stressed repeatedly the importance of explaining the text, of explaining repeatedly, of checking to see if the student has understood. A futile exercise. You do not teach how to play a game by talking about it. No one can produce meanings of unknown words. There are no dictionaries, and, more important, no habit of consulting dictionaries.

As I continued with the useless harangue, I said, 'as two of you might remember, I spent two hours explaining Nelson Mandela to you some years ago. It is important to explain'. A fleeting smile, no eye contact, passed across the face of the bright one, sitting in the last row. It is unusual for such signals to pass from her class to mine.[28]

The number of calculative moves to be made and sustained in the political sphere, with the deflecting and overdetermined calculus of the vicissitudes of gendered class-mobility factored in at every stop, in order for the irony-shared-from-below communication to be sustained at this level, would require immense systemic change. Yet, in the supplementary relationship between the possibility of that fleeting smile – a sign of the interruptive emergence of the ethical – and the daunting labour of the political calculus, we must begin with the end, which must remain the possibility of the ethical. That inconvenient effort is the uncertain ground of every just society. If the political calculus becomes the means *and* the end, justice is ill served and no change will stick. The peculiar thing about gendering is that, in Lucy's vision of 'starting with nothing', in the reproductive situation shorn of the fetishization of property, in the child given up as body's product, the ethical moment can perhaps emerge – at least so the fiction says.[29]

I have recounted this narrative to make clear that although on the literary register, the register of the singular and the unverifiable (this story, for example, is unverifiable because you have nothing but my testimony), the suggestive smile, directed by indirection and a shared experience, is a good event; it has no significance in terms of the public sphere, to which education should give access. The discontinuity between the ethical and the political is here instrumentalized – between the rhetoric of pedagogy and the logic of its fruition in the public sphere. For the smile of complicity to pass between the *adivasi* and the caste-Indian, unprovoked, marks an immense advance. But it is neither a beginning nor an end, only an irreducible grounding condition.

When I was attempting to teach in that darkening room, I had no thought but to get through. It so happened that the topic was *shoman-adhikar*, equal rights. Writing this for you, on the other hand, I put myself grandiosely in Tagore's poem: *manusher odhikare bonchito korechho jaare, shommukhe danraye rekhe tobu kole dao nai sthan* – those whom you have deprived of human rights, whom you have kept standing face-to-face and yet not taken in your arms. So, spending considerable skill and labour, to teach precisely the meaning of *shomanadhikar*, was I perhaps undoing the poet's description of the behaviour of the Hindu historical dominant, denying human rights over centuries to the outcastes (today's *dalits*) and *adivasis*? The point I am laboriously making is that it is not so. Although the literary mode of instruction activates the subject, the capital I, in order to be secured it must enter the political calculus of the public sphere. Private voluntarism such as mine remains a mongrel practice between the literary and the rational, rhetoric and logic.

And so the reader of literature asks the social scientists a question. Is it not possible for the globally beleaguered state to institute civil service positions that will call, on a regular and optional basis, upon interested humanities professionals from the highest ranks to train ground-level teachers, periodically, yet with some continuity, gradually integrating and transforming the existing training structure, thus to deconstruct or sublate private tuition and slowly make it less possible for 'a teacher of [sic] Birbhum village' to say: 'How can we carry over the training to our classrooms? *Baro baro katha bala soja* – Talking big is easy'.[30]

Before I had started thinking about the heritage of 'disgrace', I had tried to initiate the production of same-language dictionaries in the major Indian languages, specifically for ground-level teachers and students. It came to nothing, because the situation was not imaginable by those whom I had approached, and because the NRI (Non Resident Indian, Indian designation for diasporics) has other kinds of uses. Should the NRI have no role but to help place the state in metropolitan economic bondage? Is it not possible to think of subaltern single-language dictionaries as an impor-tant step toward fostering the habit of freedom – the habit of finding a meaning for oneself, whoever suggests this? Is it not possible to think, not of writing new textbooks, but of revising what is now in existence – to make them more user-friendly for the least privileged, even as such teachers and students are texturally engaged? I do not believe the more privileged child would suffer from such a change, though I can foresee a major outcry. It must be repeated, to foster such freedom is simply to work at freedom in the sphere of necessity, otherwise ravaged by the ravages of political economy – no more than 'the grounding condition [*Grundbedingung*] for the true realm of freedom', always around the corner.[31]

Shakespeare, Kafka, Tagore, Coetzee, Amartya Sen. Heavy hitters. My questions are banal. I am always energized by that paragraph in the third volume of *Capital* from which I quote above, and where Marx writes, in a high philosophical tone: 'the true realm of freedom, the development of human powers as an end in itself begins beyond [the realm of necessity], though it can only flourish with this realm of necessity as its ground'. That sentence is followed by this one: 'the reduction of the working day is its grounding condition'. In Marx's text, philosophy must thus displace itself into the everyday struggle. In my argument, literature, in so far as it is in the service of the emergence of the critical, must also displace itself thus. Its task is to foster yet another displacement: into a work for the remote possibility of the precarious production of an infrastructure, that can in turn produce a Lucy or her focalizer, figuring forth an equality that takes disgrace in its stride.

Notes

1 This chapter was first presented as a paper at the Centre for Studies in Social Sciences in Kolkata on 10 February 2003 and subsequently published in *Diacritics*, 32, no. 3–4 (December 2002).

2 Jacques Derrida, *Adieu to Emmanuel Lévinas*, tr. Pascale-Anne Brault and Michael Naas (Stanford: Stanford University Press, 1999), pp. 51–9.

3 Emmanuel Lévinas, *Otherwise than Being: Or Beyond Essence*, tr. Alphonso Lingis (Pittsburgh: Duquesne University Press, 1981), p. 58; translation modified.

4 Derrida 1999, p. 59; translation modified. There is a footnote in the text to Paul Ricoeur's *Conflict of Interpretations*, tr. Don Ihde (Evanston: Northwestern University Press, 1974), p. 99. The next quoted passage is from the same page.

5 See Derrida 1999, pp. 29–33 for a discussion of this.

6 I first learned to notice this from Derrida's article 'White Mythology' whose subtitle is 'Metaphor in the Text of Philosophy' (*Margins of Philosophy*, tr. Alan Bass, Chicago: University of Chicago Press, 1982), pp. 209–71.

7 This paper (chapter) was first given as a Deuskar lecture at the Centre for Studies in Social Sciences in Kolkata, India. In the second lecture of the series, I offered a reading of Salman Rushdie's *Midnight's Children* as a President Schreber-style critique of postcolonial political ambitions.

8 Pratichi (India) Trust, *The Pratichi Education Report*, Introduction, Amartya Sen (Delhi: TLM Books, 2002).

9 Rabindranath Tagore, Poem No. 108, *Gitanjali*, 20 Ashadh 1317 BE (i.e. approximately 1910). The title 'Apoman' would have been acquired at a later stage, as the poems in *Gitanjali* had no titles. Kshitimohan Sen's Bengali translations of Kabir were read & discussed by Rabindranath well before he published his own English translations of them. See Rabindranath Tagore, *Kabir, Songs of Kabir*, tr. from Kshitimohan Sen (New York: Macmillan, 1915).

10 *Adivasi* is the name used commonly for so-called Indian 'tribals', by general account the inhabitants of India at the time of the arrival of Indo-European speakers in the second millennium BC.

11 Diann Sichel, 'Mass, Momentum and Energy Transport (Living Space)', Dancers: Josiah Pearsall, Melanie Velo-Simpson, Singers: Wendy Baker, Erik Kroncke.

12 J. M. Coetzee, *Disgrace* (New York: Viking, 2000).

13 William Shakespeare, *King Lear* (Cambridge, MA: Harvard University Press, 1959), Arden Edition, p. 141.

14 For an analysis of this rhetorical question, see Rosalind C. Morris, 'The Mute and the Unspeakable: Political Subjectivity, Violent Crime, and "the Sexual Thing" in a South African Mining Community', in *Law and Disorder in the Postcolony* (eds), Jean and John Comaroff (Chicago: University of Chicago Press, 2006), pp. 57–101.

15 Since 1983, when I delivered 'Can the Subaltern Speak?' as a lecture at the Summer Institute at the University of Illinois in Champaign-Urbana, I have been interested in suicide as envoi. Partha Chatterjee reminded me in conversation (31 October 2003) that the 'cause' is metaleptically constructed by the suicide, as the effect of an 'effect'. My point is that Lucy is not represented as the 'subject' of a 'cause'. Her representation may be read as Lévinas's object-human as the figure that subtends all knowing, including the cognition of a cause. About suicide bombing I speculate at greater length in 'Terror: A Speech After 9/11', *boundary*, 2, 31.2 (2004), pp. 81–111; reprinted in Italian translation in *aut aut* 329 (January/March 2006), pp. 6–46.

16 Franz Kafka, *The Trial*, tr. Breon Mitchell (New York: Schocken Books, 1998). The quoted passage is from page 231.

17 Mieke Bal, *Narratology: Introduction to the Theory of Narrative* (Toronto: University of Toronto Press, 1985), p. 100.

18 Karl Marx uses this to describe why the tendency of the rate of profit to fall does not result in increasingly lower profits (*Capital: A Critique of Political Economy*, tr. David Fernbach, New York: Vintage, 1981, vol. 3, pp. 365–6 *passim*).

19 *Black Protest: History, Documents and Analyses, 1619 to the Present* (ed.), Joanne Grant, 2nd edn, Greenwich, CT: Fawcett, 1974, pp. 418–25.

20 Immanuel Kant, 'An Answer to the Question: What is Enlightenment?', in *Practical Philosophy*, tr. and ed. Mary J. Gregor (Cambridge, UK: Cambridge Univ. Press, 1996).

21 *Herculine Barbin: Being the Recently Discovered Memoirs of a Nineteenth-Century French Hermaphrodite* [no tr. given] (New York: Pantheon,1980), p. 89, translation modified.

22 For a debate over such readings, see Peter D. McDonald, '*Disgrace* Effects', and David Attwell, 'Race in *Disgrace*', in *Interventions* 4.3 (2002), pp. 321–41.

23 This possibility of an uneasy snigger (as well as the 'giving up' at the end of Coetzee's novel) may mark something irreducible, the seeming 'abyss' – we think also of the incessant back-and-forth of the abyssal – between the 'I' of the 'I think' and the presumed self-identity of the animal: 'This automotricity as auto-affection and self-relation, before the discursive thematic of a statement or an *ego cogito*, indeed of a *cogito ergo sum*, is the character recognized in the living and in animality in general. But between that self-relationship (that Self, that *ipseity*) and the *I* of the "I think" there is, it seems, an abyss' (Derrida, 'L'animal que donc je suis [à suivre]', in Marie-Louise Mallet (ed.) *L'animal autobiographique*, Paris: Galilée, 1999, p. 300). It is possible that the dull effort of a cogitative Lurie has an abyssality that must not be forgotten as we attempt to acknowledge the enigmatic historiality of the mixed-race postcolonial child of rape deliberately given up as property for the adopted father, Black Christian, a Petrus upon which rock the future, guaranteeing tenancy for the colonial

turned native, is founded. It is not the object-human as a figure with nothing that comes before all else, but the look of the naked *animot* (a word that the reader must learn from the essay by Derrida I have already cited; a word [*mot*] that marks the irreducible heterogeneity of animality). This is Derrida's critique of Lévinas. I have often felt that the formal logic of Coetzee's fiction mimes ethical moves in an uncanny way. The (non)relationship between the cogitation of animality and the setting-to-work of gendered postcolonialism in *Disgrace* may be such an uncanny miming. The 'dull decrepitude' of the former is where equality in disgrace is impossible, we cannot disgrace the *animot*. It is the limit of *apomane hote habe tahader shobar shoman*; and to call it a limit is to speak from one side. Since my ethical texts are Kant, Lévinas, Derrida, and my fictions are 'Apoman' (Tagore, *Gitanjali*, tr. Joe Winters, Kolkata: Writers' Workshop, 1998, pp. 140–1), *Disgrace*, and the uncoercive rearrangement of desire, I have not considered J. M. Coetzee's staged specu- lations about animality and the human in 'Lives of Animals' (in Amy Gutmann (ed.), *The Lives of Animals*, Princeton: Princeton University Press, 1999).

24 *Pratichi Education Report*, p. 10.
25 I have developed the idea of the role of rural education in maintaining class apartheid in 'Righting Wrongs', in *Other Asias* (Boston: Blackwell, 2008).
26 J. M. Coetzee, *Foe* (New York: Penguin, 1986).
27 Clyde Prestowitz, *Rogue Nation: American Unilateralism and the Failure of Good Intentions* (New York: Basic Books, 2003) argues that the US wants to make everyone American and there left and right meet. The same, I think, can now be said of Europe. This is too big a topic to develop here. What I urge in the text is the need to imagine a world that is not necessarily looking for help.
28 She died in 2003 of encephalitis. Her name was Shamoli Sabar. She is memo- rialized in figure 2 of my 'Righting Wrongs' (in Nicholas Owen (ed.), *Human Rights, Human Wrongs*, Oxford: Oxford University Press, 2003). She was one of the signatories of the petition. I offer this chapter to her memory.
29 We have to have an idea of how fiction can be made to speak through the transactional heading beyond the limits of the author's authority, which would expose the frivolousness of a position such as Rajat Ray's in *Exploring Emotional History: Gender, Mentality, and Literature in the Indian Awakening* (New Delhi: Oxford Univ. Press, 2001), pp. 79, 115 n.28.
30 *Pratichi Education Report*, p. 68.
31 Karl Marx, *Capital*, vol. 3, tr. David Fernbach (New York: Vintage, 1981), p. 959.

10 Self, body and inner sense

Some reflections on Sree Narayana Guru and Kumaran Asan

Udaya Kumar

I

In his autobiography, C. Kesavan recounts a story from the end of the nineteenth century. The story is that of his mother-in-law wearing a blouse for the first time:

> My sister-in-law used to live in Trivandrum. Women used to wear blouses there, and she also began wearing them. My misfortune, when she came home, she brought me a couple of blouses. Two glittering blouses. How the blouse suited her! I also liked the blouses, and wore one at once. It looked good, but I felt ticklish wearing it. I took it off, folded it carefully, and brimming with enthusiasm, showed it to my mother. She gave me a stern look and said, 'Where are you going to gallavant in this? Fold it and keep it in the box'. She did not look cheerful in the least. I was scared of my mother. She could kill me. At night I wore the blouse and showed it to my husband. He said it looked good, and told me that I could wear it. ... He left in the morning. In my innocence, I came out wearing the blouse. Twisting and turning, I looked at myself; how lovely it looked. ... I stood there immersed in a daydream. I didn't notice my mother coming. Suddenly I heard her break a piece from a coconut branch. When I turned around, she was behind me, fierce and furious. 'Take it off, you slut!', she said, 'you want to walk around in shirts like Muslim women?' And, my God, she started beating me. ... Scared of her blows, I took off my blouse that day. But I was determined as well. If my mother did not like it, my husband liked it. During the day, I did not wear the blouse, but the night was mine. When I knew that my mother had slept, I used to take out the blouse and wear it. My husband used to come only very late, like a *gandharva*.[1]

To understand the nuances of this story would be to recognize several strands of transformations that make the end of the last century a crucial turning point in the history of modern subjectivity in Kerala. Some external markers of this transition can be seen in the last two decades of the nineteenth century. Sree Narayana Guru's consecration of the temple at Aruvippuram, the publication of the first modern Malayalam novel *Indulekha*, the submission of the Malayali Memorial and the proceedings of the Malabar Marriage Commission are among them.[2] This period also marks a new articulation of forms of subjectivity, both in terms of doctrines and practices. Caste provided the primary grid for differentiation in nineteenth-century Kerala. Clothing, jewellery, hairstyle, naming, food – all these constituted an elaborate sign system that had as its basis the system of caste differentiation.[3] The spectacle of the body in public spaces was replete with caste markers. The movement of the body in public spaces was regulated through a system of distance pollution – the sacredness of the space and the purity of the body being dependent on restrictions of access to other bodies in terms of visibility, touch, hearing and clearly specified distances.

Clothing and jewellery were among the most visible signs of caste on the body and they were instrumental in identifying infringements to the system of distance pollution. The semiological status of attire is well illustrated in the controversies that emerge in the nineteenth century around the conversion of lower-caste women to Christianity. Channar women from southern Travancore who had converted to Christianity in the 1850s began wearing blouses and thin cotton shawls (*melmundu*, literally upper dhoti) across their shoulders.[4] Now, this form of dress was used at that time by upper-caste Hindus on special occasions. A royal proclamation of 1829 had allowed earlier Channar converts the right to wear a long white jacket like the Syrian women.[5] The *melmundu* worn by the new converts was seen by upper-caste Hindus as an insult to their own caste status. The Channar *lahala* of 1859 was a result of these tensions, and a royal proclamation, responding to this situation, declared that there was no objection to Channar women wearing the *melmundu* in the way they liked. However, the proclamation specified, they should not exactly emulate the dress of upper-caste women: at least some small difference should be retained.[6]

Tensions arose and riots occurred around jewellery and naming. Until the royal proclamation of 1769, and even until much later, restrictions prevailed in Travancore regarding the form of gold and silver jewellery that Sudra women could wear.[7] Even a century after the proclamation, stories were reported of a nose-ring being torn from the nose of a lower-caste woman in Pandalam.[8] These examples may suggest that upper-caste opposition was only against lower castes wearing items of attire traditionally worn by them. A counter example, which further underlines the semiological nature of clothing and jewellery, can be seen in the *nayar–pulaya* confrontations in the early decades of this century. In 1915, a reformer called Gopaladas began a campaign among *pulaya* women to reform their customs.[9] He argued that the red stone necklaces worn by *pulaya*s were indications of primitiveness and lack of culture. Many *pulaya* women followed Gopaladas's advice and relinquished their necklaces, only to invite the wrath of the *nayars* who began forcing the *pulaya*s to wear them again. This indicates that the sign system of attire and jewellery did not form an inverted pyramid with the largest number of caste markers assigned to the highest caste, and the least number to the lowest caste. The elements of the system, in their presence or their absence, could function as caste markers, and the acquisition or relinquishing of items of attire or jewellery by any caste could invite resistance from higher castes.

The same principle seems to have obtained in the case of personal names as well. The addition of *amma* to the names of Ezhava women, *panikkar* to Ezhava men, the dropping of diminutives such as *kunju* or *kutty* by lower castes – none of these changes, be it an acquisition or the relinquishing of a caste marker, had a smooth and entirely unchallenged passage.[10]

Now, if we return to the passage cited at the beginning of this chapter, we can understand some of the co-ordinates of the complex relocation that the body underwent at the turn of the century. The 'blouse' ceases to be a caste marker here, and becomes available as an object of personalized enjoyment. What makes this passage interesting is the nexus of volition, individuation and desire that seems to be present in the act of wearing a blouse. The setting aside of the semiology of attire seems to have made possible a gaze directed at one's own body ('twisting and turning, I looked at myself'). This gaze indicates a new relation to the body in the context of individuated desire and enjoyment. 'It looked lovely', 'it tickled me', says this delighted new subject. Central to the change in the relation to the body here is an act of self-possession which carves the 'night' as my own, and elaborates a system of concealment that constitutes the very experience of privacy – concealment of the body, concealment from the mother's surveillance, concealment from the day. The figure of the husband-lover merges with the image of the *gandharva*, further delineating the marital locus of this new desire in the bedroom, a more intimate space of privacy within the household.

This chapter will try to explore below some of the moments in the reconfiguration of the ideas of the body and the self that characterize this period. The chapter focuses on two figures whose work can be seen as engaging with some central aspects of this reconfiguration. Sree Narayana Guru, social reformer-sage of the turn of the century, relied on a variety of sources from tradition to redefine the body in its relations to caste and to agency.[11] His disciple Kumaran Asan provided in his poetry an elaboration of the notion of interiority, making it the proper locus of individuated erotic desire as well as of the act of self-transformation.[12] A discussion of the work of these two figures may throw some light on the complex relations between asceticism and desire that underlie the constitution of modern subjectivity. Further, it might also enable us to have a more differentiated understanding of the 'modern' moment in the history of the subject in Kerala – in terms of the elements at play in this moment, their sources and the logics of interplay between doctrines and practices of the self.

II

Sree Narayana Guru's work shows the confluence of diverse traditions. Often seen as an *advaitin*, Narayanan was also influenced by *Saiva Siddhanta* and the tradition of the Tamil *siddhars*.[13] The self-practices that underlie his work show the influence of *yogasastra*, and the stories that surround his life indicate his familiarity with yoga as well as with *siddhavaidyam* or the medical practice of the *siddhars*.[14]

The influence of these traditions, especially those of the Tamil *siddhars*, on Sree Narayanan has not been adequately understood. Sree Narayanan's poems are resonant with allusions to this tradition, and commentators have traced the strong presence of Pattinattar behind many of his verses.[15] One of Sree Narayanan's devotional compositions, *Kundalinippattu*, has clearly been written along the lines of the work of Pampatti Siddhar. Each stanza in *Kundalinippattu* ends with the refrain, 'Dance, Snake! Dance!' as in Pampatti Siddhar's work.[16] Even Sree Narayanan's most popular slogan 'One caste, one religion, one God for man' resonates with the presence of lines from Tirumular's *Thirumantiram*: 'One caste, one God'.[17]

The presence of the *siddhars* in Sree Narayanan's work is not accidental. The *siddhars* of Tamil Nadu have a long tradition of struggling against caste, as can be seen in Sivavakkiar ('what is virtue if it believes in caste distinctions?') or Pattirakiri ('O, when will come the day when we shall do without caste distinctions?').[18] Kamil Zvelebil suggests that '[t]he *siddhars* in Tamilnad are certainly not an isolated and unique body of free thinkers, but part of a very general tradition, well-spread in space and time in medieval India – the tradition of *siddhacharyas*, who are, again, part of a larger *agamic, tantric* and yogic tradition of India'.[19]

The *siddhar* tradition has been contrasted in many ways with the *bhakti* tradition. *Siddhar*'s attitudes against idol worship and their stress on knowledge, yoga practice, moral behaviour and right conduct in contrast to passionate devotion to an '*ishtadevata*' distinguish them from the bhakti cults. Sree Narayanan's writings evidence these features in a pronounced way. 'Arivu' and *jnanam*, the two words for knowledge, occur repeatedly in Narayanan's work. Often *arivu* occupies the structural space for *brahman*.[20] 'Arivu' is seen as the only essential reality, and the world and all lived reality are seen as moments in the self-searching movement of *arivu*. Sree Narayanan's experiments with unconventional idols such as mirrors and lamps can also be understood in terms of the anti-idolatrous thrust of the *siddha* tradition.[21] The stress that the *siddhars* placed on life practices can also be seen in Sree Narayanan's prescriptive and practice-related texts.

However, in Sree Narayanan, ideas from *Saiva Siddhanta*, from Tamil *siddhars*, and from *advaita vedanta* appear undifferentiated in an eclectic way. This looseness and indiscernibility of frontiers have at times also characterized the life of these traditions. Tirumular, whose *Thirumantiram* is seen as the first major source for *Saiva siddhanta*, is also seen as the first *siddha*. Further, there is a belief that he was an *advaita vedantin* who came to Tamilnad from Kashmir.[22]

Several of Sree Narayanan's texts apparently seem to paraphrase arguments enunciated in texts of the *advaitin* tradition, such as by Sankara. However, details of doctrine as well as metaphors used for illustrating doctrinal arguments, often derive from the *siddha* tradition, and the Tamil *saivite* saints such as Appar, Sambandhar, Sundarar and Manikyavacakar form prominent parts of the intertextual universe that informs Sree Narayanan's writings.[23] Often *advaitin* arguments undergo a deflection in the direction of the *Saiva* tradition and *Saiva siddhanta* arguments are recast in an *advaitin* idiom. In this process, the status of the body seems to undergo a change. While Narayanan's texts evidence an evaluation of phenomenal experience as lacking in ultimate validity, they also show the presence of the *Saivite* valorization of the world as Shiva's body. This makes the ontological status of the world different from that of illusion, and a positive characterization of the world becomes possible and necessary. The dualism of *Saivite* texts allows a certain differentiation of reality, although false differentiation is seen as an object of suspicion and criticism. As we shall see later, Sree Narayanan uses a very similar argument when he addresses the differentiation of the body of the human race on caste lines. As with the world – Shiva's body – so with the human body. The *siddha* tradition believed that *uyir* (life-force) does not exist without *utal* (body). Tirumular saw the body and its care as prerequisites for any spiritual practice:

> If the body perishes, Prana departs
> Nor will the light of truth be reached;
> I learned the way of preserving my body
> And so doing, my Prana too.[24]

For Tirumular, despising the body becomes untenable when he discovers the *porul* within *utal*. The body becomes the temple of God and the preservation of the body with infinite care becomes the new task for the enlightened devotee.[25] In another verse, Tirumular characterizes the heart as the temple and body as the house.[26] All these metaphors place the body as the locus of a set of positive practices. However, there is a strand in the classical yoga tradition, as well as in some of the later *siddhars* such as Pattinattar that shows a denunciation of one's own body as the locus of decay and filth.[27] Sree Narayanan's work is a site of these ambivalences and tensions.

Some of Sree Narayanan's early texts, notably 'Mananatheetham' and 'Siva Satakam' entreat Shiva to rescue the devotee from temptations of the flesh. In 'Siva Satakam', it is primarily the woman who epitomizes the fallen state of the body. The female body becomes a site of stench, as if the oceans had been emptied out and filled with waste.[28] The breasts are compared to boils, and life with the woman is seen as an infernal sea filled with blood and pus.[29] 'Mananatheetham' oscillates between the two poles of fear and attraction with an intense sense of urgency and desperation. The female figure is seen as an irresistible conqueror in front of which the devotee is helpless without the support of Shiva's grace. The soul is compared to a bird caught in a snare set by Kamadeva. Death and madness haunt the presence of the woman: the female body is seen as a corpse, and the woman reveals herself as a raving lunatic in the midst of fervent embraces.[30] Fear of the female merges with the fear of mortality and unfreedom. In texts such as these, the body's senses do not know what they can celebrate, what their legitimate domain can be. They constantly indicate the proximity of death and the promiscuous trap of unfreedom. To move away from this sense of fallenness and shame, of *jugupsa*, the senses need to be re-inscribed in a new relation to the body and the self. Another poem of Sree Narayanan, 'Indriya Vairagyam', tells us that neither the problem nor the solution lies in the senses. The senses do not have any suffering – it is the self that is the locus of suffering.[31] The devotee sees his body as being abused by the senses – the latter are seen as inferior beings involved without respite in the sensible world. The prayer to Shiva takes the form of a plea to salvage the devotee from untruth so that he can embrace the new, uncorrupted body.[32] This possibility of a pure body and its maintenance connects Sree Narayanan's writings to the sacralization and maintenance of the subtle body in yoga.

Sree Narayanan's most elaborate text that deals with the doctrine of the self is 'Atmopadesa Satakam'.[33] Initially circulated as *Atmabodham*, this text is believed to have reached its present form by 1897.[34] It is a practice text written in the form of advice. The title captures the constitutive ambiguities of the practice – it could mean advice to oneself or advice on the doctrine of the self, and each stanza concludes by stressing the modality of instruction, evident in locutions such as 'may be uttered', 'may be remembered' or 'may be practised'. The space of the enunciating subject in this text can be occupied by the *guru* or the *shishya*. Furthermore, the enunciating subject can oscillate between these two positions, becoming the subject as well as the object of the advice. Thus, the mode of performativity underlying the text is that of a self-practice, a set of actions performed by the self on itself, effecting and recognizing moments of transformation. The performance quality of the text is accentuated by the appearance of postures of the body several times in the text, beginning with the *pranamam* in the opening verses and ending with the *amarcha* of the closing lines, delineating a posture of active containment of energy.

Although popularly interpreted as a text propounding the *advaitin* doctrine of the self, 'Atmopadesa Satakam' is also replete with resonances that come from *Saiva Siddhanta* and from the tradition of the Tamil *siddhars*. The prominence given to *arivu* as the manifestation of God and the placing of the senses (*indriyam*), inner sense (*karanam*) and body (*kalebaram*) and the world (*jagat*) as its manifestations already pick up many of the strands from these traditions. The third verse, for example, describes the five elements first as *vivartham* in the *advaitin* tradition and then as *vibhuti* in the *Saiva Siddhanta* way. The poem delineates a phenomenology of *arivu* seeking itself and going through a series of manifestations. Traditions of *Saiva Siddhanta* and *sankhya* in their conception of the evolution of *prakriti* lie beneath this narrative of differentiation of *arivu*[35] *Ahanta* or sense of the self is seen as comprising skin, bones, excreta and volatile inner thoughts (*anthakalakal*).[36] But *ahanta* itself is a moment in the differentiation of *arivu*.[37] Even time, the very modality of this differentiation, is seen as the play of *arivu*. The temporality of the body thus gets an ambivalent new status. Even as it is the site of transience and decay, it is also a moment in the narrative of the search for the self by *arivu*. Sree Narayanan describes the body as the shadow of the soul (*atmavu*), but the soul is presented as a lamp of which the senses form the container, *vasana* from earlier life the oil and right practices the wick.[38] In this complex metaphoric of light and darkness, the body's positioning is inscribed in ambivalent ways. The shadow has a special status as a metaphor in that, while unreal in itself, it has its origin in something real and thus may serve to guide one's attention to a recognition or knowledge of that reality.[39] In other words, while its ontological status may be suspect, it may have an epistemological and axiological value in the movement towards self-reflection and self-realization.

The ambivalence of the text towards the body is expressed in detail in verses 8 and 9 of the *Satakam*. Verse 8 describes the body as a foul-smelling tube on which the five birds of the senses play tantalizingly, feeding on the five objects of the senses.[40] The verse, however, ends with another, contrasting image of the body – that of a body of light or *velivuru*. This new body annihilates the birds of the senses, and it can be rightly inhabited by the soul. The juxtaposition of these two bodies, one the subject of the self-practice and the other the object, is made possible by the availability of the distinction between *sthula sarira* (gross body) and *sukshma sarira* (subtle body). This makes possible a representation of the body inscribed in terms of the yogic tradition. Verse 9 presents the image of a sage meditating under a tree, on the two sides of which climbs a creeper bearing six blossoms.[41] The image of the tree is a *yogasastric* figuration of the body, with the two sides of the creeper being *ida* and *pingala*, and the six flowers suggesting the six stages (*muladhara, swadhishtana, manipuraka, anahata, visuddhi* and *ajna*) in the ascent of the *kundalini* towards its final destination of enlightenment, *sahasrara*.

These verses also show us the complex intertextual universe behind Sree Narayanan's metaphors. The image of the birds resonates with Pattinattar's description of the body as a cage with five birds inside.[42] Tirumular speaks of the 'six birds in the house of five' and the 'hundred birds on top of the tree' and the 'seven steps that lead to the home'.[43]

This possibility of redeeming the body through a knowledge that eliminates the attributes of the gross body allows Sree Narayanan to restore value to worldly existence as well. Sree Narayanan's *advaita* allows an identity between the worldly and the spiritual aspects of one's existence. Sree Narayanan's prescriptive text, 'Advaita Jeevitam', written on the occasion of the founding of the *math* at Sivagiri, illustrates this point well.[44] Beginning with the assertion that all human beings desire happiness, the text moves on to assert that the human soul is in general seen to prefer eternal, spiritual happiness to happiness of a transient, sensory nature. The moment of the social is introduced here, when Sree Narayanan goes on to suggest that the internal reforms of diverse communities influence the extent to which such happiness is attained. This passage is worth quoting at length, as it displays some important moves in Sree Narayanan's argument:

> For a community to achieve prosperity of all sorts – related to the body, the mind and the soul – the religious and moral rectitude of its members can be a source of great help. Temples and places of worship can be useful in developing these qualities in everybody in the community. However, the economic prosperity of the members of the community is equally essential. For this, we need to reform agriculture, trade and technical education, among other things.
>
> The worldly and the spiritual are not two separate things. In reality, both work with the same aim. The body enjoys happiness thanks to the harmonious functioning of all its parts. Similarly, for the human community to attain its ultimate goal of happiness, the harmonious functioning of various spiritual and worldly arrangements is needed.[45]

We see here two moves that Sree Narayanan's writings would rehearse repeatedly, explicitly or otherwise. First, the move from the individual to the community and from the community to the human race. The individual aspiration for well-being and the self-practices that need to accompany it in a spiritual endeavour are projected as the ground as well as the analogic model for practices of social reform. The identity established here between worldly and spiritual aspirations can be seen as emerging from the problematic of the body described in the pages above, echoing Tirumular's recognition that the body needs to be preserved in order to care for the *prana*. Second, the image of human race as a body whose organs should function harmoniously places the various activities of mankind as analogous to the functions of different bodily organs. Here, once again, the care of the body functions as the model for conceiving collective effort.

Sree Narayanan's texts and pronouncements on caste can profitably be reread in the light of these considerations. Caste is seen as one of the principles for differentiating the human race, but a false principle which produces a set of false differences. 'Jatilakshanam' ('the sign system of caste'), written around 1914, questions this false semiology built on false differentiation, and propounds a new semiology.[46] Interestingly, it is the body that functions as the basis for this new differentiation. The poem's critique of caste is based on a notion of natural law: 'all beings that embrace and procreate belong to the same caste (*jati*)'. Form, voice, odour, temperature – these are signs of differentiation that mark out humans from other species. Body, name, place, occupation – these are co-ordinates of further, individual differentiation. But 'do not ask who [what caste]' Sree Narayanan says, 'the body answers it'.[47]

Why do we need a true principle of differentiation instead of a false one? Why differentiate at all? Narayanan places differentiation, as we saw in our reading of 'Atmopadesa Satakam', as the form of evolution of *arivu*, the modality of its movement towards itself. Difference is seen as the water in the ocean of knowledge and it is also described as the mould in which knowledge casts the various forms it produces.[48] In other words, difference does have a value in the attainment of knowledge. This is why differentiation needs to be founded on true principles and not on false ones. The only true principle that Sree Narayanan recognizes here is that of natural kinds – 'humanness is to humans what cowness is to cows'.[49] Embrace and procreation function as signs of a biological, natural bond. This argument against caste echoes that made by the *siddhars*, with Siva Vakiar exclaiming 'What is caste? What is it to sleep with a Brahmin woman or a Paraya woman?'[50] This argument is similar to the one made in the Buddhist tradition, e.g. in *Vajrasuchi*.[51] In fact, Sree Narayanan's disciple Kumaran Asan will present the same argument in 'Chandala Bhikshuki', where Buddha would remind us that as a *chandali* can bear the son of a *brahmin*, there is nothing wrong in considering them the same *jati*.[52]

The interesting moment in this argument, for us, is the status occupied by the body in the process of revealing truth. Body is a sign that reveals the ground of true differentiation. In other words, it is not caste markers that constitute the true semiology of differentiation, but the body itself. The body is not a bearer of signs, it is a sign in its own right. Therefore, caste markers obscure the true signification of the body, not merely by presenting redundant signs, but by usurping the semiological function to themselves. The names *Pulaya* and Ezhava merely conceal the true identity of human beings. Sree Narayanan's arguments on caste names can be seen as pointing out the misleading nature of their semiology. At times, he suggested that the word Ezhava was not a caste name but a place name, alluding to the belief that the word Ezhavan is a corrupt form of *Sinhalan*, indicating that Ezhavas came from Sri Lanka.[53] 'If Ezhavas really want to use a place name', Sree Narayanan argued, 'why not use the appellation "Malayali" since they have been living in Kerala for such a long time?'[54] Sree Narayanan categorically asserted that the word Ezhava signified neither caste nor religion.

In Sree Narayanan's pronouncements on caste, we find three recurring concepts around which the argument is built. They are caste (*jati*), religion (*matham*) and community (*samudayam*). While pointing out that caste was a principle of false differentiation that needed to be abjured, Narayanan also argued that religion was purely a matter of inner beliefs and opinions. Here Narayanan relies on the literal meaning of the word *matham*, that is, belief, opinion. The third element, community (*samudayam*), indicates the locus of concerted action. In Sree Narayanan's writings, this concept can be seen to oscillate between specific human collectives founded on a commonality of conditions of existence or of objectives of action on the one hand, and the human race as the most truly valid, universal community. When Sree Narayanan says, 'Caste should go; there is no other way. All human beings belong to the same community', he is stressing the opposition between true and false differentiation of the body of humanity.[55] Community is founded on natural law here, on true difference. However, while discussing the argument that Ezhavas should convert to Christianity or Buddhism, Sree Narayanan uses *samudayam* in another sense. 'Religion (*matham*) has two sides: one internal and the other external', he said, 'which of these sides would you like to see changed?' He continued:

> If the desire is for change in the external aspect, it is not really religious conversion (*mathaparivarthanam*), but change in community (*samudayaparivarthanam*). As for internal religion (*abhyanthara matham*, also meaning inner belief, inner opinion), it is subject to constant and gradual change in all thoughtful people.[56]

Here, *samudayam* comes to stand for a specific collectivity; it is not identical with the human race. Sree Narayanan's own social reform movement primarily addressed the Ezhavas, appealing to them to get rid of their caste markers and to reform themselves internally into a *samudayam*. Thus, the caste identity of the Ezhava comes to be redefined as and supplanted by the identity of a community. The word Ezhava ceases to function as a sign of differentiation according to convention, but becomes the name of a community, signifying the common locus of a certain set of individual and collective practices.

The deeper ambitions and assumptions of these practices are universal – they are validated in terms of the concept of a virtuous life that pertains to the entire human race or human community (*manushya samudayam*). However, this identification with the human race becomes real only insofar as there is an eradication of false divisions such as caste. This purifying impulse gives rise to action at the level of the Ezhavas, previously understood as caste and now understood as a community, that is, the locus of a specific set of practices. This is what gives rise to the second sense of community in Sree Narayanan's writings. When he says that the progress of the human soul towards spiritual happiness is facilitated by the level of internal reform attained by different communities (*oro samudayangal*), he has this sense in mind.[57] Building places of worship, developing agriculture and trade, and spreading education constitute actions that have a specific community as their locus.

Sree Narayanan insisted on the distinction between community (*samudayam*) and religion (*matham*). 'It is wrong to subordinate matters of the community to religion or religious matters to the community. There should be no connection between community affairs and religion. Religion is a matter of the mind'.[58]

The discourse of social reform, among the Ezhavas as well as among other castes, uses this notion of the community as the ground for understanding the identity and agency of its practitioners. This distinction in grounding between the notions of caste (*jati*) and community (*samudayam*) later on allows for further redefinitions. A resolution passed in 1931 at a conference of the Nayars declared that 'anybody who speaks Malayalam and observes Malayali customs can be admitted, regardless of their caste, as members into the Nayar community'.[59] The Nambudiri reform movement's motto, 'to make Nambudiri into a human being' (*namboodiriye manushyanakkuka*) and its practices of internal reform, once again reflect similar impulses at understanding the notion of the community.[60]

Sree Narayanan's redefinition of religion as inner belief and his notion of the community as the locus of reform also discourages conversion as a strategy in anti-caste struggles. Just as the individual needed to get rid of caste markers in the form of attire or jewellery from his or her body, Sree Narayanan believed that Ezhavas as a community also needed to rid itself of caste rituals such as *talikettu* and *tirandu kalyanam*. Sree Narayanan devised new rituals for the community which were all within the larger ambit of Hindu traditions in Kerala. However, in his philosophy which stressed 'one caste, one religion, one God for man' and 'It is enough if a man is good, whatever his religion', it is difficult to find reasons directly against conversion. In 1916, Sree Narayanan even issued a statement to the effect that he did not belong to any particular caste or religion. He also clarified that his founding of temples did not entail his belonging to Hindu religion: 'We have founded some temples in response to the desire of certain Hindus. Similarly, if Muslims and Christians wish, we will be glad to do appropriate things for them'.[61] However, the redefinition of the community and the practices of reform Sree Narayanan initiated also show that for him the spiritual self-understanding and practices of Ezhavas as community should be within the horizon of the very tradition which had differentiated them as caste (*jati*) earlier.

We looked earlier at the relations that Sree Narayanan draws between the human body and the notion of the community. We saw parallels between the individual's practice of denuding the body of caste markers and the community's reformulation of rituals. Hygiene, which runs as a common thread through several reform movements as also Sree Narayanan's, can also be seen in this light as the attempt to cleanse the body of caste markers and to make it shine in its essential dignity. We saw the traditions of the sacralization of the body as the temple of God against the backdrop of which this notion of dignity can be understood. Hygiene is placed as a practice central to this problematic. It is seen by Sree Narayanan as the appropriate response to distance pollution. It rehearses the gesture of the 'polluted' man in a pre-emptive move that would invalidate the rationale used by the 'polluted' for purification. The onus of purity is assumed by the self – not of the purity of the other, but of one's own purity in an act of self-possession. 'It is not enough that one displays hygiene before others to convince them', Sree Narayanan noted, 'one should practise it at home as well; one should begin with the kitchen'.[62] Here we see hygiene becoming more than a ritualistic practice related to the body – it becomes a practice related to the family space and to what would later be more clearly seen as private life. Between the individual and the community, the space of the family emerges as a site for action. From a mere negative gesture – denudation of caste markers – hygiene becomes an element in a positive style of daily life. 'Sree Narayana Dharmam', compiled by Sree Narayanan's disciples and published posthumously in 1924, enunciates a code of conduct for the subject, with hygiene playing a prominent role.[63] The section on purity, '*shuddhi panchakam*', includes discussions of *deha shuddhi* and *griha shuddhi* (purity of the body as well as of the house).

III

We have so far seen how the body appears as a site of redefinition in Sree Narayanan's work – from being a bearer of marks of a false differentiation to being the foundation of a true differentiation on which one could found the rationale for a sense of community. This, we saw, was accompanied by the elaboration of a set of practices that individuates the body and allows its insertion in familial and communal spaces. In the work of Kumaran Asan, the most prominent among Sree Narayanan's disciples and one of the major figures in the history of Malayalam poetry, this individuation is elaborated further and given a new dimension – that of the interiority of the individual.

In this, as in his treatment of the body, Asan's poetry marks a clear departure from traditions in Malayalam poetry that were dominant at his time. This is particularly evident in Asan's treatment of the female body and of desire. The female body was a prominent object of sensual appreciation in the writings of Venmani poets, and this tradition can be seen to continue in Vallathol. Here the female body is presented as a delightful object of enjoyment, like other objects of the senses in general.[64] Just as good food delights the palate and good music the ear, the sight of a beautiful woman delights the eye, caressing her, the sense of touch, listening to her, the sense of hearing and imagining an encounter with her, the inner sense. Sexual pleasure is conceived as a combination of other sensory pleasures. This does not mean that sexual pleasure can be substituted by a combination of other objects of sensory enjoyment. However, the uniqueness of the sexual is conceived in terms that are similar to the uniqueness of extraordinarily pleasurable objects of the senses. Just as there is no substitute for the unique sensual enjoyment of a particular food prepared by a particular person in a particular sort of way, there is no other object that will function as an entirely satisfactory substitute for the enjoyment of a female body. However, the elements that constitute this enjoyment irreducibly belong to the five senses and to the combination of these elements in the inner sense.

This does not mean that a sexual encounter in Venmani is always a one-sided enjoyment of a passive object. The woman's engagement in the act is sometimes a necessary moment in the scenario of enjoyment. She often excites the subject of sensory enjoyment through feigned anger or mock challenge. 'Feigned' and 'mock' deliberately as these acts and counter-acts are given the status of reality that is less serious than that accorded to the ultimately solitary pleasure of the sensual subject.[65] The anger, the fear, the challenge and the conquest – all these belong to the realm of 'play'. The model of play allows an unfolding of the dynamic of the encounter and makes possible a gaze that can convert the details of this dynamic into aspects of enjoyment. The possibility of such a gaze is disallowed for the partner, and this asymmetry restricts the realm of play to its proper, fictional locus. One could say that in these poems, the presence of the other is inscribed in a fictional space so that a 'subject-effect' can be created to sustain the notion of play without compromising in any ultimate sense the sensory nature of sexual enjoyment.

In this problematic, the uniqueness of the object of enjoyment is understood as the uniqueness of the enjoyment of a particular sexual encounter. In other words, while enjoyable encounters are experientially particularized, the identity of the partner is not sufficiently individualized.[66] The word 'sexual' functions here in quite a different way, distant from its contemporary use in ordinary language as well as in literary discourse. A conception of subjective interiority is central to most of the contemporary uses of the term, while it is precisely this dimension which is precluded in the poems we are addressing. To collapse the distinctions between these two notions would be to foreclose an examination of the history of conceiving the sexual in Kerala and its place in the delineation of the contemporary subject. Equally, to stress this distinction as an absolute beginning would be to foreclose a further interrogation of this distinction itself. The point is rather to describe the dynamic of a transformation, the reconfiguration of earlier elements, the introduction of new elements and finally the reassignment of values that this process entails. Crucial to this reconfiguration is a revaluation of notions of the body and an elaboration and a redefinition of notions of 'inner sense'.

It is in this nexus of connections and disconnections that Asan's work forms a clear point of departure. Asan was a disciple of Sree Narayanan, and some of his early, devotional poetry partakes of the fear of the temptations of the flesh and the fear of female sexuality we found in Sree Narayanan's 'Mananatheetham' and 'Siva Satakam'. However, another motif inscribes itself like a shadow of this fear – or, perhaps, as the original of which the fear of sexuality is the shadow – that is, the fear of mortality. Even Asan's 'Vairagya Panchakam' first expresses fear at the mortality and transience of the beautiful female body before fear at its temptations.[67]

It is said that Asan, when he was twenty, completed a devotional couplet of Sree Narayanan's apostrophizing the Goddess by another couplet, pleading with her for protection against mortality. Asan's first mature poem, 'Veena Poovu' bemoans the fall of a wilted flower, extending the play of metaphor to reflect on transience. In his later work too, meditations on human life take place primarily within the horizon of reflections on death.[68] Death appears as an absolute limit, defining human life as essentially finite, and reflections on the human body and on transactions within the inner sense are carried out within this irreducible locus of finitude. In saying this, I am not overlooking the recurrent use of notions such as *vasana* 'after-life' and 'liberation' in Asan's work. As will become clear later in this discussion, even in the context of the use of these notions, death constitutes an irreducible turning point in his poetic universe.[69] Practices of reflection on life take as their point of departure the finitude of their locus, and over the gaze on the body or into one's own thoughts falls the shadow of cessation, not only of the body and of thoughts, but of one's gaze as well.

The gaze on the female body also encounters a difficult passage in Asan's work. His early heroines, Nalini and Leela, are rarely described in terms of physical detail.[70] Even for later heroines such as Seetha or Mathangi, physical description hardly allows any lingering on the body as an object of sensory attraction.[71] Breasts, the usual objects of lingering and relish, in the poetry of Kumaran Asan's times, hardly find any mention in Asan. 'Karuna', Asan's last work, is the only one which presents the heroine in terms that indicate sensory attraction.[72] However, the reader recognizes soon that this description is inscribed in terms of a mechanism of repetition, where the same parts of the body will reappear at the close of the poem, bleeding and fragmented, to underline the finitude of the body.[73]

If the body is thus merely an object of erasure, the pretext for a recognition that annihilates its validity, does it mean that it does not have any positive function in Asan? Does it mean that it merely disappears, abandoning the history of its connections with other concepts, leaving the pages of Asan's work blank for a new set of attributions? To answer this question, we need to look more clearly at the narratives of Asan's longer poems.

The first among them, 'Nalini' (1911), presents a heroine who goes into the forest in search of Divakaran, a young ascetic whom she knew well in her childhood and whom she had secretly adored for long. They do meet in the forest, but Divakaran does not recognize Nalini, and even when he does, is affectionate with her in a non-desiring, non-differentiating way. Nalini affirms her love for him, and appeals to him to let her accompany him in his life. Now, in this affirmation and articulation of love, an interesting relation between desire and the body can be seen to be at work. Desire here does and does not recognize itself as bodily – bodily desire forms a stage or a special instance of this desire. The object of desire, for the desiring subject, is not really the body of the other, nor even the bodily desire for the other, but a desire affirmed by the other's soul. However, this desire is only possible between a man and a woman, and in that sense, it profoundly depends on a differentiation of human beings into men and women, a differentiation of which the body remains the primary sign. There is a natural law behind this differentiation and this desire. Even Sree Narayanan who, as we saw, argued against false further differentiation of natural kinds, allowed at times a true differentiation within the human race, a natural differentiation, between the male and the female. Just as the body is the primary sign of this inexorable difference, bodily desire is the primary sign of a desire that is ultimately grounded as the soul's desire. The model for the soul's desire, the logic and dynamic that it emulates, the intensities it expresses, enjoys and suffers remain embedded in a discourse of bodily desire.

Divakaran rejects Nalini's plea to be accepted as his companion, saying that it is the same love, in its intensity, that makes him abandon any desire for earthly union. Nalini finds enlightenment in this moment of revelation, but paradoxically that moment becomes her moment of death as well. She collapses, her face ecstatic with joy, and dies on Divakaran's chest. Even this moment where the soul's desire finds its fulfilment in absolute separation from bodily desire, resonates with the ecstasy of bodily union: 'Unable to bear the waves of ecstatic joy that inundate her inner states, her body gave way, like a reed on the river's bank. The yogi took her in his arms, with care as if this wounded body were his own. As calm ripples merge, their hands entwined, and their bodies joined like sound to like sound, glow to like glow'.[74]

The paradox that underlies this self-negating and profoundly self-affirming gesture made by bodily desire needs further unravelling. 'Leela' (1914), Asan's next major poem, was an occasion for such unravelling. This becomes evident from the 'Preface' where Asan tells us that the protagonists of 'Nalini' had almost fully relinquished *rajas* and had attained the *satvik* stage. 'However', Asan continues, 'it is the earlier situations [lower, *rajasik* stages] that contain in greater measure the sorrows of life and the secrets of the mind. Therefore, it was about those lives situated at a stage just below where the protagonists of "Nalini" were located, that I felt writing next'.[75] The profound paradox of the relation between the body and the soul in the experience and articulation of desire, sketched in 'Nalini' in a form all too abstract, could be further explored only if its site moved closer to the bodily. Understandably, in 'Leela', emotions are more intensely defined and the paradox more sharply delineated. Leela's lover, Madanan, renounces the world and wanders like a madman after she marries someone else – in deference to wishes of her parents – a rich man, with whom she lives until his premature death. Asan's lines on the consummation of Leela's marriage are ambiguous, although he clearly indicates that Leela keeps remembering Madanan and is distraught within her marriage. As in 'Nalini', Leela goes to the forest in search of Madanan and finds him.

However, while Nalini could find an equivalent for her desire in her plea to be Divakaran's spiritual companion, Leela's affirmation of desire takes a form more closely related to the body. She senses the proximity of her lover as she feels the intoxicating fragrance of *champakam* flowers and prepares for meeting him by decorating her body with them. The site of their meeting, even within the forest, is a garden luxuriant with the treasures of spring – wild colours, maddening fragrances, the sound of birds and bumble bees, and the gentle murmur of trees – this is indeed the *topos* of a sensual tryst between lovers.[76] Yet, this sublime site of the senses is also a liminal space where bodily desire finds its limit and understands this limit as a moment of relinquishment. When Leela finds Madanan and, holding him in her arms, reminds him of their past, Madanan remains unresponsive, his mind far, far away from the present. Slowly, he remembers her, responds to her and, in a brief moment of intense passion, takes her in his arms and kisses her. This constitutes the limit of the moment – immediately he walks away as if frightened, and disappears into the torrential flow of the river to embrace his death. Unhesitantly, Leela follows him and ends her life too in the river. Later, Madhavi, Leela's *sakhi*, has a dream where both Leela and Madanan reappear with new, unblemished bodies to tell her that no one disappears from this universe, and that there is no cessation for the love-entwined bond that unites the soul to the body.[77] Spiritually transformed by this epiphanic moment, Madhavi becomes a *sanyasini*.

We need to observe at least three elements at play here to understand adequately the complexity of the moment of transformation, of which these texts seem to be a part. First, there is an irreducibly sensual or bodily quality to desire, which finds its true locus of affirmation not in the body but in the soul. The body seems to constitute a limit to the bodily, sensual intensity of desire. Once this limit is recognized, desire abandons the body and acknowledges the soul as its further habitat. This is how desire recognizes itself as 'the love-entwined bond that unites the soul to the body'.

Second, in relocating desire, Asan's focus shifts from the body to the mind. The inner transactions of the desiring soul, in moments of self-affirmation and self-transformation become the central theatre that organizes the poem's inner visibility. Even though an interlocutor appears in the form of a *sakhi* or even in the form of an object of one's desire, discourse in Asan's poetry is profoundly monological.[78] Apparent dialogism, even in the fleeting moments of its appearance, is the inner dialogism of a self-practice, those discursive acts where the subject and the object remain located within the interiority of the same person.

Third, there is a clear demarcation of gender roles in Asan's delineation of desire. The subject of desire as well as of self-practices remains female, while the male figure remains outside the pale of desire and transformation, either because he is seen as having transcended particularizing desire (as in the case of Divakaran), or because he is too weak to bear the burden of subjectivity (as in the case of Madanan). In order to draw out the implications of these three elements, we will need to pursue the trajectory taken by these elements in Asan's later work.

In many of Asan's longer poems, the central space continues to be occupied by the moment when intensities leave the body as an inadequate vehicle. This moment is isolated temporally as the pivotal moment of narration, and spatially as a liminal *topos* located away from convention and community. The forest provides such a space, again in 'Chintavishtayaya Seetha', while in other poems it is the cremation ground ('Karuna'), the *pulaya*'s hut that houses the Nambudiri woman ('Duravastha'), or the *chandala*'s well from which an upper-caste sadhu drinks ('Chandala

Bhikshuki') that constitute such spaces. This isolation, this bracketing or suspension of community and convention, functions to accentuate the individuation of the protagonists, and allows them an extension in a dimension that can be called 'private' retaining some of the original, divestment-related resonances of this word.

'Chandala Bhikshuki' and 'Duravastha' develop a discourse against caste, based on notions of natural law embedded in the human body, in terms similar to those used by Sree Narayanan in his relocation of the body. Buddha in 'Chandala Bhikshuki' argues that as a Chandali's womb can conceive a Brahmin's child, one cannot deny their belonging to the same caste.[79] This, as we saw earlier, echoes and elaborates Narayanan's dictum that 'those who embrace and procreate together belong to the same caste'. However, both in 'Duravastha' as well as in 'Chandala Bhikshuki', it is desire that constitutes the ultimate ground for validation and the deeper motive for transformation. Matangi's desire for Anandan retains its bodily resonances in the early parts of the poem, as in the source text Asan cites in the Preface.[80] In 'Duravastha' too, it is the gendered, erotic desire of Savithri that validates her union with Chathan and thus validates the very possibility of 'embrace and procreation'. Thus, once again, justifications made at the level of the body need, and are given, a deeper validation at the level of the desiring soul.

In 'Karuna' and 'Seetha', as in the early poems, we find that the consummation of the logic of desire is coterminous with death. Vasavadatta experiences a higher consummation to her intense longing, once desire recognizes that the body is inadequate as a vehicle of intensities. Seetha's desire provides a further, deeper exploration of desire itself. In its articulation, desire not only leaves the realm of the bodily, but even the object of desire, turning one's own desire into an object. Here, love would need to be understood in the sense Asan gives to this notion: in rather abstract terms, as the force that unites the soul and the body. There is an immersion into interiority within this poem, in its narrativization of inner life, that displays the development of a deep, autobiographical desire oriented towards self-articulation and self-possession.

Thus, 'Chintavishtayaya Seetha' also marks the most mature articulation of the monologue in Asan's work. Monologue in Asan is the site of a self-practice that seizes the self in a moment of recognition and transformation. This is progressively true of 'Chandala Bhikshuki', 'Duravastha' and 'Chintavishtayaya Seetha'. Through the monologue, Asan develops a language for 'the secrets of the mind', a language of thought (*vichara-bhasha*), and provides an elaboration of the notion of 'inner sense' (*anthakaranam*). We saw a sketching of the place of the *anthakaranam* in Narayanan's work where it, along with the five senses, belongs to the realm of the bodily, and is subjected to the same ambivalent judgements. Sree Narayanan's conception of *anthakaranam* echoes, among others, the Sankhya and *Saiva Siddhanta* traditions. As with the senses, in Sree Narayanan, *anthakaranam* is not individualized. Practices of the self that address the senses and the *anthakaranam* occupy a level that does not seek to individualize the agent.

The notion of '*anthakaranam*' is deployed in Asan's work in a field of words denoting personal interiority. Ranging from the flux of thought to the turbulence of emotions to the locus of inner reflection, *anthakaranam* is used in a variety of related senses in Asan. These indeed do fit with the philosophical conception of this term in tradition, but as the site of the 'secrets of the mind', *anthakaranam* acquires in Asan a clearly individualized sense that has come to be central to the use of this word in modern Malayalam. One of the functions of the monologue in Asan is to reflect on the state of the *anthakaranam*. At the same time, the monologue itself is a reflection *of* the state of the *anthakaranam*, as the monologic discourse emerges from there and is subjected to the vagaries of the inner sense. Individuation of the *anthakaranam* allows it to become the seat of self-reflection and self-possession. It is here that the bodily becomes firmly located in the interiority of the subject.

Asan seems to have been influenced by the Buddhist tradition of self-practices in his attention to inner thoughts. Again, in his reading of this tradition, Asan seems to introduce an individualizing inflection that enables him to develop the subject's perception of her intensity as the ground of truth about the self. Elaborating on the notion that the world is a reflection of the mind, Asan comments:

> The way one is, so is one's world. Each state in the universe is firmly rooted in our inner experience of that state. It is not important to look at the external state. This is because all that [external state] is a reflected image of the state of our inner sense (*anthakaranam*).[81]

This is even more pronounced in his reflections of the soul (*atmavu*):

> Each human life experiences events, helpful or difficult, depending on the quality and the strength of its inner life of thoughts. The body is a mixture (*samavayam*) of the experiences and thoughts condensed in the soul, as well as the temporary vehicle for articulating them. Therefore, our real soul (*yatharthamaya atmavu*) is none other than our thoughts.[82]

The attention paid in Asan's poems to inner thoughts and inner sense in the delineation of character-subjectivities has a certain relationship to this last move in his argument. Inner sense, with its relations to the bodily and the worldly, in its individualized sense of personal interiority, begins to be seen as the 'real soul' of the subject, and becomes the ground for unveiling the 'truth' about the subject. Monologue is the form of this 'true', 'authentic' discourse in Asan.

The third element I indicated above, the genderedness of desire, the source of erotic initiative being located in the female subject, appears in Asan's later poems as well. Whether it be Mathangi going in search for Anandan, or Savithri inviting Chathan to her bed, or Vasavadatta sending messages to Upaguptan, the pattern remains the same. In 'Chintavishtayaya Seetha', the initiatives, although not erotic, remain with the heroine. All Asan's monologues have a female subject – all the deliberations aimed at self-understanding or self-transformation have female subjects of enunciation. How do we understand this recurrent pattern where the woman is assigned the task of erotic initiative as well as of self-transformation, and man a space beyond transformation, either because he possesses a superior, ascetic virility or because he is too powerless to desire and transform himself? Is Asan relying on the Sankhya understanding of an unevolute *purusha* and a constantly evolving *prakriti*? Is it that the suspicion of the woman as temptress that underlies Sree Narayanan's 'Siva Satakam' and Asan's own 'Vairagya Panchakam' in *Siva Sthothra Mala* continues to shadow these moments? Could it be that Asan's use of the woman as the self-transforming subject belongs to larger currents in *bhakti* tradition where the devotee's soul assumes a feminine form in its relation to the virile aspect of the object of devotion? In this complex genealogy, how do we distinguish between elements from the Indian and Western traditions of figuring the woman? A detailed exploration of these would also need to address the emergence and discursive elaboration of self-practices for women in Malayalam writing – a large number of prescriptive texts did appear around this time in Malayalam, expounding and elaborating on the notion of *streedharmam*. Some of them were authored by women and several by men. Reviewing one of them, entitled *Bharyadharmam*, Asan commented in approbation that men who happen to read this book would indeed buy copies of it as gifts for their wives.[83]

A close examination of the evolution of the notion of gendered selves in Asan's times as well as in his thought, relevant as it is, lies beyond the immediate purview of this chapter. However, it is necessary to note that the possibility of finding in the female subject the locus of a self-transforming, deliberative discourse has had a profound impact on the understanding of the subject in later Malayalam writing. First, this allowed an individuation of the subject and an embedding of discourse in the personal consciousness or *anthakaranam* of the subject. Second, displacing bodily desire from the body to the inner sense on the one hand, and making that realm of the inner sense the true foundation of self-understanding, the 'real soul' on the other, made possible an interiorization of the erotic which, again, has had a history in subsequent writing and thought in Kerala that awaits inscription and interrogation. There is a relationship between *ascesis* and this new *eros* – an *eros* that is far more intense than before, but an *eros* that has disappeared into the hidden recesses and infinite folds of the inner sense – that also needs to be unravelled and understood in such a history.

IV

I have tried to indicate two moments of transformation in thinking about the body in Kerala in the decades immediately preceding and succeeding the end of the last century. Sree Narayana Guru's work, both philosophical as well as prescriptive, involved a relocation of the body away from caste markers and functioning as a foundation for true differentiation according to natural law. I have also tried to indicate some of the strands of tradition put to play in the ambivalent and complex understanding of the body in his work. Kumaran Asan effected a further transformation of the elements he inherited from Sree Narayanan as well as to Sree Narayanan's use of elements from tradition. The 'natural' foundation of differentiation is no longer found in the working of the body, but in the logic of a bodily, erotic desire. This erotic desire, in its turn, goes beyond the body and finds in the inner sense the true site of its higher intensities. An ascetic impulse shadows the elaboration of this desire, facilitating its interiorization and making human finitude the horizon within which these intensities can be felt and thought. In the elaboration of the *anthakaranam* in monologues, a new relationship begins to emerge in Asan's work between articulation, desire and moments of self-transformation.

As we saw, in this nexus, desire shifts its locus from the body to the inner sense, thus internalizing the erotic. In the same movement, our understanding of the inner sense is transformed – it becomes individualized and reveals its truths to itself through expressing desire as well as deliberating on and articulating its relation to desire, thus eroticizing the 'inner'. The valorization of inner sense as the site of eroticization, reflection and transformation constitutes an important moment in the history of self-articulation in Malayalam writing. Pleasure and pain, in their ultimate intensities, would no longer be matters of the body but of the soul; and the soul would become irreducibly individual in its task of self-articulation and in its self-affirmation as desire.

Acknowledgements

The research for this chapter was carried out during my term as a Fellow of the Indian Institute of Advanced Study, Shimla. Parts of this work have been presented in lectures and seminars in 1996. I would like to thank the discussants and participants in these presentations as well as B. Rajeevan and Oommen George for detailed discussions and valuable clarifications.

Notes

This chapter previously appeared in *Studies in History*, 13:2 (July–December 1997), pp. 247–70.

1 C. Kesavan, *Jeevitasamaram* (Life Struggle), Kottayam, 1990.
2 The Siva temple at Aruvippuram was consecrated by Sree Narayana Guru in 1888; O. Chandu Menon's novel *Indulekha* was first published in 1889; the Malayali Memorial was submitted to the Maharaja of Travancore in 1891; and the Malabar Marriage Commission submitted its report in 1891.
3 See, for detailed discussion and documentation on this, P. Bhaskaranunni, *Pathonpatham Noottandile Keralam* (Nineteenth-century Kerala), Trichur, 1988.
4 Ibid., pp. 31–4 and 743ff.
5 Ibid., p. 743.
6 Ibid., pp. 743 and 750.
7 Ibid., p. 751.
8 Ibid.
9 Ibid., p. 753.
10 Ibid., p. 752.
11 Sree Narayana Guru was born in Champazhanthi near Trivandrum in 1856. After studying Sanskrit and teaching for a few years, he left home to become a renunciant at the age of twenty-eight. Narayana Guru died in 1928. For a biography, see M. K. Sanu, *Sree Narayana Guru*, Kottayam, 1978.
12 Kumaran Asan was born in 1873. In 1891, he met Narayana Guru, who arranged for his education in Bangalore (1895–8) and Calcutta (1898–1900). Asan was the secretary of Sree Narayana Dharma Paripalana Yogam until 1919. Asan died in a boat accident in 1924.
13 For a discussion of Tamil *siddhar* poets, see Kamil Zvelebil, *The Smile of Murugan: On Tamil Literature of South India*, Leiden, 1973, p. 73ff. See also, David C. Buck, 'Siddhanta: Siddha and Saiva' in Fred W. Clothey and J. Bruce Lang (eds), *Experiencing Siva: Encounters with a Hindu Deity*, New Delhi, 1983, pp. 59–74.
14 Sree Narayanan is said to have learned yoga from Thaikkattu Ayyavu, to whom he was introduced by Chattampi Swami. See Sanu, *Sree Narayana Guru*.
15 See T. Bhaskaran's commentary in Sree Narayana Guru, *Sreenarayanaguruvinte Sampoorna Krithikal* (Complete Works of Sree Narayana Guru), Calicut, 1995, pp. 171–218, 266–72. (Hereafter, abbreviated to *Narayanan*).
16 Ibid., p. 273. See also Pampatti Siddhar's work in T. Kovendan (ed.), *Siddhar Padalgal*, Madras, 1976, pp. 220–39.
17 Tirumular, *Thirumantiram: A Tamil Spiritual Classic*, tr. B. Natarajan, Madras, 1991, v. 2104.
18 Siva Vakkiar, v. 47, and Pattirakiri, Lamentations, v. 126, cited in Kamil Zvelebil, *The Smile of Murugan*, 1973, p. 227.
19 Ibid., p. 229.
20 See 'Arivu', *Narayanan*, pp. 522–30; 'Atmopadesa Satakam', ibid., pp. 339–40.
21 See Siva Vakiar, v.126: 'Thevar kallum avaro?'; Zvelebil, *The Smile of Murugan*, p. 227.
22 See Zvelebil, *The Smile of Murugan*.
23 See 'Anukampa Dasakam', in *Narayanan*, pp. 519–21. For a selection of their writings with translations into English, see F. Kingsbury and G. E. Phillips, *Hymns of the Tamil Saivite Saints* (Calcutta: Association Press, 1921).
24 Tirumular, *Thirumantiram*, v. 724.

25 Ibid., v. 725.
26 Ibid., v. 1823.
27 Zvelebil, *The Smile of Murugan*.
28 'Siva Satakam', v. 72, *Narayanan*, p. 205.
29 Ibid., v. 71, p. 205.
30 'Mananatheetham', vv. 7–8, ibid., p. 270.
31 'Indriya Vairagyam', vv. 1–3, *Narayanan*, pp. 225–6.
32 Ibid., v. 10, p. 230.
33 'Atmopadesa Satakam', *Narayanan*, pp. 334–45.
34 Ibid., p. 334.
35 See *Sankhya Karika of Isvara Krsna*, ed. S. S. Surya Narayana Sastri, Madras, 1973, especially pp. xv–xvi and xxii–v, for a discussion of some differences between sankhya and *Saiva Siddhanta*.
36 'Atmopadesa Satakam', v. 12, *Narayanan*, p. 348.
37 Ibid., v. 33, p. 368.
38 Ibid., v. 17, p. 352.
39 Ibid., v. 85, p. 404.
40 Ibid., v. 8, p. 34. *Sabdatharavali* defines the word 'nalika' as 'gun'. See Dr T. Bhaskaran's commentary on this verse, ibid., pp. 343–4.
41 'Atmopadesa Satakam', v. 9, p. 344.
42 See Zvelebil, *The Smile of Murugan*.
43 Tirumular, *Thirumantiram*, v. 2905.
44 'Advaita Jeevitam', *Narayanan*, p. 1.
45 Ibid., p. 1.
46 'Jatilakshanam', ibid., pp. 501–9.
47 Ibid., v. 1, p. 501.
48 'Atmopadesa Satakam', vv. 41–2, *Narayanan*, pp. 373–4.
49 'Jatinirnayam', v. 1, *Narayanan*, p. 497.
50 See Zvelebil, *The Smile of Murugan*.
51 See, for a discussion of arguments presented in this text, P. Lakshmi Narasu, *The Essence of Buddhism* (1907), Bombay, 1948, pp. 91ff. This is Asan's major source for the story of 'Chandala Bhikshuki'.
52 See Kumaran Asan, *Kumaranasante Sampoorna Padya Krithikal* (Complete Poetic Works of Kumaran Asan), Kottayam, 1981, p. 672. (Hereafter abbreviated to *Asan*).
53 See Sanu, *Sree Narayana Guru*, p. 431.
54 Ibid.
55 Ibid., p. 349.
56 Ibid., p. 472.
57 'Advaita Jeevitam', *Narayanan*, p. 1.
58 *Desabhimani*, 15 July 1916, cited in C. R. Kesavan Vaidyar, *Sree Narayana Guruvum Kumaran Asanum* (Sree Narayana Guru and Kumaran Asan), Kottayam, 1993, p. 5.
59 See P. K. Balakrishnan, *Narayana Guru*, Kottayam, 1969, p. 91.
60 Ibid., p. 101.
61 C. R. Kesavan Vaidyar, *Sree Narayana Guruvum*, p. 6.
62 Ibid., p. 89.
63 See 'Sree Narayana Dharmam', *Narayanan*, pp. 657–9.
64 See, for example, the presentation of the female figures in Venmani Mahan's poems. See Seevolli Naryanan, ed., *Venmani Krithikal* (Venmani Poems), Kottayam, 1988, especially 'Pooraprabandham', pp. 59–124 and 'Srngara Slokangal', pp. 458–76. See also the description of Parvathi in Vallathol's

'Sishyananum Makanum', in *Vallatholinte Padya Krithikal* (The Poetical Works of Vallathol), vol. 1, Kottayam, 1975, pp. 205–32.

65 The sense of challenge and conquest is also shared by Narayanan and Asan in their *'vairagya'* poems. However, here the challenge is no longer feigned. It evokes in the subject an intense fear, which functions as a symptom of the ultimate fear, the fear of mortality, as we shall see below.

66 This underlies the repetitive, formulaic nature of the description of female figures in the Venmani tradition.

67 See the section 'Vairagya Panchakam' in 'Siva Sthothra Mala', *Asan*, p. 756.

68 'Veena Poovu' (1909) in *Asan*, pp. 67–79.

69 As we shall see below, in Asan, *'vasana'* also appears as a naturalizing element in the understanding of desire.

70 See 'Nalini or, A Love' (1911) in *Asan*, pp. 99–139; 'Leela' (1914), ibid., pp. 149–226.

71 See 'Chintavishtayaya Seetha' (1919), *Asan*, pp. 521–63, and 'Chandala Bhikshuki' (1922), ibid., pp. 655–76.

72 'Karuna' (1923), *Asan*, pp. 685–701.

73 Ibid., pp. 685 and 693.

74 See 'Nalini', vv. 140–1, *Asan*, p. 133.

75 See 'Preface' to 'Leela', ibid., p. 143.

76 'Leela', vv. 27–36, *Asan*, pp. 208–10.

77 'O, sakhi, no one disappears from this world; the bond that unites the soul to the body is entwined with love; it does not cease to be when the flesh is shed'. 'Leela', v. 82, *Asan*, p. 224.

78 See 'Nalini', vv. 81–117; 'Leela', vv. 1.42–1.44, 1.52–1.56, 2.37–2.43, 3.36–3.53; 'Chintavishtayaya Seetha', vv. 12–185; 'Duravastha', *Asan*, pp. 602–30; and 'Karuna', ibid., pp. 687–8.

79 See 'Chandala Bhikshuki', *Asan*, p. 672.

80 'The blessed One, understanding her sentiments towards Ananda made use of them to open her eyes to the truth, and took her among his disciples'. Lakshmi Narasu, *The Essence of Buddhism*, p. 91, quoted in *Asan*, p. 652.

81 *Kumaran Asante Gadya Lekhanangal* (ed.), N. K. Damodaran, Thonnakkal, 1982, vol. 2, p. 137.

82 Ibid., p. 138.

83 Ibid., vol. 1, p. 46. Asan also reviewed M. V. Parvathy Amma's *Sthreedharmam* (ibid., p. 29), Muloor Padmanabha Panikkar's book of the same title (ibid., pp. 20–1), and P. M. Govindan Vaidyan's *Soothikamrtham* (ibid., p. 23).

11 Postcolonial relations

Gandhi, Nehru and the ethical imperatives of the national-popular

Rajeswari Sunder Rajan

For intellectuals and activists leading anti-colonial struggles, the *ethical* could become and often was developed as an explicit agenda in the conduct of political life. Alongside their insistence that colonialism's mission was unconscionable, colonized people could also claim the moral high ground of the injured. Righteousness functioned as a compensation for the lack of material power, allowing them to go beyond the abjectness of victims or the rage and *ressentiment* of the vanquished. When anti-colonial struggles were launched, they threw up leaders marked by individual 'greatness'. Many found the rhetoric of moral *rightness* as much as political *rights* of strategic use in mass mobilization.

In this chapter though, I want to emphasize a related but different 'use' of the ethical, directed not *at* the colonizer, but inwards, as a mode of self-fashioning that was both individual and communal.[1] In anti-colonial struggles and, following their culmination in political independence, in nation-building projects as well, the 'social' and the 'national' as forms of community had to be forged across existing, indeed deeply entrenched divides of class, gender, caste, religion, language. In these enterprises nationalist leaders had to be creative in finding ways to relate to the 'people' that would avoid replicating not only colonial authoritarianism but, equally, colonialist benevolence. Finding ways of being 'one with the people' was not always easy, since relations of power have a tendency to assume similar forms across different contexts. The distance and divide between native elites and the masses were reflected in the reformist drive, the pedagogical rhetoric, and the performance of sacrifice and service that often characterized the leadership exercised by the former. I suggest that the attempt to transcend the limits of such authoritarian benevolence led to the self-conscious development of a kind of indigenous – by which I mean here an improvised and situated – ethicality; with of course varying degrees of success. The question of political ethics is therefore equally central to postcolonial politics and its forms and practices: in this instance specifically as a question that relates to the function as well as the functioning of democracy.

In India, the morality of politics is identified with the names of the two most prominent nationalist leaders of the time: Mohandas K. Gandhi and Jawaharlal Nehru. The ethico-political mode of identification that I am interested in exploring in the case of Gandhi will be directed chiefly at the idioms and practices of *giving*, in so far as it constitutes the basic structural and performative component of his adoption of voluntary poverty as a way of life – in the public eye as much as within the intimate confines of family life. Gandhi's political morality and way of life is tautologically described – since it appears so entirely *sui generis* – as Gandhianism. In the case of Nehru my interest is in the ways he both exemplified and urged upon other Indians a relationship of intimacy and responsibility between nation and people, and *among* the people, for which the word 'patriotism' will serve as shorthand. I shall invoke Gandhi at the origin of the concept of a specific technology of self that I name *dissemination*; and Nehru as the exemplification of a postcolonial national political leadership that resembles *noblesse oblige*.

I

Gandhi's morality was named by him as a series of 'experiments with truth'. It was a set of successive, lifelong exercises, physical as well as spiritual, that he performed first of all on himself, then persuaded his family and friends to follow, and sooner or later brought to the attention of a larger public through his articles, letters and speeches – in the form of confession (if he failed), or exhortation (if he succeeded). Gandhian experiments with truth resemble nothing so much as the ethical habits cultivated by the philosophers in classical Greece and early Christian Rome that Foucault (1997) has resurrected for us under the descriptive term 'technologies of self' – though with the crucial difference that Gandhi's ideas and practices were incorporated into an active political life. Gandhi's different technologies of self cohered into a single doctrine, *satyagraha* or soul-force, which he put to use in the Indian freedom struggle and, before that, in South Africa.[2] Voluntary poverty was central to achieving *satyagraha*, the first 'necessity' for a life in politics, claimed Gandhi ('Speech at Guildhouse Church', 1931, 50).

Gandhi came late and by stages to the spectacular nakedness that made him 'the greatest exponent of voluntary poverty in the world'.[3] We can follow these stages in his autobiography. In the account of his student years in London, Gandhi describes his initial comic extravagances of dress and social life, which he begins to check as soon as he realizes that his family's means will not support such a lifestyle. The changes he consequently makes in his life – moving to cheaper rooms, walking instead of taking public transport, cooking his own meals – are described with his characteristic gusto for such 'experiments' in living: 'Let not the reader think that this living made my life by any means a dreary affair. On the contrary the changes harmonized my inward and outward life ... and my soul knew no bounds of joy' (Gandhi 1982, 66).[4] But as yet the simple life was dictated only by necessity and a principled wish to live within his means.

It was later, at the peak of his successful career as a barrister in South Africa in 1906, that he began to be 'agitated' by a need to find ways of 'further simplifying my life and of doing some concrete act of service to my fellow men', as he put it in the chapter of the *Autobiography* titled 'Spirit of Service' (192). It is significant that Gandhi began to regard the simple life and service to others as going hand in hand in this way; the discipline of the body seemingly had to be simultaneously self- and other-directed. No doubt he felt that simplicity by itself would have appeared eccentric or obsessive, and conversely that service alone would be hypocritical if he continued to lead the life of the conventional householder. But when the simple life and service were combined, each legitimized and strengthened the ethical value of the other. The thought came to him that nothing less than 'giving up the desire for children and wealth and living the life of a *vanaprastha* – of one retired from household cares', was required of him if he was to devote himself completely to a life of public service (Gandhi 1982, 196).

His first steps in the life of public service were marked however by dissatisfaction, trial and error. He tells us of taking into his home a leper, tending his sores and looking after him himself at first, but then deciding to send him off to the Government Hospital. Though the reasons he gives for abandoning this project (and the leper) are practical ones, the admission 'I lacked the will to keep him always with me' makes it clear that the experience was coded in a spiritual (specifically Christian) symbolic register, as abjectness and singularity of contact, that was not congenial to his needs at this time (Gandhi 1982, 192). He was casting around instead for 'some humanitarian work of a permanent nature', seeking a larger field of operation (ibid.). In these years from 1893 to 1906, he served successively as a part-time medical dispenser, volunteered his services as a stretcher-bearer in an ambulance corps in the Boer War and nursed wounded Zulus in the so-called Zulu 'rebellion'. The troubled reflections during the early years in South Africa led to his setting up the Phoenix ashram. The crucial exposure to Ruskin's *Unto this Last*, described in terms of religious conversion, was the prelude to this decision: 'I could not get any sleep that night. I determined to change my life in accordance with the ideals of the book. I arose with the dawn, ready to reduce these principles to practice' (Gandhi 1982, 274–5). In the middle of his endeavours during the Zulu rebellion he took his vow of *brahmacharya* or celibacy, which was the 'preliminary as it were to Satyagraha' (Gandhi 1982, 291). He regarded the remainder of his life in South Africa (which he left in 1915) to be in the nature of an experiment using *satyagraha* as a political instrument. This new life, we must note, was not to be primarily humanitarian in focus but broadly *political* as he emerged as a leader of the Indian community in their struggle for their rights.

In what follows I examine the implications of Gandhi's ideology and practice of voluntary poverty and his doctrine of service separately for analytic purposes. But their logics were actually deeply imbricated in a unique public life, one that was not free of contradictions. Let me begin with an episode that he narrates in the *Autobiography* which will serve as a parable about the attitude to possessions that he had adopted. When travelling to India by ship in 1914, in the company of his Phoenix ashram friend Kallenbach, Gandhi began to nag Kallenbach about a pair of costly binoculars that the other owned. 'Rather than allow those to be a bone of contention between us, why not throw them into the sea and be done with them?' he wheedled; whereupon an exasperated Kallenbach replied: 'Certainly throw the wretched things away'. 'And forthwith', writes Gandhi, 'I flung them into the sea' (314–15).[5]

What the episode shows us is that voluntary poverty was for Gandhi less an act of *giving* than of *ridding oneself of things*. When he came to write at length about it, it is in these terms of self-dispossession that he primarily described it: 'I must *discard* all wealth, all possessions' (Gandhi 1931 ('Speech at Guildhouse Church'), 51, emphasis mine). He goes on to use other terms similar to 'discard' – 'give up ... things' (note: not 'give away'), 'things slipped away from me', 'I threw overboard things which I used to consider as mine', 'a great burden fell off my shoulders'. And he comes to the conclusion: 'Possession seems to me to be a crime' (ibid., 52).

Gandhi's position, if taken to its extreme logical conclusion – which he does (its extremity provoking C. F. Andrews to compare Gandhi to Savonarola![6]) – raises some obvious issues, of which he has anticipated and addressed several as moral dilemmas. I shall identify the most significant of these as they relate to the following: the conditions of possibility of a life of voluntary poverty, which include the necessity of living on charity; the consequent issues of dependency, debt and gratitude; the problem presented by 'real', that is *involuntary*, poverty; and the status of the physical body.

Let me begin with the first of these, that is, with the problem of how one might *become* poor. Gandhi is confronted by the difficulty that the man without possessions must still find a means of subsistence, and decides that he has no option except to 'live purely on the charity of the world' (Gandhi 1931, 53). To be a recipient of charity under *these* circumstances is, however, a different matter from being a 'real' beggar. About beggary and dependency he expresses a fairly conventional view, quite unlike the radical defence of the case of the voluntarily poor man (himself) living on charity:

> The grinding poverty and starvation with which our country is afflicted is such that it drives more and more men every year into the ranks of the beggars, whose desperate struggle for bread renders them insensible to all feelings of decency and self-respect. And our philanthropists, instead of providing work for them and assisting them on their working for bread, give them alms. (Gandhi 1982, 391)

Alms-taking and alms-giving must, it seems, be restricted only to those who are voluntarily poor like himself. In this Gandhi is able to build upon Hindu and Buddhist religious practices that enjoined giving to *sanyasis* or *bhikhus* (religious mendicants, renunciants), men who have rendered themselves voluntarily poor (and are consequently allowed to live *only* on charity), within a closed and self-serving system of donors and donees. The novelty of Gandhi's chosen poverty was that he was not a religious *sanyasi*, but one who was, on the contrary, active in secular public life. Such activity would be felt to be incumbent upon a non-religious person living on charity if he was not to exist as a parasite on society. Living on charity is a contingent, chancy affair that entails subsisting literally from hand to mouth, from day to day. As he became established in national public life, Gandhi's life of poverty naturally became less risky in this sense;[7] nor was his poverty projected as a matter of dependency – it became an emblem, rather, of agential self-sufficiency.[8] These differences, however, did not prevent Gandhi from embracing the identity of a 'poor man' whole-heartedly – a comment not to be viewed as an accusation of hypocrisy but as an acknowledgement of a constitutive contradiction in the unique position he constructed for himself, as simultaneously poor man (subject) and public figure (object, of universal charity).

As in the matter of living on charity, Gandhi was unflinching when it came to handling debt and the accusation of ingratitude. For instance, having once taken out an insurance policy for his family at a time of financial insecurity, he experienced a great crisis of conscience: did such an act of worldly prudence not betray a lack of confidence in God, in his brother who had always supported the larger family, and even in the self-reliance of his wife and children? He could breathe easily only when he finally brought himself to cancel the policy. As in the case of charity, dependency had to be accepted with humility; and once again, a form of living contingently, on the brink, was the ethical demand of poverty that he felt obliged to respond to. In the same breath he wrote to inform his older brother Lakshmidas that his vow of poverty meant that 'henceforth he should expect nothing from me' (Gandhi 1982, 245). Having lived on the resources provided by this brother during his student years in London, Gandhi had been expected to take on the responsibilities of the larger family once he became an established lawyer. His abdication led to a rift between the brothers. As a grandson, Arun Gandhi, explains it in his memoir of Kasturbai: 'His [Gandhi's] ingratitude was a cruel blow, a humiliation for the whole family' (A. Gandhi 2000, 129). Gandhi argued that he was in fact supporting his family – only, 'the meaning of "family" had but to be slightly widened and the wisdom of my step would become clear' (Gandhi 1982, 245). Gandhi's unilateral cancellation of the debt replaces the obligation of repayment by a different obligation – that of service to a different (wider) set of recipients. Rather than confine the debt/gift – the gift that is always implicitly a loan – within the intimate closure of return and reciprocity, he sets it in motion on a different and dispersed trajectory.

The trickiest aspect of advocating voluntary poverty is of course the existence and prevalence of real, that is, *involuntary* poverty. Gandhi is quick to refuse any idealization or compensatory view of poverty *as such*: 'I would not go among my fellows who starve and talk of voluntary poverty; I do not tell them how blessed they would be if they changed that involuntary poverty into voluntary … these men have first of all to have the necessities of life before I can talk to them of voluntary poverty' (Gandhi 1931, 57). There is therefore a profound paradox that lies at the heart of Gandhi's position: in order to *become* poor, one cannot be poor to begin with. It is choice, not lack, which is the key ethical aspect of voluntary poverty. And since Gandhi thought himself able to determine and dictate an ideal measure of needs and wants, he recast poverty in absolute rather than relative terms, that is, in terms of a universally acceptable standard of sufficiency.

Admittedly, Gandhian voluntary poverty is not a new idea. Gandhi himself alluded to the number of sources, Hindu and Christian, indigenous and foreign, from which he drew with characteristic eclecticism: Christ's teachings; Ruskin; Tolstoy; Thoreau; the Vaishnava saints; the Bhagavad Gita; Dadabhai Naoroji; his spiritual mentor Raychandbhai.[9] But neither was it exactly like any of these other sources and examples. Nowhere do we see in him any desire to store up merit through good deeds; there are no overtones of Christian otherworldliness or of Christian idealization of (natural, involuntary) poverty; it was more than only a choice of the simple life;[10] nor is it a version of Hindu asceticism;[11] he distinguished his credo from socialism;[12] and he rarely spoke of sacrifice except in the sense of renunciation.[13]

What remains may be called a kind of ethical self-centredness. This chosen poverty's justification is its practitioner's *own* 'happiness, the bliss, the ability that it gives one', without any reference to the good it might do to others (Gandhi 1931, 58). 'Benevolence', he believed, should have no 'taste of favour about it'. 'To serve without desire is to favour not others, but ourselves' (Gandhi 1930, 259). Voluntary poverty is not charity, and it is not a redistributive project (hence his advocacy of trusteeship rather than communism);[14] it is not about sharing one's wealth but sharing the other's poverty; not a giving *to* but a giving *up*. Its practice, as he repeatedly emphasized, results not in (personal) deprivation but (universal) self-sufficiency, which is why he never described it as sacrificial. His poverty would act like a 'dissemination': a going forth (casting, broadcasting) without return, but also without recipients (or only accidental recipients). Through dissemination one does not seek to forge a relationship with a designated 'other', one loses one's self.

The word 'dissemination' is an echo but not an invocation of Derrida. The invocation would be legitimate, nevertheless, authorized by the heterogeneous sources Gandhi himself drew on to enunciate his practical philosophy, but also by Derrida's own repeated returns to the question of (the impossibility of) the gift which come close to capturing Gandhi's endeavours. Derrida posits a radical benevolence that would have to lie entirely outside the motivations, contexts and conditions in which benevolence is usually viewed. It should not emerge, for instance, from a mere superfluity of possessions, or get caught up in the circuits of exchange (cf. Derrida: 'the gift must remain *aneconomic*' (1992, 7)); and furthermore, unlike acts of philanthropy or charity, it would have to be free of moral calculation.

In one place Derrida succinctly describes what I have laboured to convey through my exposition: the gift is 'that which one does not have' (1994, 27). Why is it viewed as such a crucial ethical project, this giving without expectation of return, and why is it also 'impossible'? As Derrida explains the gift/gifting in *Glas*, 'when *someone* gives *something* to *someone*, one is already long within calculating dialectics and speculative idealization' (1986, 244a, all emphases in original). The contamination of even the 'pure' gift is inescapable. 'At the limit, the gift as gift ought not to appear as gift: either to the donee or to the donor ... If the other perceives or receives it, if he or she keeps it as gift, the gift is annulled' (Derrida 1992, 14). The gift 'puts the other in debt, with the result that giving amounts to hurting, to doing harm' (12). Derrida might be speaking on Gandhi's behalf, in the matter of Gandhi's unilateral cancellation of his debt to his brother, when he insists that the true (impossible) gift requires that 'the donee not give back ... The donee owes it *to himself* even not to give back, he *ought* not *owe*' (13, emphases in original).

It is this care about refraining from gift/ing or returning the debt, but despite it entering the *circuit* of the gift – which is nothing less than the social itself – that Gandhi 'impossibly' managed in his life's experiments.[15]

Tracking the philosophy and practice of voluntary poverty further in Gandhi's life, we can see that it changes – grows stricter, more absolute – from 1915 onwards when he began his political life in India. From being a lifestyle of simplicity adopted primarily as a matter of integrity in public life, poverty in India became for Gandhi a more explicitly political issue and then an issue of nationalist politics. It was Dadabhai Naoroji's

Poverty and Un-British Rule in India (1901) that gave him, he writes, his 'first acquaintance with the extent of Indian poverty' (Gandhi 1924, 103). Poverty, in other words, ceased to be simply the tautological condition of the poor, but was, if not newly, certainly more acutely perceived as a consequence of the immiseration of the people caused by colonial rule and capitalist exploitation.[16] Gandhi's attempt to reconcile his structural understanding of poverty with its existential and ethical aspects produced contradictions that became particularly acute in his public-political life.

Thus, while there could be no question that involuntary poverty must be alleviated wherever it was found, how could the project of allevia-tion be effected, or how would it be even affected, by a political leader's example of self-chosen poverty? The life of poverty was an essential condition, in Gandhi's view, for a leader of the Indian masses (though it was not merely a strategy as some analysts have reductively suggested). Gandhi adopted (some would say usurped) the very identity of the poor as well as, as we shall see, the untouchable and, on occasion, the female; he sought nothing less than to *become* the figure of the oppressed through identification. Identification with the poor came to mean, for Gandhi the political leader, adopting a number of symbolic outward marks of poverty, the most famous being his dress (the homespun loin-cloth),[17] his diet (vegetarian: fruit, nuts and goat's milk), his dwelling (the ashram), his programme of spinning (*khadi*) and his favoured modes of transportation (walking and third-class train travel), all of which have been extensively analysed for their meanings and their efficacy, not least by himself.[18]

The public, performative aspect of voluntary poverty was achieved through the precise modalities of *exemplarity* and *service*. The simple life would not only allow him to live in the midst of the masses and gain cred-ibility among them, it would also serve as an inspiration and bring hope to the poor: 'They would say: "He is happy though he possesses nothing; how is it?" I do not need to argue with them; they begin to argue for themselves' (Gandhi 1931, 57).[19] He impresses by simply *being* (i.e. by authenticity, or the non-contradiction between practice and preaching). Gandhi's remarks indicate, in addition, that he is not poor as the 'poor' are poor: he simultaneously fashions himself as an exemplary model of the condition he embraces.[20] He often urges, for instance, that simple cleanli-ness and contentment will make poverty tolerable as well as virtuous.

Under most circumstances the authenticity of being (poor) should have absolved Gandhi of any obligation to act. He surely had no need to exert himself any further in acts of service, especially when service, like exemplarity, was bound to intrude the differences of status and power, whereas through identification he sought sameness with the people. But in Gandhi's case as we saw there was a compulsion to serve, closely allied with the ethical imperative of voluntary poverty and indeed instigated by it.

Physical service by means of the body's performative labours is the only form of 'gifting' left to a donor who has renounced all worldly possessions, and even then it remains ambiguous as a form of giving. When Gandhi confronted the ontological question of the body's relationship to the self, he decided in favour of a separation of the body as such from self. 'In order to realize that ideal [of voluntary poverty] in its fullness ... I must not possess anything on this earth as my property, not even this body, because *this body also is a possession*' (Gandhi 1931, 54, emphasis mine). Since one does not own even one's own body, one must treat it, he says, as a 'temporary possession' which, while it is at one's disposal, 'must be used ... for service and service the whole of our waking hours' (ibid., 54). The body has a central place in his schema. It must be worn out like a pair of slippers with continual use, as the proverb has it. It is through the body's performative labours that he offers his service to suffering humanity.

Seva, or service, has recently been theorized by Ajay Skaria as an aspect of a broader Gandhian political philosophy.[21] Skaria presents *seva* as Gandhi's response to the 'incoherence and injustice' of the application of liberalism's ideals of equality to the subaltern. Gandhi, by contrast, would acknowledge and subscribe to the hierarchies of social relations.[22] The religious idioms in which he described the subaltern – *daridranarayan* (the divine poor) and *harijan* (children of God, referring to untouchables) – allowed him to offer them, instead of a false liberal equality, the devotion of *seva* through physical labours such as spinning (Skaria 2002, 979–81).

Seva nevertheless produces an insuperable contradiction when conceptualized – as how can it not be? – in terms of service *to the other*. Though distinct from forms of giving (wealth), the body labouring on behalf of the other (as opposed to indulging itself by using its labours to serve only oneself), comes close to constituting itself as a gift. Whereas voluntary poverty is solipsistic and self-centred (so much so that Gandhi could take a unilateral decision about adopting it as his condition in life), service, like friendship, is tied to the other. Can one unilaterally decide to serve or befriend the other? Is not service predicated on acceptance of service, as friendship is on reciprocity? Can it, even, ever be anything more than a *response*, though prompt and unequivocal, to a request framed by the other – unlike friendship which implies spontaneity followed by mutuality? There is every likelihood that help proffered without reference to the other's will, will render the other impotent: *helpless*.

We may follow the implications of this a little further as it applies, specifically, to the issue of caste. Gandhi's stand on untouchability has become one of the key issues for understanding the history of caste politics today. Gandhi presented untouchability as uniquely a problem for caste Hindus, and hence called for reform within Hinduism by means of 'service' to untouchables and other forms of reparation to be performed by them. (In this matter Gandhi's attitude shows a return to the abject version of service, coded as singularity and contact, which he had rejected in seeking a larger, more impersonal public and political field of action in South Africa.) Gandhi's hegemonic sway over the caste issue did not go unopposed, however. B. R. Ambedkar, the leader of the untouchables, was caustic in his disapproval of the upper-caste Hindu 'service' that turned many dalits into 'mere recipients of charity' (Prashad 2000, 128). Gandhi's position, as Vijay Prashad has argued, 'did not argue for emancipation *from* dalithood, but for reform *within* dalithood' (117). Gandhi's refusal to address untouchability in any except upper-caste Hindu reformist terms, like his refusal to support any attack on private property or its owners, meant that he successfully contained both dalit and peasant politics within the ambit of bourgeois and upper-caste *seva*. *Seva* may counter liberal equality, but in doing so it also checks the revolutionary agency of subalterns themselves.

Gandhi's emphasis on upper-caste *seva* claimed monopoly over the caste issue, to the extent that he opposed any lower-caste activism such as *satyagraha*, or political initiatives such as separate electorates, that addressed aspects of caste other than untouchability. Thereby he sought to retain caste within the ambit of reformability. The intractable obstacle to seeing *seva* as a response to untouchability analogous to voluntary poverty as response to involuntary or 'real' poverty, lies in caste's immutability. Even when Gandhi undertook to perform the degraded labours of the untouchables, it could not make him untouchable as voluntary poverty could make him poor; he could only occupy the upper-caste position as *seva* became reparation.

Gandhi's doctrine of *seva*, like his economic prescriptions, was evidence equally of his anti-statism, reinforced by the auto-didacticism of his ethics.[23] His non-revolutionary praxis, fearing violence, sought to retain the *status quo* of class, gender and caste relations, relying instead on a change of heart which would put the onus of transforming social structures on those who are in possession of power and privilege. This much, by way of limits, is obvious.

What I wish to propose nevertheless is the likelihood that Gandhi was not oblivious to the possibility, and the shape, of the recalcitrant subaltern response to such initiatives. Though *seva* could not but descend into gift, and although Gandhi was thwarted by the inability to find a moral strategy similar to voluntary poverty in his response to caste, there is nothing in the logic of his positions on either trusteeship or *seva* that scripts gratitude or acquiescence as the recipient other's only possible response. At any rate, he had little to say about his expectations of the recipient of *seva*, concentrating instead on the behaviour expected of those whose duty it is to perform it. We might even say that resistance articulated as 'ingratitude', of the kind expressed by many dalits to the programmes of the Harijan Sevak Sangh, would cancel debt most effectively, restoring *seva* to the domain of giving without benevolence. Such non-expectation of return is a key teaching of the Bhagavad Gita, one of Gandhi's major intellectual and spiritual resources.[24] Consider also as a variation of this, by way of a more active *expectation of non-return*, Lévinas' description of the self's transcendent relation to the 'other', which requires a 'movement without return' of the kind Derrida posits for the gift: 'A work conceived in its ultimate nature requires a radical generosity of the same who in the work goes unto the other. It then requires an *ingratitude* of the other' (Lévinas 1986, 349, emphasis in original). Inherent in the communitarian self-sufficiency and the worker non-cooperation that Gandhi so staunchly supported, is an intransigent ingratitude that functions as a practical ethics of subaltern response to the gift of service as much as to the injustice against which it is more overtly directed.

II

The political history of India as it changed from colony to independent nation also marked a regime change from Gandhi's leadership and influence to those of Jawaharlal Nehru.[25] The shift in the dominant ethico-political thought, from Gandhi's anti-colonial 'anarcho-communitarianism' and 'non-statist idiom', to Nehru's idea of a *state*-sustained postcolonial Indian identity (Khilnani 1998, 166) – in other words, towards the idea of liberal citizenship – marks a major difference of emphasis.[26] Though there were continuities as well as changes – Nehru had always been Gandhi's disciple and presumptive heir, and deeply affective bonds united them – the demands of defining and leading a hugely diverse and profoundly underdeveloped nation that was to adopt a democratic republican state form, as much as temperamental and ideological differences from Gandhi, led Nehru to chart a distinctively different path. It was a path that led Nehru, as leader of India's postcolonial democracy, to explore the ideal and praxis of *responsibility*. Whether its expression predominantly in terms of patriotism and *noblesse oblige* indeed functioned as an alternative to benevolence, or whether it was instead simply its surrogate, is the question that concerns me in this analysis.

Nehru's first speech as leader of free India, delivered to the Constituent Assembly on 14 August 1947, the eve of Independence, acknowledges Gandhi's legacy, but marks at the same time the nuanced departures from it that Nehru's perception of his new role as elected representative of the people required. This famous speech, both stirring and sober, was delivered as a pledge to serve the people: the 'responsibility' that comes with 'freedom and power', Nehru declared, 'rests upon this assembly, a sovereign body representing the sovereign people of India'. Nehru goes on to invoke Gandhi movingly in this short address: 'The ambition of the greatest man of our generation has been to wipe every tear from every eye'. That wish is both honoured and reframed thus: 'That may be beyond us, but as long as there are tears and suffering, so long our work will not be over'.[27] Nehru is scrupulous to mark the difference between Gandhian *seva* – which he views here in terms that recall Lévinas's invocation of Dostoevsky's phrase, 'insatiable compassion' ('he does not say "inexhaustible compassion"'), (1986, 351) and his own more limited but nevertheless onerous responsibility as a political leader of this new nation (Nehru 1949, 3).

And yet Nehru could not always contain the dutifulness expressed in these carefully constructed terms of political responsibility from over-flowing into the language of affect. It is instructive to turn to another of Nehru's writings, his last will and testament, in order to illustrate the overpowering, and complicated, nature of his feelings for his country (1997).

Written as early as 1954, the will was made public at his death ten years later. It has since become a much-admired text, frequently anthologized, for example, in school and college textbooks. This document allows me now to make the move to a different set of problematics, that of national identity, which is closely linked in postcoloniality to the sentiment of patriotism. Patriotism is a relationship to the national body – to the land and its people – that is rhetorically coded here as both claim and allegiance.

In its form and content the will is a conventional one: it bequeaths Nehru's property to his heirs, expresses his love for the people and land of India, and leaves instructions about his funeral. Since, unlike Gandhi, Nehru did not adopt voluntary poverty (he both inherited wealth and earned money from his writings), or refuse political office, his commitment to the nation is neither as total nor as disinterested as Gandhi's could be said to have been. Questions of divided loyalties, and of power, can therefore be found reflected in each of these aspects of the will.

Despite Nehru's anxious reiteration that he has few assets and little property to leave because of the distracted public life he has led, he is clearly uneasy about the disposition of his famous ancestral house, Anand Bhawan, as he debates the rival claims of nation and daughter. The large house in Allahabad that his famous nationalist father Motilal Nehru had built, was connected intimately with the national struggle for freedom: 'within its walls great events have happened and great decisions have been reached'. Hence it ought to be, he feels, a national property, 'more than a private possession'. But in the event it is to his daughter Indira and her sons that he leaves it, with the stipulation, however, that 'whoever lives in Anand Bhawan must always remember this [i.e. its historical associations] and must not do anything contrary to that tradition'. He hastens to add, 'This wish of mine [is] not intended to be in any way a restriction on the proprietary rights conferred upon my daughter'.[28] (Indira Ghandi donated it to the nation in 1970 and it is now a national museum of the Nehru family.)

The conflict between the public and private personae of the nationalist figure could not be clearer and more poignant, especially when it is a question of being a 'father' – of the people, but also of biological offspring.[29] *Not* leaving Anand Bhawan to the nation then, he turns to the question of how he might, despite this, acknowledge gratitude, debt, and return. 'I have received so much love and affection from the Indian people that I have been overwhelmed by it ... nothing I can do can repay even a small fraction of it ... there can [of course] be no repayment of so precious a thing as affection'. Nevertheless, we can discern in these lines the unspoken assurance that this affection is his due, the return for *his* services and sacrifices during the nationalist struggle. Writing this document in the early years of political office, he can still look forward to deserving the people's love and gratitude with continued service as the nation's Prime Minister. 'I can only express the hope that in the remaining years I may live, shall not be unworthy of my people and their affection'.

It is in the same affective register – love which dissolves debt and return – that he asks that his body be cremated and a handful of his ashes thrown into the Ganges, not because of any religious sentiment, he clarifies, but because of an entirely secular emotional attachment to the great river from childhood, as a symbol of India, like the Himalayas from which it flows. He asks that the rest of the ashes be scattered from a plane 'over the fields where the peasants of India toil', so that 'they may mingle with the dust and soil of India and become an indistinguishable part of India'.

The wish to merge into the largeness of physical India, its rivers, mountains and fields, is an expression of abjection, while at the same time it assumes an identification between the individual and the nation that amounts almost to a proprietary relationship. The intimate sense of belonging that he felt to India was therefore also, always already, a form of ownership.[30] It is an attitude not unknown among other colonial elites. But what distinguishes Nehru's attitude from colonialist paternalism – though his tortuous prose is arguably inflected by rhetoric of a similar kind – is the inchoate feeling that we call patriotism.

Patriotism is less a matter of 'practical morality' than of 'sentiment', Anthony Appiah would argue (Appiah 1997, 622). In Nehru's case we might modify this to describe a morality *inflected by* sentiment. This primordial sense of belonging to the land is one he had detected also in the Indian masses and written about in *The Discovery of India* (1946). At that time he had held it insufficient to ground a new sense of Indianness. In a passage that has become well known, he writes of his pedagogic mission to create the sense of a modern Indian identity which located it in the *people*, both individually and in their relations as an 'imagined community', rather than in simply an atavistic sense of belonging to the land. At the vast gatherings he addressed all over India, he would ask his audience:

who was this Bharat Mata, Mother India... ? At last a vigorous Jat, wedded to the soil from immemorial generations, would say that it was the *dharti*, the good earth of India, that they meant .... I would endeavour to explain that India was all this that they had thought [mountains, rivers, forests, broad fields]... but it was much more. What counted ultimately were the people of India, people like them and me, who were spread out all over this vast land ... You are parts of this Bharat Mata, I told them, you are in a manner yourselves Bharat Mata. (1946, 39)

Though Nehru speaks here of 'people like them and me' in an attempt at finding the democratic levelling essential for forging the nation as community – as Khilnani has observed, Nehru was no populist but instead someone who promoted the 'idea of an abstract, historically durable "people" or "nation"' (1998, 41) – there can be no doubt that he related to the people from a position that placed him above and apart from them.

Nehru's love of India was essentially that of a cosmopolitan. He represents what Anthony Appiah terms the 'cosmopolitan patriot', a type that, as he observes, is familiar among nationalist elites in South Asia and Africa, whose 'roots' are local but who is intellectually nourished by 'Europe and its Enlightenment' (1997, 636). Offering a similar diagnosis, Sunil Khilnani astutely remarks how fitting the title of Nehru's *Discovery of India* is in that, although it reflects India as 'indubitable presence', it acknowledges that 'it could not be taken for granted by people of Nehru's class and background – its contours had to be actively plotted' (1998, 168). It is this acquired and self-conscious love – none the less intense or authentic for that – which marks Nehru's identification with the land (which can also be read as a claim) as being different from that of his interlocutor, the 'vigorous Jat'. From this same-but-not-quite position he can offer to the people a share in the identity 'Indian', the grounds for the nation-as-community and for his own identification with the people. That the implications of such a pedagogic discourse, marked as it is by condescension, paternalism and self-righteousness, could be problematic from the point of view of a truly egalitarian relationship, hardly needs pointing out.[31] The term *noblesse oblige* helps to capture some of the contradictory aspects of responsibility in this mode.

Noblesse oblige (literally, 'nobility obligates') is a dictum derived from European feudalism; 'nobility' itself describes a class ('the quality, state, or condition of being noble in respect of rank or birth': *The Shorter OED*), but in course of time it yields to a description of a meritocracy. The English 'have no equivalent phrase in English to "*noblesse oblige*"', Evelyn Waugh held; instead 'everything turns on "the grand old name of gentleman"' (1956, 73). Nancy Mitford, in her famous little book bearing the phrase as its title – essentially a disquisition upon class – described the 'aristocrat' thus: 'The purpose of the aristocrat is to lead, therefore his functions are military and political'. In war, accordingly, English noblemen have fought bravely, and in politics they 'have worked hard for no reward and done their best according to their lights' (1956, 47–8). This sums up English *noblesse oblige*. In America, in 1867, Emerson had eloquently praised the new democratic elite he was addressing as an assembly of 'educated, reflecting, successful and powerful persons'. He went on to invoke *noblesse oblige*: 'Yours is the part of those who have received much. It is an old legend of just men, Noblesse oblige; or, superior advantages bind you to larger generosity', going on to outline the great responsibilities borne by 'good men' in a society such as America's (1876, 235).

These meanings of the term, both the meritocratic Emersonian inflection and the feudal English connotations of 'gentleman', had particular resonance for those leading anti-colonial nationalist struggles, for whom political freedom was itself associated with responsibility. For instance, Sarojini Naidu, poet, prominent Congress nationalist, and one of Gandhi's closest associates, wrote as follows in a letter to her young daughter in 1921:

> Only remember that you are an Indian girl and that puts upon you a heavier burden than if you were an English girl born to a heritage of freedom. Remember that you have to help India to be free and the children of tomorrow to be free-born citizens of a free land. Therefore if you're true to your country's need you must recognize the responsibility of your Indian womanhood.... You are not free – no one is – in the sense of being a law unto yourself in defiance of all existing tradition in our country – for freedom is the heaviest bondage in one sense – since it entails duties, responsibilities and opportunities from which slaves are immune ... *Noblesse oblige*! And the ampler the liberty the narrower the right to do as one pleases. You have in you all the seeds of true greatness: be great my little child ... but always remembering that you are a symbol of India. (Naidu 1996, 157)

Middle-class Indian children of Nehru's generation and those belonging to the following generation ('midnight's children'), have heard variations on this exhortation reminding them of obligations of service to the nation.[32] But sometimes there was more: as in Naidu's case, there could also be a feeling of a calling to 'greatness'.

One need not resort to cynicism to discern how deeply implicated *noblesse oblige* is in structures of class or privilege; or how, apart from the hierarchies it establishes, it is also inseparable from authoritarianism. In a pseudonymous essay titled 'The Rashtrapati', published in the *Modern Review* in 1937, Nehru discovered in himself the 'makings of a dictator', stemming from his very assets as a leader: 'vast popularity, a strong will directed to a well-defined purpose, energy, pride, organizational capacity, ability, hardness'. Nehru castigated himself for 'an intolerance of others and a certain contempt for the weak and inefficient', this despite 'his love of the crowd'. The wish to serve or to lead the people – the difference becomes irrelevant – is reflected in an 'overmastering desire to get things done, to sweep away what he dislikes and build anew' (Nehru 1937, 522).

While undeniably perceptive and morally admirable, Nehru is not unique in finding that *noblesse oblige* both arises from and breeds power, that it can legitimize the quest for power and its exercise. The criticism itself is in some ways banal. The answer cannot lie in a disavowal of privilege and the responsibility that attends it – such a move can only be disingenuous.[33] The ethically complex issue is whether privilege and responsibility can be handled differently, and how. The contrast with colonial benevolence brings out the specific features of postcolonial responsibility: where the former arises from plenitude and certitude, 'responsibility' in postcolonial relations is marked by efforts to determine its own ethical limits.

Therefore, to my mind the most interesting part of Nehru's essay lies in his insight that his impatience 'will hardly brook for long the slow processes of *democracy*' (1937, 522, emphasis mine). He was quick to see that democracy, as the rule of the people, must remain forever in conflict with and resistant to the rule of elites, however benevolent their leadership. Any attempt to reconcile the two can only be wishful and dangerous.

The recent influential argument of Fareed Zakaria stands as an instance of the troubling logic of the attempt to resolve the conflict. Zakaria, pitting the 'illiberalism' of the masses ('the tyranny of the majority') against liberal democracy, opts for the latter. He is nostalgic for a time when *noblesse oblige* in America was expressed in the public school credo 'to serve is to reign', and its followers believed that 'public service was a responsibility that came with power' (Zakaria 2003, 233–4). In the different context of India, Zakaria harks back to the Nehruvian era when democracy was still an elite prerogative – only to yield, to his dismay, in the decades since then to the growing power of new voters, 'almost all from poor, rural, lower-caste backgrounds' (108). Therefore, he recommends that democracy be (once again) made the responsibility, and entrusted to the leadership, of the elites, 'those with immense powers in our societies' (256).

Nehru was very far from seeking a solution to his dilemma conceptualized in terms such as these. On the contrary, the 'Nehru era', Khilnani maintains, 'was permeated by the rhetoric of democracy and social reform, and indeed Indian democracy was exemplary as a system of government then; parliamentary and party procedures were priggishly followed, there were few scandals, enough Indians voted to give the system legitimacy without overtaxing its capacities' (1998, 40). A genuine attempt was made by the national leadership 'to pass the burden of reform down to the lowest levels, through "community development projects" and local democracy, *Panchayati Raj*, or rule by village councils' (79). Where Nehru did seem to be supporting elite hegemony, was through his increasing reliance on a powerful bureaucracy and technocrats, chiefly economists and scientists, in promoting the nation's 'development' (81). As far as his political style of functioning was concerned, Judith Brown speaks of his failures only in terms of an exacerbated sense of responsibility, but not of any temptation to take away power from the people (as his daughter, Indira Gandhi, was to do through the notorious Emergency): 'in the highest political office in the country he developed a vast and unsustainable role for himself. He proved incapable of delegating authority and effectively sharing power among colleagues' (343).

It is tempting to map Weber's distinction between 'Gesinnungsethik' and 'Verantwortungsethik' (translated as 'absolute ethics' and 'ethics of responsibility') on to Gandhi and Nehru respectively (Weber 1964).[34] But while 'ethics of responsibility' does in a sense capture Nehru's endeavours, it is not by scanting means for ends as Weber's heroic leader would, that Nehru enacted such a responsibility.[35] As we saw, the fear of dictatorial behaviour – and, implicitly, the recognition of the anachronism of *noblesse oblige* in an age of democracy – informs Nehru's self-criticism in 'The Rashtrapati'. Nevertheless Weber's posing of the problem as the constitutive conflict of ethics and politics is central to our understanding of Nehru's dilemma. Even if 'power' in his case was benevolent rather than 'demonic' as in Weber's argument, its inevitable authoritarianism, as he himself realized, was personally corrupting and could, moreover, endanger the idea of democracy.[36]

Democracy is often claimed to be the 'gift' of the West to the rest of the world, either through the instrumentality of colonialism or simply through its own benign example. In the postcolonial world, it tends to be perceived as the 'gift' of political equality offered to a largely poor and illiterate population by those who (are *elected* to) rule – rulers who often came to power as a result of their service and perceived sacrifices in anti-colonial struggles. This sequence mimics, on the stage of history and politics, the dynamics of the gift and its reciprocities. But democracy is not the thing that exists prior to its gifting. Rather, as Derrida repeatedly emphasizes, it is that which comes into being through ceaseless negotiation, always as a democracy-to-come (1997, 306). In Nehru's pioneering efforts in India to make democracy work – against the grain of his own inherited *noblesse oblige*, and despite the constraints of postcolonial underdevelopment, both political and economic – we can begin to discern the outlines of an ethics of responsibility that was more difficult than benevolence, and well in excess of the demands of mere political office.

Notes

This chapter was previously published in a slightly different form in Gilbert Helen and Chris Tiffin, eds. *Burden or Benefit? Imperial Benevolence and Its Legacies* (Bloomington, IN: Indiana University Press, 2008), pp. 136–59.

1 Sunil Khilnani explains attempts at such self-fashioning, as reflected for instance in Gandhi's writing of an autobiography, in terms of the crisis produced by modernity: 'For Gandhi, as for his fellow intellectuals … an insistent challenge was that of how to translate this alien world [of modernity] into one which was comprehensible, a world where it was possible to find one's moral bearings, and over which Indians, collectively and individually, might gain some control and even mastery' (Introduction to M. K. Gandhi, *The Story of my Experiments with Truth*, 1982, 5).
2 *Satyagraha*, translated into civil disobedience and marked by non-violence or *ahimsa*, has received extended attention from Gandhian scholars (see, for example, Bondurant 1988; Steger 2000).
3 Gandhi is quoting Dr Maud Royden, a 'progressive social reformer, who was in the chair' ('Speech at Guildhouse Church', 53), (editor's note, Iyer, 1993, 125).
4 Typically also, in these endeavours, Gandhi writes that he consulted 'books on simple living'. An aspect of Gandhi's modern, or at least unorthodox ways was his willingness and ability to consult do-it-yourself manuals on a variety of matters. This made him very much an autodidact. More particularly, it reduced his dependence on servants and service-providers.
5 He had earlier recorded, in a tone half-comical, half-tragical, a much more fraught struggle of wills with his wife over some costly gifts that were given to him: 'We had been fast simplifying our life … What was I now to do with the jewellery that had come upon me?' He finally overcomes her resistance and places the gifts in a trust for the community's needs (Gandhi 1982, 208).
6 The Rev. C. F. Andrews, one of Gandhi's closest friends and associates, invokes the comparison while describing Gandhi's *swadeshi* campaign for the boycott of foreign goods in India: 'with his mind aflame at the sufferings of the poor and the luxuries of the rich, [Gandhi] ordered bonfires to be made of foreign clothes and ornaments on the beach at Bombay … Then he mounted the great pile and himself applied the flaming torch at night, while the vast crowd raised shouts that rent the sky'. Though he is quick to qualify his criticism – 'such puritanical fervour is never the deepest thing about him' – Andrews' insight into Gandhi's fanaticism about the *destruction* of wealth is to be borne in mind (Andrews 1929).
7 We can say, without trivializing the real difficulties and sacrifices involved in the life he followed, that the very fact of being a figure in public life, well known and admired as a Mahatma, made Gandhi's life of poverty an elegant and reasonably comfortable one. The quip made by Sarojini Naidu is well known: 'You will never know how much it costs us to keep that saint, that wonderful old man, in poverty!' (reported by Shirer 1993, 38).
8 Gandhi is unashamed also to be engaged in a more modern form of begging, fund-raising. To be a beggar for a cause, as he undertook to be on occasion, is a matter indeed for pride: 'I have got this reputation of being one of the best beggars in India. At one time I collected one crore of rupees, some horribly large sum, but I had no difficulty in collecting it', he boasts (Gandhi 1931, 55).

He attributes his success to the '*scientific result* of this vow of non-possession or vow of voluntary poverty' (ibid., emphasis added).

9 Raychandbhai – poet, businessman, scholar and spiritual guide – was the person Gandhi came closest to adopting as his own *guru* (Gandhi 1982, 92–3).

10 The misapprehension has, however, gained ground – Gandhi is recuperated in the West today mainly as a *guru* of counter-cultural, New Age, anti-consumerist and eco-anarchist movements.

11 See his letter of 17 March 1945: 'Asceticism in the English sense is not needed at the present time. But there is all the need for renunciation' ('Note to Gope Gurbaxani', 1945, 261).

12 He often compared his programme to socialism without the violence of its means (for example, 'Who is a Socialist?', 1947b, 283).

13 Gandhi did quite often enjoin 'sacrifice' in the usual sense of giving up something on behalf of others' well-being, but he was quick to warn of the perils of such sacrifice: for instance, expectations of reciprocity that may potentially approximate tyranny (see 'Letter to Narandas Gandhi', 1930, 260).

14 Trusteeship meant that those who are given wealth may keep it, but in a spirit of 'trusteeship', intending their wealth not for themselves but for others. To 'end economic disparity without violence' is the chief justification Gandhi offered for his espousal of trusteeship ('Answers to Questions at Gandhi Seva Sangh Meeting', 1939, 219). But it is not the aversion to force alone, we may surmise, but also the idea of owning-without-having that appeals to him in trusteeship; his advocacy of trusteeship is animated by the same sense of non-obligatory (non-)giving as his practice of poverty. Even the problematic option of *keeping* one's wealth (but in discomfort) seems to him preferable to doling it out (comparatively, a painless action).

15 It is in some ways trivial to point out that if Gandhi was able to be thus *theoretically* pure in his ideal of voluntary poverty, there were contradictions and limits, as well as costs to its *practice*. I shall not elaborate here on the most obvious consequences of Gandhi's public life, his failures as a family man. Arun Gandhi's memoir describes the travails of his sons, whom he denied a proper education and on whom he imposed strict rules of poverty.

16 Imperialism's complex political and economic networks had consequences even in the home country, as Gandhi saw for himself with distress during a visit to England in 1931 – he spent three days in the 'devastated areas' of the Lancashire mills, lying idle because of the Indian boycott of mill goods (see Shirer 1993, 152).

17 He explained his reasons for the change to his trademark attire, in 1921, thus: 'In order... to set the example I propose to discard at least up to the 31st of October my *topi* (cap) and vest, and to content myself with only a loin cloth and a *chaddar* (shawl) whenever found necessary for the protection of the body.... I consider the renunciation to be also necessary for me as a sign of mourning, and a bare head and a bare body is such a sign in my part of the country' (Bean, cited in Chakrabarty 2002, 52).

18 For an extensive treatment of *khadi* and Gandhi's dress, see Emma Tarlo (1996). On the ashram, see Andrews (1929), Skaria (2002) and Thomson (1993). On Gandhi and Gandhi's body, with a special focus on his celibacy and diet, see Joseph Alter (2000) and Khilnani (1998, 'Introduction'); and on all these Gandhi's *Autobiography* (1982).

19 It is worth noting, at least as a curious footnote, that while Gandhi intended his example of voluntary poverty to reconcile the *poor* to their lot, he does not seem to have expected it to inspire the *wealthy* to emulate him.

20 Where I have been speaking of exemplarity as a matter of performance, Akeel Bilgrami shows how exemplarity is central to Gandhi's moral *philosophy*. The *satyagrahi* privileges conscience over principle. He sets an example to others by his actions and by doing so he too, like the man of principle, universalizes his choices. But the concept of the exemplar is able to provide an ethical alternative, Bilgrami explains, to the concept of principle in moral philosophy: it makes the 'psychology surrounding our morals' a more 'tolerant' one (Bilgrami 2003, 4162–3).

21 See also Srivatsan (2006). Srivatsan develops '*seva*' as an important dimension of the politics of the Indian nationalist movement including Gandhi's *harijan* uplift.

22 Skaria constructs two other Gandhian categories: '*mitrata*' (or friendship) which is the appropriate response to those who are one's equals, and '*satyagraha*' (or non-cooperation) as the response to those in dominance. All three responses thus sidestep the demand for equality.

23 Gandhi's position, Skaria explains, stems largely from his anti-statist prejudice: conflicts of inequality, in his view, would have to be settled between the two parties concerned *without reference to* the liberal state's mechanisms of law and rights. The anti-statism of Gandhi's politics is equally evident in his blueprint for a national economy, a far more controversial agenda for independent India than his idiosyncratic personal lifestyle. Gandhian large-scale economics emphasized village *swaraj* (independence or autonomy): 'My idea of a village *swaraj* is that it is a complete republic, independent of its neighbours for its own vital wants, and yet interdependent for many others in which dependence is a necessity' (Gandhi 1942, 308). Towards the end of his life he was exhorting Rajendra Prasad, the soon-to-be President of the free republic, that 'it is better for us to starve than to import even a single grain of rice from outside'. 'But mine', he mourned, 'is a voice in the wilderness' (Gandhi 1947a, 159).

24 This is expressed in the well-known injunction that the doer must be detached from the fruits of his labour (see, especially, Chapter 18).

25 Jawaharlal Nehru (1889–1964), India's first Prime Minister and leader of the ruling Congress party. In the seventeen years of his leadership of the country, he formulated and put in place independent India's major economic, political and social policies: socialism, industrialization, non-alignment and secularism, broadly the projects of modernity.

26 For the line of argument I am following here, Alisdair Macintyre's contrast between the Stoic and Aristotelian conceptions of morality in ancient Greece can serve as a suggestive heuristic (with obvious necessary qualifications) to illustrate the differences between the values represented by Gandhi and Nehru respectively. The Stoics sought to do 'what is right for its own sake', Macintyre explains. For them 'the good man is a citizen of the universe; his relation to all other collectivities, to city, kingdom or empire is secondary and accidental' (Macintyre 1987, 169). Aristotle on the other hand developed the notion of the 'virtues' essentially in civic and political terms (see especially chapters 11 and 12).

27 Nehru speaks in the context of the Partition of the subcontinent which attended independence, marked as it was by enormous turmoil – riots, loss of life, the displacement and migration of millions across the newly drawn borders of India and Pakistan. Gandhi was at the time in riot-torn Bengal, far from the scene of the official celebrations of Independence in Delhi.

28 I have been unable to find this opening section of the will in any of the official editions of Nehru's writings and speeches. It is likely to have been

dropped because it brings up the vexed question of Anand Bhawan as national property. I have used the unexpurgated original version, as cited in www.partitionofindia.com/_archive/00000064.htm (accessed 24 June 2010).

29 The obvious contrast is to the *failed* relationship of Gandhi to his children.

30 An outraged response from a present-day Nehru-basher: 'No doubt Nehru thought of India and whatever she stood for as his own creation. There was no room for anyone else, other than himself and his family, who had any right to claim the slightest love and ownership to our land', www.partitionofindia. com/_archive/00000064.htm (accessed 24 June 2010).

31 Judith Brown's analysis of Nehru's leadership in her recent political biography emphasizes this aspect: 'Nehru sought to spread his vision of a new India by means other than his personal lifestyle. He also adopted a pedagogic role, exhorting and teaching Indians ... His tone was often one of exasperated paternalism' (2003, 192).

32 In her recent reflections on the women's movement, Vina Mazumdar provides some insights into this situation for women of her generation, those who came of age at the time of independence. Their entry into careers was viewed as a return for what 'this poor country' had invested in their training. Thus the middle-class, educated woman of privilege in India internalized a certain idea of citizenship, as equality, public service and patriotism (Mazumdar 1999, 343, note 9).

33 Introspection about the role of the so-called ruling classes is most conspicuous today among activists in social movements and NGOs (non-government organizations). For example, Aruna Roy, a prominent figure in rural development, realizes, despite her conviction that the people must 'manage things themselves', that she will continue to have a major role in social transformation, not only because of the experience and expertise she has acquired, but also because of her 'useful' position as a member of the class that dominates decision-making (quoted in Bakshi 1998, 36–7).

34 The analogies have already been noted by Gandhi scholars (see Steger 2000, 193); Brown invokes Weber obliquely, in comparing Nehru to Luther (2003, 340).

35 For a defence of Nehru's 'deep moral anxiety about politics as a career', see Khilnani, 'Nehru's faith' (2002). Judith Brown also comes to the conclusion that at the end of his life, in the 1960s, Nehru 'increasingly turned to many of the Mahatma's teachings when confronted with his own failure to transform party and country as he had wished' (2003, 334).

36 For the exposition on Weber I have depended on Verstraeten (1995), especially page 183.

References

Alter, Joseph S. 2000. *Gandhi's Body: Sex, Diet and the Politics of Nationalism*. Philadelphia: University of Pennsylvania.

Andrews, C. F. 1929. *Mahatma Gandhi's Ideas, Including Selections from his Writings*. London: George Allen and Unwin Ltd. Excerpt from www.mkgandhi.org/articles/influence.htm (accessed 20 June 2010).

Appiah, Kwame Anthony. 1997. 'Cosmopolitan Patriots', *Critical Inquiry* 23, 3: 617–39.

Bakshi, Rajni. 1998. *Bapu Kuti: Journeys in Rediscovery of Gandhi*. New Delhi: Penguin Books.

Bilgrami, Akeel. 2003. 'Gandhi, the Philosopher', *Economic and Political Weekly*, 27 September 2003: 4159–65.

Bondurant, Joan. 1988. *Conquest of Violence: The Gandhian Philosophy of Conflict*. Princeton, NJ: Princeton University Press.

Brown, Judith M. 2003. *Nehru: A Political Life*. New Delhi: Oxford University Press.

Chakrabarty, Dipesh. 2002. *Habitations of Modernity: Essays in the Wake of Subaltern Studies*. Chicago: University of Chicago Press. Reprinted New Delhi: Permanent Black.

Derrida, Jacques. 1986. *Glas*. Trans. by John P. Leary Jr and Richard Rand. Lincoln and London: University of Nebraska Press.

——. 1992. *Given Time: 1. Counterfeit Money*. Trans. by Peggy Kamuf. Chicago: University of Chicago Press.

——. 1994. *Specters of Marx: The State of the Debt, the Work of Mourning, and the New International*. Trans. by Peggy Kamuf. London and New York: Routledge.

——. 1997. *Politics of Friendship*. Trans. by George Collins. London: Verso.

Emerson, Ralph Waldo. 1876. Address read before the B. K. Society at Cambridge, 18 July 1867. In *The Complete Works of Ralph Waldo Emerson*. Volume VIII, *Letters and Social Aims*. London: George Bell and Sons, 1883, pp. 224–37.

Foucault, Michel. 1997. *Ethics, Subjectivity and Truth*. Volume I of *Essential Works of Foucault, 1954–1984*. Paul Rabinow (ed.). New York: New Press.

Gandhi, Arun. 2000. *Kasturba: A Life*. New Delhi: Penguin Books.

Gandhi, M. K. 1924. 'The Birth Anniversary of Naoroji', *Navajivan*, 7 September 1924, in *The Collected Works of Mahatma Gandhi XXV 1924–25*, pp. 102–4.

——. 1930. 'Letter to Narandas Gandhi', 28 October 1930, in *The Collected Works of Mahatma Gandhi XLIV 1930*, pp. 257–61.

——. 1931. Speech at Guildhouse Church, under the auspices of the Franciscan Society, *The Guildhouse*, 23 September 1931, in *The Collected Works of Mahatma Gandhi XLVIII 1931–2*, pp. 50–8.

——. 1939. 'Answers to Questions at Gandhi Seva Sangh Meeting', Brindaban, 6 May 1939, in *The Collected Works of Mahatma Gandhi LXIX 1939*, pp. 218–28.

——. 1942. 'Question Box', *Harijan*, 26 July 1942, in *The Collected Works of Mahatma Gandhi LXXVI 1942*, pp. 308–9.

——. 1945. 'Note to Gope Gurbuxani', 17 March 1945, in *The Collected Works of Mahatma Gandhi LXXIX 1945*, p. 261.

——. 1947a. 'A Letter', 15 June 1947, in *The Collected Works of Mahatma Gandhi LXXXVIII 1947*, p. 159. From *Bihar Pachhi Dilhi*, p. 142.

——. 1947b. 'Who is a Socialist?', *Harijan*, 13 July 1947, in *The Collected Works of Mahatma Gandhi LXXXVIII 1947*, pp. 282–3.

——. 1982. *An Autobiography or My Experiments with Truth*. Trans. from the original Gujarati by Mahadev Desai. Harmondsworth: Penguin Books; copyright Navjivan Trust, 1927.

Iyer, Raghavan (ed.). 1993. *The Essential Writings of Mahatma Gandhi*. Delhi: Oxford University Press.

Khilnani, Sunil. 1998. *The Idea of India*. New Delhi: Penguin.

——. 2001. Introduction to M. K. Gandhi, *The Story of my Experiments with Truth*. Harmondsworth: Penguin Classics, pp. 1–10.

——. 2002. 'Nehru's Faith'. *Economic and Political Weekly*, 30 November 2002: 4793–9.

Lévinas, Emmanuel, 1986. 'Trace of the Other' (1963). Trans. By A. Lingis. In Mark C. Taylor (ed.), *Deconstruction in Context: Literature and Philosophy*. Chicago: University of Chicago Press, pp. 345–59.

Macintyre, Alisdair. 1987. *After Virtue: A Study in Moral Theory*. London: Duckworth.

Mazumdar, Vina. 1999. 'Political Ideology of the Women's Movement's Engagement with Law', in Amita Dhanda and Archana Parashar (eds). *Engendering Law: Essays in Honour of Lotika Sarkar*. Lucknow: Eastern Book Company, pp. 339–74.

Mitford, Nancy. 1956. 'The English Aristocracy', in Mitford (ed.) *Noblesse Oblige: An Enquiry into the Identifiable Characteristics of the English Aristocracy*. London: Hamish Hamilton, pp. 39–61.

Naidu, Sarojini. 1996. *Sarojini Naidu: Selected Letters 1890s to 1940s*, selected and edited by Makarand Paranjape. New Delhi: Kali for Women.

Nehru, Jawaharlal. 1937. 'The Rashtrapati', reprinted in *Selected Works of Jawaharlal Nehru*, First Series, edited by S. Gopal. New Delhi: Orient Longman, 1972–82. Volume 8, pp. 520–3.

——. 1946. *The Discovery of India*. London: Meridian Books.

——. 1949. 'Tryst with destiny', in *Independence and After: A Collection of the More Important Speeches of Jawaharlal Nehru from September 1946 to May 1949*. Delhi: Government of India, pp. 3–4.

——. 1997. Last will and testament. Cited in Shashi Tharoor. *India: From Midnight to Millennium*. New York: Arcade Publishing.

Prashad, Vijay. 2000. *Untouchable Freedom: A Social History of a Dalit Community*. Delhi: Oxford University Press.

Shirer, William L. 1993. *Gandhi: A Memoir*. Calcutta: Rupa & Co.

Skaria, Ajay. 2002. 'Gandhi's Politics: Liberalism and the Question of the Ashram', *The South Atlantic Quarterly* 101 (4, Fall): 955–86.

Srivatsan, R. 2006. 'Concept of "Seva" and the "Sevak" in the Freedom Movement', *Economic and Political Weekly*, 4 February 2006: 427–38.

Steger, Manfred B. 2000. *Gandhi's Dilemma: Nonviolent Principles and Nationalist Power*. New York: St. Martin's Press.

Tarlo, Emma. 1996. *Clothing Matters: Dress and Identity in India*. Chicago: University of Chicago Press.

Tharoor, Shashi. 1997. *India: From Midnight to Millennium*. New York: Arcade Publishing.

Thomson, Mark. 1993. *Gandhi and his Ashrams*. Bombay: Popular Prakashan.

Verstraeten, Johan. 1995. 'The Tension between "Gesinnungsethik" and "Verantwortungsethik": A Critical Interpretation of the Position of Max Weber in "Politik als Beruf"', *Ethical Perspectives* 2: 180–8.

Waugh, Evelyn. 1956. 'An Open Letter to the Hon. Mrs. Peter Rodd (Nancy Mitford) on a Very Serious Subject', in Mitford, pp. 65–82.

Weber, Max. 1964. *Politik als Beruf*. Berlin: Duncker and Humblot.

Zakaria, Fareed. 2003. *The Future of Freedom: Illiberal Democracy at Home and Abroad*. New York: W. W. Norton.

12 Humiliation

The politics and cultural psychology of the limits of human degradation

Ashis Nandy

Years ago, Giri Deshingkar, distinguished Sinologist and peace researcher, told me a story that may be, for all I know, apocryphal. When diplomatic negotiations took place after the Opium Wars between the defeated Chinese regime and the triumphant Western powers, they ended in a humiliating treaty for China. However, the Chinese diplomats looked at it differently. They had sawed off an imperceptible length from the legs of the chairs on which the Western negotiators sat, so that they spoke to the Chinese from a lower height. The Chinese were convinced that *they* had decisively humiliated the Western powers in the negotiations. The Western diplomats, of course, knew nothing about this, and naturally did not feel humiliated at all.

It is possible that while thinking they had triumphed over the imperial powers, the Chinese also knew they had lost. That awareness may have powered their politically impotent, self-congratulatory venture. I am also ignoring the possibly quasi-therapeutic role the humiliation played for the Chinese, who were facing traumatizing disgrace and national crisis. The European diplomats may not have been affected, but the very attempt to humiliate them protected Chinese self-esteem. Human nature is a multi-layered affair; people respond to or acknowledge events at many levels. I am merely proposing, as a basic assumption of this chapter, that humiliation in human relation can never be a one-way exchange. Unless the humiliated collaborate by feeling humiliated, you cannot humiliate them, however hard you try. No humiliation is complete unless the humiliated oblige their tormentors by validating their desire to humiliate. The Boxer treaty did not fully humiliate the Chinese, and the Chinese did not humiliate the victorious powers either. Those trying to humiliate may get a kick by doing what they do, but unless there is consensual validation from the humiliated, humiliation remains one-sided or takes place only in the eyes of a third party.

It follows, counterintuitive though this may sound, that the humiliated, too, have some control over their tormentors. This control is not overt, given that in a game of humiliation the parties involved often have asymmetric power relations. Yet, sensitive ethnographers and littérateurs have frequently come close to acknowledging that, in India's caste system for instance, while the Savarnas apparently control the varna system, the Dalits also have traditionally controlled the Savarnas through their power to pollute by touch or presence, and through the Savarnas's constant fear of pollution.[1] This dyadic relationship explains why, at moments of crisis or conflict involving Dalits, so much venom is released. Conflicts bring to the fore what is tacit in caste relations and creates in the Savarnas a crippling fear of losing control. When Gandhi insisted that anyone joining his ashrams had to first clean toilets, he was not practising, despite appearances, reverse humiliation as a penance. He was striking at the heart of the compact of humiliation that has tied the Untouchable to the 'Touchable'. He was redefining the idea of pollution. In 1973, the Government of Karnataka banned the practice of carrying night soil. If the Government had been sensitive to Gandhi's project, it would have made the ban applicable only to Dalits.

Some are uncomfortable with the proposition that successful humiliation needs acknowledgement from the humiliated that they are being dishonoured. They believe that persons or groups may be so numbed by institutionalized and regular humiliation that their sensitivities are blunted, and so they do not feel humiliated. A third party has the right, they feel to declare a situation as humiliating. Such an argument apparently has some validity; those who use it usually have in mind the Dalit predicament – what V. Geetha calls 'the dark narcissism of untouchability'. However, appearances notwithstanding, the argument is absurd and antidemocratic. If some victims do not feel humiliated, others have the right to convince them of their situation. But that gives no one the right to declare, on behalf of someone else, that humiliation has taken place, that the victim has become too used to humiliation to sense it, and, therefore, that one can act or speak on behalf of the victim. Let us not forget that Hindu nationalists, too, argue on behalf of all Hindus that Muslims have humiliated Hindus for centuries, and that Hindus who do not admit this are benumbed. Even when not invoking the idea of numbing, the assumption of the right to speak on behalf of the humiliated has its hazards. During the Emergency in 1975–7, when civil rights were suspended in India, sycophantic bureaucrats and ruling party functionaries decided, on behalf of Prime Minister Indira Gandhi, that Gulzar's *Andhi*, a film based on her complicated relationship with her husband, deserved to be banned because it was humiliating to a democratically elected prime minister.

Rajeev Bhargava pushes the argument about numbing further. He declares that a third party has the right to intercede when a person or group being humiliated cannot sense it, for they are already 'socially dead'.[2] This is a cure worse than the disease, though in recent years it has acquired a certain legitimacy, thanks to the intellectual climate created by the growing global concern with victims of trauma in general, and post-traumatic stress disorders in particular. 'Such is the preoccupation with trauma', says Vanessa Pupavac, 'that over the last decade, trauma victims have displaced famine victims in Western imagination'.[3] These diagnoses of victimization give social analysts the right to 'pathologize' not only individuals but entire communities and declare them socially dead. When a psychiatrist declares a person as having been numbed by years of oppression, or as overly sensitive to perceived humiliation due to deep feelings of inferiority, the diagnosis at least does not generally involve a summary trial of an essentialized collectivity.[4] The use of the idea of social death does.

The situation in India is complicated by a number of excellent and suggestive studies that show that sycophancy or ingratiation, one of the key indices of passive acceptance of humiliation, is often deployed as a Machiavellian tactic to control the powerful and to limit their options.[5] This is specially so when the institutional context is bleary or ill-defined, as inter-caste relations have become in recent times, and also in situations of resource scarcity.[6] Those seemingly gulping or inviting humiliation do so, these studies suggest, not because they are reconciled to their lot but because they consider it legitimate manipulative behaviour when confronting the powerful: they think it a small price to pay, to neutralize or contain the dominant in a fluid politics of hierarchies, and to gain privileged access to power.

Finally, if we grant a third party the right to declare a situation humiliating, independently of the victims' point of view, what happens when an ethnic or religious community claims it does not mean to humiliate anyone by following age-old practices or conventions? Do we accept the claim at face value, or grant others the right to proclaim the community dishonest or hypocritical? Conversely, when some groups claim to have been humiliated, do others have the right to deny those claims? Such questions are becoming important because globalization today is bringing communities into more regular and close contact. The scope for unintended humiliation is growing. The dog-loving English have to now deal with the dog-eating Koreans. The pork-loving Germans and Chinese cannot avoid the pork-shunning Muslims and Jews. The chances of humiliating someone unintentionally have increased enormously.

However, if we accept humiliation as one side of a reciprocal relationship, humiliation can be an interpreter's nightmare. Who humiliates whom, when, and how? Does humiliation have anything to do with changing times and moral standards? When one brings up the subject of colonialism, does one demean only the former colonized societies or also the former colonizing societies? Is a record of victimization more shameful to victims or to those who victimize? Can we assume that colonialism truly ends when both colonizers and the colonized acquire the psychological capacity to see colonialism as a more embarrassing or humiliating memory for the former colonizers?

Thus, I confess that I have always felt uncomfortable with American Blacks changing the name of their community according to their changing ideas of what is humiliating and what is not. They were first Negroes, and many of them did not like the name because it was associated with slavery, and, later, racial discrimination. They became Blacks and, after a while, some of them did not like that either because it ironed away ethnic distinctions. Since then, they have become African Americans. This kind of response declares the locus of control to be outside oneself: the response is a reaction to what others think and an attempt to revise one's self-definition accordingly.

Yes, the term 'negro' was associated with slavery, and with the term of contempt 'nigger'. But negro also means black and it is still associated with the self-definition of Francophone Africans, who have no option but to use the term because it is the only one available to them in French. 'Noire' just does not have the same ring as black. More importantly, the term 'negro' has been associated with much resistance, protest against oppression, and creativity against immense odds. It is associated with Leopold Senghor's idea of negritude; with Paul Robeson's negro spirituals; with W.E.B. Du Bois's work on the African cultural heritage of the negroes, their cultures of survival and protest under slavery and after, when slavery ended but discrimination and humiliation did not. 'Black' does not carry these associations. The term African American is, in some ways, worse. It blurs the entire recent past of violence, torture, and exploitation through which Black Americans have passed and links them to their African heritage, about which they know little.

What I dislike most is the tacit admission in such renaming that the memories of slavery and racism are more shameful for Blacks than for Whites. It is as if Blacks have to erase their past more carefully and diligently than those who practised slavery. The Whites have not changed their name or ethnic tag, though they carry the heavier historical baggage of slavery. No White has resented being called a White on the grounds that that name has been associated with oppression, exploitation, and genocide in most parts of the world and can be used as a term of abuse. I cannot but suspect that the attempt of American Blacks to rename themselves is partly based on the belief that it is more honourable to be a master than a slave. At the same time, I am also vaguely aware that, in a future society, after the collapse of racism, calling oneself a Negro may be considered an attempt to insult the White by recalling the days of slavery. Symbols of defiance do sometimes enshrine entire worldviews.

I

This brings me to my second proposition. While civilization as a process means the gradual abolition or dilution of master–slave relationships, it also means a growing awareness that it is more honourable to be a slave than a master, if not as a viable social or personal choice, at least as a normative and cognitive frame. (To secure wider acceptability for this proposition, I am willing to rephrase it to state that it is less dishonourable to be a slave than a master.) This is a position different from the one that asserts that it is as dishonourable to be a master as to be a slave. The first presumption – that the slave is morally and cognitively superior – allows a collectivity to 'work through' its past, as psychoanalysts describe the process, and opens up the possibility of the wide-ranging creative use of the past. The latter – in practice a facade for the entrenched belief in the master's moral infirmity but cognitive superiority – often prefaces reactive ethnonationalism, built on defences such as projection, displacement and identification with the aggressor. Above all, it leads to a constant effort to beat the master at his own game.[7]

I have discussed this issue elsewhere in some detail.[8] Let me confine myself here to its implications for communities trying to escape humiliation and protect their dignity.

Humiliation in South Asia is usually a story of separation and the pain of separation. But like the post-Opium War treaty negotiations in China, that story too has a built-in Roshomon effect.

Caste and religion are seen as the main sources of separation in our part of the world. Most people hope that both will dissolve obligingly in an egalitarian modern society giving way in separations based on non-ascriptive, secular, social divisions that, for some reason, are presumed to be less painful and squalid. Yet, paradoxically, most serious battles waged against caste and religious bigotry have used caste and religion, and not secular social categories like class. These battles have weakened caste and religious bigotry socially but also strengthened them as principles of political mobilization. The dramatic rise of the numerically preponderant lower castes in Indian public life has come through caste mobilization, with its attendant problems. It is only our self-serving, cultivated blindness that stops us from acknowledging that the same may be the case with religion, that we may have to cope with problems associated with religion by deploying religion itself – as an input into the culture of politics and as a principle of political mobilization. Even a hardboiled, modern secularist like B. R. Ambedkar had, in order to fight religion-based discrimination and exclusion, to make a statement by converting to Buddhism, a religion neither immune to exclusion and chauvinism nor to caste-based discrimination (as the Sri Lankan experience shows). In our times, the Dalai Lama and Desmond Tutu have shown how this can be done.

We like to believe that all principles of separation humiliate. They may not. As an old, poor Muslim riot victim living in Delhi's Jama Masjid area said some years ago in a television interview. 'Previously we did not eat together, but our hearts met. Now we eat together but our hearts do not meet'.[9] Nearness may not merely sour but also implode. Let me go back to the story brought to us by Dipesh Chakrabarty, which I consider in many ways paradigmatic.[10] I seek the reader's indulgence to use the story once again.

Jasimuddin was the best-known folk poet of Bengal of the twentieth century who was also a devout supporter of the Muslim League and the idea of a separate homeland for the Muslims. He came from a humble background and was a fellow student of the famous radical film director Mrinal Sen at a school in Faridpur (now in Bangladesh). Mrinal's father spotted Jasimuddin's brilliance early and the young Jasimuddin began to visit the Sens, soon becoming virtually a member of the family. An indicator of the intimacy between the budding poet and the Sens was that Jasimuddin used to call Mrinal's mother 'Ma' and the Sens in turn called him by his pet name, Sadhu (literally, 'world renouncer'). As communal politics began to warm up in the 1940s, Jasimuddin and Mrinal's father often had fierce debates, his father supporting conventional nationalism, Jasimuddin its ethnonationalist version.

One day, during the course of such a debate, Jasimuddin asked why the Sens, if they considered him a member of their family made him eat separately when he dined at their house. This embarrassed everyone, for it was true. Mrinal's mother, with tears in her eyes, explained that it was the servants who objected to Jasimuddin eating with the rest of the family. Indeed, the servants resisted washing the plates he used: she had been washing Jasimuddin's plate herself.

We have no clear picture of how the dialogue ended, nor of the fate of the relationship after the event. However, we can make a few guesses. First, the Hindu servants, themselves of uncertain social status in the family, tried to protect their self-esteem by separating and humiliating Jasimuddin. They must have felt threatened by the closeness of a Muslim to the domestic power structure and insisted on their right, as Hindus, to observe the principles of purity and pollution, to reaffirm a social hierarchy that was getting dangerously fuzzy. They were making a point by humiliating the new member of their employer's household who dared to call the mistress of the house 'Ma' – not the way servants in a Bengali household call their women employers, but the way a surrogate son does. Indeed, one suspects that they were protecting themselves from humiliation by humiliating the new-found 'son' of the family and reducing him to his 'true' stature – a poor Muslim patronized by the family.

The result was that Mrinal's mother's moving gesture – an upper-caste woman washing the plate of her son's Muslim friend, and humiliating herself vis-à-vis her servants to protect her adopted son from humiliation – did not get its due either from an angry young partisan of ethnonationalism, or from her own modern son. Jasimuddin *did* feel humiliated, and even the self-abnegation of Mrinal's mother could not erase the hurt beyond a point. However, it is also clear from the story that Jasimuddin felt humiliated at least partly because he had come close and entered the circle of commensality and kinship, and was expecting a different kind of behaviour from the family. It was not distance but nearness that created the problem in the first place.

Do separations, encrypted in principles of commensal taboos, automatically lead to humiliation, as Jasimuddin seemed to believe? Had he not felt humiliated, would it have been because he was numbed to the demands of ritual hierarchy in the closed circles of Touchables? A part-answer lies in an interview Saba Khattak carried out in Pakistan with a woman victim of Partition for a collaborative project on mass violence.[11] The victim firmly denied that the observation of rules of purity, impurity, pollution and touch had anything to do with Hindu–Muslim tensions or the violence of Partition. Hindus did not eat with most Hindus in any case, she said. In another variation on the theme, Prafulla Sen, a refugee from the former East Pakistan, though he himself did not believe in caste-based checks on commensality, remembered with great fondness his Muslim friend Sirajuddin Ahmed's father, who was once furious with his son for hosting Prafulla and helping break Prafulla's commensal taboos. The relationship between the two families had spanned two generations; Prafulla's late father too had been a friend of Sirajuddin's father. The latter on hearing of the transgression, lamented. 'How will I show my face to your father after I die? How shall I tell him that my son helped your son to lose his religion?'[12]

One sees in these episodes three faces of humiliation in a political culture. In the last case, both sides accept separation in some areas of social life as almost a cultural eccentricity, the odd but unavoidable religious practice of a community. The distance that so humiliated Jasimuddin does not poison social relations in the other two cases. One is tempted to add that, if one is not committed to a melting pot model and is ready to view public culture partly as an interplay of contending, incompatible cultures of communities that observe inbuilt limits on interaction, one has to be prepared to confront situations where some degree of tolerance will have to be exercised for rituals and practices that look hierarchical or humiliating from within a melting pot model. I remember my late friend Jaidev Sethi, an activist-scholar and Gandhian, telling me that he virtually had to starve when visiting his ancestral village in Pakistan after a gap of fifty years. No longer having Hindu neighbours, the villagers went by their memories and reduced Sethi, who did not know how to cook, nearly to tears by affectionately gifting him a huge mass of uncooked green vegetables and cereals. They expected the returning son of the village to observe caste taboos and cook his own food. They did not believe him when he said he ate everything and was perfectly willing to eat at anyone's place.

Such tolerance presumes, however, two relatively autonomous, self-confident communities or persons, something that cannot be said in the case of Dalits. Saba Khattak's case strengthens the argument. In it, familiarity with other cultures assures the respondent that separation is not targeting the respondent or her community specifically. Separation becomes acceptable because two generic, already internally fragmented entities called 'Hindus' and 'Muslims' have emerged and one is able to say, as Khattak's respondent said, that 'they' treat their own kind the way they treat 'us'. In Jasmuddin's case, the closeness of the budding poet to the future film director's family gives separation a different meaning. The threshold of tolerance has been lowered because the two parties have redefined their communities. Both sides are modernized to the extent that they cannot have asymmetrical relationships with each other and hierarchy-tinged separation becomes a marker of humiliation.

I am emboldened to add that Jasimuddin's story is paradigmatic also in the sense that most modern social scientists can empathize with Jasimuddin and Mrinal Sen's point of view, not with the predicament of Jasimuddin's adopted mother or that of her servants. The 'strange', politically incorrect categories of those at the receiving end of a social order are an embarrassment and must be quickly forgotten, presumably for the benefit of the victims themselves. It is a bit like the consistent forgetfulness I have found in the plethora of reports and studies that came out after the massacre of Sikhs at Delhi in 1984. None mentions a recurrent theme in the testimonies of Sikh victims when talking of the complicity of the Indian National Congress and the Rajiv Gandhi regime in the pogrom – 'they got us beaten up and killed by the Bhangis (Untouchables)'. Some kinds of humiliation, we implicitly recognize, no respectable victim should complain of.

Insensitivity to such situations is what makes the psychological measures of social distance so vacuous in a country like India. Scores of studies were done at one time on intercaste and interreligious relations here with such measures, particularly the Bogardus Social Distance Scale. All of them assumed a graded relationship between different kinds of social interaction. (For instance, if I accept my daughter's marriage to your son, I am closer to you than if I am willing only to dine with you.) In a complex, pluricultural, traditional society, such simple linear relationships do not obtain. Emory Bogardus would have been surprised to hear that in many South Asian communities, despite intermarriage, commensality may not always be possible. An obvious example is of a parent who does not eat at his or her married daughter's place, because custom demands restraint.

Intermarriage itself makes some kinds of commensality impossible. (Even in a modern setting, there is George Bernard Shaw's crypto-biblical injunction, 'Do not do unto others what you would that they do unto you. Their tastes may be different'. I have heard of at least one French family that is happy that their progeny has married into an Indian family, but has resisted eating at the home of their in-laws, lest they have to eat Indian food.)

This flux in the meaning of humiliation is well exemplified by one of the darkest periods in South Asia. Pollution and purity acquired entirely different meanings during the Partition riots when by most conservative estimates, 100,000 women were abducted. Strangely, a very large proportion of the abductors married their victims in Punjab. All these abductors could have raped and killed their victims (as many of them did). Why did they marry their victims? How did communities and the families of abductors accept women from enemy communities in a caste society? Unlike Bengal, in Punjab abduction was a three-way traffic. All three religious groups – Hindus, Muslims and Sikhs – participated in the game, and in all three cases a large number of families, clans and communities accepted the abducted women. Some of us have identified villages and urban ghettos where a majority of the elderly women, even today, are women abducted during the Partition. Presumably, these women live with their traumata and memories of humiliation. Yet they live with them not as aliens or strangers, but as insiders. How have concepts of pollution and purity worked in these cases? One possibility is that, after humiliating their enemies by stealing their women, the abductors felt morally obliged to protect a semblance of the dignity of their victims by marrying them. Another is that marriage could establish 'honourable victory' or seal the social superiority or equality of the abductors. The concept of a *rakshasa*, or demonic, marriage in India's epic traditions might have supplied a framework of justification for such feelings. Perhaps, for some abductors, the humiliation of the enemy was not complete if they had only raped and abandoned their victims or remained anonymous rapists and killers. Losing one's own woman of capturing others' women took place within a common frame of humiliation and counter-humiliation, defeat and victory. But these are guesses; we do not really know.

Compare this experience with rapes during the 2002 riots in Gujarat where, in many cases after raping a woman, the rapists set her on fire. Some of the killers justified this by saying they were advised to prevent the multiplication of Muslims through unwanted pregnancies. The game in Gujarat was not humiliation, but annihilation. In Bosnian genocide, too, rape was used as a well-organized technique of dishonouring and polluting the other, and as a means of systematic deracination. As part of a jury in the Women's Court Against Racism, set up in Durban, South

Africa, in 2001, I heard testimonies on the chronic culture of rape under slavery in the United States.[13] One testimony based on the diaries, autobiographical records, notes and letters of plantation slaves in the United States claimed that many women knew their mothers and grandmothers had been raped; they were raped themselves; and they could see that their daughters would be raped too. Rape was a part of normal life. It included a component of amoral, nihilistic, destructive humiliation that was anti-life. In the same category fall the cases of two Dalits at Thinniyam, Tiruchi, forced by those belonging to the non-Brahminic, upwardly mobile, Thevar community, to eat human excreta in Tamil Nadu; and the Dalit domestic help who underwent the same treatment in Eastern Nepal at the hands of a Chhetri couple.

Finally, to be aware of the instrumental use of the rhetoric of humiliation, one must also be aware of voluntary or invited humiliation as a technique of political mobilization and consolidation. Humiliation can be imagined and cultivated in response to contemporary political and social needs. First, a record of humiliation can become a badge certifying one's identity and membership of an in-group. Violent nationalism has always carefully nurtured feelings of humiliation, Nazism being its best-known example. However, there are less diabolic versions of cultivated humiliation used as the means of political and social mobility. Some Cochini Jewish immigrants in Israel talk about centuries of oppression in Kerala, whereas their own community in Cochin talk of 2000 years of non-discrimination and a life of dignity. Indeed, the Cochin Jews are surprised and amused by the history of oppression that some Israeli Jews of Indian origin have concocted.[14] But, in Israeli public culture, there is a rat race among communities flaunting their experience of oppression and humiliation; not having a record of ill-treatment is a misfortune in that society. In that rat race, European Jews have the edge because their persecution, over the centuries, is one of the key images around which the self-definition of the Israeli nation-state is built.

When the creation of a feeling of humiliation is part of a political programme, it is not always equally necessary to possess a genuine record of oppression and violence. Ethnonationalists know this. Hindu nationalism, for instance, talks of many instances of humiliation that look contrived and fictitious, or as projections into the past of more recent feelings of inferiority vis-à-vis Islam and Christianity. Empirical evidence to the effect that no genetic category called Hindus faced these humiliating instances in pre-modern times – because the vast majority of Hindus did not even define themselves as Hindus until the nineteenth century – fails to cut much ice with Hindu nationalists. The sense of humiliation and feelings of inferiority in recent times are real, history serves as a projective test and political propaganda works.

II

I have already mentioned the growing use of the technique of pathologization. That technique is quickly becoming a postcolonial version of the colonial technique of infantilization. It is therefore important to remember that though the pathologies of humiliation attract public notice because of their incendiary potential, humiliation can also open up new, creative possibilities. If the capacity to feel humiliated presumes minimum self-esteem, the capacity to withstand or stand up to humiliation, too, presumes ego strength, a sense of mastery over oneself and one's environment.[15] An incapacitating or crippling fear of humiliation may also indicate low self-esteem. This is the other side of Geetha's formulation that humiliation is fundamentally an experience that questions and recasts one's relationship with oneself.

There are many instances when attempts to diminish or narrow the target's self have ended up expanding it. When a racist, white conductor threw Gandhi out of a train compartment in Pietermaritzburg in South Africa, despite Gandhi holding a first-class ticket, the conductor did not know that he was gifting the world a new political weapon for the oppressed – militant non-violence. That humiliating encounter in a lonely South African railway station turned out to be a boon not only to the world but also to Gandhi himself. It woke him, as it were, from a stupor. Some forms of humiliation – such as the crawling order enforced in Punjab in the wake of the Jalianwallabagh massacre in 1919 – degrade and silence the victims, but may also help consolidate new political formations. Others directly create new openings. These consequences have as much to do with the nature of the humiliation as with the nature of the victim.

The experience of Pietermaritzburg may have also sensitized Gandhi to the pedagogic possibilities of milder forms of humiliation. During India's freedom struggle, many found Gandhi's dress disgraceful and his negotiations with the Viceroy on an equal footing humiliating. Winston Churchill felt offended by the antics of 'the half-naked faqir'. Others found it provocative and humiliating when, after the famous Salt March and the successful movement against a newly imposed salt tax, while negotiating with the Viceroy, Gandhi took out and sprinkled some illegally made salt on the snacks he was served by the viceregal kitchen. To remove all humiliation from human affairs seems a doubtful possibility. Someone somewhere is always going to feel humiliated. We probably shall have to console ourselves by acknowledging that sometimes some humiliations can be a means of renewal and re-education for both sides in an unequal partnership.

These creative potentialities exist because humiliation, when it is not an isolated case but a chronic ailment, is usually a political statement. Some forms of playful counter-humiliation in such circumstances can be a means of defiance. However, to identify such counter-humiliation – often essentially the non-destructive refusal to play assigned roles – one must first acknowledge the contexts in which humiliation becomes chronic. Humiliation breaks out in an epidemic form when the humiliated refuse to abide by well-established institutionalized rules. Humiliation then becomes a means of reasserting old hierarchies increasingly under stress. That is the crux of the Dalit problem in India today. The humiliation of Dalits does what in other situations is sought to be done through mass murder.

Humiliation becomes a substitute for genocide partly because, unlike the American Indian, a good Dalit has never been a dead Dalit. Though outcastes, Dalits remain within the caste system by being a collection of service castes. If they do not supply these services, others have to perform them, or one would have to opt for self-service. In either case, the result is a quick loss of social status. Humiliating Dalits is a means of avoiding that status loss and the resulting humiliation. This leads to strange anomalies. While studying the Partition violence of 1946–8, we found out how the Karachi elite and Pakistan's political leadership had to cajole the Hindu Dalits of Karachi to stay on in the city when ethnic cleansing was taking place all over northern India. In fact, when, after the destruction of the Babri mosque in 1992, some people targeted the Karachi Dalits, they struck work and reduced the city to a stinking slum. In no time, they were provided armed security. In a caste society, fears of pollution can supersede fanaticism.[16]

In the classical Hegelian master–slave relationship, one can build upon Octave Mannoni and affirm that the slave, to survive, cannot but be sensitive to the moods, foibles and personality dynamics of the master. The master, on the other hand, can to an extent afford to objectify his possession; he does not have to internalize the slave. This splits the slave into two. One part of his or her personality wants to equal the master, to do to the master and to others what has been done to him as a slave. Gandhi, in *Hind Swaraj*, identifies this as the eagerness to acquire the tiger's nature, without the tiger.[17]

Building upon the original psychoanalytic construct, we can call it identification with a 'remembered' aggressor, an ego defence that can be seen in full play in today's Israel and in the cosmology of *Hindutva*.

In this identification with the aggressor, there is often an attempt to undo history, real or imaginary, by re-enacting it – with oneself on the winning side. This is accompanied by a search for scapegoats, by humiliating whom one can undo the past. Yet, even when such re-enacting and scapegoating succeed, one cannot forget or overcome the past and move on, because one has in the meanwhile redefined oneself and given a central place in one's self to the repeated attempts to re-invoke and undo the past through violence; these attempts have become the means of holding together one's self-definition. Even successful genocidal revenge, directed against real or imaginary enemies, cannot square the balance. For without the triad of scapegoating, undoing and acting out, such a self-definition faces collapse.

Valentine Daniel describes how, while combating the aggressive evangelism of Christian missionaries, all other religions have in the last hundred years internalized some key categories and features of European Christianity, including the European meaning of religion, turning the twentieth century into a cultural triumph of Western Christianity.[18] To fight humiliation and acquire respectability, according to European concepts of respectability, every major religion in the South has sought to retell itself to conform to a standardized definition of religion.

Daniel's formulation prompts one to question the idea of respectability itself, because, in this instance, respectability means respect from within the Hegelian master's world itself. Such respectability inextricably ties the victims of humiliation in the 'tiger's nature', creating, in the long run, new targets of humiliation. Perhaps the true counterpoint to humiliation is not respect, unless we mean by it self-respect of the kind that goes with what psychologists call ego strength, that too of an order that can survive experiences of humiliation. Perhaps the counterpoint to humiliation is empathy. As it happens, empathy is neither a political category nor can be inculcated through institutional means. In everyday politics, it is probably safer to presume that the 'normal' counterpoint to humiliation is the absence of humiliation. This is particularly true of societies where communities are not dead and people expect, from fellow citizens belonging to other communities, not brotherly love but some degree of distant tolerance.[19]

This emphasis on the idea of self-respect is not incidental. In India at least, when one talks of humiliation, one invariably has in mind the Dalits. And when the Dalits talk of humiliation, there is always the presence of a derecognized psychological reality: hostility towards one's own culture and vocation inculcated in the Dalits over generations. Hence, no rhetoric of recovery of indigenous cultures or protection of artisan skills goes far among them. The Dalit commitment to modernity may sometimes be fuzzy and uninformed, but it is usually total. Modernist social reformers have endorsed this self-image by constantly describing the Dalits along only two dimensions: they are poor and they are oppressed; as if the Dalit communities did not have their gods, caste *puranas*, legends, cuisines and systems of knowledge; as if empowering their culture was to disempower the Dalits. It was against this flattening of the image of the Dalit that the likes of D. R. Nagaraj protested.[20]

To return to our core metaphor, there is the other part of the slave's personality that fights the master by refusing to internalize him, even while acknowledging the master's humanity. It is as if the slave recognized, as a key to survival, that in the long run it was better to be a slave than a master. That is the ultimate meaning of rebellion and the guarantee of the destruction of the master–slave relationship, not glib talk of equality and justice.

Thus, we come back to square one and to the proposition that the growth of civilization itself is defined by the growth of the awareness that the slave enjoys not merely moral but also cognitive superiority over the master. The master has more reasons to refashion his identity than the slave has. This is what I meant when I confessed my discomfort with African Americans changing their name because of the history of slavery.

However, I should not end this chapter without taking note of a basic contradiction in the master's personality. It arises from the basic incompatibility between humiliation and what Aimé Césaire calls 'thingification'.[21] Institutionalized slavery requires thingification. One has to objectify a human being to efficiently use him or her like a machine or a domesticated animal; one has to redefine the slave as only a factor in production. But then, one cannot humiliate things or animals because, as I have argued already, the victims must grasp their humiliation for humiliation to succeed. Humiliation is a human situation, it can never be extra- or trans-human. To humiliate someone, you have to grant your target human sensitivity. To that extent, you also have to be willing to be a captive to the will of the humiliated. In this respect, humiliation is a bit like torture. One is a successful torturer only when one's victim begs for forgiveness and screams for mercy to satisfy the torturer's sense of power, control or sadism and thus endorse the torturer's sense of mastery over himself. But think of the torturer whose victims laugh at him and deny his ability to inflict pain and, thus, gradually reduce the torturer to a frustrated, desperate and even humiliated being, struggling to maintain his dignity.[22]

Humiliation can destroy people only by bringing them closer and inducing them to share categories and establish common criteria. Humiliation cannot survive without some degree of consensual validation. Humiliation dissolves when the dyadic bonding – and the culture that scaffolds it – is disowned by at least one of the two sides.

Notes

From *Time Treks* (Delhi: Permanent Black, 2007).

1   There are, of course, subtler fears that plague oppressors in any system of dominance. V. Geetha talks of accusations of witchcraft against Dalit women as another instance of oppression. This can be read as another admission of oppression by the oppressive and their haunting fear of retributive justice. V. Geetha, 'Bereft of Being: Humiliation and Untouchability', paper presented at the conference on Humiliation, Ranikhet, 7–9 September 2002.

2 Rajeev Bhargava, 'The Moral Significance of Humiliation', paper presented at the conference on Humiliation, Ranikher, 7–9 September 2002.
3 Vanessa Pupavac, 'Pathologizing Populations and Colonizing Minds: International Psychosocial Programs in Kosovo', *Alternatives*, vol. 27 (2002), pp. 489–511 (p. 489).
4 Though even such trials are now no longer rare. Entire populations are sometimes now declared politically 'incompetent' because of a history of violence and trauma. See the suggestive paper by Pupavac, 'Pathologizing Populations and Colonizing Minds' for the larger issues involved; see also Elien Herman, *The Romance of American Psychology: Political Culture in the Age of Experts* (Berkeley: University of California Press, 1995).
5 For example, Janak Pandey and R. Rastogi, 'Machiavellianism and Ingratiation', *The Journal of Social Psychology*, vol. 108 (1981), pp. 221–5; Janak Pandey, 'Ingratiation as Expected and Manipulative Behaviour in Indian Society', *Social Change*, vol. 10 (1980), pp. 15–17; and 'Ingratiation Tactics in India', *The Journal of Social Psychology*, vol. 113 (1981), pp. 147–8; R. C. Tripathi, 'Machiavellianism and Social Manipulation', in Janak Pandey (ed.), *Perspectives on Experimental Social Psychology* (New Delhi: Concept, 1981), pp. 133–87. See also K. Bohra and Janak Pandey, 'Ingratiation toward Strangers, Friends, and Bosses', *The Journal of Social Psychology*, vol. 122 (1984), pp. 217–22.
6 Janak Pandey, 'Effects of Machavellianism and Degree of Organizational Formalization on Ingratiation'. *Psychologia*, 1981, vol. 24, pp. 41–6; Janak Pandey, 'Social Influence Processes', in Pandey, *Perspectives in Experimental Social Psychology*, pp. 55–93; and 'Cross-Cultural Perspectives on Ingratiation', in B. Maher and W. Maher (eds), *Progress in Experimental Personality Research* (New York: Academic Press, 1986), pp. 205–29.
7 The ways in which the memories of British colonialism in South and South East Asia are deployed constitute an example. As a general rule, countries, regions and communities that are more self-confident and less plagued by memories of real or imagined humiliation like persons with robust ego strength, need less symbolic reparation and ritual and/or compulsive 'undoing' of the past. Even their nationalism reflects the lighter burden of the memories they carry. There is a difference between a nationalism built on an underlying strain of anti-imperialism that sees itself as heir to an anticolonial movement and a nationalism that seeks constant national and cultural security by bending or distorting the entire machinery of state and the entire culture of politics to equal the former colonial powers in statecraft and diplomacy. Gandhi, officially remembered in India mainly as a nationalist leader, was sensitive to this issue. Nationalism, to be genuinely anti-imperialist, had to be non-violent, he openly claimed, for armed nationalism was the other name of imperialism. M. K. Gandhi, *Collected Works of Mahatma Gandhi* (New Delhi Publications Division: Ministry of information and Broadcasting, 1967), vol. 25, p. 369. What remained unsaid was that non-violence was the natural political stance of the psychologically healthy, not of political eccentrics and the politically weak who had a poor grasp of the reality around them. To opt for violence as the 'proven' technology of the master is to admit defeat even when the master has been formally defeated.
8 Ashis Nandy, *The Illegitimacy of Nationalism: Rabindranath Tagore and the Politics of Self* (New Delhi: Oxford University Press, 1994); and Ashis Nandy, *The Intimate Enemy: Loss and Recovery of Self Under Colonialism* (New Delhi: Oxford University Press, 1983).

9 In the case of caste, D. L. Sheth has attempted an insightful stocktaking that explores the long-term political consequences of the process. See D. L. Sheth, 'Secularisation of Caste and Making of New Middle Class', *Economic and Political Weekly*, vol. 34, no. 5 (21–28 August 1999), pp. 2502–10.

10 Dipesh Chakrabarty, 'Remembered Village: Representation of Hindu Bengali Memories in the Aftermath of Partition', *Economic and Political Weekly* (10 August 1996), pp. 2143–61. I discuss this story also in the book *Time Treks*: see Chapter 3, 'Telling the Story of Communal Conflicts in South Asia: Interim Report on a Search for Defining Myths'.

11 Saba Khattak, paper presented at the workshop of the project, 'Reconstructing Lives', Centre for the Study of Developing Societies, Delhi, 2001.

12 Anindita Mukhopadhyay, Interview with Prafulla Sen, Delhi, 1997.

13 World Court of Women, *Singing in the Dark Times* (Bangalore: Asian Women's Human Rights Council; and Tunis: El Taller, 2002).

14 Ashis Nandy, 'Time Travel to a Possible Self: Searching for the Alternative Cosmopolitanism of Cochin', *Time Warps: The Insistent Politics of Silent and Evasive Selves* (Delhi Permanent Black, 2002), pp. 157–209.

15 Geetha, 'Bereft of Being'.

16 Unpublished case study presented by Suchitra Subramanyam Sheth at the Conference on Life History Construction and Mass Violence, organized by the project on Reconstructing Lives, Centre for the Study of Developing Societies at Udaipur, 25–29 July 2000.

17 M. K. Gandhi, *Hind Swaraj* in *Collected Works of Mahatma Gandhi* (New Delhi: Publications Division, Government of India, 1963), vol. 4, pp. 51–208.

18 Valentine Daniel, 'The Arrogation of Being by the Blind Spot of Religion', paper presented at the Conference on Twentieth-Century Dreams and Realities, organized by the Graduate School of Social Science, Hitotsubashi University, Tokyo, 2 December 2000.

19 Nandy. 'Time Travel to a Possible Self'.

20 For instance, D. R. Nagaraj, 'From Political Rage to Cultural Affirmation: Notes on the Kannada Dalit Poet-Activist Siddalingaiah', *India International Quarterly*, vol. 21, no. 4 (1994), pp. 15–26.

21 Aimé Césaire, *Discourse of Colonialism*, trans. Juan Pinkham (New York and London: Monthly Review Press, 1972).

22 In Romain Gary's novel *The Dance of Genghis Cohn* (Harmondsworth: Penguin, 1978), the anti-hero, the former SS officer Schatz, is possessed by the ghost of Genghis Cohn, a Jewish comedian, who became Schatz's victim when an inmate of Auschwitz. Cohn remains, even in death, defiant and insolent. He haunts Schatz by displaying his only apparently impotent comic defiance.

Part IV

Global/cosmopolitan worlds

Introduction

Elleke Boehmer and Rosinka Chaudhuri

In his important 2007 study, *The Triumph of Modernism*, which explores the arrival of a self-conscious avant-garde in the Indian visual arts from 1922, Partha Mitter proposes a new way of looking at cosmopolitan cultures across the world in this period, one that resonates with other important post-2000 investigations of the transcultural dimensions of cosmopolitanism.[1] On the strength of the lively interaction of avant-gardes in different urban centres in the early decades of the twentieth century, Mitter suggests that far from belonging exclusively to the metropolis/the centre of empire, or to the West, cosmopolitan sites (and their values, approaches, perspectives) should instead be regarded as multiply located and engaged with rich vernacular as well as imported traditions. Modernity, he writes, has always been marked by 'a two-way dialogic transaction', in which so-called periphery and centre are fully involved as both generators and recipients of meanings and influences. Primitivism, for example, which offered artistic elites in the West a mode of interrogating industrial and urban cultures, was also deployed in places like India and Brazil to develop a critical diagnosis of colonial malaise. This view of what might also be termed a diffused and hetero-geneous cosmopolis, or a singular modernity, with which the insights of Rasheed Araeen, Nestor Garcia Canclini, Dipesh Chakrabarty and Elleke Boehmer, amongst others, accord, represents an important new departure in postcolonial criticism, one that permanently disturbs the neat binary margin-centre distinctions that, until quite recently, tended to govern postcolonial critique.[2]

The four chapters in this section explore the borderline, 'postnational' and culturally heterogeneous interactions that make up the protean and vernacular cosmopolis which Mitter was concerned to espouse. Extending Mitter's insights, novelist and essayist Amit Chaudhuri offers a thoughtful, unexpected cosmopolitan take on the complicated, even contrary affini-ties and affiliations of India's writers across the twentieth century – affini-ties and also idiosyncrasies which the bald term postcolonial does not for him begin to encapsulate, though it may anticipate them. In particular, Chaudhuri is interested in how the sensibilities of writers who work in sharp awareness of literary traditions at several international removes from their immediate location, are, if anything, at the same time, and in consequence, more responsive to vernacular conditions, and local, contingent events. 'Transverse mappings across [cultural] territories', an interest in 'the fragmentary, the concrete and a certain quality of the aleatory': these are quintessential features of the heterogeneous, transcultural and interconnected modern worlds which these writers embrace, and to which they declare belonging. Indeed, writes Chaudhuri, given that any cosmopolitan writer is in a state of internal exile, distanced from many of his or her native sources, he or she identifies with the rootlessness or alterity of the Jew.

Moving back in time, Santanu Das's chapter explores the massive Indian contribution to the First World War, and considers in particular how this experience was represented in the complexly inflected lyric poetry of the nationalist Sarojini Naidu, in soldiers' transcribed letters, and in Mulk Raj Anand's iconic novel *Across the Black Waters* (1949). His careful reading points out not only how going to war represented for Indian soldiers participation in a vast new multiracial hubbub, as well as in 'the exhilaration and trauma of industrial modernity', but also that the fault lines thrown up in India by the war effort, where nationalist sentiment cut across imperial loyalty, zigzags even through the sinuous lines of Naidu's verse: here the native contribution is subtly aligned with global events in a quintessentially cosmopolitan way. Das's chapter implies a conception of the national imaginary that Irish historians and scholars too have outlined in their work: the paradoxical fact that the nation is often a cosmopolitan construction, imagined by diasporic elites working at a distance from their homelands.

The terrain of the 'beyond nation' (whether temporal or spatial) is of particular interest to Nivedita Menon in her farsighted and topical chapter, 'Thinking through the postnation', in which she casts the 'postnation' as referring to the sometimes cross-national, sometimes subnational, sometimes cosmopolitan material locations from which we all now speak. Interrogating the world picture of transnational and corporatized flows that has allegedly superseded the static organization of the world into nation-states, Menon insists on the postnation as a viable ethical horizon projected beyond the violence and homogenization involved in any process of national emergence. At the same time, however, she concedes that non-, sub- and even national identities continue to be expressed in seeming postnational situations, such as within India's northeastern borderlands. For Menon, the postnational, broadly speaking, has two dimensions, one 'over the nation' and one 'under the nation', and resists inclusion in this homogenizing entity by 'insisting on space/

time trajectories that do not manifest within the progression of dominant narratives of nation and history' – and may well, we as editors would add, take on in certain contexts the forms of a *local* cosmopolitanism.

Persisting with the thread of interwoven and heterogeneous space/time trajectories, though once again in colonial times, Ranajit Guha writing on the 'colonial city' of Calcutta considers how different experiences of time were overlaid upon or subtended others in imaginative literature. Here the official, 'grid' time of timetables and train schedules, for example, was mixed in with the more fluid time of indigenous society (in contrast to the deeply historic European accounts of the city, as in Dickens), or with the reiterative time of festivals, necessarily always celebrated and described in the moment, as charted in Bhabanicharan Bandyopadhyay's *Kalikata Kamalalay* (1829), or Kaliprasanna Sinha's *Hutom Pyanchar Naksha* (1861). The latter's prose, Guha suggests, is fully involved in the life of the city, its language loaded with diverse voices and different registers: it is in effect already cosmopolitan in style and form. Whereas in Dickens the dominant and uniform unfolding of time imposes an order of things where inanimate objects, individuals' lives and the narratives of those lives become metonymic of each other, Sinha's historical perspective is subject to an exuberant immediacy of presence, gossip and shared festival-time in an 'incessantly unsettled contemporaneity'.

Notes

1 Partha Mitter, *The Triumph of Modernism: India's Artists and the Avant-garde 1922–1947* (London: Reaktion, 2007), pp. 12–13. See also, for example, Kwame Anthony Appiah, *Cosmopolitanism: Ethics in a World of Strangers* (London: Penguin, 2007); Carol Breckenridge, Homi Bhabha and Dipesh Chakrabarty (eds), *Cosmopolitanism* (Durham, NC: Duke University Press, 2002).

2 Ziauddin Sarkar, Rasheed Araeen and Sean Cubitt (eds), *The 'Third Text' Reader on Art, Culture and Theory* (London: Continuum, 2002); Elleke Boehmer, *Empire, the National and the Postcolonial: Resistance in Interaction, 1880–1920* (Oxford: Oxford University Press, 2002); Nestor Garcia Canclini, *Hybrid Cultures: Strategies for Entering and Leaving Modernity*, trans. C. Chiappari and S. Lopez (Minneapolis, 1995); Rosinka Chaudhuri (ed.), *Derozio: Poet of India* (New Delhi: Oxford University Press, 2008).

13 The alien face of cosmopolitanism

An Indian reading of Cynthia Ozick on the Woolfs

Amit Chaudhuri

Let me begin with a series of recent conversations. In fact, these are snatches of conversation from larger discussions, in almost all of which the subject of cosmopolitanism and modernity – in their locations both in and out of Europe – were broached, explored and argued over. In one of them (the venue was a bookshop), I was trying to articulate my unease with the term 'postcolonial writer'; not only as a description of myself, but as a description of a generic figure. Both the affiliations and the oppositionality of the 'postcolonial writer' seemed too clearly defined; while, for most of the more interesting canonical writers of twentieth-century India, the complexity and unexpectedness of their opposition-ality took their affiliations to unexpected territory – for the Urdu writer, Qurratulain Hyder, therefore, there was Elizabeth Bowen; for the Bengali poet, novelist, and critic Buddhadeva Bose, who adored Tagore and also adored Eliot, there were the compensatory, contrary figures of the poet Jibanananda Das, a contemporary he did much to champion, and of D. H. Lawrence and Whitman. The richness of the various power strug-gles to define the literary within India in the time of modernity, and the robust, often contradictory creative opportunism that took place in the interests of that struggle, is, alas, considerably reduced and simplified by the terms 'colonial' or 'postcolonial'. If one were to map the strategic affinities of these writers, those terms would gradually lose their mythic integrity; what would begin to appear (almost accidentally, as not every point of the map would be known to the other) is a sort of trade route of vernacular experimentation, a patois of the concrete, an effervescent cherishing of the idiosyncratic. If we were to trace the lines radiating from one writer or location to another on this map, we, for instance, might find that, often, a high degree of attention and erudition had been brought to bear upon the commonplace.

Of course, no such map exists. But the fact that these forms of 'commerce' (Pound's word for his curious relationship with Whitman) did characterize literary activity in the late nineteenth and in the twen-tieth centuries comes back to us even today, in, as I've just suggested, unpremeditated instants. One of them occurred at the end of the discussion I just referred to, when, in that bookshop in Oxford, a young Bangladeshi graduate student said to me: 'I've spoken to Indian writers who write in Bengali' – and, here, he mentioned Sunil Ganguly, the leading poet, novelist, and ageing *enfant terrible* who lives in Calcutta, and Ketaki Kushari Dyson, poet, translator of Tagore, erstwhile star student, who lives in Oxford where she was an undergraduate, and who was in that audience – 'I've spoken to these people, and they aren't happy with the term "postcolonial"'. He suggested this might be because of the sort of transverse mappings and affiliations I'd mentioned, and which these writers had pursued in the interests of arriving at the recognizable tone and metier of their enterprise, lines of contact that couldn't be contained by the orthodox demarcations of the 'postcolonial'. But it was, still, chastening and something of a salutary shock to be reminded of actual, specific individuals, and to become conscious of them in a new way, as I began to become aware of Ketaki Kushari Dyson that evening, sitting not a great distance away from me, in her seventies now. In constructing my argument, I'd thought about myself, about history and the great canonical writers of the Indian past, and even, in general terms, of writers like Ketaki Dyson; but I hadn't thought of her in particular, and, for whatever reason, it had never occurred to me to speak to her, or to query her, about the subject. I knew her opinions on a range of things; but, on this, there had been an inadvertent silence. Now, to hear from another source, during a public conversation (she, wordless, as if she had some of the sphinx-like instructiveness of history or the archive), that she was unhappy at being termed a 'postcolonial' was at once vindicating and, as I've just confessed, disconcerting.

In attempting to think about the alien face of cosmopolitanism, I've had to have recourse to moments such as this one, to impressions rather than hard historical fact. Something not spoken of, a question not asked, something you thought you'd forgotten, and remembered later in a different way: these are almost all that is left of the residual cosmopolitanisms of the world – an odd sense of discomfiture, and, in lieu of a definitive language, personal reminiscences that appear to have implications, but remain isolated and arbitrary. I'm interested in exploring whether these moments – essentially afterthoughts from itineraries that have almost been erased – can mark the beginnings of an admittedly desultory enquiry, as much as the assignation of an actual historical date might: a date such as the Indian art historian Partha Mitter fixes, for instance, when he argues that the Bauhaus exhibition in Calcutta in 1922 led to the formation of an artistic avant-garde in India. The exchange that evening in Oxford, and my failure to follow up with Ketaki Dyson, who disappeared quickly after the event, have made me alert to the conversations I've had since with writers in, for the want of a better term, the Indian vernaculars – they being, often without quite knowing it, the sole remnants in our country of those vanished cosmopolitanisms. But there are remnants adrift everywhere – and, so, overheard remarks and incomplete confessions from people, especially writers and academics, from various parts of the world also shape my interpretation. I am not, in doing this, hinting that the rumours of the death of the cosmopolitan are exaggerated; nor am I simply arguing for his or her survival. I am registering the persistence of a worldview as an angularity, resurfacing constantly, at a time when the old dichotomies that defined and animated it (for instance, the 'cosmopolitan' in relation to the 'provincial') have become largely irrelevant. How does one think of the cosmopolitan in the global world?

Let me cite three conversations, beginning with the most recent one. Not long ago, I had dinner with C. S. Lakshmi, who was visiting Calcutta from Bombay, where she lives; Lakshmi is better known by her pseudonym 'Ambai', and is one of the most sensuous and experimental short story writers in the Tamil language. My wife had begun to talk about a little, comical altercation Salman Rushdie had initiated with me recently in print, while I, without irony, protested my admiration for *Midnight's Children*. 'But you can't just bring in these forms by force', said Lakshmi, scolding an invisible third party. 'Firstly, you have to see if there's any such thing as "magic realism" in your tradition or not'. She'd clearly decided this was doubtful. She confided, perturbed, scandalized: 'Do you know, it's begun in the languages as well'. By 'languages' she meant the Indian ones. 'Even Tamil and Kannada writers are now trying to be "magic realist"'.

Before I reflect on these statements, let me quickly move on to the second conversation. This took place over the telephone, again in Calcutta; my interlocutor was Utpal Kumar Basu, probably the most accomplished and – if I might use that word – interesting living poet in the Bengali language. We were discussing, in passing, the nature of the achievement of Subimal Misra, one of the short-story writing avant-garde in sixties Bengal. 'He set aside the conventional Western short story with its idea of time; he was more true to our Indian sensibilities; he set aside narrative', said Basu. 'That's interesting', I observed. 'You know, of course, that, in the last twenty years or so, it's we Indians and postcolonials who are supposed to be the storytellers, emerging as we do from our oral traditions and our millennial fairy tales'. 'Our fairy tales are very different from theirs', said Utpal Basu, unmoved. 'We don't start with, "Once upon a time ..."'.

In both cases, Basu's and Lakshmi's, a cultural politics to do with a more or less unexamined category, 'Indianness', was being used to advance a politics of the modernist avant-garde; both writers, in effect, were offering a throwaway polemic against what the postmodern and the postcolonial had largely rehabilitated – narrative and the fairy tale. A second glance at their remarks, and the suggestive way the word 'our' is used in them – 'our tradition', 'our stories', 'our sensibilities' – tells us that it's not the essential and changeless that's being gestured towards, but the contingent and historical; a cosmopolitanism of the avant-garde that had been located in an India which, since the late nineteenth century, had been making those transverse mappings across territories in the pursuit of certain objectives: the fragmentary, the concrete, and a certain quality of the aleatory that narrative couldn't accommodate. If the didacticism of the postmodern and the postcolonial had taught us that narrative – especially in its guise as epic – was liberating, that storytelling was 'empowering' in its expression of identity, the cosmopolitan avant-garde all over the world in the twentieth century had repeatedly drawn our attention to the tyranny, the enforcements, of narrative: it was to the latter that C. S. Lakshmi and Utpal Basu were referring when using that pronoun, 'our'.

Using the rhetoric of cultural nationalism in the service of the interests of the avant-garde has a long history in the non-West, almost as long a history there as that of modernity itself, and I've written about this elsewhere. There is, for example, Tagore's strategic celebration of the fourth-century Sanskrit poet Kalidasa, as a great, possibly the supreme, describer of the 'real' (Tagore's word for the 'real' is 'nature'), a celebration undertaken while demonstrating that Western poetic language – especially Shakespeare's language – repeatedly falls short of the Flaubertian task of description. This praise is formulated in the first decade of the twentieth century; but even earlier, in 1895, to be precise, Tagore is already attacking rationality and teleology, and enshrining the aleatory, in his essay on Bengali nursery rhymes. Here, drawing the reader's attention to the presence of random associations that so-called 'grown up' writing often lacks, he borrows from, or echoes remarkably, William James's famous essay in *Psychology*, which had been published just three years earlier. The rubric of Tagore's meditation is shored up by forms of cultural nationalism (the invention of a literary tradition with regard to Kalidasa; the construction of a Bengali childhood in connection with the nursery rhymes), but the interests are the interests of the avant-garde (through Kalidasa, a privileging of the image and the 'here and now'; through the nursery rhymes, a celebration of the disruption of linear time, and of the mysterious importance of the 'superfluous'). And these interests, intriguingly, are being articulated right at the inception, worldwide, of the avant-garde, and, coincidentally, at the crossroads, or confluence, at which both political nationalisms and cosmopolitanisms are everywhere coming into being. The nationalism makes possible Tagore's cultural politics as a colonized subject, and the cosmopolitanism a certain kind of journey and mapping (for instance, the crucial and unprecedented borrowing of the notion of the 'stream of consciousness', '*nityaprabahita chetanar majhe*', the first known literary transposition of the idea, in fact).

Against what the nationalisms of the colonies are being fashioned we are certain, but to what end, and against exactly what, the anarchic play, the space for the superfluous, promoted by the various cosmopolitanisms are being posited we are still not entirely clear about; but it's clear that the urgency of the mission leads to an intricate and intense reciprocity over and across the values imposed by colonialism.

Here, I should also mention the Japanese writer Junichiro Tanizaki's brief, dream-like manifesto, *In Praise of Shadows*, where a civilized cultural politics carries forward an essentially modernist programme. Tanizaki is speaking of Japanese, even, occasionally, Eastern, architecture, habitation, allocation of domestic space, and domestic appurtenances in opposition to Western conceptions and traditions of the same things; in doing so, he's positioning shadows, indefiniteness, a desire for decrepitude and recycling, against the definiteness, the clarity, the newness treasured by the West. It is really a modernist dichotomy, a modernist polemic; in speaking of the East and the West, Tanizaki is subtly, richly, delicately, conflating the Japanese with the modernist. We should remember that, from the late nineteenth to the early twentieth century – when neither modernism nor the avant-garde had been ascribed the denominations, the locations, the histories and epiphanic moments by which we know them today – the West, for both European radicals and non-Western artists and thinkers, was identified with linearity, rationality, and naturalism. The Bauhaus painters' works – Klee, Kandinsky, and others – were brought to Calcutta on Tagore's behest; the latter had, Partha Mitter tells us, seen these paintings on a visit to Austria and recognized a concordance, a convergence, of temperament and intention with his own; Mitter also reminds us of Klee's secret but deep absorption in Indian philosophy. Once the paintings were exhibited, they were reviewed in Calcutta's major English-language daily, the *Statesman*, by Stella Kramrisch, an art historian of Austrian-Jewish descent, who was also spending time in India at Tagore's invitation. In her review, Kramrisch told her readers that these paintings might reveal to them 'that European art does not mean naturalism and that the transposition of forms of nature in the work of an artist is common to ancient and modern India'. The attack on linearity and naturalism cannot be characterized as a Western development alone, with occasional epiphanic and opportunistic uses of 'other' cultural resources by Western artists: Picasso with his African mask, Gauguin and Van Gogh with their Japanese prints.

A history of cosmopolitanism and modernism has to take into account both the incursion of the Japanese print into Van Gogh's painting and the peculiar mixture of identity-making, cultural politics, and modernist rhetoric in people like Tanizaki and Tagore: that both were happening at the same time, and, importantly, that the modernism we're aware of in different ways today was being fashioned in the same world. What is common to Picasso, Gauguin, Kramrisch, Klee, Tagore, Tanizaki and others is an impatience with a certain kind of hard and finished object, a cosmopolitan profligacy and curiosity, a renewed, all-consuming attention directed to the contingent, the 'here and now', the particular, and a stated or secret flirtation with 'otherness' or 'difference', at a time when no language exists to do with 'difference', except the one dealing in terms like 'East', 'West', 'progress', 'materialism', and the 'primitive'. It is no historical coincidence that the avant-garde and the modernist was created everywhere in the time of colonialism. One exists in the other, in hidden ways – but not interred simply, as, in Edward Said's reading, the West Indian plantation is hidden in Jane Austen's work; a suppressed, indubitable truth that, once brought to light, would clarify and redress at once.

I had mentioned a third conversation. More enigmatic comment than conversation, I remember it dislocated me because of its suggestive rather than categorical nature, and because it gave me an intimation of lines of contact I should have known more about. It also hinted at a problem of language that is always with us, and prohibits a discussion of modernity without the use of certain catch-words and oppositions: 'Western', 'derived', 'mimicry', 'elitism'. The context here is my visit to the Wissenschaftskolleg in Berlin for lunch almost three years ago, as a preamble to a talk I would deliver in early 2006. My very generous hosts that afternoon all happened to be, fortuitously, Egyptian academics: probably because, given my own interests, all three – two women and a man – were from cultural studies, postcolonial studies or literary departments. Predictably, at some point, the conversation hovered around and then moved gently, but headlong, towards Indian literature, Salman Rushdie and 'magic realism'; as predictably, my contribution introduced a note of uncertainty in relation to the question of unacknowledged modernisms. The women nodded; I sensed that their own trajectories and career choices would have ordinarily distanced them from my preoccupations, but that erstwhile literary investments, perhaps (who knows) buried family histories, and, more noticeably, Rushdie's recent pro-American politics in relation to Iraq had also alienated them from the project of epic fantasy. The man, however, was slightly different; unlike the women, at least one of whom seemed to have spent a lot of time in America, he taught in a department of literature in Egypt; his dilemmas, his biography, would have been somewhat unlike theirs, which is probably why it was in private that he told me: 'We have the same problem in Egypt. We find it difficult to talk about the cosmopolitanisms and modernisms in our tradition'. As I revisit the scene now, I become aware of distinctions and contrasts that my mind had suppressed at the time. The women were globalized individuals, and spoke English fluently: one of them, I think, was a naturalized American. The man, on the other hand, with all his unprepossessing sophistication, evidently spoke and wrote English as a second language.

This reminded me of certain parallels in India, and the way the English language inflected histories there: the women, with their possible elite and global backgrounds, their command of English and their smattering or more of Arabic, echoed the contexts in India in which postcoloniality and notions of hybridity had been consolidated; the man, comfortable in Arabic, with more than a cursory knowledge of English, deeply engaged, in fact, with European literature, reminded me of an earlier, superannuated context in my country, in which, largely, our cosmopolitan modernity had been formed, and from which, with cultural inflections very similar to the Egyptian man's, writers like the poet Utpal Basu and the short-story writer C. S. Lakshmi had emerged.

What do I mean, or, for that matter, understand by the word 'cosmopolitan'? The primary sense that is operational in India is, as I've pointed out elsewhere, a constitutional one: it is related to a governmental guarantee that heterogeneous faiths, communities, and cultures might cohabit peacefully, even vibrantly, within a visible space – usually, the city – in the nation. In this, it is not unlike 'multiculturalism', or the special Indian post-Independence version of the 'secular'; a domain not outside of religion, but a constitutionally protected space of interreligious, intercommunal co-existence. Perhaps the word 'cosmopolitan' also makes a gesture towards the urban middle classes; and, as a result, it is often Bombay (where I grew up), and whose educated middle class encompasses a multifariousness of faiths and provincial identities – Gujarati, Maharashtrian, Parsi, Tamil, Bengali, Bohri Muslims, 'East Indian' Christians, to name some of them – that is called the most 'cosmopolitan' of Indian cities.

I, however, for the purposes of this writing, have an idea of the word somewhat different from the constitutional one; it has to do with the notion of inner exile at the core of the 'high' cultures of the twentieth century. If one were to keep this notion in mind, the city of Calcutta would come powerfully into the frame; and a history of Bombay cosmopolitanism beg to be written that is more than, or distinct from, an account of variegated urban co-existence. I will return to these two cities later. But the theme of 'inner exile' reminds us that the bourgeois cosmopolitan (most profoundly, in our imagination, the European cosmopolitan) – whether artist or intellectual or writer – was never entirely at one with himself or herself. Let's stay with the European cosmopolitan for a moment, as an apparently founding, fundamental type. He or she presents a characteristic twentieth-century embodiment of Europeanness, but also an intriguing modulation upon it; in fact, a testing of the very limits and recognizable features of Europeanness, because the cosmopolitan, by his or her very nature, is constantly telling us they belong nowhere. In what way? One of the main reasons for this, as we know, is that at the heart of the hegemonic 'high' cultures of modernity is the Jewish artist or intellectual; simply put, the Jew, the Other. With the crucial involvement of the figure of the Jew – and I use that term metaphorically as well as literally, introducing all its specific physical dimensions – in the shaping of cosmopolitanism, European modernity becomes, at once, characteristically itself, with its unmistakable eclectic tenor, as we know it today, and deeply alienated from itself. All that is canonically strange about the European twentieth century – its avant-garde, its artistic disruptiveness, its experimentation – opens up, if we linger with the figure of the Jew for a while, into the strange that is not canonical, that is not European, that always carries within it the unrecognizable texture of the minority. But this pursuit cannot be an exercise where we eventually rip off the mask to reveal the true face underneath, fair or dark; because we have to reconcile ourselves, in a new way, to the fact that cosmopolitanism does not, and never had, a true face; its characteristic domain, and achievement, is the defamiliarized.

Before I go any further, I should quickly distinguish what I'm doing here from the many excellent scholarly studies available on the role of Jewishness in modernity. My attempt is less rigorous and more impressionistic, and has, inescapably, to do with facets of who I am: raised in Bombay, a middle-class Bengali, located, as both a writer and a reader, in the histories of modernism in a putatively postmodern age. Chancing upon an old essay by Cynthia Ozick, 'Mrs Virginia Woolf: A Madwoman and her Nurse', from her 1983 collection, *Art and Ardor*, set into motion a train of thoughts that had been with me for a while, to do with Jewishness as well as the India I'd grown up in. It also made me think further into what, in the context of the conversations I've reported, I'd already been thinking about: who is the non-Western cosmopolitan? Did he or she, as it were, vanish thirty years ago into postcolonial identity and ethnicity? Or does the dichotomy of the Western and the non-Western, as we understand it today, actually fall apart in the cosmopolitan?

Ozick's essay is a review of Quentin Bell's biography of his aunt Virginia; and it is, as the title implies, an account of a difficult marriage held together by significant companionship. But it also contains a surprisingly large digression on Leonard Woolf's Jewish identity in particular, and Jewishness in general, the compulsive reflections of a commentator who, a privileged insider in American letters (and, increasingly, a passionate proponent of Zionism), must, at this moment of all moments, confront the spectre of non-Europeanness. Ozick, however, doesn't speak of herself directly; instead, she dwells on the ministering husband in the very heart of Bloomsbury, and, specifically, on faces and appearances. She introduces the theme, the hiccup, the rupture, after briefly sketching the educational background of the Bloomsbury set, and then narrowing upon Leonard: 'Cambridge was not natural to him, Bloomsbury was not natural to him, even England was not natural to him – not as an inheritance; he was a Jew'. And then these comments, on the biographer's failure to properly imagine Leonard Woolf, leading to an unexpected consequence, an opening up; for, Ozick would have it, Bell's inability to 'get' Leonard makes him present to us, while aunt Virginia, whom Bell might understand intuitively, becomes distant: 'Quentin Bell has no "authority" over Leonard Woolf, as he has over his aunt; Leonard is nowhere in the biographer's grip … The effect is unexpected. It is as if Virginia Woolf escapes – possessing her too selectively, the biographer lets her slip – but Leonard Woolf somehow stays to become himself'.

And in what way, in Ozick's essay, does he 'become himself'? She describes the strange courtship, the really very distinct worlds, domestic parameters, and lineages the husband-and-wife-to-be belonged to, Virginia's trademark enervating uncertainties, the careful and polite abstention, in their set, from any remark being passed either on Leonard's religion or his agnosticism, and, in spite of this, Virginia's bewildered admission: 'You seem so foreign'. Now, Ozick begins to discuss the inescapable marks of Jewishness, and, in doing so, almost accidentally touches upon an element in the fashioning of the cosmopolitan in the twentieth century that is rarely acknowledged; the way the cosmopolitan could, poetically, 'belong nowhere', be in a state of inner exile, while the subconscious responded to a register, an actual mark, in her or him, which it could never express itself about with the candour that Virginia Woolf, from her position of agitated intimacy, could: 'You seem so foreign'. This is the mark of alterity or difference: not antithetical to cosmopolitanism's homelessness, its internationalism, but, I hope to suggest, fundamental to it. Ozick brings us to the incontrovertible piece of evidence, the face, tracing its passage and vicissitudes from Woolf's paternal grandfather's time to his own. In connection, again, with his contemporaries, Ozick points out that 'if his own origins were almost never mentioned to his face, his face was nevertheless there, and so, in those striking old photographs, were the faces of his grandparents'. Ozick quotes Leonard Woolf's own words, from his autobiography, on his paternal grandfather: 'a large, stern, black-haired, and black-whiskered, rabbinical Jew in a frock coat' with a 'look of stern rabbinical orthodoxy'. According to Ozick, he preferred his Dutch-born maternal grandmother's face, 'the round, pink face of an incredibly old Dutch doll', and he also wondered if this grandmother might have had 'a good deal of non-Jewish blood in her ancestry. Some of her children and grandchildren were fair-haired and facially very unlike the "typical" Jew'. About his grandfather, though, he was resolutely without illusions: 'No one could have mistaken him for anything but a Jew. Although he wore coats and trousers, hats and umbrellas, just like those of all the other gentlemen in Addison Gardens, he looked to me as if he might have stepped straight out of one of those old pictures of caftaned, bearded Jews in a ghetto'. And so, in his unconvincing 'coats and trousers, hats and umbrellas', Leonard's grandfather is already working his way towards that secular modernity that his grandson will come to inhabit, almost naturally, but whose neutral 'Englishness', in turn, even in the temporary persona of the colonial officer, a figure of authority, does not deceive Ozick. She is, again inadvertently I think, gesturing towards a history of the secular from the nineteenth century onwards that is as characteristic of the non-West as it is, as we see, of the heart of Empire itself; the fusing of ethnic identity, as in the case of the grandfather, with a European paradigm, an almost proud fusing, one can't help feeling, in spite of the grandson's misgivings; and then, two generations later, with the fashioning of the cosmopolitan, the modern, and the modernist, we have the grandson's invisibility, which, as Ozick shrewdly points out (without unfolding any of its consequences), is also a form of visibility. The process was taking place, let's say, in Bengal as much as in London; it is often called 'Westernization', which is an almost meaningless term, not only because the process meant very different things to, say, Leonard Woolf's grandfather and to Woolf himself, but because it does not catch the intricacy, the cultural and emotional complexity, of the way 'difference' directs the process. It is something that could equally, and as validly, be called 'non-Westernization', without any of the assertiveness of the postcolonial discourses.

Ozick now turns to a photograph, part of what she calls a 'pictorial history of Bloomsbury'. Before she offers her reading, she offers her caveat: 'One is drawn to Leonard's face much as he was drawn to his grandfather's face, and the conclusion is the same. What Leonard's eyes saw [that is, when they confronted his grandfather] was what the eyes of the educated English classes saw [that is, when regarding Woolf]'. Ozick is right to alert us to this; but there is also the question of what her eyes see, and what ours do. Ozick studies the 'arresting snapshot' of Leonard Woolf and Adrian Stephen, brother of Virginia Woolf. 'They are', says Ozick, 'both young men in their prime; the date is 1914 ... They are dressed identically (vests, coats, ties) and positioned identically – feet apart, hands in pocket, shut lips gripping pipe or cigarette holder ... Both faces are serene, holding back amusement, indulgent of the photographer'. At this point, we come to the anticipated turn in the portrayal: 'And still it is not a picture of two cultivated Englishmen, or not only that. Adrian is incredibly tall and Vikinglike, with a forehead as broad and flat as a chimney tile; he looks like some blueblood American banker not long out of Princeton; his hair grows straight up like thick pale straw. Leonard's forehead is an attenuated wafer under a tender black forelock, his nose is nervous and frail'. After a moment's reflection on what the correct analogy might be, Ozick decides to be, as she puts it, 'blunt': 'he looks like a student at the yeshiva. Leonard has the unmistakable face of a Jew'.

Ozick is absolutely right, I think, in her preternatural and prickly sensitivity, to exhume the Jewish identity of the 'cultivated Englishman'; but she is perhaps wrong to give it such fixity. There is another kind of movement taking place in this image, this picture, which Ozick says nothing about, and which would consign Adrian Stephen's type – blonde, tall, 'Vikinglike' – into history just as Woolf's grandfather had been consigned to history; it involves, in the unwitting figure of Woolf, the emergence of the cosmopolitan – the person who belongs nowhere, the person whose alterity and state of exile are hidden but unmistakable. The old distinction between the 'student at the yeshiva' and the 'cultivated Englishman' may have been true of Woolf's grandfather's time, but it is, already, no longer of Woolf's: to be modern, increasingly, will be to be impure, to both conceal and exhibit that impurity. The great project of 'high' modernity, defamiliarization, and the principal discourse of postcoloniality, alterity, had always, we'd presumed, been distinct from each other, belonging to distinct phases of twentieth-century history, and even embedded in worldviews at war with one another. A second glance at the cosmopolitan – especially at the Jewish writers and artists who lived in Europe, many of them transplanted to America from around the time of the Second World War, or who died shortly before (Walter Benjamin, Kracauer, Adorno, Schoenberg, Bloch, Hannah Arendt, to name a few) – reminds us that alterity is an indispensable and intimate constituent of the 'high' modern, that it is the hidden twin of what is already hidden but powerfully definitive of 'high' modernity – the defamiliarized. To be modern, Ozick accidentally reminds us, is to be foreign, to be 'different': not only figuratively, but, in significant ways, literally; and it is of course the literal, for obvious reasons of her own, that Ozick is here fiercely concentrated on. As far as appearances are concerned, the misfit in the picture, the one who is already beginning to date, is Adrian Stephen, not Leonard Woolf.

Let me, here, address my own recollections of cosmopolitanism; for Ozick's essay is of interest to me because, primarily, it makes me realign what I already know. I wish to refer to faces and styles of appearance in Bombay that gradually decided for me, as I was growing up in the sixties and seventies, what the lineaments of cosmopolitanism and bohemianism might be. In the light of Ozick's essay, I am led to wonder what made me take those decisions: for no clear or definitive catalogue of features had been put down. Of course, one identified an artist or writer of the avantgarde through their work, but there was clearly another realm involved, or else I wouldn't have registered the adolescent shock I did at the discrepancy between T. S. Eliot's appearance and his poetry, the canonical unfamiliarity and experimental nature of the latter, and the unfamiliar or unexpected conventionality of the former. We are aware, certainly, that Eliot made deliberate comic use of this discrepancy, in 'Prufrock', of course, but pointedly in 'Lines for Cuscuscaraway and Mirza Murad Ali

Beg': 'How unpleasant to meet Mr Eliot! / With his features of clerical cut, / And his brow so grim / And his mouth so prim'. Here is the American exile, in middle age, a man who has, for long, deliberately emptied his appearance of signs of exile, and who seems to be mocking the visible features of cosmopolitanism (not in his poetry, but in his personal style), who seems to be refuting (and I'm making no easy connection with his publicized anti-Semitism) the subterranean ethos of alterity.

The realm of the visible, then, is an important one in recognizing the cosmopolitan, because it comprises both carefully orchestrated markers and intrinsic lapses. Visible signs also help us to distinguish between cosmopolitanism as inner exile, and the other, constitutional form of cosmopolitanism I mentioned earlier, a state-sponsored multiculturalism. As the decades after Independence went past, this second form became the authoritative one in India, and especially definitive, in a clichéd way, of society in Bombay; what the history of cosmopolitanism as a state of inner exile might be in that city has become increasingly difficult to remember or articulate. The visible markers of constitutional cosmopolitanism were symbolic and straightforward, as in a Hindi film set in the seventies, signifying sub-nationalisms that added up to the nation: there was the Sikh in his turban, there was the Muslim in his skull cap, there was the Christian crossing herself, and there the hero, at once Hindu and everyman, embodying the secular space – the film, the story, the nation – in which, despite tribulations and challenges, these particular elements unite. With the cosmopolitan as exile, the visible elements – the blue jeans, the handspun *khadi kurta*, the sandals, the filterless cigarette between the fingers, the copy of Lorca in one hand – did not add up; they did not cohere, as the constitution had foretold the heterogeneous fragments of the nation would; they were casual signs of belonging nowhere. I will elaborate on this in a moment.

I realize that, as I was growing up, I began to identify the cosmopolitan avant-garde and the bohemian artistic fraternity in seventies Bombay not only by their practice, but also as a consequence of what they looked like. That tutoring had come to me from desultorily studying members of this subclass from a distance, as well as both the works and faces of the American, especially, the New York, artists and poets; in fact, a certain kind of American person who happened to be quite distinct from the 'tall, Vikinglike' American banker prototype Ozick compares Adrian Stephen to. In this latter group, whose features I'd been subconsciously absorbing, I'd include a whole range of practitioners, whose work, at the time, I didn't necessarily admire: Allen Ginsberg (who'd visited India in the sixties and hung out with the Bombay and especially the Calcutta poets, including Sunil Ganguly, whom I described as an 'ageing *enfant terrible*'), as well as figures from pop culture and entertainment, like Bob Dylan, Woody Allen, Groucho Marx, and, with his diverse racial background and his benign belligerence, a sort of honorary Jew, Frank Zappa. There seemed to be an air of the outsider, of difference, about these people: I ascribed this to their practice, and to the persona being an extension of that practice. To be an outsider, in the twentieth century, was also often to have a curious combination of, on the one hand, the awkward, the pedagogical, the pedantic, and, on the other, the anarchic and comic, and, often, the two were interchangeable: thus, the anxious academic air of Woody Allen and Groucho Marx, and the quietly comic appearance of Albert Einstein. These were signs of the fine balancing act through which alterity was shaping modernity: a seriousness that was out of place and therefore foreign, mirroring a foreignness that was altogether too serious. The result could be comic, as is evident from Ozick's pitying, acerbic: 'he looks like a student from the yeshiva'. The modern, marked and pursued by difference, also makes a mess of things: 'under the sign of Saturn' is how Susan Sontag describes the condition in connection with Walter Benjamin, who is less than adept at the technology of everyday life ('my inability even today to make a cup of coffee'), botching up too, with the yeshiva-student's seriousness, his final, attempted escape to the United States. In India, this serio-comic figure of the modern, singled out at once by modernity and difference, emerges in the nineteenth century with the Bengali babu, and is parodied by Bengalis and Englishmen alike – most savagely, for the Anglophone reader, by Kipling in *Kim* at the beginning of the new century.

As for myself, I didn't dwell on the fact that many of the faces I was studying, by some coincidence, belonged to Jews, though this was often a part of their self-advertisement; Jewishness, hidden or anxious, if ineluctable, in the Europeans, seemed to have become, with these Americans, a more acknowledged secular component, sometimes a subversive one, of defamiliarization. Many of the poets who lived or studied in Bombay, and wrote in English in the sixties and seventies – set apart in those relatively early decades after Independence, therefore, by the curious double prestige and disgrace of writing in a colonial language and an international one – this strange microcosmic minority (comprising, among others, Arun Kolatkar, Arvind Krishna Mehrotra, Nissim Ezekiel) were unmistakably cosmopolitans. They reminded me in some ways of the Americans, but this I might have taken to be a family resemblance, integral to the texture of the time. I may have also assumed that there were elements in their visible and intellectual make-up that they'd fashioned after the Americans; certainly, Kolatkar and Mehrotra had studied, respectively, William Carlos Williams and Pound in order to create a vernacular that would allow them to move away from both Orientalist poetry and King's English, a language of defamiliarization, of finding the uncanny in the Indian mundane. Something in them also very powerfully echoed the Jewishness of American artists; but I was not conscious of this fact – nor do I think were they – except subliminally. The Jewish artist created a space that many non-Western cosmopolitans, especially in Bombay in the sixties, came to rework seamlessly in their own milieu, without anyone either clearly noticing it, or being able to remark on it except in inadequate terms such as 'Westernization'. I say 'inadequate', because the Jew had almost unknowingly introduced a dimension of racial and physical alterity to the modern, which, almost unknowingly, the sixties Indian English poets and bohemia presented their modulation upon. It was not simply towards the European or the Western that poets like Kolatkar and Mehrotra were aspiring, but a condition of twentieth-century modernity that crucially brought together what are seen to be incompatibles: defamiliarization and difference, modernist experiment and ethnicity, Europeanness and non-Europeanness. It also occurs to me here that the modernities and cosmopolitanisms that I am familiar with were all shaped by disenfranchised elites; that is, by groups of people who, in the contexts they found themselves in, had no natural – or had a somewhat ambivalent and subterranean – access to political power. This was true of the Jews in Europe and even America; it was true of the Bengali in the time of colonialism; it was true of the odd minority position of the Indian poets who wrote in English in the sixties, at a time well before English was the 'boom' Indian language it would become twenty-five years later, being reproached by the canonical writers in the Indian vernaculars and Ginsberg alike for employing a foreign tongue. It was in these contexts of disenfranchised elitism that other, cultural modes of power were fashioned by these cosmopolitans. The question of legitimacy raised by each of the elites I've mentioned finds its odd, and possibly logical, counterpart in the constant question of the legitimacy of the artwork itself in modernism – is this art? – a challenge which has, of course, been domesticated in the triumphal narrative of European modernity.

Among the Bombay poets were a number of people who belonged to liminal religions: for instance, the founder poet of the group, the late Nissim Ezekiel, was Jewish, a descendant of the Bene Israel sect that had sought refuge in Gujarat in the second century BC; and there was Adil Jussawala, one of the most intellectual of that set, a Zoroastrian and a Parsi. I'll only point out here that their minority status played itself out in two ways: firstly, in a semi-visible relationship to the secular, largely Hindu nation, and, secondly, in connection to the prism of cosmopolitanism, where it also merged into their roles as sometimes derided deracinated writers in the English language. Occasionally, and this is only a hunch, being part of a minority seems to have given them, particularly Ezekiel, privileged access to international cosmopolitanisms; at least, this is what these lines from Ezekiel's autobiographical poem, 'Background, Casually', seem to indicate: 'The Indian landscape sears my eyes. / I have become a part of it / To be observed by foreigners. / They say that I am singular, / Their letters overstate the case'. 'Singular' is a word Ezekiel uses more than once; it encompasses both the resonance of the minority and of the privileged cosmopolitan. Living in India, being Indian, you almost feel that Ezekiel is aware of Jewish cosmopolitanism, but has forgotten the problem of Jewish alterity.

Interestingly, all these artists and poets – whether they were Hindus, Muslims, Parsis, Jews, Christians – made cosmopolitanism visible in a new way in the sixties and seventies, in that brief period when the old disenfranchised vernacular elites began to lose their intellectual hegemony in India, and before a new empowered post-Nehruvian ruling class emerged in the eighties with Rajiv Gandhi; they fashioned a style called the 'ethnic', and, in doing so, complicated the relationship between the Indian and the deracinated, between authenticity and foreignness. 'Ethnic', at the time, used to indicate, generally, non-Christian, non-European identity; with the bohemian set in India, it denoted the condition of belonging nowhere. Among the visible symbols of the ethnic were handspun *khadi kurtas*, sometimes worn in conjunction with long *churidar* pyjamas, sometimes blue jeans, cotton Bengali *tangail* saris, and, on the foreheads of bohemian women, large vermilion Fauvist *bindis* or dots, the feet of both men and women in Kolhapuri *chappals* or sandals. The conventional Western clothes of the Indian middle class – shirts, trousers, suits, shoes – were set aside, not in the interests of nationalism, but for a combination of clothing that, individually, could be overdeterminedly 'Indian', but were now suddenly transformed into a signature of deracination. The 'ethnic', then, is a peculiarly sixties' Indian modulation of alterity's delicate relationship to the cosmopolitan and the defamiliarized.

On this matter of the visibility of the cosmopolitan, and its surprising allocations of the recognizable and the unrecognizable, I wish to end with a tiny coda on the city of Calcutta, and on the Bengali *bhadralok* or bourgeois – the descendant of the babu. The Bengali *bhadralok* emerges more or less parallel to the Jewish cosmopolitan in Europe; in him, once again, as in the Jew, we find the 'high' cultural defamiliarized merging with the irreducibly non-European. Unlike, for instance, the Japanese modern, the *bhadralok* eschews the Western suit; the suited Bengali, in fact, is often seen to be a government official, or a functionary of the Raj. The *bhadralok*'s visible mark of deracination, of defamiliarization, is the once-feudal costume, the white *dhuti* and *panjabi* or kurta; at what point the transition took place from the feudal to the cosmopolitan is difficult to pinpoint, but once it had, it became increasingly difficult to mistake, from a distance, the wearer of that costume as anyone except a person belonging to a particular history that was, indeed, unfolding worldwide. The fact that – unlike the flowing Persian or Oriental robes worn by Rammohun Roy or the Tagores, or, for that matter, the club-goer's suit – the *dhuti* and *panjabi* were the attire of the Bengali everyman was important; for, like the 'cultivated Englishman', Leonard Woolf, it made the *bhadralok* at once invisible and newly visible. The worldwide history this person belonged to was a history of the modern, certainly, but it was also a history of the different; it was a narrative of 'high' culture as well as being a narrative of otherness. That narrative, as was to be expected, had a limited life; the figure in the *dhuti* and *panjabi* has all but disappeared. This makes it possible to consider afresh the contraries that were visible but never fully declared in its appearance.

Note

This chapter previously appeared in *New Left Review* 55 (January–February 2009), pp. 89–106.

14 India, empire and First World War writing

Santanu Das

At the heart of Kolkata, between the brown-green stretches of the Maidan (with the floodlight platforms for the Eden Gardens cricket ground rising in the distance) on one side and a multi-lane traffic-spewing thoroughfare on the other, stands the memorial to the soldiers killed in the First World War (Figure 14.1). Flanked on either side by the statue of a soldier marked by his Saxon features and Western military uniform (not visible in Figure 14.1), the memorial at once invites and resists assimilation into the cultural fabric of the city. Between memory and the monument falls the shadow, at once of colonialism and of class. The statues of the British Tommies and the Latin dates inscribed on the memorial are for the people of the city symbols of the Great European War; they are also symptomatic of the strange gap in much of Indian middle-class metropolitan memory (except in places such as Punjab) about the country's own role in the conflict.

India contributed approximately 1.5 million men, including 900,000 combatants and 600,000 non-combatants. According to the governmental records of the time, the total number of Indian ranks recruited during the First World War and up to 31 December 1919 was 877,068 combatants and 563,369 non-combatants, making a total of 1,440,437.[1] Between August 1914 and December 1919, India had sent overseas for purposes of war 622,224 soldiers and 474,789 non-combatants, who served in France, Mesopotamia, Persia, East Africa, Gallipoli and the Far East.[2] This is a momentous event in early twentieth-century history and culture, as hundreds of thousands of semi-literate, plebeian Indians voyaged 'across the black waters', to adopt the title of Mulk Raj Anand's war novel; it is also a singular event in Indo-British imperial relations. But coming largely from the peasant-warrior classes of the northern parts of the country and falling on the wrong side of the political line in post-independence India, these men and their stories have been doubly marginalized. They have been largely ignored in Indian nationalist-elitist historiography as well as in 'modern memory' of the war that, until recently, has remained largely Eurocentric.

History, according to T. S. Eliot in 'Gerontion', 'has many cunning passages, contrived corridors'.[3] Eliot wrote 'Gerontion' in 1919 – the year following the end of the war – and one cannot help noticing the shadow of the trenches across Eliot's maze of metaphors. Post-war memory has a similar labyrinthine, subterranean structure; it too exists silently, persistently. In the village of Lehri in Northern Pakistan, a simple plaque commemorates the 391 men from the area who went to the war; opening the diary of the Private Charles Stinson, 1st Australian Light Horse Brigade in the Australian War Memorial, one comes across a page where an Indian had signed his name 'Pushkar Singh' in Urdu, Gurmukhi and English.[4] A search through my extended family revealed the war mementoes of Captain Dr Manindranath Das: his military uniform, a dispatch signed by Winston Churchill, a German shell case and several medals, including the Military Cross. Most poignant of the archival findings were a pair of broken bloodstained glasses, and a photograph of a young man in military uniform wearing them that I came across in a display cabinet in a small, dilapidated museum in the former French colony of Chandernagore (Figure 14.2). The label identified him as 'Dr. J. N. Sen, M.D., M.R.C.S., Private, West Yorkshire Regiment ... he was the first Bengalee, a citizen of Chandernagore killed in 1914–1918 War'.[5] Meaning and materiality here are fused and confused; so are imperial war service, cultural identity and a regional consciousness. It refuses to fit the oppositional categories of 'imperialism' and 'nationalism', or the models of 'hybridity' or 'mimicry' so influential in postcolonial theory, and instead points to what Raymond Williams calls a 'complex structure of feeling'.[6] These archival discoveries were, however, the fruit of my adult academic enquiry: they did not impinge on the emotional world of my early youth. As I was growing up in Kolkata, my mind fastened instead on the statues of the Tommies who, with their downcast visage and forlorn majesty, stirred adolescent fantasy: they blended seamlessly with the poetry of Wilfred Owen and Siegfried Sassoon that we were taught at Presidency College, Kolkata, which some believed to have the oldest English department in the world.

In recent years, as we move towards the centennial commemoration of the First World War, there has been a swell of interest in its colonial, particularly multi-racial, dimensions.[7] The opening of the Memorial Gates at Hyde Park Corner in London in 2002 to commemorate the contributions of the Indian subcontinent, Africa and the Caribbean to the two World Wars, the increased space devoted to the Native Labour Corps in the museum for the South African troops in Delville Wood in France or the exhibition 'Man–Culture–War: Multicultural Aspects of the First World War' (2008) at the Flanders Museum at Ypres are powerful examples. Indeed, if one had visited Ypres during the war years, one would have seen Indian sepoys along with *tirailleurs Sénégalais*, North African *spahis*, Chinese and Indo-Chinese workers, Maori Pioneer battalion and First Nation Canadians, in addition to white troops and workers from Europe and the British dominions. Over two million Africans were involved in the First World War. The French empire mobilized around 600,000 colonial troops to its army, including 293,756 North Africans, 170,891 West Africans, 48,922 Indochinese, and employed over 200,000 non-white workers to work in its factories and farms.[8] In France alone, more than one million non-white men were present between 1914 and 1918, mobilized by France, Great Britain, and later the United States. However, of all the colonies in the British, French and German empires at the time, the contribution of India in terms of manpower, estimated at around 1.5 million men, remains the highest. In a grotesque reversal of Conrad's vision, hundreds of thousands of non-white men were voyaging to the heart of whiteness to witness the 'horror, the horror' of Western civilization.

The nature of the 'Great War and modern memory' would look quite different if, instead of the over-articulate intensity of an Owen or a Remarque, we take as our guide the following comment of the Indian sepoy Mausa Ram writing in April 1915 from the Kitchener's Indian Hospital in Brighton: 'The state of affairs here is as follows: the black pepper is finished. Now the red pepper is being used, but, occasionally, the black pepper proves useful. The black pepper is very pungent, and the red pepper is not so strong. This is a secret but you are a wise man'.[9] 'Black pepper' refers to Indian soldiers while the 'red' to English: it is a coded advice meant to hoodwink the colonial censors and warn fellow-villagers against further recruitment. On the other hand, Indian soldiers haunt the writings of European war-writers, such as Siegfried Sassoon, Edmund Blunden and Ernst Jünger. Sassoon notes in his diaries: 'I watched the Indian cavalry in the horse-lines by the river: their red head-caps made occasional spots of poppy-colour: the rest was browns and duns and greys – like the huddle of horses and wagons and blankets, and the worn grassless earth'.[10]

This essay is part of a larger project that aims to recover and examine the Indian experience of the First World War and the way in which these sepoys were configured in the cultural and literary consciousness of the time, in India and in Europe.[11] These men, I argue, were the conscripts of both modernity and empire for it was the conjunction of modern transportation and availability of cheap non-white labour in the colonies that resulted in their being drafted. How was the war understood and represented in India, and what was the experience of the men who suddenly found themselves transferred from small villages in northern India to the killing fields of France? My aim here is to investigate these issues as well as to unearth certain structures of feeling – the experiential, intimate, and the affective – as engendered by the intertwined histories of race, empire and the war. There is a related methodological concern. In a context where we do not have the thousands of diaries, poems and memoirs that form the corner-stone of European war memory, when the colonial archives are remarkably silent, a dialogue between different kinds of sources – archival, oral and the literary – becomes particularly important to recover and understand the texture of the past.

Indian responses to the war

India joined the war as part of the British Empire. As Great Britain declared war on Germany in August 1914, Lord Hardinge, the Viceroy of India, immediately declared that India also was at war. However, apart from a few, isolated revolutionary activities centred on the activities of the Ghadr party in North America,[12] the responses in India were largely enthusiastic. In August 1914, when the 'King-Emperor' sent a message to the 'Princes and People of My Indian Empire',[13] the native princes, still ruling one-third of India, started almost competing with each other with their extravagant offers. Vast sums of money flowed in from these 700-odd princes, from the Nizam of Hyderabad's contribution of over a million rupees for the maintenance of two cavalry units in France to five lakhs from the Maharajah Gaekwar of Baroda for the purchase of aeroplanes for the use of the Royal Flying Corps.[14]

From the perspective of gender and war, particularly in the colonial context, the responses of the woman rulers of some of the princely states were striking. Consider the following two speeches, the first from the Hindu princess, Taradevi, made in Calcutta on 25 December 1914 and the second from the Begum of Bhopal at the Delhi War Conference in April 1918:

> Gentlemen, though I am a lady of such an advanced age, yet I am Kshatriya and when my Kshatriya blood rises up in my veins and when I think I am the widow to the eldest son of one who was a most tried friend of the British Government, I jump on my feet at the aspiration of going to the field of war to fight Britain's battle. It is not I alone, I should say, but there are thousands and thousands of Indian ladies who are more anxious than myself, but there is no such emergency, neither will there be one for the ladies to go to the front when there are brave men who would suffice for fighting the enemies.[15]

> Is it not a matter for regret then that Turkey should … join hands with the enemies of our British Government? All gentlemen like you have read, I suppose, in the papers, how the British Government is now, as ever, having Mohammedan interests at heart … India will leave

nothing undone to justify the confidence, the love, the sympathy with which the King-Emperor has always honoured us. The need of the Empire is undoubtedly India's opportunity ... Now that the war has entered upon a more intense phase we assure you that it will never be said that in this supreme crisis India when weighed in the balance was found wanting.[16]

In the first extract, we have the image of the Hindu warrior-queen invoking ideas of the 'martial race' ('Kshatriya' is the martial caste) and the gender politics of a patriarchal, feudal society for recruitment. The second quotation points to a specific religious issue: the Allied powers became anxious about the possibility of a global *jihad*, especially with the entry into the war in November 1914 of Turkey whose sultan bore the title of *Khalifa* or religious leader for the Muslim population around the world. Here, the local leader is being used to ensure the continuing loyalty of the Indian Muslims, particularly for those fighting their religious brethren – the Turks – in Mesopotamia. Echoing the Begum's exhortations, we have similar appeals from the Nizam of Hyderbad, the Nawab of Palanpur as well as the Aga Khan, telling their subjects that 'it is the bounden duty of the Mohammedans of India to adhere firmly to their old and tried loyalty to the British Government'.[17]

While the responses of these powerful men and women are extensively recorded, as in *India's Services in the War* (1919), we know very little about the responses of thousands of poor, village women whose husbands, sons or brothers actually fought; indeed, civilian war responses in the villages of Asia and Africa remain some of the least explored areas in First World War history.[18] Among the Indian soldiers, the highest rate of recruitment was in the villages in Punjab which contributed around 360,000 soldiers, that is, almost 50 per cent of the total number of Indian combatants. Among certain communities, such as the Jat Sikhs, the rate of recruitment varied between 30 and 50 per cent.[19] Lieutenant Colonel D.G.Rule, recruiting officer in Amritsar district, mentioned in his diary several cases of women who would follow recently enlisted men for miles, waiting for the right opportunity to lure them back.[20] Such instances point to a tantalizing area, but apart from these occasional references, we have no records at all as we reach the limits of archival knowledge and the traditional tools of historical research. What, however, do survive from these villages are folksongs about the war and recruitment – songs of female lament – pointing to a subcutaneous but powerful layer of memory and protest against the war. Consider the following Punjabi First World War folksong, recently excavated and translated by the distinguished Punjabi poet, Amarjit Chandan:

My husband, and his two brothers
All have gone to *laam*. [l'arme]
Hearing the news of the war
Leaves of trees got burnt.
Without you I feel lonely here.
Come and take me away to Basra.
I will spin the wheel the whole night.

Come back from *laam*.
Drop in some time like a guest.

War destroys towns and ports, it destroys huts
I shed tears, come and speak to me
All birds, all smiles have vanished
And the boats sunk
Graves devour our flesh and blood.[21]

Such songs give insights into female emotional history, and point to an alternative lyric tradition of anti-war protest and mourning absent from the archives or standard narratives of India and the war.

Between these two extremes are the responses of the political bourgeoisie and the educated middle class. As I have argued at length elsewhere, such responses, extensively documented, were varied and complex, but on the whole enthusiastic.[22] The Indian National Congress, dominated at the time by political moderates, pledged their full support. Different political parties and communities such as the All India Muslim League, Madras Provincial Congress, Hindus of Punjab, the Parsee community of Bombay as well as senior nationalist leaders such as Surendranath Banerjea and Madan Mohan Malaviya concurred. Addressing a big gathering in Madras, Dr Subramania Iyer claimed that to be allowed to serve as volunteers is an 'honour superior to that of a seat in the Executive Council and even in the Council of the Secretary of State'.[23] Fund-raising was organized and meetings were held in cities such as Calcutta, Bombay, Lahore and Allahabad. Pamphlets were produced pledging support, one typical title (1915) being 'Why India is Heart and Soul with Great Britain'.[24]

The First World War catches the Indian political consciousness at a fragile spot between a continuing (though increasingly qualified) loyalty to the British Raj and early concerted nationalist movements, such as the Home Rule Movement, launched during the war years by Annie Besant and Gangadhar Tilak. According to Besant, support for the empire at this critical juncture would later be repaid with greater political recognition, as set forth in her article 'India's Loyalty and England's Duty':

When the war is over and we cannot doubt that the King-Emperor will, as reward for her [India's] glorious defence of the Empire, pin upon her breast the jewelled medal of Self-Government within the Empire. It will be, in a sense, a real Victoria Cross, for the great Empress would see in it the fulfilment of her promise in 1858, and the legend inscribed on it would be 'for valour'.[25]

Mahatma Gandhi however demurred. In his autobiography, he notes: 'I thought that England's need should not be turned into our opportunity, and that it was more becoming and far-sighted not to press our demands while the war lasted',[26] thus clearly distancing his position from that of the Irish nationalists. But it was quite widely assumed that India's war services would lead to greater national autonomy and self-determination.

But at the same time, political shrewdness is not the only explanation as it is often made out to be retrospectively: reading the political treatises with other kinds of writing shows a much more messy emotional space. Underlying the political calculation was also a complex colonial anxiety, captured succinctly in a piece of doggerel verse: 'Who calls me now a coward base, / And brands my race a coward race?'[27] Signed by a Bengalee, and possibly written in the context of the theory of the 'martial races', it nonetheless speaks of the sense of 'psychological damage' wrought by the internalization of the racist, colonial ideology that theorists such as Frantz Fanon and Ashis Nandy have analysed powerfully.[28] In much of Indian war writing – ranging from the works of Sarojini Naidu (discussed below) to the censored letters of the sepoys or the diary of Prince Amar Singh who was attached to the 9th Sirhind Brigade in France, the First World War becomes an opportunity to set aright the racial slur. National honour can paradoxically be salvaged through imperial war service, by fighting alongside the European masters in a European war. This sentiment was expressed powerfully in an article written in 1915 in the black Jamaican journal *Grenada Federalist*: 'As Coloured people we will be fighting for something more, something inestimable to ourselves. We will be fighting to prove to Great Britain that we are not so vastly inferior to the white'.[29]

Patriotism, poetry, politics: Sarojini Naidu

How did the war affect the socio-cultural and literary imagination in India at the time? What is astonishing is the enthusiasm and rigour with which the educated middle classes and the colonial administrators addressed, absorbed, debated and wrote about India's role in the war. Many of the contemporary articles are collected into the compendious war volume *All About the War: The Indian Review War Book* (n.d. (1915?)) edited by the Madras-based publisher G. A. Natesan. Indian war writings range from documentary histories such as Bhargava's *India's Services in the War* (Allahabad: 1919) and *Patiala and the Great War* (London: 1923) to pamphlets, poems and short stories to later literary responses such as Mulk Raj Anand's *Across the Black Waters* (1939). In fact, during the war, a recruitment play titled *The Bengal Platoon* (1916) was written by the Bengali novelist Satish Chandra Chattopadhyay and was played to full houses at the Presidency theatre in Calcutta. Even an anti-colonial and anti-nationalist writer such as Rabindranath Tagore – who would later decry the violence of the war and blame it on European nationalism – was moved to publish in the 1914 issue of the Calcutta-based war journal *Indian Ink* poems such as 'The Trumpet' with its exhortation, 'Come fighters carrying your flags'.[30] However, it is in the wartime writings of the Indian nationalist leader and poet Sarojini Naidu that the ambivalences and the anxieties underlying the Indian middle-class responses to the war find one of their most complex testimonies.[31]

Sarojini Naidu was an internationally celebrated figure in the early years of the twentieth century. An eminent poet in English, she was christened the 'Nightingale of India' by Mahatma Gandhi, and her admirers included Rabindranath Tagore, Arthur Symons and Edmund Gosse; an ardent feminist, she led the All-India Women's Deputation in 1917 to Montagu, Secretary of State for India, arguing for the political franchise for Indian women; one of the foremost leaders of the Indian nationalist movement, she went on to become the president of the Indian National Congress in 1925. In 1931, she accompanied Gandhi to London for the Second Round Table Conference, and her engagements included an invitation to Buckingham Palace and reading poetry at the Poetry Bookshop.[32] She worked closely with Gandhi, but, in fact, it was the First World War that led to her first encounter with him in London. Naidu was then actively involved in the war effort through the Lyceum club and Gandhi at the time was raising an ambulance corps.

During the war, she went back to India and at the Madras Provincial conference in 1918, she made the following appeal:

> It is, in my opinion, imperative that India should give the flower of her manhood without making any condition whatsoever, since Indians were not a nation of shopkeepers and their religion was a religion of self-sacrifice … Let young Indians who are ready to die for India and to wipe from her brow the brand of slavery rush to join the standing army or to be more correct, India's citizen army composed of cultured young men, of young men of traditions and ideals, men who burnt with the shame of slavery in their hearts, will prove a true redeemer of Indian people.[33]

The smarting phrase 'nation of shopkeepers' leaps out of the page. It perhaps reveals why this nationalist leader who declared that her aim was to 'hold together the divided edges of Mother India's cloak of patriotism' would support India's war service. Consider 'The Gift of India', written for the Report of the Hyderabad Ladies' War Relief Association, December 1915, and later collected in *The Broken Wing: Songs of Love, Death and Destiny 1915–1916*:

> Gathered like pearls in their alien graves,
> Silent they sleep by the Persian waves.
> Scattered like shells on Egyptian sands
> They lie with pale brows and brave, broken hands.
> They are strewn like blossoms mown down by chance
> On the blood-brown meadows of Flanders and France.
>
> Can ye measure the grief of the tears I weep
> Or compass the woe of the watch I keep?
> Or the pride that thrills thro' my heart's despair
> And the hope that comforts the anguish of prayer?
> And the far sad glorious vision I see
> Of the torn red banners of Victory?
> When the terror and tumult of hate shall cease
> And life be refashioned on anvils of peace,
> And your love shall offer memorial thanks
> To the comrades who fought in your dauntless ranks,
> And you honour the deeds of the deathless ones,
> Remember the blood of thy martyred sons![34]

A lush war lyric in a late Victorian vein becomes curious when produced by a nationalist Indian woman. What is remarkable is the way the nationalist/feminist image of the abject Indian 'mother' – a recurring trope in Naidu's poetry – is here exploited to legitimize and glorify India's 'gift' to the empire: a standard trope of anti-colonial resistance flows into and fuses with imperial support for the war with breathtaking fluency.

The poem remains a powerful example of how literature illuminates the faultlines of history, exposing its contradictions and ambivalences: Anglicization and indigenousness, residual colonial loyalty and a burgeoning nationalist consciousness, martial ardour and female mourning are all fused and confused in the above poem. More than a tribute to India or the war, Naidu's poem is an ode to the complex and intimate processes of colonialism. The most articulate Indian woman-nationalist is here seen to be steeped by virtue of her class and education in the English patriotic and poetic tradition, played out through the sounds and images of her lyric poetry. In the early nineteenth century, British colonial education in Bengal produced a class of Anglicized, indigenous elite immersed in the English cultural and literary traditions. An example is the Indian poet Michael Madhusudhan Dutt who declared: 'Yes – I *love* the language – the glorious language of the Anglo-Saxon in all its radiant beauty'.[35] Though this adoration would significantly change in the latter half of the century with the swell in nationalist feeling, one could see the continuation of this Anglicized sensibility in Naidu. While clichés such as 'drumbeats of duty, sabres of doom' and the 'torn red banners of Victory' are reminiscent of the school of poetry associated with Jessie Pope that Owen so famously ridiculed, the aestheticization of the dead soldiers in the second stanza with its sensuous vocabulary – 'pale brows', 'broken hands', 'blossoms mown down by chance' with their murmur of labials and sibilance – looks back to Tennyson, Swinburne and Yeats.

In fact, the knotted relation between the tropes of gender, nation and war in the poem is resonant with Owen's war poem 'The Kind Ghosts'. Owen imagines Britannia as a *femme fatale* who lures her men to death:

> She dreams of golden gardens and sweet glooms,
> Not marvelling why her roses never fall,
> Nor what red mouths were torn to make their blooms.[36]

Naidu's poem – sharing a similar vocabulary with Owen ('doom', 'torn', 'red' 'bloom') and the rich use of sibilance and labials – shows a common Georgian inheritance. But at the same time, it is also Owen's poem turned upside down. Naidu at once inherits and interrogates the stock images and phrases of Victorian verse. 'To be Anglicized is *emphatically* not to be English' notes Homi Bhabha while discussing the ambivalence of colonial discourse, and how it opens up an unsettling space between 'mimicry and mockery'.[37] The nation is no longer Britannia as *femme fatale* but 'Mother India' with whom the female poet and implicitly the Indian reader identifies: the affective power of the image of the war-bereaved mother in this poem is here rooted in the native trope of Mother India 'fettered' by the colonial yoke. Thus, while pro-war and seemingly derivative, it is at the same time slyly subversive: imperial war service becomes a route to its opposite, the restoration of national prestige and through it to national autonomy.

Within the nationalist context, phrases such as 'the pride that thrills through my heart' or the closing line 'Remember the blood of martyred sons' gather particular intensities of meaning, especially when read alongside her political writings. Indeed, the final line of her poem recurs in a speech she made in 1916 to protest against the government ban on the right of Indians to carry arms to defend themselves:

> Have we not, the women of India, sent our sons and brothers to shed their blood on the battlefields of Flanders, France, Gallipoli

and Mesopotamia, when the hour comes, for thanks, shall we not say to them for whom they fought ... *remember the blood of martyred sons*, and remember the armies of India and restore to India her lost manhood.[38]

This manifesto is a continuation of the central plea in the poem, with the nationalist agenda made more explicit. War service is openly used as an emotional and political lever, but Naidu also capitalizes on her position as a woman and a mother. When she concludes, 'Remember thy martyred sons', is she asking India to remember her sons martyred in the war, or, is the empire called upon to remember India's 'gift': the maternal metaphor binds together empire, nation and the female poet. The poem is also significant for the imagination of the nation and the writing of Indian history. Naidu brilliantly uses the war to align native contribution with global events. Her poem is not an aria for the death of the high European bourgeois consciousness but rather for the just recognition of the Indian soldiers: they fight not only in 'Flanders and France' but also in Egypt and Persia, revealing a different and more international geography of the war than in canonical First World War verse. The war panegyric, associated with empire and patriarchal glory, is ruptured through the inscription at its heart of a powerful nationalist consciousness as well as the plaintive notes of female mourning.

Letters and palimpsests: war-thoughts from abroad

The first two Indian divisions – renamed Lahore and Meerut – arrived at Marseille during September and October 1914 to joyous cries of 'Vivent les Hindous'. Drafted to fill in the gaps left by the heavy losses in the British Expeditionary Force, they initially totalled 24,000 men – of whom 75 per cent were sepoys and 25 per cent British. They formed the Indian Expeditionary Force 'A' and were put under the command of Lt-General Sir James Willcocks. Controversy has marked the performance of the Indians on the Western Front, including sagging morale, and a high number of hand wounds, often believed to be self-inflicted. But at the same time, the Indian sepoys took part in some of the severest fighting, including the battles at Neuve Chapelle, Festubert and Loos, incurring heavy casualties and earning the first Victoria Crosses to be awarded to Indians.[39]

A total of 138,608 Indians served in France between October 1914 and December 1915 and attention has recently focused on their performance and cultural experience. But before moving onto them, it is important to remember that it was not France, but Mesopotamia to which the majority of the Indians – some 588,717 men, including 295,565 combatants and 293,152 non-combatants (often forming porter and labour corps)

– were sent.[40] According to one estimate, at the time of General Charles Townshend's surrender on 29 April 1916 at Kut-al-Amara, the number of Indians in the 6th Division was around 10,440, including 204 officers, 6988 rank and file and 3248 followers. The siege at Kut-al-Amara and the subsequent captivity of Indian and British troops in Mesopotamia have gone down as one of the most infamous episodes in First World War history, marked by an unnatural degree of depravation, and brutality from the Turks. However, apart from a few interviews, the sources have been exclusively British. In recent years, a new source has emerged – the letters of the Dr Captain Kalyan Mukherjee, who served there, and whose letters are extracted in full in the remarkable biography *Kalyan Pradeep* written by his grieving 80-year-old grandmother Mokkhada Devi after his death in 1917.[41]

The letters of Dr Kalyan Mukherjee are some of the finest in the whole pantheon of First World War letters. Trained partly in England and a member of the Indian Medical Service, he was appointed a military doctor to the Indian Expeditionary 'Force D'. He was among the several highly trained and talented Indian doctors serving in Mesopotamia. He served in Mesopotamia from his arrival at Basra on 9 April 1915 until his death from high fever in 1917 and was posthumously awarded the Military Cross. His letters show a gradual process of disillusionment with the British occupation of Mesopotamia in the initial stages of war, but soon they harden into powerful anti-war views as well as a critique of imperialism. Consider the following extract, written to his mother on 20 October from Aziziya after the battle of Kut-al-Amara:

> Great Britain is our educator. The patriotism that England preaches, the patriotism that all civilized nations celebrate – that patriotism is to be blamed for this bloodshed. All this patriotism – it means snatching away another's land. This way, patriotism leads to empire-building. To show patriotism and nationalism by killing thousands of people and to get hold of a bit of land, well, it's Great Britain who has taught us this.
>
> And the youths of our country, seeing this, have started to practise this brutal form of nationalism. Killing people or throwing bombs at an innocent overlord – all these horrific things have started now. Shame on patriotism. … Whether a man throws a bomb from the roof-top or whether fifty men start firing from a cannon-gun – this bloodshed, this madness have the same cause.[42]

The level of intellectual sophistication places the letter alongside the pacifist missives of an Owen or Sassoon. But it is essentially different – the radicalism is two-fold. It is not just a condemnation of violence or patriotism. A colonial subject, he exposes the intimate relationship between patriotism and imperialism. However, his critique of imperialism, even as he acknowledges the deep educational influence of England upon the Indian bourgeoisie, cannot be equated with nationalism. Through acute reasoning, he associates imperial aggression with its obverse – nationalist terrorism. For Mukherjee, imperialism, revolutionary nationalism and the European war are all implicated in the same vicious cycle of violence.

Mukherjee's letters, with their subtle analysis of political ideologies, are, however, more of an exception. Our main sources of information about the inner lives of the sepoys are the censored extracts from their letters, written home from France or Mesopotamia. These letters, either written in the native languages by the sepoys themselves or dictated to scribes, were translated into English for the censors and, ironically, the English versions are what survive today, housed in the British Library. This heavily mediated nature of these documents somewhat undermines their testimonial value but, as David Omissi notes in the introduction to his important anthology *Indian Voices of the Great War: Soldiers' Letters, 1914–1918*, 'The crucial issue is, surely, less what we cannot learn from these letters, than what we can learn from them'.[43] These letters open up the emotional world of these men, providing glimpses into an area of experience and consciousness for which very few written documents survive. Their emotional range is astonishingly wide, ranging from excitement and rapture to horror, homesickness and mourning.

Consider the following two letters which, written at different points in the war, suggest the range of the emotional responses:

> Listen to one little thing. Here, no one drinks water. ... So many apples are produced that the people press the juice and store it in barrels, [from] which they drink throughout the year. ... Barrels upon barrels are full of it. Moreover, there are barns full of apples. If I return alive I will tell you all about this country. You shall be staggered at all I shall tell you. It is a real heaven.[44]

> There are heaps and heaps of dead bodies, the sight of which upsets me. The stench is so overwhelming that one can, with difficulty, endure it for ten or fifteen minutes. ... Nevertheless, the warriors, undismayed, continue their onward course, despite the hail of shot and shell, and the numbers that fall on the way wounded or killed.[45]

The first extract is a good example of the metaphysical wonder at the riches of the Occident that recurs in the letters of the newly arrived sepoys. But at the same time, the letters cannot be read, as some historians have done, as the transparent envelope of sepoy experience in France; moreover, apart from their multiple sites of textuality, there are complex narrative strategies. The attraction of France is registered not through the lights of Paris but through agricultural modernity whose products are quantified for the appropriate emotional response of the anticipated reader from the Indian rural community. The hyperbolic description of the apples may indeed be a faithful index of the sepoy's sense of wonder. But what happens when the initial shock of wonder wears away? The second letter bears more semblance to what we think of as the quintessential First World War letter. The phrase 'shot or shell', perhaps quarried out of Tennyson and occurring in other letters, is possibly an embellishment from the scribe. What is important to remember is that these letters are not unmediated 'authentic' voices but rather palimpsests: they are overwritten documents with layers of textual intervention where traces of the original intent can nonetheless be discerned.

Moreover, rather than treating the sepoys as passive receptacles of either Occidental wonder or war trauma, it is perhaps more productive to view them as thinking and active agents who, with their limited authority and knowledge, try to negotiate Western norms, people and institutions; occasionally, they also register their protest against the brutality of the war and may well have taken recourse to desperate measures. In late October and early November 1914, of the 1848 Indian soldiers who have been admitted to the hospital, 1049 or 57 per cent were suffering from hand wounds, widely suspected to be self-inflicted. The rate dropped dramatically after five sepoys were shot that winter, but again the rates increased when new sepoys arrived from India in May 1915.[46]

The experience of these soldiers finds one of its most evocative accounts in Mulk Raj Anand's novel *Across the Black Waters* (1939). Anand wrote it while working for the Socialist side in the Spanish Civil War. He is now largely forgotten in accounts of literary history, but he was an important figure in early twentieth-century literary London, hovering on the fringes of the Bloomsbury group.[47] Anand dedicated the novel 'to the memory of my father Subedar Lal Chand Anand, M.S.M, (late 2/17th Dogra)' who underwent training for the First World War though he possibly was not sent overseas. However, many of his friends fought in the war, men Anand would have known as a child.

Across the Black Waters is written in the shadow of British anti-war writing. But at the same time it opens up a whole new world in First World War fiction written in English as Anand shows Lalu Singh and his associates – a group of villagers from Punjab – disembark at Marseille and negotiate Western culture for the first time, including a visit to a pub and a brothel. The first third of the novel is an exhilarating read as he aligns Indian village history with Europe's Great War with the villagers bringing with them the structure of an extended Indian family – Uncle Kirpu or Daddy Dhanoo – to the trenches in France. The novel is also an exploration of Lalu's complex subjectivity:

So we have come across the black waters safely [said Lalu] ... It seemed
as if God had spat upon the universe and the spittle had become the
sea. The swish of the air as the ships tore their way across the rough
sea seemed like the fury of the Almighty at the sin which the white
men had committed in building their powerful engines.[48]

Anand draws on Indian folklore and mythology to show how they shape
Lalu's structures of feeling. The black sea was safe; the white man's land is
where they are all going to die as Anand subverts the conventional associations of 'black' and 'white'. This is Conrad's *Heart of Darkness* turned
upside down; it is one of the earliest examples of the empire writing back.
At the same time, Anand is remarkably attentive to the insidious class and
caste politics within the Indian camp. The novel ends with most of Lalu's
comrades dead – including a suicide – and Lalu himself is taken prisoner
by the Germans. Anand's novel is not a lament for the lost generation but
rather about finding a voice for the working-class Indian sepoy.

In April 1999, a large group of Sikhs from Britain, France and Belgium
made a pilgrimage to Ypres; there was an air of celebration about the
event, and an ethnicization of identity through the donning of saffron
robes.[49] It was a passionate gesture on the part of these men to commemorate the contributions of their forefathers who fought in the war and to
integrate their ethnic identities with mainstream European history. It was
also a representative moment in European multicultural and multi-faith
life. But at the same time, it is important to remember that the war was a
singularly traumatic experience: the Indian sepoys were at once victims
and perpetrators of violence. As we prepare for the centennial commem-
orations of the First World War, it is important to recover these different
voices and embed the 'modern memory' of the First World War in a more
international and multi-racial framework. But it is equally important to
remain alert to war's fundamental story of killing, and consequently be
ever vigilant about the uses to which its legacy is being put.

Figure 14.1
First World War Memorial in
Kolkata.

Figure 14.2 Memorabilia of Dr J. N. Sen, Private, West Yorkshire Regiment.
Courtesy of The Indo-French Cultural Institute and Museum, Chandernagore,
West Bengal.

Notes

1 'India' and 'Indian' in this chapter refer to the land and people of undivided British India, which today would include India, Pakistan, Bangladesh and Sri Lanka. The above figures are from *Statistics of the Military Effort of the British Empire during the Great War, 1914–1920*, London: His Majesty's Stationery Office, 1920, p. 777, and reproduced in *India's Contribution to the Great War*, Calcutta: Superintendent Government Printing, India, 1923, p. 79. This number is in addition to soldiers already in the British Indian army at the time of the outbreak of the war, estimated at 239,561 (p. 777).

2 *Statistics of the Military Effort*, p. 777.

3 T. S. Eliot, 'Gerontion', *Inventions of the March Hare: Poems 1909–1917*, edited by Christopher Ricks (New York: Harcourt Brace, 1996), p. 350.

4 Lehri, Pakistan; Charles Stinson, 'Diary', Australian War Memorial, Canberra, PR84/066.

5 Dr J. N. Sen, 'Papers', The Indo-French Cultural Institute and Museum, Chandernagore, West Bengal.

6 See Raymond Williams, *Marxism and Literature* (Oxford: Oxford University Press, 1977), particularly chapter 9 ('Structures of Feeling'), pp. 129–33.

7 Apart from Hew Strachan's majestic *The First World War: To Arms* (Oxford: Oxford University Press, 2003), the first volume of his projected trilogy of the war, there has been some excellent work on individual countries and communities. The colonial war experience and memories are brought together in Santanu Das (ed.), *Race, Empire and First World War Writing*, (Cambridge: Cambridge University Press, 2011). Also see Marc Michel, *L'Appel à L'Afrique, contributions et réactions à l'effort de guerre en A.O.F. 1914–1918* (Paris: Publications de la Sorbonne, 1982).

8 The above figures are from Michel, *L'Appel à L'Afrique*, p. 404.

9 David Omissi (ed.), *Indian Voices of the Great War: Soldiers' Letters, 1914–1918* (Basingstoke: Macmillan, 1999). This important anthology brings together many censored letters, mainly archived in the British Library, London.

10 Siegfried Sassoon, *Diaries 1915–1918* (Bristol: Faber and Faber, 1983), p. 96.

11 Part of this chapter shares research material published in Das, 'Lest we forget: colonial voices of the Great War' in Kaustav Bakshi, Samrat Sengupta and Subhadeep Paul (eds), *Anxieties, Influences and After: Critical Responses to Postcolonialism and Neocolonialism*, (Delhi: Worldview Publications, 2009). There has been some interest in India and the First World War: see S. D. Pradhan and Ellinwood (eds), *India and World War I* (Delhi: Manohar, 1978); David Omissi, *The Sepoy and the Raj* (Basingstoke: Macmillan, 1994); Omissi (ed.), *Indian Voices of the Great War: Soldiers' Letters, 1914–1918*; Gordon Corrigan, *Sepoys in the Trenches: The Indian Corps on the Western Front 1914–1915* (Staplehurst: Spellmount, 1999); Rozina Visram, *Asians in Britain* (London: Pluto Press, 2002); George Morton Jack, 'The Indian Army on the Western Front, 1914–1915: A Portrait of Collaboration', *War in History*, 2006 13: 329–62; Radhika Singha, 'Finding Labour from India for the War in Iraq', *Comparative Studies in Society and History* 2007, 49:2, 412–45; K. Bromber, D. Hamza, H. Liebau and K. Lange (eds), *The World in World Wars. Experiences, Perceptions and Perspectives from the South* (Leiden: Brill, 2010).

12 The most prominent activities in this regard were that of the Ghadr party settled in North America as well as the Komagatamaru incident: see West Bengal State Archives, Home (Political) Confidential, File 26 (1–39). Also see Bose, 'Indian Revolutionaries during the First World War' in *India and World*

War I, pp. 109–126, and F. C. Isemonger and J. Slattery, *Account of the Ghadr Conspiracy* (1913–1915), Delhi, South Asia Books, 1998.

13 Quoted in *India and the War* (London: Hodder and Stoughton, 1915), pp. 40–1.

14 Foreign and Political, 1915, Internal B, April 1915, Nos. 319. National Archives of India, Delhi (hereafter NAI); Political (Confidential), 1915 Proceedings 505, West Bengal State Archives, Kolkata.

15 Quoted in M. B. L. Bhargava, *India's Services in the War* (Allahabad: Standard Press, 1919), p. 205.

16 *India's Services*, pp. 278–80.

17 G. A. Natesan (ed.), 'Indian Mussalmans and the War' in *All About the War: The India Review War Book* (Madras: Natesan, n.d., perhaps 1915), p. 269. For a detailed account, see Yuvaraj Deva Prasad, *The Indian Muslims and World War I* (New Delhi: Janaki, 1985).

18 There has been important work on responses to the war in African villages, often based on interviews: see Melvin Page, *The Chiwaya War: Malawians and the First World War* (Colorado: Westview Press, 2000).

19 S. D. Pradhan, 'The Sikh Soldier in the First World War' in *India and World War I*, p. 217. Also see Omissi, *The Sepoy and the Raj*, p. 39.

20 Cited in Tai Yong Tan, *The Garrison State: Military Government and Society in Colonial Punjab, 1849–1947* (London: Sage, 2005), p. 108.

21 This song is quoted from Amarjit Chandan, 'How they Suffered: World War One and its Impact on Punjabis', available at http://apnaorg.com/articles/amarjit/wwi (accessed on 22 September 2009). This song has been translated by Amarjit Chandan, and Amin Mughal. Chandan also presented the above article as a paper at a conference in the School of Oriental and African Studies in London, 2009.

22 See Santanu Das, 'Imperialism, Nationalism and the First World War in India' in Jennifer Keene and Michael Neiberg (eds), *Finding Common Ground* (Brill, Leiden, forthcoming).

23 Quoted in *India and the War* (Lahore: Khosla Brothers, n.d.), pp. 34–5.

24 Bhupendranath Basu, *Why India is Heart and Soul with Britain in this War* (London: Macmillan, 1914).

25 Natesan (ed.), *All About the War*, p. 267.

26 Gandhi, M. K. *An Autobiography or, The Story of My Experiments with Truth*, trans. Mahadev Desai (Harmondsworth: Penguin, 1982), p. 317.

27 Bhargava, *India's Services*, p. 218.

28 Nandy, Ashis, *The Intimate Enemy: Loss and Recovery of Self under Colonialism* (Delhi: Oxford University Press, 1983), pp. 3–4.

29 The *Grenada Federalist* (27 October 1915), quoted in Glenford Howe, *Race, War and Nationalism: A Social History of West Indians in the First World War* (Kingston: James Currey, 2002), p. 17.

30 'The Trumpet', *Indian Ink*, 1914, 4. *Indian Ink: Splashes from Various Pens* was a singular, though short-lived, Kolkata-based journal where both the British and prominent Indians submitted poems, paintings, polemic and various other ephemera.

31 My discussion of Sarojini Naidu here draws substantially on my chapter '"Indian Sisters! … Send your husbands, brothers, sons": India, Women and the First World War' in Alison Fell and Ingrid Sharp (eds), *The Women's Movements: International Perspectives, 1914–1919* (London: Palgrave, 2007), pp. 18–37.

32 The standard biographies are Baig, Tara Ali, *Sarojini Naidu* (Delhi: Publication Division, Government of India, 1974) and Hasi Banerjee, *Sarojini Naidu:*

The Traditional Feminist (Calcutta: K. P. Bagchi, 1998). Also see R. Bhatnagar, *Sarojini Naidu: The Poet of a Nation* (Allahabad, n.d).

33 Quoted in Bhargava, *India's Services*, pp. 208–9.

34 'The Gift of India', *The Broken Wing: Songs of Love, Death and Destiny 1915–1916* (London: William Heinemann, 1917), pp. 5–6.

35 Michael Madhusudhan Dutt, *The Anglo-Saxon and the Hindu* (1854), quoted in Rosinka Chaudhuri, 'The Dutt Family Album and Toru Dutt' in Arvind Krishna Mehrotra (ed.), *A History of Indian Literature in English* (New York: Columbia University Press, 2003), p. 53.

36 Jon Stallworthy, *The Poems of Wilfred Owen* (Oxford: Oxford University Press, 1990), p. 158.

37 Homi Bhabha, 'Of Mimicry and Man' in *The Location of Culture* (London: Routledge (1994), 2002), pp. 85–92.

38 'The Arms Act', Naidu, *Speeches and Writings* (Madras: G. A. Natesan), pp. 102–3, my italics.

39 See Morton Jack, 'The Indian Army on the Western Front', pp. 329–62.

40 *India's Contribution to the Great War* (Calcutta: Government of India, 1923), pp. 78, 96.

41 Mokkhada Devi, *Kalyan-Pradeep: The Life of Captain Kalyan Kumar Mukhopadhyay*, I.M.S. (Calcutta: privately printed, 1928); translation mine. I am grateful to Dr Kaushik Ray for allowing me to use his copy of this rarely available book.

42 Letter dated 20 October 1915, extracted in *Kalyan-Pradeep*, p. 334. My translation

43 Omissi, *Indian Voices of the Great War*, p. 9. Also see Omissi, 'Europe Through Indian Eyes', *English Historical Review*, 122:496 (2007), pp. 371–96.

44 Bakhshish Singh, Sialkot Cavalry Brigade in France, letter to Sher Singh, 27 February 1916, quoted in Omissi, *Indian Voices*, p. 157

45 Asim Ullah, 19th Lancers, France, letter to Hassan Khan, 16 October 1916, quoted in Omissi, *Indian Voices*, pp. 245–6.

46 War Office 154/14, 'Return Showing Court-Martial Convictions in Indian Corps from October 1914 to February 1915', Public Records Office (PRO); War Office 256/4, Field Marshal Sir Douglas Haig, Western Front Diary IV, 5 May 1915, PRO. See Jeffery Greenhut, 'The Imperial Reserve: the Indian Corps on the Western Front, 1914–1915', *Journal of Imperial and Commonwealth History* 12 (1983), p. 57.

47 See Saros Cowasjee, *So Many Freedoms: Major Fiction of Mulk Raj Anand* (Delhi: Oxford University Press, 1978).

48 Mulk Raj Anand, *Across the Black Waters* (Delhi: Orient, 1949), p. 8.

49 See Bhupinder Singh Holland, *How Europe is Indebted to the Sikhs* (Waremme: Sikh University Press, 2005).

15 Thinking through the postnation

Nivedita Menon

The idea that the nation-state is a historically contingent if enduring institution is hardly a new one. When I use the term postnational, therefore, I both build on and depart from scholarship that has problematized the nation-state in various ways. It will also become clear in the course of this paper that the term postnational provides a way of escaping the limited swing between Empire and Nation that the term 'postcolonial' increasingly runs up against.[1]

I will begin with an incident that strikingly illustrates the most familiar of current globalization narratives, in an effort to distinguish from it my own usage of the term postnational. In April 2007, Infosys, one of India's largest IT companies, organized a function at its Global Training Campus in Mysore, attended by the President of India, A. P. J. Abdul Kalam. According to press reports, a shoddy keyboard rendition of the national anthem was played at the entry and exit of the President. Media-persons, ever alert to potential threats to national pride, questioned Infosys chief Narayana Murthy as to why a more melodious vocal performance was not organized. Narayana Murthy, habituated to absolute and unquestioning media adoration, replied quite confidently: 'Indeed, we had arranged for five people to sing the anthem. But then we cancelled it as we have foreigners on board here. They should not be embarrassed while we sing the anthem'.

There was a national furore caused by this remark from a person considered at the time to be in the running for the post of President of the Indian Republic. In addition, a private organization lodged a complaint against him under Section 3 of Prevention of Insults to National Honour Act 1971, claiming his statement was defamatory and an insult to the anthem. But on the eve of Independence Day, on 14 August 2007, the Karnataka High Court quashed lower court proceedings, holding that playing an instrumental version of the national anthem is not prevented by the Act. In doing so, the High Court sidestepped the really contentious issue by referring only to what happened at the function, and not to Narayana Murthy's controversial statement afterwards. Thus, the embarrassment for the Indian state, of taking on one of the most powerful and charismatic of India's corporation chiefs, was avoided.[2]

This story illustrates a well-known opposition in globalization debates: 'the national versus the post-national' in which on the one hand, there is the static nation, defined forever by symbols of identity produced in the now-irrelevant era of nation-states; on the other, the dynamic post-national corporation, located everywhere and nowhere, resisting the parochialism of national pride and national symbols.

The sense in which I will use the term 'postnational' in this chapter, however, is very different from this sense in which corporations and the self-defined 'global civil society' conceive of spaces above and beyond the nation-state. I will use the term post-national with a hyphen to refer to arguments of this sort. I am aware that both with and without a hyphen, the term has come to acquire a particular meaning in that part of the world where nation-states initially came into being – Europe. Two centuries after blood flowed to create France, Italy and Germany, those nation-states are being dismantled, and various kinds of global and transnational institutions are in the process of coming into being. In the debates around the idea of the European Union, both terms, post-national and postnational, can only mean one thing – the end of nation-states and the rise of supranational entities.

However, in a world in which dominant discourses valorize 'flows', 'fluidity' and 'translatability', the term postnational as I try to develop it here, may offer us a vantage point that insists on location in the face of translatability. Let me add as the last prefatory remark here, that the term *location* does not imply *indigeneity* or *authenticity*. The point is not to claim authenticity for being located in the non-West. Rather, with the term location, I mean to gesture towards the *materiality* of spatial and temporal co-ordinates that inevitably suffuse *all* theorizing. A sensitivity to location would invariably lead to a productive contamination of the purity of empty universalist categories and challenge their claim to speak about everywhere from nowhere.

In the first section, I look at the discourse on the 'end of the nation-state' and the different views on this that emerge, particularly in the debates on the European Union. Etienne Balibar points out that the end of the nation-state is understood by some (he cites Hobsbawm), as a positive phenomenon bringing the 'great universalist project of modernity to a fitting conclusion' whereas for others, precisely because of the strong affiliation between nation and modernity, the decline of the nation-state is a symptom of regression and crisis (Balibar 2004: 13).

My usage of the term 'postnational' would outline itself very differently from both of these, not lining up with narratives of triumphant post-nationalism rendering national borders obsolete, but at the same time, not retreating to a reconstituted national space in the face of this triumphalism.

Enlightened Europe contra American empire

One version of the view that celebrates the end of the nation-state is evident in debates over the new Europe, through a reading of which, from our location in the non-West, I attempt to outline the terrain in which the idea of the postnational would emerge. Why engage with European debates? The reason is not that theorizing in the West is central to, or even necessarily a reference point for understanding our own situation. Rather, it is the case that in the self-understanding of these debates, they play themselves out on grounds designated as universal – they speak about the globe in a manner which assumes that European concerns and experiences are translatable everywhere.

Jurgen Habermas has been a prominent voice theorizing the 'postnational constellation' in the context of Europe,[3] conceiving of a world citizenship posed in opposition to the imperialist agenda of the United States of America. Here he distinguishes between the USA 'enforcing the global implementation of human rights as part of the national mission of a world super-power' and a European vision of 'enforcement of a politics of human rights ... aimed at establishing the rule of law in international relations' (1999). However, from the perspective of the global South in an unequally structured global economy, the distinction between US hegemony and European hegemony does not appear to be a significant one.

Habermas suggested in the celebrated statement against the US invasion of Iraq, written by himself, signed also by Jacques Derrida (in the *Frankfurter Allgemeine Zeitung*, 31 May 2003, later published with responses as a wider debate in 2005), that a 'core Europe' (France, Germany and the Benelux countries), should play an avant-gardist role, and 'be the locomotive' to 'endow the EU with certain qualities of a state' (Habermas and Derrida 2003/2005: 4–5).

What, according to Habermas, are the qualities of a distinctively European, as opposed to an American public sphere? These are: secularism in politics ('Citizens here regard transgressions of the border between politics and religion with suspicion'), broad popular agreement on the crucial role of the state in controlling capitalism's destructive qualities, a proper sense of cynicism about the possible achievements of technological progress (Europeans having 'a keen sense of the "dialectic of enlightenment"'), and the desire for a multilateral and legally regulated international order within the framework of a reformed United Nations (Habermas and Derrida 2005: 9).

The statement concludes with a rejection of Eurocentrism, and a 'Kantian hope for a global domestic policy', urging that the European experience of imperialism should give European powers the chance to 'learn from the perspective of the defeated to perceive themselves in the dubious role of victors who are called to account for the violence of a forcible and uprooting process of modernization' (2005: 12).

Some of the responses to this statement, brought together in the volume cited here, highlight the sharp disagreements within Europe itself over the very idea of an avant-gardist core Europe, particularly from the perspective of East Europeans (Esterhazy 2005), but also from those who term the idea as 'Euro-Gaullism', or a form of elitist privileging of some part or parts of Europe (Garton Ash and Dahrendorf 2005).

One is also struck by Habermas's unproblematic definition of secularism that begs the question of Europe's internal Other, Islam. The controversy over the French state's attitude to the headscarf ('conspicuous religious symbols') in schools surely has produced discussion of sufficient complexity to counter Habermas's simple assertion that 'citizens here regard transgressions of the border between politics and religion with suspicion'. Disagreement over what exactly constituted the transgression of that border – the state's *banning* of religious symbols or citizens' *wearing* of them – was precisely at the heart of the controversy. Moreover, it was apparent that the category of 'citizen' was internally split – the question of which groups of citizens objected, and to what, brought every tension in the classic European conception of secularism into focus.

Further, Iris Marion Young objects to the reference to imperialism in the concluding paragraph cited above, as an 'uprooting process of modernization', which makes it sound, she says, like 'colonialism is an unfortunate by-product of the otherwise universalistic and enlightened project Europe led to establish the principles of human rights, rule of law, and expanded productivity'. She reminds Habermas that colonialism was not just a 'vicious process of modernization, but a system of slavery and labour exploitation' (2005: 157).

The rejection of the EU constitution, termed by Antonio Negri a 'constitution of multinational corporations' (at the *Conference on the Constitution of Europe*, Rome 2004), by the people of France and the Netherlands in 2005 was recognized by analysts as reflecting not a simple nationalism but several different, perhaps mutually contradictory strands – distrust of the liberalization and free trade policies of the EU, of its lack of democratic accountability, but also simultaneously, fears of being overrun by immigrants from those internal Others – East Europe and Turkey. The rejection has further sharply brought into view the impossibility of a shared European voice.

What the debate on post-nationalism in the European context alerts us to, is the fact that the assertion of a grand identity that transcends 'smaller' identities is necessarily insensitive to the powerless and the marginal, even when articulated in the best traditions of the Enlightenment – or perhaps especially then. For after all, the Habermas who speaks of a 'core Europe' and of secularism as if it is a simple given, also argues that modern self-understanding (in contrast to the universalism of old empires which had a centralizing perspective) 'has been shaped by egalitarian universalism that requires a decentralization of one's own perspective' (Habermas 2005: 25). If despite this insight he is unable to decentralize his perspective, we must question the very possibility of the universalist project.

Nancy Fraser has pointed to the difficulties inherent in the idea of a transnational public sphere, and in doing so, unintentionally exposes the impossibility of even the national public sphere as a normative ideal. She points out that Habermas's public sphere theory, conducted simultaneously at the empirical-historical-institutional level and at the normative level, was implicitly conceptualized as co-extensive with a territorial nation-state. It assumed a national state apparatus and economy, national citizenry resident on the national territory, a national language and literature and a national infrastructure of communication. She has earlier tried to rescue this ideal from the limits set by bourgeois democracy, but today, she argues, the critique must go beyond that. Each of these assumptions is problematic if not counterfactual. The 'who' of communication is no longer a national citizenry but a collection of dispersed subjects of communication; the 'what' of communication, previously theorized as a national interest rooted in national economy, now stretches across the globe; the 'where' of communication is no longer national territory but deterritorialized cyberspace; the 'how' of communication, far from being a national print media, is 'a vast translinguistic nexus of disjoint and overlapping visual cultures'; and finally the addressee of communication once theorized as state power to be made accountable to public opinion, is now a mix of public and private transnational powers that is neither easily identifiable nor rendered accountable (Fraser 2005: 39–45). She believes, therefore, that the transnational public sphere cannot be assumed to exist; it is necessary to bring it about by 'major institutional renovation' that needs to be thought through carefully.

What is interesting about this critique is that it brings to the fore the problems inherent in the very idea of a public sphere as a normative ideal even at the level of the nation. The assumption of a national citizenry with common and shared interests, with a shared language and values, as a given, or as a desirable goal, obscures the violence by which nation-states produced such homogeneity even in the limited cases where it existed. It is at this point that we may glimpse the critique that we may offer of the national as the counter to the trans/postnational, which will be expanded on a little later.

Global civil society contra the nation-state

A different post-national understanding from the Eurocentric one outlined above is the idea of 'global civil society' in different forms. For instance, Daniele Archibugi promotes the idea of 'cosmopolitical democracy' through which he attempts to apply the principles of democracy internationally. Faced with problems that transcend national borders, such as the protection of the environment, the regulation of migration and the use of natural resources, Archibugi argues, democracy must transcend the borders of single states and assert itself on a global level (2003: 7).

What institutional forms can cosmopolitical democracy take? Some examples that Archibugi suggests are a world parliament, peace assemblies that invite representatives of peoples rather than states, the International Criminal Court. Inevitably though, when action is to be taken against erring states, whether European or non-European, the actors are conceived of as existing nation-states. Although their actions will require corroboration by world citizens in assembly, 'world citizens' are not imagined as being agential themselves, in the form of cross-border political movements or struggles.

Arjun Appadurai's understanding of 'globalization', on the other hand, does take cross-border initiatives seriously. However, in his formulation of globalization from below, there is a conflation of political movements with funded NGOs (non-government organizations). He refers to 'new sovereignties' that are 'definitely postnational' in *Modernity at Large* (1997) and in a later essay uses the term 'grassroots globalization' to refer to a worldwide order of institutions of which the most recognizable are NGOs (2001). These differ in their size, legitimacy, influence and relationship with nation-states, but by and large he characterizes them as progressive. Some of these have now emerged as transnational advocacy networks (TAN) – 'part movements, part networks, part organizations' – and according to Appadurai, these forms are the 'crucibles and institutional instruments of most serious efforts to globalize from below'. Successful TANs might, he argues, 'offset the most volatile effects of runaway capital'. The reason they have not been able to do so is because they lack the assets and planning that global capital has. One of the biggest disadvantages for 'activists working for the poor in fora such as the World Bank, the UN system, the WTO, NAFTA and GATT is their alienation from the vocabulary used by the university-policy nexus' (2001: 16–20)

Thus Appadurai offers 'globalization from below' through NGOs and TANs as an alternative both to 'globalization from above' as exemplified in institutions such as the World Bank, as well as to the nation-state. But the conflation referred to earlier is problematic from the notion of post-national politics this chapter offers. It is crucial to recognize that people working with funded NGOs, including 'activists working for the poor' in the World Bank, are salaried employees, while cross-border non-funded political movements have a radically different character. It is our understanding that this distinction is crucial to recognize and maintain if we are to retain the idea of the postnational as an ethical horizon. It could even be argued, I suggest, that TANs, in performing the valuable function Appadurai identifies as 'offsetting' the 'most volatile effects of runaway capital', thus play a critical role in stabilizing global capital.

Very revealing in this context is a startling analysis of currently popular moves by governments in the global South to create formal titles in land for the poor, provided by Timothy Mitchell in a closely argued paper, 'The Properties of Markets' (2004). On the face of it, these programmes use progressive and leftist language to justify the creation of formal property rights in land for people who have hitherto lived on these lands in semi-formal and informal ways. NGOs all over the world are being funded by bodies like the UNDP's High Level Commission on Legal Empowerment of the Poor, in order to promote this agenda. The ideologue behind this campaign, Hernando de Soto, believes that assets held informally are 'defective', and that the absence of property title and the mechanism of credit it enables are the principal reasons for the failure of capitalist development outside the West. What property titling is intended to do is to bring the assets of the poor from the 'outside' to the 'inside' of the capitalist economy, thus bringing into being opportunities for speculation, concentration of wealth and for the accumulation of rents. However, the NGOs working on this agenda see their work as promoting 'empowerment of the poor'. The use of leftist/Marxist language is particularly noteworthy because De Soto is from Peru, and his intervention was promoted by the government also as a way of cutting the ground from beneath the Maoist Shining Path with its own agenda of land rights.

The fact that transnational NGOs are funded means that the question of the funders' agenda can never be far from the surface. More often than not, they are co-opted into the project of fulfilling the agenda of global capital, even if sometimes unwittingly. This is why we insist that a clear distinction must be maintained between cross-border political movements and transnational funded NGOs if we are to retain the idea of the postnational as an ethical horizon. The term 'postnational' as I use it here suggests currents running counter to both Nation and Capital.

Tom Mertes offers a microexample of the fragile process that 'organizing from below' is, threatened by both TANs as well as powerful states. When activists based in Los Angeles tried to get in touch with workers in Mexican maquiladoras (sweat shop factories), they found they were being blocked not just by the Mexican state and global capital, but by the moderate NGOs that controlled the funds for transport and translators, who wanted to control the LA activists' interaction with the workers (2002). In what seems to me to be an interesting postnational twist, Mertes refers to the Los Angeles-based American activists as 'Angelenos' and to the Mexican workers as 'their Tijuana counterparts'. This nomenclature dismantles the national identities of both partners by foregrounding the localities where they are based. This is consistent with the understanding of the postnational that I work with, which involves recognizing currents going 'under' and not just 'over' the nation, a point to which I will return in the last section of this chapter.

The nation-state as the bulwark against global capital?

In response to arguments such as those outlined above, which in different ways suggest supranational alternatives to the thrust of global capital, one kind of position seeks to reinstall the nation-state as 'the only concrete terrain and framework for political struggle' (Jameson 2000).

Timothy Brennan, in his response to Archibugi's suggestion outlined above of a global civil society that will monitor the system of states, asserts that national sovereignty is the only way under modern conditions to secure respect for weaker societies or peoples (2003: 42). Like Jameson, he knows what nation-states are: 'discrete units for the organization of profit-making, resource extraction, and the perpetuation of unequal social relations' (2003: 47). But he holds nevertheless, that within a world system of unequally powerful nation-states, the only chance that local or indigenous peoples have 'to draw a boundary between what is theirs and what lies beyond' (2003: 47), is offered by national governments.

Whatever happened to Marxist internationalism? Although that tradition too, eventually took a form that legitimized existing nation-states, Jameson and Brennan seem to have given up even on its attenuated form. Brennan's assumption that indigenous and local peoples can unproblematically lay claim to what is 'inside' a nation is puzzling. More often than not, such people are engaged in continuous struggles to stake a legitimate claim to 'national' resources, even when these resources are located within territories in which they have lived for centuries. Such resources, whether forest produce, minerals or rivers, are harnessed by nation-states for the project of 'national development', leaving the areas depleted and ecologically devastated, often displacing the local people or leaving them impoverished. When Brennan argues therefore, that '[n]ations are "manageable" in both directions. They allow the state to manage the subalterns and the subalterns to petition the state, with a rhetoric of the "popular" that appeals to a shared cultural identity' (2003: 47–8), there appears to be an amnesia about the history of actually existing nation-states, how 'shared cultural identity' was produced if it exists at all, and how nation-states have engaged with subalterns.

Etienne Balibar points out that the construction of European nations involved the constitution of a 'fictive ethnicity' (2004: 8) through the nationalization of cultures, languages and genealogies with different histories, leading to 'permanent rivalry' from the inside. Similarly, Crispin Bates points out that the English believe their own history to be continuous, but

> the so-called 'English' culture is a congeries of Celtic, Pict, Angle, Saxon, Viking, Norman, Asian, Caribbean, Polish, Italian, Huguenot, French, East European and of course, American cultures, and of the different gender biases within each. By selecting from this mélange however, a set of ideas is upheld that somehow enshrines the 'exceptionalism' that is held to be 'English'. (2001: 22)

The Indian project of 'nation-building' has been similarly beleaguered. In the next section I will discuss some points of resistance to this project as well as some examples of postnationalist currents running 'under' the nation, as an illustration of the historical impossibility of attaining nationhood.

When was India?[4]

Sudipta Kaviraj has pointed out how 'European models of nation formation', in which cultural unification preceded the coming into being of the nation-state, were understood by Indian nationalist leadership of all shades to be paradigmatic and universal. Consequently, the nationalist myth, whether secular-Nehruvian or *Hindutvavaadi*, involved the idea of an already existing Indian nation formed over thousands of years, waiting to be emancipated from British rule. In this understanding the Indian nation had been for millennia 'an accomplished and irreversible fact' and any voices that questioned this were of necessity 'anti-national' (Kaviraj 1994: 330).

However, there are regions and peoples residing in the territory that came to be called 'India', which have histories autonomous of the Indian nation-state, and which had independently negotiated relationships with the British colonial government. One of the significant achievements of the nation-building elite of what subsequently became India was the incorporation into the Indian nation of these peoples and regions, at varying degrees of willingness. The hegemonic drive of the anti-imperialist struggle as well as the coercive power of the Indian state after independence was deployed to enforce the idea of India as a homogeneous nation with a shared culture. Its very diversity was supposedly its strength, the popular nationalist motto being 'Unity in Diversity'. However, the idea that all the multiple identities and aspirations in the landmass called India are ultimately merely rivulets flowing into the mainstream of the Indian nation was never an unchallenged one. The project of nation-building, therefore, sixty years down the line, continues to be a fraught exercise.

It would be misleading to assume that the two well-known 'trouble spots' on the borders of India – Kashmir and the North-East – are unique instances of the crisis of the nation-state. Many other instances illustrate the perpetual anxiety generated by the need to preserve a nation – assumed to be simultaneously eternal and perpetually under threat of disintegration. Ranabir Samaddar terms this a 'particular kind of post-colonial anxiety' – the anxiety of 'a society suspended forever in the space between the "former colony" and the "not-yet nation"' (Samaddar 1999: 108).

Consider just two instances. One is the linguistic reorganization of states in the 1950s under pressure from popular movements that mobilized all the passion and emotiveness associated with nationalist sentiments. The fear of the nationalist leadership was not entirely without basis then that linguistic states could lead to 'Balkanization'. Since then there have been other new states created under pressure from mass movements, the latest being Uttaranchal (from UP), Chhattisgarh (from MP) and Jharkhand (from Bihar) in 2000. The renaming of Uttaranchal as Uttarakhand in 2007 is another revealing instance of the identities that run *under* 'the idea of India'. While *anchal* in Hindi suggests 'region', *khand* means 'piece' or 'fragment', suggesting a breakaway portion. The popular movement had demanded 'Uttarakhand', but the ultra-nationalist BJP was in power at the centre when the state came into being, and it was named as Uttaranchal. Seven years down the line, the State Legislative Assembly decisively reasserted the *khand*.

Innumerable and continuing disputes over water-sharing between states, which go beyond bickering between state governments and often take a popular form, are another indicator that the idea of India cannot be assumed but must be subject to a 'daily plebiscite' (Renan 1996: 53). One instance of this is the dispute over the waters of the Kaveri River between Tamil Nadu and Karnataka, resulting in rioting and violence against Tamilians in Karnataka in 1991 (P. Menon 2002). Another dispute, on-going at the end of 2006, is between Kerala and Tamil Nadu over the Mullaperiyar dam on the Periyar river arising from an agreement between the British government of Madras Presidency (now Tamil Nadu) and the Princely State of Travancore (now part of Kerala). Significantly, the opposition of the Kerala government to Tamil Nadu's rights to Periyar waters is sometimes expressed in the language of independent nation-states – that the colonial government had arm-twisted Travancore into an agreement that was disadvantageous to it, and that Kerala today should consider its own interests first (Special Correspondent 2006: 1). Thus, there are several simultaneous levels at which 'non', 'sub' and 'cross' national identities manifest themselves, all of which contribute to our idea of the postnational. I will end this section with a brief, but hopefully suggestive, discussion of one of the two most dramatic flash-points continually inter-rogating the nation – the 'North-East'. Kashmir, the other flashpoint, is much written about, and for reasons of space I will not go into it here.

The most important recognition for a postnational perspective on the 'North-East' may be drawn from scholarly work suggesting that the region cannot be understood solely as the 'north-east' of India. It is after all, also the 'north-west' of South East Asia. Ninety-eight per cent of the borders of North-East India are international borders. Like other such border regions, this one too exemplifies the tensions produced by the idea of bounded nation-states. From the viewpoint of nation-states, cross-border affinities can only be 'anti-national' and unregulated movement across borders can only be 'illegal immigration'. As Walter Fernandes puts it, 'the North-East' could be understood as a gateway to closer ties with South East Asia and China, but the Indian state 'seems to be obsessed with security and treats this diversity as a threat and the region only as a buffer zone against China' (Fernandes 2004: 4610).

Most movements here are armed struggles for independence from India, which is regarded as an occupying power that moved in after the British left. For example, in 1947 the kingdom of Manipur had been constituted as an independent constitutional monarchy with a demo-cratically elected assembly, but the king was arrested under instructions from the Indian government and the state forced into a merger with India in 1949.

Similarly, the Naga National Council (NNC) had met the Simon Commission (set up to examine the feasibility of self-government for India) as early as 1929 to petition against Indian rule once the British pulled out. When a Naga delegation met Mahatma Gandhi in 1947, he supported the Naga's right to independence. He said – 'I believe you all belong to one, to India. But if you say that you won't, no one can force you ... I will go to Naga Hills and say that you will shoot me before you shoot a single Naga' (Baruah 2005). Of course, by that time, Gandhi's distrust of the emerging nation-state was already irrelevant to main-stream politics. Under the Hydari Agreement signed between the NNC and the British administration, Nagaland was granted protected status for ten years, after which the Nagas would decide whether they would stay in the Indian Union or not. However, shortly after the British with-drew, independent India proclaimed the Naga Territory to be part of the new Republic. Thus, it is important to note that insurgent groups such as ULFA of Assam and NSCN-IM of Nagaland[5] insist that they are not 'secessionist' movements, asserting rather, that Assam and Nagaland were never part of India. Both of these consider themselves to be inde-pendence struggles for self-determination against the occupying army of a colonial force.[6]

At the same time, the logic of the nation-state is overwhelming and each insurgent movement tends to 'think like a nation'. In a context of extreme economic and cultural alienation of indigenous or local populations, the 'foreigner' issue is on top of the agenda of many ethnic movements in the North-East. The claim to indigenous identity has come to play a central role in the politics of this region because of the need to lay claim to local resources. Many conflicts such as the Naga–Kuki conflict in Nagaland and the Naga–Meitei conflict in Manipur are all about land and exclusive control over depleted resources, as land increasingly becomes the only reliable long-term capital (Fernandes 2006; Misra 2000; Oinam and Thangjam 2006: 66). Similarly, the claim to Nagalim, a 'greater homeland' for the Naga peoples, that would bring all Naga-dominated areas in the North-East under one administrative mechanism, brings NSCN-IM into conflict with other ethnic groups in Assam, Manipur and Arunachal Pradesh. On the other hand, the Indian government's decision to recognize Nagalim *de facto* through the extension of the ceasefire agreement with the militants to all Naga-dominated areas, can only be seen as an attempt to further dissension among ethnic groups in the North-East.

It seems the movements in the region are replicating the logic of the nation-state and the notion of the sanctity and integrity of national borders, the very logic against which their struggles began in the first place. As Bimol Akoijam puts it, 'the region called the North East of the postcolonial Indian state ... is a theatre' in which the actors can only 'make sense of each other in terms of an intelligible shared world of colonial modernity' (Akoijam 2006: 117), that is, the world of clearly bounded, homogeneous nation-states.

Postnationalism as counter-hegemony

Balibar argues that historical nations at a given moment put to work only '*one of the existing possibilities* for uniting populations in the framework of the same institution'. But it is never the only possibility – 'other possibilities that seem to open new historical and political perspectives ... can always recover their credibility – whence the frequency of "divisions" or "separations" and "fusions" or "federations"' (2004: 17). The nation-form as a type of social formation is only one of the models in history for 'administering the economy and managing the symbolic' (others have been the city-state, the empire), nor has there ever been a time when it was the only existing form or even the only dominant form at work everywhere to the same degree (2004: 18). He urges that democratic politics should avoid becoming enclosed in representations such as the nation-state, that have historically been associated with emancipatory projects and struggles for citizenship, but have now become 'obstacles to their revival' and that prevent their 'permanent reinvention' (2004: 10).

The politics of the postnationalism I have outlined here can be represented by any idea that is counter-hegemonic, whether that hegemony
refers to development, sexuality, caste/community or any other. But
equally importantly, it can be manifested in one of two dimensions – one,
'over' the nation, across national borders, and two, 'under' the nation,
resisting inclusion into the 'larger' national identity, insisting on space/
time trajectories that do not mesh with progressivist dominant narratives
of nation and history.

The first dimension is easier, in a sense, to recognize as a subversive
strategy, for it begins with the assumption of existing nations, which it
then interrogates. For example, Black Laundry, an Israeli anti-occupation queer group, positions itself differently from other Israeli gay/
lesbian groups that presented themselves as part of the mainstream. It
also distinguishes itself from the Israeli Left, with its universalist understanding against which Black Laundry posed its 'concrete social positioning' as a platform for critique. Amalia Ziv, in a study of the group,
suggests that Black Laundry tied together 'sexual deviance' and 'national
deviance' with slogans like 'Free Condoms, Free Palestine', 'Bull Dykes,
Not Missile Strikes', 'Transgender not Transfer' (forced deportation of
Palestinians) – which break down the hierarchies of Nation and Sex, challenging queer politics with anti-occupation politics and vice versa. Ziv
argues that through the twin strategies of national betrayal and sexual
depravity, Black Laundry deliberately situated itself outside the discursive
community of Israel/Palestine as well as hetero/homosexual (Ziv 2005).

The diasporic location too, is one that offers rich insights from 'over'
the Nation. An instructive example is the relationship of gay and lesbian
people of Indian and South Asian origin in the USA, to something called
'India'. The Federation of Indian Associations, a private organization
dominated by Indian businessmen in the US, refused permission for
years to South Asian Lesbian and Gay Association (SALGA, formed in
1992) and Sakhi (an organization that addressed the question of domestic
violence against women in the South Asian community), to march in the
Indian Independence Day parade in New York City. The presence of
SALGA and Sakhi would have disrupted narratives of the Indian nation
in two crucial ways, as the reasons given for their exclusion attest – one,
they insisted on the South Asian identity, which would have meant that
Bangladeshis and Pakistanis would have marched in the Indian parade.
Two, SALGA is gay and lesbian, identities that could not, by definition, be
'Indian', since homosexuality did not exist in India. Sakhi was, evidently,
additionally problematic because it exposed disjunctures in the family,
the cornerstone of the Indian nation. After sustained pressure, Sakhi was
'allowed' to join, but SALGA had to carry on struggling for much longer,
until in 2000, it won the right to participate. The presence of SALGA
and Sakhi in the India Day parade in New York is a constant reminder

that the idea of the unified and homogeneous Nation has the potential to unravel through feminist, queer and counter-nationalist politics (Shah 2001, Gopinath 2005).

Another example of postnational politics 'over' the nation is the move by Dalit groups in India to take the issue of caste to the United Nations conference on Racism and Related Forms of Discrimination, first held in Vienna in 2001 and then in Geneva in 2009. This move provoked outraged reaction from the government and other nationalist circles, leading in turn to a vigorous public debate. The argument put forth by the nationalists was primarily that this was an 'internal matter' of the nation and could be redressed within the forums provided by the law of the land. This argument is of course, too bitter to swallow for Dalits who have had first-hand experience with the biased operation of the law and governmental machinery since Independence. Others – among them academics and journalists of some standing – joined the debate with the argument that 'caste' unlike race, is not a biological matter. Contemporary theoretical developments in critical race theory have shown how thin this dividing line is, and how race too, is a matter of social construction rather than a simple biological phenomenon. Moreover, Dalit groups emphasized the common feature caste shares along with the Burakumin of Japan, that of being discriminations based on descent (and to that extent, caste as a 'related form' of racism) (Thorat and Umakant 2004). The Dalit leadership did succeed, in the teeth of major opposition, in raising the issue at Durban, but at Geneva the Indian government managed to have caste excluded from the final resolution. While being under no illusion about the politics of the United Nations and 'global civil society', nor about the actual efficacy of getting caste recognized as race in such fora, the point here is that Dalit politics, by thus transgressing the limits set by nationalism and national sovereignty, offers yet another illustration of what I term postnational politics 'over' the nation.

The other dimension of postnational politics – 'under' the nation – is less obvious as a strategy, because *it does not assume the prior existence of the nation*. The history of the Nation is simply an irrelevance in the case of identities and politics that are produced and work at the level of the everyday. For instance, a significant contribution to what I term postnational thinking is feminist work on abducted women during the partition of India. The governments of India and Pakistan set up administrative mechanisms to recover these women and the children born to them. However, many of these women had been absorbed into the families of the men who had abducted them, and refused to return. Nevertheless, both governments intervened to ensure that as far as possible, abducted Hindu women were 'returned' to India and abducted Muslim women to Pakistan, regardless of their own desire in the matter. Feminist studies, by insisting on uncovering the voice and agency of these women, disrupt nationalist narratives of citizenship on both sides of the border (Butalia 1993; Menon and Bhasin 1993; Das 1995).

More significantly, the subversive edge of 'under' the nation may lie in the exact opposite of what animates the politics of 'over' the nation, which is the strategy of exit and movement across borders. The interrogation of the nation from under may involve, rather, the *refusal to move*, as for example, in the struggles of tribal people and villagers against big dams, Special Economic Zones or mining operations that involve massive dislocation of populations. This dimension may involve claiming histories that run parallel to, that do not intersect with, that of the nation. Or claiming forms of family and kinship that produce identities that are splintered and fluid, that resist inclusion into larger formations. A startling moment, de-normalizing the idea of family, is produced when *hijras* contesting elections claim that precisely because they cannot have children, they will be less selfish and corrupt.[7] Sex-workers refusing to shift their work-premises in the face of intimidation by local communities force a recognition of the imbrication of sex-work in everyday life.[8] This *politics of refusal* thus implies the simultaneous transformation, through practices of everyday life, of the place where you insist on staying.

In conclusion, let us briefly consider the debate in India over the Indo-US nuclear deal as a tragic instance of the deliberate silencing of a voice that has the potential to link postnational currents both over and under the nation. As the mainstream media presents it, there are only two views possible – for the deal (UPA, pro-US hawks), and against the deal (the BJP, the Left). The concern of these positions against the deal at both ends of the political spectrum has to do with the fact that the Hyde Act (the basis for the final version of the Indo-US nuclear deal), places India in a subordinate position to the world's sole remaining super-power (Jayaraman 2006; Kulkarni 2006).[9] What has been wiped off the map of public discourse in this manner of posing of the debate are the long-standing debates within the country on nuclear disarmament and the desirability of nuclear energy. In the sound and fury around the Indo-US deal, which mobilized all the familiar and widely popular tropes of nationalism and sovereignty, the crucial strand of thought in India, Pakistan and the US committed to global disarmament and universal nuclear non-proliferation as well as to ecologically sustainable forms of energy (Bidwai 2006, 2007; Hoodbhoy 2006) has been rendered invisible. This strand consists of scholars and activists who consider themselves as part of the global anti-nuclear peace movement rather than as representing nation-states. The anti-nuclear energy campaign has the potential to link global anti-nuclear movements with the local struggles of communities against 'their own' governments, through their resistance, for example, to the devastation of uranium mining (in Jaduguda in Jharkhand and in the state of Meghalaya),[10] and against being incorporated into the nation-state's agenda.

We have yet to test the imaginative horizons of the postnational as concept and as practice.

Acknowledgements

I would like to thank the Postnational Collective, with whom extended conversations over some years followed by an intensive workshop in Delhi, led to a set of papers being published in *Economic and Political Weekly*, 7 March 2009. Thank you to Malathi de Alwis, Satish Deshpande, Pradeep Jeganathan, Mary John, Aditya Nigam, M. S. S. Pandian, Akbar Zaidi, for your friendship, intellectual stimulation and shared political vision.

Notes

From *Economic and Political Weekly* 44:10 (7–13 March 2009), pp. 70–7.

1 This chapter has emerged from a long-running conversation with a set of intellectual interlocutors – Malathi de Alwis, Satish Deshpande, Pradeep Jeganathan, Mary John, Aditya Nigam, M. S. S. Pandian and Akbar Zaidi – which eventually termed itself the Postnational Collective. This conversation resulted in a set of papers around the theme of the postnational, which was published in *Economic and Political Weekly* Vol 44 No. 10, 7–13 March 2009.

2 'Proceedings against Narayana Murthy quashed' *The Hindu*, 15 August 2007. Available online at http://www.hindu.com/2007/08/15/stories/2007081553290500.htm

3 Habermas himself uses postnational without a hyphen, but the sense in which he uses it is, within the frame of my argument, *with* one.

4 This section is based on part of a book jointly authored with Aditya Nigam, *Power and Contestation. India Since 1989*, Zed Books, London and Orient Longman, Hyderabad.

5 ULFA is the United Liberation front of Assam and NSCN-IM is the National Socialist Council of Nagaland (Isaac-Muivah).

6 See Homepage of ULFA www.geocities.com/CapitolHill/Congress/7434/ulfa.htm. Downloaded on 10 December 2006; and Homepage of NSCN www.nscnonline.org/nscn/index-2.html downloaded on 25 December 2006. The ULFA homepage is now www.oocities.com/capitolhill/congress/7434/ulfa.htm. The NSCN homepage is currently inactive, but NagalimVoice expresses the views of supporters of the demand for a greater homeland for the Naga people: www.nagalimvoice.com.

7 See interviews with *hijra* candidates, www.thewe.cc/contents/more/archive/aruvani.html, downloaded on 22 March 2006.

8 For an extended discussion of postnationalism in the context of feminist politics, see my 'Outing Heteronormativity. Nation, Citizen, Feminist Disruptions' in *Sexualities* (ed.) Nivedita Menon, Women Unlimited, 2007.

9 Sudheendra Kulkarni, ideologue of Hindutva (2006) commends both BJP's Arun Shourie and the CPI(M) leader Prakash Karat for having 'publicly aired convergent views on an important national issue'.

10 See Nivedita Menon and Aditya Nigam *Power and Contestation* op. cit. pp. 132–3 for a brief discussion of resistance to uranium mining in these two areas.

References

Akoijam, Bimol A. (2006) 'Ghosts of colonial modernity: Identity and conflict in the eastern frontier of South Asia' in Prasenjit Biswas and C. Joshua Thomas (eds) *Peace in India's North-East. Meaning, Metaphor and Method* New Delhi: Regency Publications.

Appadurai, Arjun (1997) *Modernity at Large*, Delhi: Oxford University Press.

—— (2001) 'Grassroots Globalization and the Research Imagination' in Arjun Appadurai (ed.) *Globalization*, Durham and London: Duke University Press.

Archibugi, Daniele (ed.) (2003) *Debating Cosmopolitics*, London: Verso.

Balibar, Etienne (2004) *We the People of Europe?* Princeton: Princeton University Press.

Baruah, Sanjib (2005) 'Nations within nation-states', *Hindustan Times*, 13 October.

Bates, Crispin (2001) 'Introduction: Community and Identity among South Asians in Diaspora' in Crispin Bates (ed.) *Community, Empire and Migration: South Asians in Diaspora*, Hampshire and New York: Palgrave.

Bidwai, Praful (2006) 'Nuclear disadvantage', *Tehelka*, 15 July 2006.

—— (2007) 'Drifting into nuclear blunderland' South Asians Against Nukes Available at http://groups.yahoo.com/group/SAAN_/message/999.

Brennan, Timothy (2003) 'Cosmopolitanism and Internationalism' in Daniele Archibugi (ed.) *Debating Cosmopolitics*, London: Verso.

Butalia, Urvashi (1993) 'Community, State and Gender: On Women's Agency during Partition', *EPW*, 24 April.

Das, Veena (1995) 'National Honour and Practical Kinship: Of Unwanted Women and Children', *Critical Events: An Anthropological Perspective on Contemporary India*, New Delhi: Oxford University Press.

Esterhazy, Peter (2005) 'How Big is the European Dwarf?' in Daniel Levy, Max Pensky and John Torpey (eds) *Old Europe, New Europe, Core Europe: Transatlantic Relations after the Iraq War*, London and New York: Verso.

Fernandes, Walter (2004) 'Limits of law and order approach to the north-east' *Economic and Political Weekly*, 16 October, 4609–11.

—— (2006) 'Shortages, ethnic conflicts and economic development in north-eastern India' in C. Joshua Thomas (ed.) *Engagement and Development. India's Northeast and Neighbouring Countries*, New Delhi: Akansha Publishing House.

Fraser, Nancy (2005) 'Transnationalizing the Public Sphere' in Max Pensky (ed.) *Globalizing Critical Theory*, New York: Rowman and Littlefield Publishers.

Garton Ash, Timothy and Ralf Dahrendorf (2005) 'The Renewal of Europe. Response to Habermas', in Daniel Levy, Max Pensky and John Torpey (eds) *Old Europe, New Europe, Core Europe: Transatlantic Relations after the Iraq War*, London and New York: Verso.

Gopinath, Gayatri (2005) *Impossible Desires: Queer Diasporas and South Asian Public Cultures*, Durham: Duke University Press, pp 16–17.

Habermas, Jurgen (1999) 'Bestiality and Humanity: A War on the Border between Law and Morality', translated from the German, Franz Solms-Laubach, *Die Zeit* 54, 18 April. English version available at Global Library, 2000, www.theglobal-site.ac.uk.

—— (2005) 'Interpreting the Fall of a Monument' in Max Pensky (ed.) *Globalizing Critical Theory*, New York: Rowman and Littlefield Publishers.

Habermas, Jurgen and Jacques Derrida (2005) 'February 15, or, What Binds Europeans Together: Plea for a Common Foreign Policy, Beginning in Core Europe' in Daniel Levy, Max Pensky and John Torpey (ed.) *Old Europe, New Europe, Core Europe: Transatlantic Relations after the Iraq War*, London and New York: Verso.

Hoodbhoy, Pervez (2006) 'South Asia needs a bomb-less deal' *Economic and Political Weekly*, 15 April.

Jameson, Frederic (2000) 'Globalization and Political Strategy', *New Left Review*, 4, 49–68.

Jayaraman, T. (2006) 'Journey from Pokhran II to Hyde Act' *Economic and Political Weekly*, 23 December.

Kaviraj, Sudipta (1994) 'On the structure of nationalist discourse' in T. V. Sathyamurthy (ed.) *State and Nation in the Context of Social Change Volume I*, New Delhi: Oxford University Press.

Kulkarni, Sudheendra (2006) 'Accepting America's nuclear hegemony', *The Indian Express*, 24 December.

Menon, Nivedita (ed.) (2007) *Sexualities Women Unlimited*, Delhi and London: Zed Books.

Menon, Nivedita and Aditya Nigam (2007) *Power and Contestation: India After 1989*, London: Zed Books.

Menon, Parvati (2002) 'A difficult turn on Cauvery' *Frontline*, Volume 19, Issue 21, 12–25 October.

Menon, Ritu and Kamla Bhasin (1993) 'Recovery, rupture, resistance: Indian state and the abduction of women during Partition', *EPW*, 24 April.

Mertes, Tom (2002) 'Grass-Roots Globalism', *New Left Review* 17, September–October.

Misra, Udayon (2000) *The Periphery Strikes Back. Challenges to the Nation-State in Assam and Nagaland*, Shimla: Indian Institute of Advanced Study.

Mitchell, Timothy (2004) The Properties of Markets. Working Paper No. 2, Cultural Political Economy Research Group, University of Lancaster.

Oinam, Bhagat and Homen Thangjam (2006) 'Indian "nation state" and crisis of the "periphery"' in Prasenjit Biswas and C. Joshua Thomas (eds) *Peace in India's North-East. Meaning, Metaphor and Method*, New Delhi: Regency Publications.

Renan, Ernest (1996) 'What is a nation?', in Geoff Eley and Ronald Grigor Suny (eds) *Becoming National: A Reader*, New York and Oxford: Oxford University Press.

Samaddar, Ranabir (1999) *The Marginal Nation. Transborder Migration from Bangladesh to West Bengal*, New Delhi: Sage.

Shah, Svati P. (2001) 'Out and out radical. New directions for progressive organizing', *Samar*, 14 Fall/Winter.

Special Correspondent (2006) 'Mullaperiyar: chief Minister rejects preconditions for talks' *The Hindu*, 25 October.

Thorat, Sukhdeo and Umakant (eds) (2004) *Caste, Race and Discrimination: Discourses in the International Context*, Jaipur and New Delhi: Rawat Publications.

Young, Iris Marion (2005) 'De-centering the project of global democracy' in Daniel Levy, Max Pensky and John Torpey (eds) *Old Europe, New Europe, Core Europe: Transatlantic Relations after the Iraq War*, London and New York: Verso.

Ziv, Amalia (2005) 'Performative Politics in Israeli Queer Anti-Occupation Activism' Paper presented at Center for the Study of Gender and Sexuality, New York University, 4 October.

16 A colonial city and its time(s)[1]

Ranajit Guha

Our story of the temporal displacements caused by colonialism had to begin in the countryside not only because the conquest which started it all had been fought in a mango grove, but also because rural society was the first to be seriously affected by the East India Company's mercantile time and its fiscal timetable. Yet, the signs of the resulting discrepancies were perhaps far less obvious to villagers than to those living closer to the urban and semi-urban seats of British power in the subcontinent. Here, that power was represented directly by the white employees of the regime and their families, as well as by the administrative and social institutions of the Raj. Consequently the time of civil society found itself flanked by a stranger, that is, the time of the so-called civil lines at every *sadar* station and *mufassil* town. In many respects, life in the bungalow and the cantonment kept itself scrupulously apart from that of the native settlement, both as a matter of official policy and cultural choice, a segregation documented well in Anglo-Indian literature. Inevitably, however, the schedule of parallel lives had to buckle under the imperatives of an alien regime's dependence on local services, skills, and even goodwill for its survival. So, from the bustle of *chota hazri* synchronizing the attendance of cooks and servants at the elaborate ritual of English breakfast through the sound of hours beaten on bell-metal gongs announcing the beginning and end of the administrative day, to the cries of night-watch on its rounds, the new *sarkari* time would overlap native time as a matter of course in any small town.

However, it was in the principal cities that the design and drama of such intersection were most pronounced, for the authority of the *sahib* radiating from these urban centres rested squarely on the back of a bureaucracy made up of Indians at its lowest levels. The very structure of governance made it necessary, therefore, that official time should impinge on the time of civil society. What makes such impingement interesting and exciting to study (however confusing it might have been to live) is that it did not, indeed could not, replicate the general configuration of power in anything so neat as a nexus of dominance and subordination. On the contrary, it amounted to a tangle of two braided temporalities, requiring each to resist as well as accommodate the other.

The patterns of that braiding had been an object of curiosity to both British and Indian observers since the early colonial days. However, their views slanted at somewhat different angles. What the former saw in this phenomenon was a native sense of time characterized by delays, inexactitudes, unpunctualities, and other vagaries which were a constant source of irritation to them. The sahibs and memsahibs wrote on this subject obsessively in myriad jokes, insults, innuendoes or plain comment, regarded often as ethnological or political wisdom by other sahibs and memsahibs. Whatever the form, it all added up to a comprehensive attribution of unreliability to an Indian attitude, behaviour and personality made up of abstractions and prototypes. What were the Indians supposed to be unreliable for? For those services required of them as *khansamans*, *bawarchis*, *ayahs*, *darzis*, *dhobis*, *peons*, *saises*, *malis*, orderlies, *babus*, and so on, every day in and around the bungalows, *kachehris*, cantonments, clubs and other institutions that affirmed the presence and power of their rulers in a colonial city. From the rulers' point of view, all that inconvenience and confusion were due entirely to the peculiarities of an indigenous time prone to slowing down, interrupting and otherwise hindering the smooth and effective flow of a master time governed by rules which the colonized, as a population of servants, could never understand or grasp.

An early literary response to changing times

The temporal scene looked confusing in the eyes of the natives as well, but with a difference. No one amongst them blamed the sahibs for the peculiarities of *their* sense of time. The problems it created for the indigenous society were all regarded by the latter as its own problem – a problem of failure on the part of the Indians themselves to adjust to the alien temporality introduced by the Company Raj. There was a comic side to this maladjustment, and the natives used it to make fun of themselves in satire, farce and parody. There was a serious side to it as well, and the vernacular literatures of the nineteenth century inscribed its anxieties copiously for a growing indigenous urban middle-class readership.

An early instance of that literary response, Bhabanicharan Bandyopadhyay's *Kalikata Kamalalay*, dates back to 1823.[2] Written in Bangla, it is a dialogue between a villager on his first visit to Calcutta and a local resident. The title of the work testifies to the reputation the city had already acquired by then as the abode of Kamala, the goddess of wealth. Paradoxically, the wealth so blessed by her presence belonged to the foreign merchants and financiers for whom the East India Company's capital in the subcontinent served, in this period, as an important base of their global transactions. Not surprisingly, therefore, there were many amongst the indigenous elite who felt threatened by such unprecedented and rapid economic development, and the word had gone out – helped to an extent by a vernacular press – that all was not well with the Hindu way of life – or *achara* – in Calcutta. The visitor interrogates his host closely on some matters of urgent concern. Is it true, he asks, that the residents of this city go out to work after an early meal and don't come back home until fairly late at night, and that too, simply to eat and sleep in before leaving for work first thing next morning?[3] Isn't it a fact that most of them have no use any more for the traditional Hindu codes of conduct, including those concerning morning and evening worship, and that even things like the funerary ceremonies (*shraddha*) required to end the state of ritual pollution caused by a death in the family have all been abandoned? How is it, he wonders, echoing rumours circulating in the outback, that they all dress like foreigners in Calcutta, eat meals prepared for them by Muslim cooks, drink brandy on ritual occasions, ignore shastric literature published in Bangla, and read nothing other than what is available in English and Persian?[4]

The resident townsman tries to allay these fears as best as he can. Villagers have been misinformed about life in the city, he suggests. Yes, there are some Hindus who have been affected by those new ways, he admits, but by and large the older tradition is still intact amongst the higher castes. In reassuring his interlocutor thus, he was no doubt voicing the opinion of the conservative elements amongst the city elite, of whom the author was himself a leading representative. But the fact that such reassurance was at all called for is important. It speaks of changing times, indeed of changes indexed in popular perception, with the advent of a new temporality rivalling one that was habitual and sanctified by custom.

The prose in which that perception was registered was itself contemporary to the new rhythm of time. Fostered by the East India Company's administration for the training of its officers at the Fort William College, and nurtured at schools set up to educate a native middle class as clerks and collaborators, Bangla prose, though older than British rule, owed its modernization primarily to the colonial city. As such, it was not only witness to those alien objects and institutions that had made their way into the language as loan words, listed at length in *Kalikata Kamalalay*, but was sensitive to contemporary anxieties as well. The dialogue in that text serves both as a measure of such anxieties and the means to deal with them. It confronts the city-dweller with the villager as his alter ego, and his self-doubts with questions asked by a country bumpkin. A relatively new discursive form, one that would enable mirror images and divided selves to be inscribed more and more frequently in literary works, this prose is true to the changing times.

However, with all its complicity, that discourse still has an air of aloofness about it. Less than eager to own up to its provenance in the world and times which are its object, it acknowledges change, but is not itself integral to it. It is a judgemental, reticent prose still not fully involved in the life of a colonial city at its formative phase. With that phase decisively over by the middle of the century, Calcutta was to celebrate its coming of age in writing adequate to the surge of its urban ethos. Far from holding back, it would spill over into the streets, join the crowds and defy the over-Sanskritized sensibilities of the literati by adopting the mode of everyday speech as its vehicle.

Hutom Pyanchar Naksha

The text which announced that outrageously brilliant debut was *Hutom Pyanchar Naksha*.[5] Published in 1861, it was immediately hailed as the signal of a radical turn in Bangla literature, and age has done nothing to dim that reputation. Unfortunately, however, the racy colloquialism on which the work relies for its diction is precisely what has made it inaccessible so far to those not familiar with the language of the original. It resists translation. Attempts to render it into English did not proceed beyond a few extracts, which is a shame, considering that the author was obviously interested in getting himself heard on both sides of the linguistic divide.[6] In Calcutta, as in the rest of Britain's subcontinental empire, English served the regime both as an instrument of dominance and an agency of persuasion. As the language of the rulers, it stood for all that set them conspicuously apart from the mass of their subjects, who spoke only in the local tongues. Yet, at the same time, as the principal medium of an officially sponsored education (which had, by then, come to mean English-style education, according to Bankimchandra Chatterjee), it was the means used by the Raj to induce a very small, but affluent and socially powerful, minority amongst the colonized to favour collaboration.[7]

Kaliprasanna Sinha, author of *Hutom* (the book was published under a pseudonym, but that, like the text itself, was part of a characteristic playfulness that made it all the easier for the author to be identified by his contemporaries), was one of that elite, the crème de la crème. Scion of a leading and wealthy family of the city, he was educated at the Hindu College. Its standing as the premier Western-style school in India at the time relied to no small extent on the reputation of its teachers of English literature. It is perhaps to them that Kaliprasanna, like some of the illustrious alumni before him, owed his knowledge of Shakespeare and Beaumont and Fletcher cited in his epigraphs. But more than anything else, it is a work by Charles Dickens to which his book has been linked ever since its publication.[8] The Dickensian connection cannot be confirmed by any direct references or citations. However, there is some evidence to show that the young Calcutta author must have been acquainted with the work of his older London contemporary. He alludes to Dickens obliquely, yet transparently enough, to acknowledge his debt, just as the inclusion of an occasional clip from Hitchcock in one of his own films has been, in our own time, young Truffaut's way of honouring the master and relating to him.

Hutom and Boz

This intertextuality, which straddles two very different linguistic codes and literary traditions, not to speak of the unequal power relations corresponding to them, is displayed clearly on the title page of the second edition of the book, published within a year of the first. The title is given in both Bangla and English.[9] The former translates as 'Sketches by Hutom the Owl', or perhaps as 'Sketches by the Hooting Owl'. But compare it with the English. Printed in capitals, it reads, 'SKETCHES BY HOOTUM ILLUSTRATIVE OF EVERY DAY LIFE AND EVERY DAY PEOPLE'. How does one account for the omission of the owl and the addition of nine other words here? For an answer, one has only to insert a hyphen between 'EVERY' and 'DAY', and replace 'HOOTUM' by 'BOZ', to realize how the title was rewritten in English in a self-conscious attempt to echo that of Dickens's work, published 25 years earlier.[10]

The junior (only 25 when he published *Hutom*) had obviously found his master. The land which he, an Anglicist (labelled so by Bankimchandra), had been educated to look up to as the very source of enlightenment, provided him with a model to emulate with a project of his own. But what was it that made him undertake that project in the first place? His interests ranged on a wide front, from publishing to philanthropy and social reform. He was taken up with myriad public activities. Even as a writer, he moved easily between genres as a dramatist, journalist and translator.[11] With so many other things to do and such a many-sided talent to invest in them, did he have to write about his city at all? To ask this is already to wonder if the choice was entirely his own, or made for him by the spirit of an age that had thematized the city for the literatures of the West, and given Paris its Balzac, London its Dickens. By comparison, Calcutta was of course just incipiently urban. But that did not take away from its importance as an issue of that historic movement which required every modern empire to site a colonial city. Caught up in that web of complementarity, the latter and its restless muse, both children of their time, had to have a Hutom to match the metropolitan Boz.

Realism and historicity in Boz

Our interest in this obscure lineage has nothing to do with any design to make amends for the oversights of literary history. We simply wish to point out how, in the colonial era, the discourse of power intersected with the discourse of the city. This was not of course central to J. Hillis Miller's concern in his influential essay, which helped, some 30 years ago, to focus academic attention on *Sketches by Boz* more than ever before.[12] Yet his argument is not without relevance to us. He sets out to examine the standing of his work as an epitome of realism. Contemporaries, he says, were impressed by its 'inimitably faithful observation and inimitably faithful reproduction' of the details of London life, especially as it was lived by its middle and lower classes. The accolade has continued for over a century until our day, with critics competing with each other to highlight what they consider its 'startling fidelity' to real life, its near 'documentary' character, its recording of 'facts observed with an astonishing precision and wealth of detail'.[13]

Responding to this Cratylean chorus which backs up, in effect, Dickens's own representationalist claim that 'his object has been to present little pictures of life and manners as they really are'.[14] Miller focuses on one particular arrangement of those 'little pictures'. Life and manners are depicted here by a massive accumulation of things, which is no doubt appropriate for an age distinguished by the production, exchange and the general proliferation of commodities as its hallmark. If, therefore, things clutter up this text, they do so in much the same way that they overload the space in a genre of sixteenth- and seventeenth-century European painting.[15] But this parallelism serves, sadly, as the measure of a certain pathos of distance as well. It parodies, in a Nietzschean manner, an earlier and complacent phase of modernity by one more recent and bitter; the self-assurance of the mercantile era by the anxieties of the industrial, the images of abundance decorating the larders and tables of Amsterdam's burghers by those of destitution in the slums of the London poor – the pawnshop, the broker's shop, the junk shop, as described by Dickens.

The objects that crowd this description are precisely those on which *Sketches by Boz* relies for its so-called objectivity. Household goods for the most part, they exude a sense of the familiar. Their plenitude stands for the density of the real. Even the randomness of their deployment is taken as an authentic index to the disorder of London life. Indeed, as Raymond Williams has remarked, that city 'could not easily be described in a rhetorical gesture of repressive uniformity'. Quite to the contrary, its miscellanea, variety and randomness were, according to him, 'the most apparent things about it, especially when seen from the inside'. Underlying all that, however, was a deep structure embodying a system – 'a negative system of indifference; a positive system of differentiation, in law, power and financial control'. It was this coexistence of surface agitation and systemic depth, randomness and regularity, 'the visible individual facts' and 'beyond them, often hidden, the common condition and destiny', which made London something of 'a contradiction, a paradox'. Dickens dealt with that paradox by creating 'a new kind of

novel', adequate to 'this double condition; the random and the systematic, the visible and the obscured, which', says Williams, 'is the true
significance of the city, and especially at this period of the capital city, as
a dominant social form'.[16]

A sense of that 'double condition' informs Miller's approach to the
Sketches as well. This is not surprising in view of the fact that the latter
is regarded, in some ways, as 'a characteristic expression of Dickens's
genius', an 'embryo' which anticipates, even in the journalistic mode,
much of what was soon to emerge as distinctive about his novels.[17] But
the duplexity highlighted in this reading works at the textual rather
than the social level. The interplay between the obvious and the hidden,
the contingent and the necessary is, in this instance, referred to as that
between the unruly miscellaneousness of things and the control imposed
by the narrative. This transcendental move, so essential to any description whatsoever, enables the critic to ask how such a 'confused jumble'
could yield so neatly ordered a series of tales. How do the multitude and
diversity of things which, in his view, 'stand for the apparent disorder of
London as a whole', not prevent the author from fashioning well-crafted
stories out of them? What is the logic of this production? The answer
lies, for Miller, in what he calls the 'law of metonymic correspondence',[18]
based, he says after Roman Jakobson, on 'the assumption of a necessary similarity between a man, his environment, and the life he is forced
to lead within that environment'.[19] Guided by that law, the author first
posits a 'scene with its inanimate objects, then the people of whose lives
these objects are the signs, and finally the continuous narrative of their
lives, which may be inferred from the traces of themselves they have left
behind'.[20]

Order of things and order of time

What interests us most about this graduation is the manner in which it
allows the order of things to take over from the order of time. There is a
good deal in the *Sketches* that shows this narrative strategy at work, as in
the well-known article, 'Meditations in Monmouth Street'.[21] On one of his
walks through that street, 'the only true and real emporium for second-
hand wearing apparel', Boz falls into a reverie before a collection of used
footwear, 'fitting visionary feet and legs … into boots and shoes', until,
moving from things to people, he matches a sturdy pair of boots to a delicate pair of satin shoes, and goes on to translate that as a tale of friendship
between a Covent Garden coachman and a servant girl – a tale with just
a hint of a happy ending, of course. There are other cameos of this kind,
but none that illustrates the process of metonymic substitution as well as
the story inspired by 'a few suits of clothes ranged outside a shop-window'
farther up the street.[22]

Those clothes, says the author, 'must at different periods have all belonged to, and been worn by, the same individual'.[23] With nothing else to support that assertion, he proceeds to assign the suits – five in all – to the presumed owner, beginning with the smallest for infancy through the next two sizes corresponding successively to adolescence and early youth, until with suit no. 4, '[a] long period had elapsed, and ... [t]he vices of the boy had grown with the man'.[24] The last item, made up of 'articles of clothing of the commonest description', suggests a sad and violent closure to the series, with the poor protagonist, now a criminal, sentenced to banishment or the gallows. The end of the tale was not at all clear, but it was easy, according to Boz, 'to guess its termination' in 'a lingering death, possibly of many years' duration, thousands of miles away'.[25]

Easy to guess, because it was predictable. As Miller observes, 'the row of old clothes ... in Monmouth Street gives rise ... to a wholly conventional narrative, the story of the idle apprentice', rehashed over and over again in eighteenth-century English fiction and drama.[26] This, he says, clinching the argument on realism, 'is not the metonymic process authenticating realistic representation[,] but a movement deeper and deeper into the conventional, the concocted, the schematic'.

For us, however, the matter is not quite settled yet. It begs a further question about that movement itself, which allows a description of things as they are to slip into the schematic, the quotidian into the conventional. How does an arrangement of clothes translate into the stages of an individual's life? What is it that brings about the substitution of spatial contiguity by the temporal? The order of time has obviously taken over from the order of things in this narrative, with a little help from the author himself. He has used some familiar tricks of the trade, such as falling into a reverie *in medias res*, to switch from the present to the past, and let his account of everyday life and everyday people drift into history. Indeed, he leaves his reader in no doubt about his historicizing intention, as Boz begins his story of the hapless apprentice by saying. 'There was the man's whole life written as legibly as on those clothes, as if we had his autobiography engrossed on parchment before us'.[27] And, true to the tradition of assimilating biography and autobiography generically to historical discourse, he refers to the last of the five suits as that which 'completed the history'.[28]

The everyday dissolved in history

It is a condition of this move deeper and deeper into history that it must dissolve the here and now of everydayness. Yet, the latter is what the book is about, as the title page shows. Is there a contradiction here? Or is it enough to say, as Miller does following Roland Barthes, that the 'reality effect' of the story based on 'referential illusion' has simply worn out in the process of the telling? For, even if that were true (and there is no reason to doubt it), it still leaves us with the paradox of the everyday fluctuating, in its concept, between a specified day in the calendar as it follows another and a dateless, nameless average which stands for all days, but is identical to none. It rains every day during the monsoon in Calcutta, but the everyday misery of the city's street-dwellers is not confined to any particular day of the wet and dry seasons. The phrase 'everyday' stands today, in this instance, for a contemporaneity, a sense of shared time spread over three generations since the Famine and Partition, bonding myriad refugees into a community which has only the pavement for its home. It is this contemporaneity that constitutes their being-with-one-another in a shared world. It enables every lived instant, every 'now', to escape the discipline of linear succession occasionally, to hark back and look ahead. Therefore, the temporality of everydayness allows the present to host the past and its forward-looking historicities.

The objects contemplated by Boz too, were witness to a world defined by the co-temporality of everydayness. Useful things, they had served a community of users. Insofar as the latter shared their time with others as the very condition of their worldhood, the household and other goods of everyday use were themselves elements of that temporality. Afloat in the tide of time, these were 'the ballast of familiar life, the present and the past'.[29] Commuting between the two, Boz's narrative picked its way through the junk of flea markets, slotting things dispersed by the force of circumstance back into their contexts in time. It was thus that an emergent mode of literary discourse, something between the journalistic and the novelistic, restored many a humble life to its historicality ignored by historiography. By sounding the lower depths of London society, it added depth to the ongoing historicization of the great metropolitan city in English literature.

Raymond Williams traces the historicizing tendency back to Wordsworth who, he says, had already inaugurated 'a permanent way of seeing any historical city'.[30] That was, of course, very much a grand vision. 'A sight so touching in its majesty', like the panorama of 'Ships, towers, domes, theatres, and temples' viewed from Westminster Bridge early one morning in 1802.[31] The sense of distance persists even when the poet finds himself in a crowd and regards. 'The face of every one / That passes me' as a mystery.[32] Dickens, on the other hand, speaks of London with an easy familiarity. The 'speculative pedestrian', child of his imagination, could point to a man in the street and say, 'We knew all about him'.[33] Between *The Prelude* and *Sketches by Boz*, a whole generation had grown up. An observer, given to what he himself called 'amateur vagrancy', could now refer to a slummy quarter of the capital as 'the only true and real emporium for second-hand wearing apparel'.[34] If this echoed the tribute paid by the older muse to 'the vast metropolis' as '[t]hat great emporium' and

'[f]ount of my country's destiny and the world's',[35] it was no mocking allusion. It only showed that the great city was perhaps a shade less numinous
than it had been in the Age of Commerce, and that it had adjusted itself
to the everydayness of a modern industrial and administrative capital. It
had been historicized. Literature in the imperial West could no longer
deal with the city without history breathing over its shoulder.

The present in the *Naksha*

By contrast, the historicist imperative is conspicuous by its absence in
Hutom Pyanchar Naksha. That is not to suggest that it is ahistorical in some
sense. Far from it, the *Naksha* affirms its historicality by deploying time in
a manner strikingly different from the *Sketches*. The latter, we have seen,
traces its way back from the day-to-day to connect itself by a direct linear
nexus to the past. The actual, assimilated thus to the bygone, adds to its
density, and the shards of broken lives, picked up from the backstreets
of London, are fitted ingeniously into the tale of England's expansion
overseas. Nothing could be more different from the temporal strategy of
the *Naksha*, based on a total involvement with the present, which, instead
of being overtaken by the past as in the *Sketches*, does the overtaking
itself. The past is by no means left out, but no sooner does it make its
appearance than it is absorbed into the ongoing surge of the present. The
aspect of light, the present or *vartamāna*, contrasted in Indian thought
and language with the more obscure aspects of the past and the future,
affirms its authority by letting some of the characteristic phenomena of
urban life disclose themselves as they make their way through the narrative, for 'The present is a path that is like light itself' (*vartamāno' adhvā
prakāśavat*).[36]

One of these phenomena, designated as *hujuk* or sensations, is a miscel-
lany made up of a couple of dozen items.[37] These range from rumours
and panics through anecdotes about upstarts, tricksters and impostors,
to even something like political news in a few instances. What they have
in common, cutting across diversities, is their role as gossip in Hutom's
Calcutta. Exploited for its content, it has been grist so far either to the mill
of social history (as evidence), or to that of a feuilleton literature of scandals
(as *kechha*). Between the earnestness of one and the triviality of the other,
what remains unacknowledged is the immediacy of presence disclosed
in such gossip. As a phenomenon, it lives only for the day, literally as an
ephemeros or *adyatana*, in a state of utter transience. Consequently, it is
the 'now', the vehicle of its circulation, rather than the messages circulated, that enables this discourse to weld the mass of its interlocutors
together into an urban public. The instantaneous exchange of information in myriad bits, with no particular demand to make on reflection,
generates a concern which, for all its indefiniteness and volatility – or,

precisely because of these – constitutes the very ground of that publicness. It is not what people are talking about that is vital to such gossip, but the fact that they are talking to one another in a state of average intelligibility. It is this that creates a sense of shared time out of the sum of short-lived sensations, and helps, together with other factors, to form the worldhood of a colonial public.

Gossip feeds on curiosity and is driven by it. Whether it is about a seven-legged cow, or the prospect of dead souls returning to earth in the year of the Mutiny, or the lifestyle of the local parvenus, or an occasional fracas involving natives and whites, gossip, in this text, is the public voice of curiosity. Curiosity, like gossip, belongs to the present, but with a distinct inclination towards the future. Ever on the lookout for the new and for what is to come, its absorption in the present is, in every instance, an awaiting for a possibility in which to consummate itself. However, the awaiting does not last long enough, since there is always another object to chase. The moment of consummation never comes.[38] Cursed thus by incompleteness, curiosity is constantly on the move. That, of course, is not conducive to the sedimentation history requires for its seedbed. Nothing germinates in this incessantly unsettled contemporaneity. Fragments of the past show up in it from time to time as tradition, genealogy or plain nostalgia, but are burnt up at once. In contrast to the serene and monumental historicity of the metropolitan capital to which Wordsworth paid his tribute, the capital city of the Raj, driven by gossip and consumed by curiosity, is rocked, according to Hutom, by a perpetual restlessness.

This restlessness, with the present always on the move along a path going nowhere, has a temporal register made out for it in many languages. Pāṇini offers us an insight into this point in the well-known sutra, *vartamāne lat* (3.2.123), with the *vṛtti* defining the present as what has commenced, but not been completed (*ārabdho' āsamāptaścha vartamānaḥ*). For Bangla, the same progressive aspect, *ghataman bartaman*, has been defined by Sunitikumar Chattopadhyay in identical terms.[39] In this language, the unfinished state of the present shows up clearly in verb phrases ending with -*techhi*, -*techho*, -*techhish*, and -*techhe*, or colloquially, with the -*te* elided, as in the *Naksha*. The present progressive, reiterated thrice in three consecutive clauses, inaugurates this text, setting it to the mood of the narrative to follow. This is an attunement which, like the opening phrase of a raga, is also an invitation, for it is the start of a festival. Hutom announces it in his very first words: 'The sound of drums is being heard from every quarter of the city of Calcutta'. A lot is going on in what, according to his description, is the site of a continuous bustle. Unlike Boz, who constructed his scenes and tales out of lists stacked with the names of things, our narrator relies on arrays of verb phrases to produce interweaving sounds and telescoped sights, noises and crowds always in a state of agitation, testifying to the urban festival as a scene of endlessly recursive activity, all starts and no stops.

It is hard to fit this image of the city into the everydayness the author claims to have illustrated in the *Naksha*. The work is dominated, in volume and in spirit, by a turbulence incompatible with the routine and the regular that had come to characterize everyday life in Hutom's time. Following the logic of a conquest normalized into rulership, the everyday of this capital of the Raj stood for a firm, if alien, order. The principal organs of government – the army, the bureaucracy and the judiciary – all had their headquarters there. Many of the big financial institutions and mercantile houses, too, operated with Calcutta as their base. These, like the state apparatus to which they were closely linked, relied critically on the local population to keep the regime and its accessories serviced, and the wheels of power turning in every department, from law and order through banking and trade to education. Six days a week, this vast collaboration was visible in the movement of these native employees commuting in large numbers between the residential parts of the city and its administrative and commercial quarters, known popularly as the *ophish-para*. Now, *para* is an old and intimate word which means, in Bangla, a close-knit neighbourhood of families who had long known one another, sometimes for generations, and were bonded in some instances by kinship, craft or trade.[40] For such a word to be compounded with a signifier borrowed from English, and associated directly with the power-houses of imperial authority, must be a measure of the extent to which the indigenous speech-community had come to accept the site of its daily pen-pushing as a second community. Language testifies to such habituation by other usages as well. A kind of horse-drawn vehicle hired by the babus for transport to *ophish-para* had their status written into its name. It was called *keranchi-gari*, that is, carriage for *keranis*, after the occupation of its passengers, clerks or *kerani* – a generic term subsuming a wide variety of salaried personnel employed by governmental and commercial agencies.[41]

Corresponding to such designations for the place of everyday work and everyday transport was also a phrase for office time, that is, *ophisher bela*. In this coupling, again of Bangla and English, there are two connotations of particular interest to us. One of these concerns the urgency that *bela* could convey sometimes to suggest that the *kerani* could be late for work, and must hurry up. The other, more basic though not entirely unrelated, idea is that of *bela* as a portion of the everyday allocated to the office, and the use made of it as a part of one's job. *Ophisher bela*, or office time, amounts thus to a deduction in favour of official time imposed by the regime at the expense of the lived time of the indigenous civil society. The latter is not and cannot be fully assimilated to the colonial state, a dominance without hegemony. Consequently, it is forced to subsist on the remainder left to it after the appropriation of a considerable part of its time by the bureaucracy each day – each 'ten-to-five day' (as the *keranis* call it themselves) – of the working week. The everyday is thus hollowed out, creating an emptiness for all those not directly involved in the day-return trip to *ophish-para*. The first to be trapped in this vacuum is, of course, the woman of the house. When she tries to overcome the weight of the lonely segment of the day, the privative foil to office time, and transform it creatively into a hiatus made her own by reading or some other occupation of her choosing at home or in the world beyond, that initiative is opposed by all the powers of patriarchy.

Thus, the everyday was irreparably split in the middle, with one part assimilated to official time and alienated from the civil society. How, then, could everyday life and everyday people be inscribed in the discourse of the colonial city? What made the author claim, implausibly as it seems, that the *Naksha* was 'illustrative of everyday life and everyday people' when it was nothing of the kind, and had indeed the very different phenomenon of festivals for its theme? It is not that he did not know what he was doing. On the contrary, the echoing allusion to *Sketches by Boz* in the title of his own work was, as we have seen, altogether deliberate. If so, was it just an instance of mimicry, with an Indian writer gilding his work with a title borrowed from the imperial metropolis? Or was it a case of parody, using imitation to affirm difference? For a master of parody, which Kaliprasanna Sinha was, the latter would indeed be quite in character.

Parodia Sacra

The *Naksha* is rich in parody. It is in fact an outstanding example of this genre in Bangla, as recognized by readers, critics and historians alike. A wide range of rhetorical modes, from irony and wit to satire and plain farce, has been deployed here with a virtuosity stunning in its parodic effect. The material used to produce that effect is just an unsorted medley of anecdotes, events and characters. Yet, if the text has not dissipated in diversity or sunk under its weight, it is because of the concept that holds it together. This is the concept of the festival as a *shong*. The latter is Bangla for a masked representation, in which the display has what is hidden for its referent. Many of the images on show at the stalls set up for the occasion or taken out in floats doing the rounds, *para* after *para*, throughout the city, have this double meaning. By highlighting the not-too-veiled gap between what is concealed and what is not, they amuse and instruct the spectators. However, the spectators are in masks themselves. No one in the crowd is what he appears to be. Everybody has dressed up for the *shong*. So has Hutom, as he confides to the reader. He, too, is out to enjoy himself, like anyone else looking up the exhibits and commenting on them. However, unlike the others, it is not only the images made of straw and clay that he comments on, but the lively crowd milling around in masks as well. For the entire city, with all that is human in it, has been transformed into a masquerade by the festival. It is easy, of course, to regard this representation of the *shong* as a critique of the discrepancy between appearance and reality, which is characteristic of urban life itself. That is how the *Naksha* has been read so far, almost exclusively in these terms – a reading that relies for the most part on the author's reformist views to justify itself.

However, such a reading is perhaps unduly restrictive. Driven by its concern with nineteenth-century literature as only a documentation of social reform, it fails to take into account the full measure of the parodic intention of the book as announced on its title page. The parody begins there. It is a part of the *shong* itself that a work on the festival should come out masked as an illustration of the everyday. Equally, if not more, of a *double entendre* is the curious fact that the mask is not even homemade. It is a *bilati* (foreign or British) mask, modelled on a master narrative and put on deliberately to mock it. To parody something so specific to the language, literature and culture of the colonial masters, so mighty and elevated, is to move daringly close to that perverse genre, the *paradia sacra*, in which the Ave Maria and the Pater Noster could easily turn into 'liturgies of drunks and gamblers, liturgies about money', and evangelical readings into 'highly indiscreet stories'. Such profanation, says Mikhail Bakhtin, to whom we owe our understanding of that medieval European phenomenon, was typically bilingual. The Latin of the sacred text served as its vehicle in the main, but turned into a macaronic hybrid when projected against the vulgar national language and penetrated by its accentuating system. According to Bakhtin, this hybridity testifies to the essentially dialogical character of parody, in which 'two languages are crossed with each other, as well as two styles, two linguistic points of view, and in the final analysis two speaking subjects'.[42]

Parody does not rely for its effect on hybridization in the *Naksha* (as it did, for instance, more or less in the same period, in the burlesque of Rupchand Pakshi). Its Bangla, youthful and audacious in the full swing of its growth, makes no concession to the English. It takes on the latter from time to time, but only to engage it playfully in punning. The vernacular is fully in charge here. Yet the text, for all its linguistic autonomy, commits itself to a dialogue the moment it adopts the title of the *Sketches* by putting them in invisible quotation marks on its own title page. That quotation, a tactic used in all manner of travesties, is meant to draw attention to a typically metropolitan way of looking at the city. That way, a 'new' way, 'an *authentic* way of seeing not just a city but the capital city', is traced by Raymond Williams to the seventh book of *The Prelude*.[43] But London, the capital city of that great poem, had grown in size and population since then. The urban theme, celebrated by the poet, has a new dimension added to it now by Dickens's prose. Squalor claims a place for itself in literary description dominated so far, if not quite monopolized, by grandeur. Yet, for Williams, 'the noise of the working day' does not take away from the importance of the older vision as 'a *permanent* way of seeing *any* historical city ... Paris ... Naples, Vienna, Berlin, Rome, St Petersburg, Budapest, Moscow ... [t]he cities of civilization, in this capital sense'.[44] A peculiarity of English society and culture in the Age of Empire has thus been generalized beyond its national territorial boundaries, and elevated to the status of a universal truth. What concerns us about this universalist conceit is, first, that a 'new' and 'authentic' way of seeing the British capital during the first half of the nineteenth century should so easily turn into 'a *permanent* way of seeing *any* historical city', and second, that only European cities should qualify as objects of this selective gaze.

Calcutta's everyday and its festivals

Calcutta was, of course, excluded from this list by definition. Yet it was the capital of the Raj, the jewel in the crown. It could thus be said to have earned a place for itself in history, and become a 'historical city' according to some version of what Williams called 'this capital sense'. As such, it too merited a look. This was the point of Hutom's parody. Parody, as we know, is 'a dialogue between points of view'.[45] Accordingly, the dialogue engaged in the *Naksha* was clearly between two ways of seeing a capital city in the Age of Empire. Boz, for his part, saw it in terms of everyday life and everyday people. But imperial London's everyday was not and could not be the same as colonial Calcutta's, which, as noticed above, was already annexed for the most part to an externally imposed official time. What was still left to the subject population to live outside the working day, which was taken up with servicing an alien state machine, was only a truncated and diminished everyday. It was restored to its fullness only when official time, embodied in the *kerani*'s six-day week, was suspended, that is, when there was a festival in the city.

'Festivals', wrote Henri Lefebvre, 'contrasted violently with everyday life, *but they were not separate from it*. They were like everyday life, but more intense'.[46] That intensity, which is temporal in essence, makes itself felt first as a plenitude. All the dispersed moments of the day-to-day occupied with individual pursuits, each in its own discrete time, are gathered in a festival to make up the fullness of a community's time. This may be celebrated, as it often is, with excess and abandon. It is as if the celebrants have all the time in the world – an indulgence that compensates for the strict temporal economy of the everyday in all societies. However, the sense of compensation was all the more heightened in a colonial city like Calcutta, if only because it was proportionate to the impoverishment of an everyday life occupied with the administrative routines of an alien power.

Here, the drudgery of office work contrasted sharply with the exuberance of the festivals – the Charok, the Durga Puja and the Ramlila as described by Hutom. By the same token, his parody highlights the contrast between London and Calcutta to show how, on the festive occasions, the purloined everyday returns to the subject people to constitute a time of their own, a plenitude resistant to colonization and fragmentation.

Festivity and community

The everyday, intensified into festival, is thus a communitarian experience for the colonized. That is to say, the festival welds the latter into a community of celebrants, since 'A festival exists only in being celebrated', as Hans-Georg Gadamer has observed.[47] To celebrate is to be present at what is celebrated together with others. A kind of bonding, 'a festival', to quote Gadamer again, 'unites everyone. It is characteristic of festive celebration that it is meaningful only for those actually taking part. As such, it represents a unique kind of presence'.[48] It is, in other words, a sharing presence, and its time a participatory 'now' in terms of which the participants define themselves. Considered thus, the festival of the colonial city is a moment of self-assertion on the part of the colonized in an elevated and intensified presence inaccessible to official time. Hutom's parody was a gesture of that self-assertion in all its desperate pride.

It is a measure of such desperation and pride that the *Naksha* was published at a time uncomfortably close to the Mutiny. It was 1861. The rebellion had been put down, but the Raj was still busy picking up the pieces to repair its battered authority. Punitive measures had blown up into a comprehensive revanchism. It was working its way through the disturbed regions, systematically confiscating rebel property and redistributing it among collaborators. Throughout the land, fugitives from the sepoy army were still being hunted down, hanged at drumhead courts martial, or simply being shot on sight. The air was heavy with the smell of gunpowder. This, the native knew, was no time for confrontation. Defeated and disarmed, he had recourse to language as the last, but inalienable, armoury of the weak, and parody as one of the most effective weapons still available to him. Its use, in the *Naksha*, is meant to give assertiveness the neutral air of simple observation. Yet, even that does not read quite as the innocuous dialogue it pretends to be. He is keen to press the point against his imaginary interlocutor that unlike in the metropolis, life and people 'as they are' in the colonial city can never be adequately represented by descriptions of the everyday as an integral time. With the everyday reduced to official time under the alien regime, its subjects have nothing other than their festivals, in which alone they are represented in the fullness and authenticity of a shared communal time. In other words, contrary to what the literati of metropolitan Britain believed, their way of seeing their capital and other European cities in the Age of Empire was not, and could not be, the same as the way the colonized in South Asia saw their own cities. For them, official time and indigenous time were two distinct entities, and called for rather different interpretations – official and indigenous – with little in common.

Two ways of seeing Calcutta

Thus, the thrust of Hutom's parody goes significantly beyond upholding the indigenous festival against the metropolitan everyday. Underlying that alternative point of view is a more radical assertiveness, keen on distinguishing between the indigenous and official ways of seeing Calcutta. With the strengthening of British paramountcy in the subcontinent, that city too gained in importance, decade by decade, throughout the nineteenth century. As the capital of the Raj, it was the most obvious exemplar of its power and opulence. Its value as a showpiece was therefore not lost on the rulers. Already in 1833, Lord William Bentinck, one of the more far-sighted of India's Governors-General, urged his administration to encourage 'members of ruling and influential families' to visit the city and spend some time there.

> A twelve months' sojourn of such persons at our seal of government, viewing *our* arts and arms, the arrangement and magnificence of *our* buildings, the order and suitableness of *our* business establishments, *our* institutions for education, the ingenuity displayed in such machinery as has reached the east, and the ships carrying on *our* commerce, would do more to diffuse just notions of *our* power and resources, of the importance of *our* alliance than any measures we can pursue. By such means *we* should have a chance of becoming truly known throughout this great empire as the powerful people *we* in fact are.
>
> Seeing all these things too with their own eyes, it would be reasonable to expect that visitors would return to their homes improved both in knowledge and feelings, and therefore better qualified to discharge those duties for which providence has destined them.[49]

The official view of the city could not be more clearly and comprehensibly stated. As Bentinck saw it – and wanted the native elite to see it 'with their own eyes' and for their own edification – Calcutta was the very epitome of Britain's power in the East. Everything it had to show – its arts, arms and education, its business, transport and technology – was governmental, and stamped 'ours'. The second person plural stands here for the Raj as rulers and proprietors – as 'the powerful people *we* in fact are' – dominating this representation completely and exclusively. There is no room in it for any of *them*, that is, any indigenous will or interest or activity that is not slotted into the grand imperial design.

The reduction of the colonial city to an entity which can be claimed as 'ours' from the standpoint of colonialism is exclusive because it is contained in official time and cannot see beyond it. A kind of theorizing, it is defined negatively by what it cannot see. What it is blind to is the city of the festival. The latter requires, for its representation, another theory, another way of seeing the world, which Hutom brings to it. He is able to do so because he belongs to that world in the plenitude of its own time, that is, festival time. His competence to represent it derives also from the primordial and inalienable privilege of a native speaker. For time and language work together in that world as the very condition of its narrative possibility.

However, in the Age of Empire, that possibility is always and necessarily precarious, as the world with which the indigenous discourse is concerned can no longer remain hermetically sealed. Even the festival, with the native speaker as its poet and participant, must learn to live with alien intrusions. Colonialism would not allow it to forget its presence. Hutom's narrative, set in the present progressive, is interrupted at regular intervals by the gun fired thrice every day at the Fort William, the supreme headquarters of the British army in the subcontinent. It is the gun which reminds the subjects, morning, noon and evening, that official time rules, never mind the native festivals. The *Naksha* transcribes that warning phonetically every now and then in the course of an ongoing yarn, 'There goes the gun *ghrm*'. 'There goes the gun *ghpsh*', or, '*ghpsh korey top porey gelo*', '*ghrm korey top porey gelo*', as in the original.[50] The contrast between the mellifluous vowels of Bangla and the harsh consonants packed into the voice of the hour-gun could not be emphasized more. It left the colonized in no doubt as to who was in command even at that moment of total absorption in festival time – a time they had always considered their own.

Notes

1 This chapter was written in 1997 and previously published in *Indian Economic Social History Review* 45, 3 (2008): 329–51.
2 The text used in this chapter is Bandyopadhyay, *Kalikata Kamalalay* (hereafter, *KK*).
3 *KK*, p. 8.
4 Ibid., pp. 10–11.
5 References are all to Sinha, *Satik Hutom* (hereafter, *Hutom*). This is by far the best edition of the work available, and is based on the 1868 recension of the original, which was the third and final version to have been published during the author's lifetime.
6 Arun Nag, editor of *Hutom*, refers to two of these partial translations, one in the *Hindoo Patriot* of 1862, presumably by Krishnadas Pal, and another, published anonymously in 1864 and attributed to Lal Behari De. *Hutom*, pp.

287–8. (The first English translation, by Swarup Roy, of the full text has now been published in 2008 as *The Observant Owl*.)

7 For an elaborate discussion of education as an instrument of persuasion, see my *Dominance without Hegemony*.

8 Bankimchandra Chattopadhyay was one of his contemporaries to suggest the change. In a review article. 'Bengali Literature', published in the *Calcutta Review* (Nos. 104, 106) of 1871, a year after Kaliprasanna Sinha's death, Bankim described *Hutom Pyanchar Naksha* as 'a collection of sketches of city-life, something after the manner of Dickens's, *Sketches by Boz*, in which the follies and peculiarities of all classes, and not seldom of men actually living, are described in a racy vigorous language, not seldom disfigured by obscenity'. *Bankim Rachanabali*. Vol. 3, p. 112.

9 *Hutom*, pp. 284–5.

10 The first edition of Dickens's *Sketches by 'Boz', Illustrative of Every-day Life and Every-day People* was published in 1836. Our references to this work, hereafter *Boz*, are to the 1839 edition published in Penguin Classics as *Sketches by Boz*.

11 In a short life of 30 years, Kaliprasanna founded and edited journals, patronized the new Bengali stage, translated the *Mahabharata* into Bangla in collaboration with Sanskrit pundits, and became a major philanthropist who was particularly active in famine relief and widow remarriage. *Hutom*, p. 7.

12 Miller, 'The Fiction of Realism', pp. 85–153.

13 Citations are from Miller, 'The Fiction of Realism', pp. 89–91, and *Boz*, pp. xii–xiii.

14 *Boz*, p. 7.

15 *The Well-stocked Kitchen* (1566) by Joachim Beuckelaer at the Rijkmuseum, Armsterdam, and *Woman Looking at a Table* by Wolfgang Heimbach (c. 1610–c. 1678) at the Staatliche Gemaldegalerie, Kassel, are fairly representative of this genre.

16 Williams, *The Country and the City*, pp. 190–1.

17 Miller is quite explicit on this point, as he writes: 'In spite of ... later works of Dickens'; Miller, 'The Fiction of Realism', p. 93.

18 Ibid., p. 100.

19 Ibid., p. 98.

20 Ibid., p. 96.

21 *Boz*, pp. 96–104.

22 Ibid., p. 98.

23 Ibid., p. 98.

24 Ibid., pp. 100–1.

25 Ibid., p. 101.

26 Miller, 'The Fiction of Realism', p. 119.

27 *Boz*, p. 99.

28 Ibid., p. 101.

29 Wordsworth, *Prelude*, p. 286.

30 Williams, *The Country and the City*, p. 188.

31 *Works of Wordsworth*, p. 269.

32 Wordsworth, *Prelude*, p. 286.

33 *Boz*, p. 102.

34 Ibid., p. 96.

35 Ibid., p. 339.

36 See Bhartṛhari, *Vākyapadīya*, Kālasamuddeśa, 53: *dvau tu tatra tamorūpāvekasyā lokavat sthitiḥ*; and Helārāja's commentary on that verse in *Vākyapadīya of Bhartṛhari*, p. 60.

37 Twenty-three items, to be precise, taking together the contacts of the three rubrics called 'Hujuk' 'Bujruki' and 'Babu Padmalochan Datta orofey Hathat Avatar'. *Hutom*, pp. 123–213

38 See Heidegger, *Being and Time* (p. 397): 'The craving for the new is of course a way of proceeding towards something not yet seen, but in such a manner that the making-present seeks to extricate itself from awaiting. Curiosity is futural in a way which is altogether inauthentic, and in such a manner, moreover, that it does not await a *possibility*, but, in its craving, just desires such a possibility as something actual. Curiosity gets constituted by a making present which is not held on to, but which, in merely making present, thereby seeks constantly to run away from the awaiting in which it is nevertheless "held" though not held on to.'

39 Sumitikumar Chattopadhyay, *Bhasha-Prakash*, pp. 321–2.

40 Some of the older street names of Calcutta testify to this connotation for example, Bosepara Lane (after the Bose a Kayastha caste group), Kansaripara Lane (after the Kansari, a caste group of traditional craftsmen and traders in bell metal), and so on.

41 For *keranchi-gari*, not to be confused with the *office-jaun* used by white employees, see Mitra, *Kalikata-darpan*, p. 174. The following are some of the various kinds of *keranis* mentioned in the *Naksha*: ship-*sarkar*, booking clerk, clerk, *kerani*, head writer and writer.

42 Bakhtin, *Dialogic Imagination*, pp. 74–7.

43 Williams, *The Country and the City*, pp. 184, 185. Emphasis added.

44 Ibid., p. 188.

45 Bakhtin, *Dialogic Imagination*, p. 76.

46 Lefebvre, *Critique of Everyday Life*, p. 207.

47 Gadamer, *Truth and Method*, p. 110

48 Gadamer, *Relevance of the Beautiful*, p. 49. The idea is elaborated further in pp. 39–42, 58–61.

49 Bentinck's minute of 5 August 1833. *Correspondence*, p. 861. Emphasis added.

50 For the Fort William hour-gun, see the text and notes in *Hutom*, pp. 40, 42–3, 77, 89, 199, 207, 244.

References

Bakhtin, Mikhail, M. *The Dialogic Imagination*, trans. Caryl Emerson and Michael Holquist, Austin, 1981.

Bandyopadhyay, Bhabanicharan, *Kalikata Kumalalay*, Brajendranath Bandyopadhyay, ed., Calcutta, Bengali Year 1343 [1936–7].

Bentinck, William, *The Correspondence of Lord William Cavendish Bentinck*, C. H. Philips, ed., Vol. II, Oxford, 1977.

Bhartṛhari, *Vākyapadīya of Bhartṛhari with the Prakīrṇakaprakāśa of Helārāja*, Kāṇḍa III, Part II, K. A. Subramania Iyer, ed., Poona, 1973.

Chattopadhyay, Bankimchandra, *Bankim Rachanabali*, Jogesh Chandra Bagal, ed., Vol. 3, Calcutta, 1969.

Chattopadhyay, Sunitikumar, *Bhasha-Prakash Bangala Vyakaran*, Calcutta, 1945.

Dickens, Charles, *Sketches by Boz*, Dennis Walden, ed., Harmondsworth, 1995.

Gadamer, Hans-Georg, *Truth and Method*, trans. Joel Weinsheimer and Donald G. Marshall, New York, 1988.

—— *The Relevance of the Beautiful and Other Essays*, trans. Nicholas Walker, Robert Bernasconi, ed., Cambridge, 1986.

Guha, Ranajit, *Dominance without Hegemony: History and Power in Colonial India*, Cambridge, MA, 1998.

Heidegger, Martin, *Being and Time*, trans. John MacQuarrie and Edward Robinson, Oxford, 1962.

Lefebvre, Henri, *Critique of Everyday Life*, trans. John Moore, London, 1992.

Miller, J. Hillis, 'The Fiction of Realism: *Sketches by Boz, Oliver Twist*, and Cruikshank's Illustrations', in Ada Nisbet and Blake Nevius, eds, *Dickens Centennial Essays*, Berkeley, 1971, pp. 85–153.

Mitra, Radharaman, *Kalikata-darpan*, Calcutta, 1980.

Sinha, Kaliprasanna, *Satik Hutom Pyanchar Naksha*, Arun Nag, ed., Calcutta, Bengali Year 1398 [1991–2]

—— *The Observant Owl: Hootum's Vignettes of Nineteenth-century Calcutta*, trans. Swarup Roy, New Delhi, 2008.

Williams, Raymond, *The Country and the City*, Frogmore, 1975.

Wordsworth, William, *The Prelude*, Ernest de Selincourt, ed., London, 1971.

—— *The Works of William Wordsworth*, Hertfordshire, 1994.

Index